❋ FROM REFUGEE TO OBE ❋

From Refugee to OBE

Charles G. Strasser

KELLER PUBLISHING
Marco Island, Florida

Copyright © 2007 by Charles G. Strasser
All rights reserved

ISBN 13: 978-1-934002-03-2
ISBN 10: 1-934002-03-8

Designed and composed in Warnock Pro at
Hobblebush Books, Brookline, NH, USA
Printed in China by Sunquest (Shanghai) Inc.

Distributor for the United Kingdom and the Channel Islands
Procurement International Ltd.
Falcon House
30 Ivanhoe Road, Finchampstead
Berkshire RG40 4QQ
01189734422

Published by

KELLER PUBLISHING
590 Fieldstone Dr.
Marco Island, FL 34145
www.KellerPublishing.com
800-631-1952

To the memory of my wife, Maureen.

And to all those others who have made my climbing of the mountain possible.

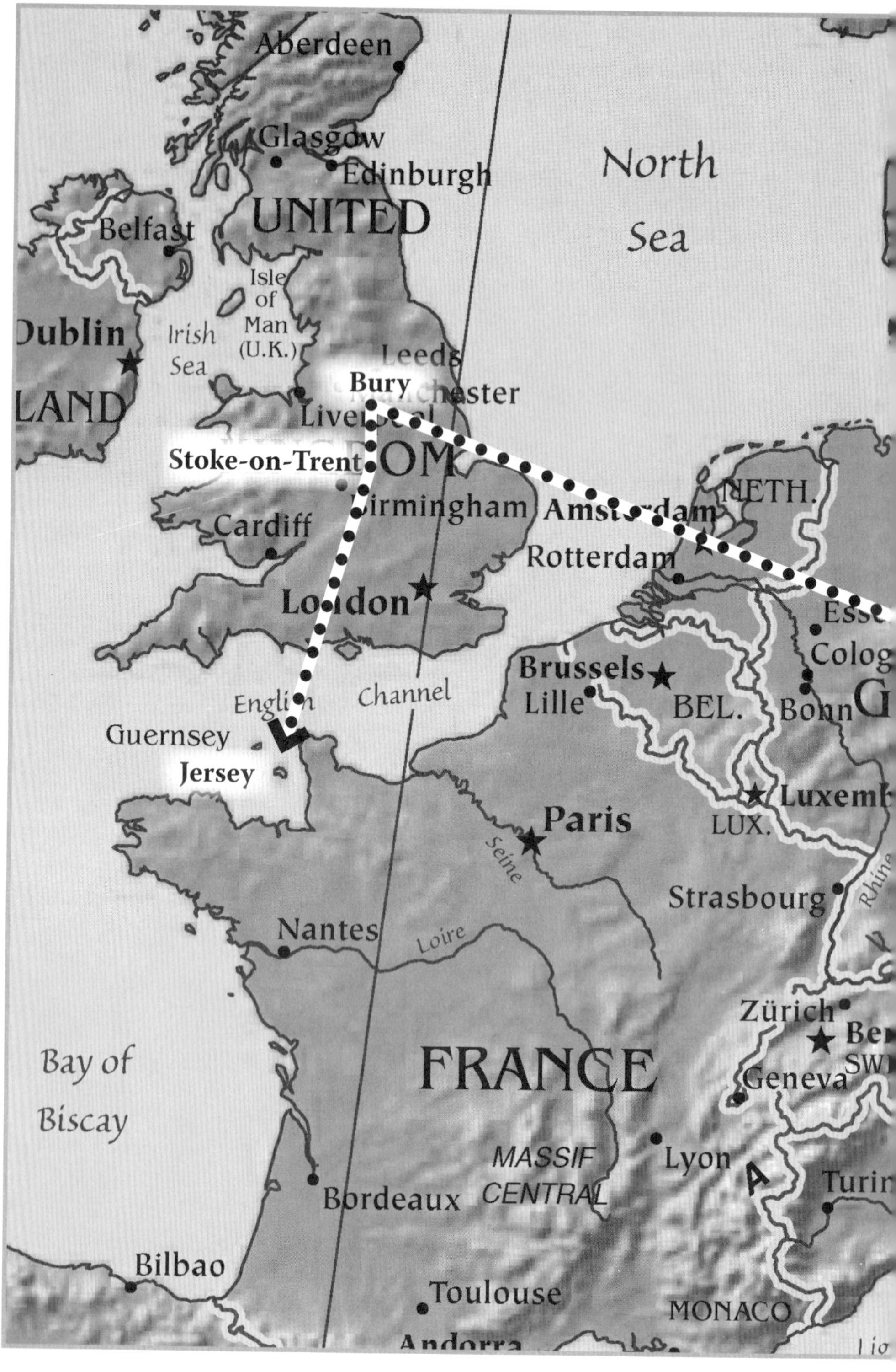

Göteborg
Gotland
Riga ★ LATVIA
Baltic Sea
Öland
LITHUANIA
Vilnius ★
NMARK
Malmö
Kaliningrad
penhagen ★
RUSSIA
Bornholm
B
Hrodna
Gdańsk
Hamburg
Berlin ★
Poznań
Warsaw
Brest
Bremen
POLAND
Łódź
Oder
Leipzig
Wrocław
L'v
Elbe
Vistula
Teplice
RMANY
Prague ★
Kraków
rankfurt
Che
m Main
CZECH REPUBLIC
rg
Brno
SLOVAKIA
CARPA
Stuttgart
Bratislava
Danube
Munich
Budapest
Cluj-
Vienna ★
Napo
LIECH.
AUSTRIA
Vaduz ★
HUNGARY
ROM
Ljubljana
★ Zagreb
Milan
SLOVENIA
Venice
Po
BOSNIA AND
Belgrade
HERZEGOVINA
★
enoa
CROATIA
SERBIA
SAN
Sarajevo ★
MARINO
ian Florence
MONTENEGRO

Contents

LIST OF ILLUSTRATIONS   xii
PREFACE   xiii
ACKNOWLEDGEMENTS   xiv

1 ⬥ Origins   3
2 ⬥ Raised Under a Brewing Storm   5
3 ⬥ Fleeing Before the Storm   8
4 ⬥ Safe in England with New 'Parents'   11
5 ⬥ Reunited   13
6 ⬥ War and Education   16
7 ⬥ Joining the War   21
8 ⬥ Crossing Germany   25
9 ⬥ Searching for Ghosts   28
10 ⬥ Farewell To an Arm   31
11 ⬥ Salute to the President   33
12 ⬥ Doors Open in Nuremberg   36
13 ⬥ An Airborne Thrill—Almost   39
14 ⬥ My First Exposure   44
15 ⬥ Cameras—Not Made But Assembled   50
16 ⬥ On the Climbing of Mountains   54
17 ⬥ Setting Up Shop   57
18 ⬥ Meeting My Match   61
19 ⬥ "I'd Like To Be Your Sole Agent in the UK"   65
20 ⬥ Every Lock Has a Key   67
21 ⬥ Expanding   72
22 ⬥ Quotas, Quotas   76
23 ⬥ Agencies and Products   80
24 ⬥ Diversification   83
25 ⬥ Moving into London   88
26 ⬥ Computerisation   92
27 ⬥ Part of the Establishment   97

CONTENTS

28 ♦ Going Public   99
29 ♦ Buying Groups   108
30 ♦ Clip-O-Matic   111
31 ♦ Terminating the Soviet Agency   114
32 ♦ Photokina Exhibitions   117
33 ♦ British and Other Exhibitions   122
34 ♦ Photokina Leads to Cokin   126
35 ♦ Paul Plus and More   129
36 ♦ A Road Not Taken   137
37 ♦ The Auctioneer's Hammer   139
38 ♦ The Japanese Market Opens   141
39 ♦ Doing Business, Japanese Style   144
40 ♦ When Things Don't Go As Planned   148
41 ♦ Japanese Agencies   152
42 ♦ Minolta and the Great KT   157
43 ♦ A Spot in Piccadilly Circus   160
44 ♦ Finding Ricoh   163
45 ♦ Subsidiaries   166
46 ♦ Expanding Beyond Japan   170
47 ♦ Industry Revolutions   174
48 ♦ Making My Shares Bankable   179
49 ♦ The Captain Never Goes It Alone   183
50 ♦ Ousted   190
51 ♦ The Wheel Turns Full Circle   193
52 ♦ My Family   198
53 ♦ My Grandchildren   204
54 ♦ A Shadow Falls   207
55 ♦ Dear Friends   209
56 ♦ A Country of Choice: All about Jersey   211
57 ♦ Learning To Fly   224
58 ♦ My First Wings   230
59 ♦ Flying Brings Us To Jersey   234
60 ♦ Airfield Hopping   240
61 ♦ Further Certification   243
62 ♦ St. John Ambulance Air Wing   245
63 ♦ My Last St. John's Flight   248
64 ♦ The End of the Ambulance Air Wing   256
65 ♦ The "Strasser Scheme" for AOPA   258

x

CONTENTS

66	◆	Fired Again!	261
67	◆	More Flying Adventures	268
68	◆	Combining Two Interests	277
69	◆	Skylog	281
70	◆	Rotary International	286
71	◆	Joining Rotary	290
72	◆	Travelling the Rotary Connections	293
73	◆	The Flying Rotarians	299
74	◆	For the Love of Flying	312
75	◆	Jersey Pride	324
76	◆	Godfather	326
77	◆	Liberation Day	329
78	◆	Words with the Bailiff	335
79	◆	Persistent Optimism	337
80	◆	The Paul Harris Award	343
81	◆	Rotary Fellowships	345
82	◆	Community Service: Trade and Professional Associations	347
83	◆	Making a Difference: The Joy of Giving	351
84	◆	Other Clubs & Charities	358
85	◆	The Jersey Joint Christmas Appeal Auction	364
86	◆	Keele University	368
87	◆	Marco Island	377
88	◆	My Business and Life Philosophy	379
89	◆	More Quotes & Personal Observations	381
90	◆	Charles G. Strasser OBE	388
		EPILOGUE	397

APPENDIXES

A	◆	Offer Document to Become a Public Company	403
B	◆	Extract from Chairman's 1969 Report and Accounts of Government Impositions	409
C	◆	Photopia International Ltd Dealer Charter	413
D	◆	List of Clubs & Associations Past and Present	415
E	◆	List of Aeroplanes Flown	419
F	◆	"Strasser Scheme" Press release	423
G	◆	Personalities of the BPIA & Photo Trade	427
H	◆	Inflation Table	431

Illustrations

Group A Personal History
Group B Family
Group C Rotary and Flying
Group D Company

◈ Preface ◈

MY LIFE SPAN OF 80 years covers the period of the most remarkable changes in human endeavour, technology and medicine in the history of the world. In this period, we saw the start of space exploration, man's first landing on the moon, the phenomenal growth of air travel, the invention of the computer and the discovery of antibiotics. On the other side of the scale, I witnessed man's inhumanity to man in the Holocaust and the growth of fanatical terrorism.

The idea of recording my life experiences, triggered mainly by the encouragement of others, came at a time when I started to reduce my time given to other matters and, therefore, it came rather late. Indeed, I only started seriously to put pen to paper in the year 2005. As I never kept a diary, a lot of memory searching was involved. To use computer terms, I do have a fantastic memory for events, but my recall system could be better. This applies particularly to dates and names. So if I get some events out of order and omit some names, my recall system is to blame.

This autobiography is mainly written for my family, friends, ex-employees and the many members of clubs and committees I have served on and to record for them and other readers the various stages of my life.

Many have asked would I have done things differently had I the opportunity to live life again. Some decisions were taken for me and those for which I was responsible I would not wish to change as they have given me such a wonderful, exciting and varied life. I am happy with what I have achieved and particularly the contributions I have been able to make to the community at large.

Acknowledgements

FIRST OF ALL TO MY two daughters, Suzanne and Dianne, for their encouragement and help in the concept and preparation of this book.

My special thanks go to the following proof readers who have so diligently undertaken this very onerous task: Tony Allchurch, Beth Lloyd and Paul Liddiard.

My grateful thanks also go to the many on whom I have called to be memory joggers and they include: John Battison, Max Blakeman, Rupert Cartlidge, David Cohen, David Coupe, Pauline Hancock, Mike Hanson, Mark Heintz, Marie Joyce, Lord Stanley Kalms, John Kirk, Sam Kusumoto, Chris Mason, Sue Mason, David Morgan, Sheila Ottolini, Jeff Pickford, Ian Rosewell, Mike Shailes, David Shaw, Geoffrey Snow and David Uwins.

Besides my own photographs many pictures in this autobiography are acknowledged with thanks to: Sue Falloon, Sue Keller, David Reynolds, and Peter Trenchard FBIPP AMPA.

Last but not least my thanks to Wade Keller, my publisher, for his many innovative suggestions and continuous encouragement of my efforts.

And finally with apologies to all the contributors to my life story whose names I have not mentioned individually, I do sincerely thank each of you.

❈ FROM REFUGEE TO OBE ❈

1

◆ 1 ◆

Origins

MY FATHER, HANS "HASTRA" STRASSER, was born in 1899 in the Czechoslovakian town of Usti nad Labem (Aussig an der Elbe in German). He had gone to the asparagus growing area of Hanover in Germany to learn to be a blacksmith. There, he met my mother, Hanna Gottlieb, who was born in 1904. Soon after, they travelled to what was known then as the British Mandate of Palestine, later to become Israel. Because of their strong idealistic beliefs in communal living and equal shares for all, they joined the Bet Alfa kibbutz. My father performed duties there as a blacksmith, a tractor driver and a night time guard against marauding Arabs. My mother was assigned to cooking duties. I, Charles Gad Strasser, was born there on 23rd of April 1927, in the nearby hospital of En Charod. I spent my first four months in the crèche, or nursery, of the kibbutz. My birth date is shared with William Shakespeare—whose poem lyric "All the world's a stage" was my inspiration for the ages-of-man concept on the back cover—and Shirley Temple—who was later the U.S. ambassador to the Czech Republic—and it is also St. George's Day in England. As to the establishment of the State of Israel, my place of birth, I was pleased that after so many years of struggle and particularly following the suffering of the Holocaust—the Jewish people had at long last got a home of their own. I fervently hope that Jews in Israel and Arabs in Palestine will, in the not too distant future, finally live in peace together as good neighbours.

Kibbutz philosophy was, in a way, more of a communist, socialist, volunteerism philosophy. Clearly, my parents were young idealists. I've studied the history of the kibbutz, which has a basic philosophy of sharing everything with your neighbour. My parents were allowed no personal possessions because everything was shared. Everybody had to perform some task, allocated by the elders or committee. The children did not live with their parents. They lived in a children's community. After a time, my parents became disillusioned with the realities of kibbutz life and because of that and my mother's illness after my birth, they decided to return to Czechoslovakia. I am told this occurred four months after my birth and that I was transported back in a Moses basket. I am not surprised that my parents, with many of their friends, became disillusioned and returned to Czechoslovakia. Over time, others acclimatised to the system, but many kibbutzim eventually changed their strict communal lifestyles and became more like co-operatives.

The first 11 years of my life were spent in Czechoslovakia. I identify with having originated in Czechoslovakia, but I consider myself now to be British. I suppose, what counts at the end of the day, is where you've spent the bigger portion of your life. When I talk now, my accent is much more pronounced. As you get older, you tend to have the accent of your original language. It's much more pronounced than when I was 30 or 40. When people ask me now where I come from, I always say I'm a Cosmopolitan, because what am I? That fills the feeling that I'm not a person from any one particular place. However, I am British by naturalisation, of Czech origin and a proud resident of Jersey in the Channel Islands.

The Czechoslovak Republic was founded in 1918 after the First World War. Its territory consisted of Bohemia, Moravia, Silesia, Slovakia and the Carpathians—all of which were, prior to that, part of the Austria-Hungarian Empire. The Czechs and Slovaks had a centuries-long history of oppression, until independence was gained on 28th October 1918, under the leadership of Thomas Garrigue Masaryk, subsequently the first President of the republic, which was established on 14th November 1918. The Czech language is one of the West Slavic languages, along with Slovak, Polish, Pomeranian and Serbian. It is spoken by most people in the Czech Republic and by Czechs all over the world (about 12 million native speakers). Czech is very close to Slovak and Polish; Czech and Slovak speakers are usually able to understand each other.

Today the Czech Republic consists of only Bohemia, Moravia and Silesia.

❖ 2 ❖

Raised Under a Brewing Storm

WE PROSPERED IN OUR NEW home town in Northern Bohemia called Teplice-Sanov (Teplitz-Schoenau in German), a quite famous spa town and later renamed Teplice-Lazne to reflect that. My father went through several career changes, from a butchery machine salesman to an area manager of that concern. At that time, we lived in an attic flat, and I started going to a nearby local elementary school. My mother started a branch of a dry-cleaning concern.

My father later became a bank clerk. A customer of the bank was at the point of bankruptcy, and my father was sent in as a "company doctor" to fix it. Later, he stayed on as its manager. This company, producing pottery and figurines, was named B. Bloch. To the satisfaction of the bank, my father quickly rescued B. Bloch from potential financial disaster.

The B. Bloch factory was in a nearby village called Dubi (Eichwald in German). It was at the southern edge of the northern Bohemian mountain region known as Krusne Hory (Erzgebirge in German) which formed the mountainous border with Germany. This area had wonderful skiing right up to the German border at Cinovec (Zinwald in German). We had a large house on the company's extensive factory grounds. My father became the managing director and initiated a very extensive export of their products, including to both the United States and the United Kingdom.

Life for me was great. I had lots of friends of similar age who were all children of the wide circle of my parents' professional friends. Weekends were spent skiing in the mountains, and summer holidays invariably included participation in youth camps by some river in Bohemia, like the Sazava. When we still lived in the town and I was going to the local elementary school, an extensive police search was made for me one day because I had apparently been lost. In truth, I had hidden under some cushions in the living room. The search was called off, and I received a suitable scolding for my prank.

From 1933, when Hitler came to power in neighbouring Germany, ominous events took place. After the German annexation (Anschluss) of Austria on 9th March 1938, Hitler began making claims on the Sudetenland (Sudety in Czech), a part of northern Czechoslovakia. The first stage occurred when Hitler had talks with then British Prime Minister Neville Chamberlain. Hitler told Chamberlain that part of Czechoslovakia—which was populated by a number of German-speaking Czech citizens—belonged to him. He promised that if he was given that part known as Sudetenland he would have no further territorial claims in Europe. Chamberlain, desperate to avoid war, believed him. So started the ill-fated "appeasement."

Chamberlain came back from Munich and talked of "that far off country of which we know little" and had given away a part of it. He exited the aircraft waving a piece of paper, a picture which became quite famous, and proclaimed "peace in our time." The Czechs had already mobilised their army and wanted to fight, and they relied on the help of their allies, as there was a pact in existence between the French, the British and the Czechs. My father was mobilised when a call for ex-soldiers to report to their units came by radio broadcast. If they owned a car, they had to bring it with them. My father drove his Tatra (a Czech-built car) there. They were issued uniforms and everyone was ready to defend the country. Then, only eight to 10 days later, they were stood down.

Hitler knew that once having been given the Sudetenland, the natural defence ring of mountains which protected Czechoslovakia in Northern and Western Bohemia bordering on Germany, the rest was easy for him to invade whenever he wished to. Indeed, he subsequently marched into the rest of Czechoslovakia five months later. Only when Hitler also attacked Poland did Chamberlain finally declare war on Hitler's Germany on 3rd of September 1939.

During this time my parents deemed it prudent to move from Dubi to Prague, the capital of Czechoslovakia. Many refugees, mainly political ones, escaped from Germany and took up residence in Prague.

To my young mind, it was just another move, even though it was explained to me. A lot of German refugees were coming to Prague, and that started people thinking something must be happening. Sure enough it did. German troops occupied the Sudetenland in October 1938 and the rest of Czechoslovakia in March 1939.

◆ 3 ◆

Fleeing Before the Storm

IT BECAME OBVIOUS THAT THE end was near for freedom and democracy in Czechoslovakia. My parents could see what was coming, so they sent me to England. I left in a train known as a Kinder Transport, one of a number of transports organised to send children out of the country for their safety. I was sponsored by a Rotarian family in Bury, Lancashire, England. To get Home Office permission for me to enter the United Kingdom, they had paid the necessary £50 and undertook to accept responsibility for me up to the age of 18.

In November 1938, I left Prague at the age of 11. My train departed from the Prague Wilsonovy Nadrazy—the main railway station named after U.S. President Woodrow Wilson. My parents took me to the station, and they didn't know if they would ever see me again. I joined the other children, most of whom would never see their parents again. We travelled across Germany and Holland and sailed on to England. At Waterloo station in London we were then distributed to the families who had agreed to take us in.

A young British stockbroker named Nicholas Winton, now Sir Nicholas, later organised many Kinder Transports. He was recently (finally) recognised for that and was knighted. Winton visited Prague in late 1938 at the invitation of a friend at the British Embassy. When he arrived, the British team working in newly erected refugee camps asked him to lend a hand. He spent only a couple of months in Prague but was alarmed by the influx of refugees, endangered by the imminent Nazi invasion. He immediately recognised the advancing danger and courageously decided to make every effort to get the children outside the reach of Nazi power. He arranged with UK voluntary organisations to get the £50 per child required for sponsorship, and he arranged transports right up to the start of the war.

Over 50 years later, Nicholas Winton's wife, Greta, came across an old leather briefcase in an attic and found his diary and lists of the children and letters from their parents. He hadn't told her of his role in arranging the transports. He helped save 664 Czech children from certain death in concentration camps. The majority of the children were Jewish.

Winton didn't think much of what he did. He just thought it was the normal, decent thing to do. After finding the diary and lists in the attic, Greta asked him what it was all about. "Oh," he said, "I just helped some children to escape." Then the story unfolded how he had badgered people for the £50 and the guarantee of sustenance up to the age of 18 required by the Home Office for each entry permit. In certain cases, he forged entry document applications and arranged the transports, and that was itself a most interesting story. There is a book by Eva Gissing, one of "his children" who wrote his biography. Also, a film entitled "The Power of Good" was made of his remarkable efforts. I went to the London premiere of it and met Sir Nicholas there. The well-known English TV personality and investigator Esther Rantzen was the first to be made aware of the story, and she thought it might be interesting to find some of these now grown up Czech children and bring them together in one of her surprise programmes. She found about 30 and put them in the audience and invited Sir Nicholas to be there on some pretext. She then introduced them to him one by one, and they told him how grateful they are and how he saved their lives. They gave their individual stories. The whole place was in tears. Quite a number of those Czech children became very famous people. The film's commentator, Joe Schlesinger, also one of Winton's children, became a very famous Canadian CBC broadcaster.

On my Kinder Transport to England, a tall military-type Englishman was a chaperone. He took all our passports and UK entry permits as we travelled to England. I don't know who arranged him, who employed him, or whether he was a volunteer. All I know is that because we weren't allowed to take money out of the country, my parents bought a Leica camera and gave it to me to take to England and turn into cash if necessary. This tall Englishman took my camera. I got my passport back, but I never saw my camera again.

◆ 4 ◆
Safe in England with New 'Parents'

GILBERT AND GLADYS HEYWOOD, A family in Bury in Lancashire, adopted me. Gilbert was a member of the local Rotary Club and I'm sure the benevolence of the Rotary spirit that I experienced at that early age influenced my later devotion to Rotary. They had a daughter named Doris, with whom I stayed in touch through the years. Quite some time after my arrival, they adopted another boy, Herbert, who came from Austria. The Heywood house, on the outskirts of Bury, was quite large and at the top end of Walmersley Road. Gilbert Heywood was the owner of a musical instrument shop in the centre of town. It was a large double-fronted shop with grand pianos in the windows. I lived with this wonderful family for a year as their adopted child. They were very good to me. They treated me like their son. They knew my parents might not make it out and I could be with them permanently.

When I first came to Bury, I couldn't speak a word of English. I was sent down Walmersley Road to a little Church of England village school, which doubled for Sunday school. No one spoke Czech or German, either in my new home or at school. This total immersion is a good way to learn a new language, especially when you are young. Within six months, I was top of the class in English. I was, therefore, transferred to the local grammar school, Bury Grammar School, rather than staying on at the village school. Bury Grammar was a very good school, and I stayed there for six months, learning, among other things, how to play that very English game of cricket and wearing a school uniform for the first time.

My father and then my mother escaped from Czechoslovakia just after it was invaded but before the war started. After that it wasn't possible to travel from Germany to England. My father had been a pottery factory manager in Czechoslovakia at B. Bloch, He, with the help of an American customer, got a similar job in February 1939, in a pottery factory in Cobridge, Stoke-on-Trent. Once in England, he was able to get entry permission for my mother, and she came to England in May of 1939.

My father always played around with bits and pieces of pottery manufacturing equipment. One of the most labour-intensive processes in making tea cups and mugs is attaching the handle. Whether the cup was made by a turning process or a moulding process, at the end you still had to stick on the handles. They were stuck on through the use of a liquid clay called slip. It was a manual process, and the amount of pressure required to attach the handles was such that it had to make it stick. On the other hand, if it was too strong, it would indent the soft clay on the side of the mug. It was done on a conveyor belt with women sticking on handles as cups passed by. My father invented a machine, the main part of which was a bicycle wheel, that could be put on the conveyor belt as a station and it could attach the handle precisely. The actual pressure of the handle onto the cup was determined by the amount of air you put into a bicycle tyre. He patented the process, and a local engineering company produced it under licence from him. It was used extensively in the British pottery industry. Later, a German pottery machine manufacturer took it up as well, so it was used on a worldwide basis. It became known as the Strasser Cup Handling Machine. My father left a legacy in the pottery industry.

◆ 5 ◆

Reunited

WHEN MY PARENTS WERE ESTABLISHED in Stoke-on-Trent, I left the Heywood family and our family was reunited. The City of Stoke-on-Trent is an amalgamation of five or six towns. One of those towns is called Burslem, and we lived at 218 Waterloo Road, Burslem in a small terrace house.

Next door to us lived a City Councillor of Stoke-on-Trent. His name was Austin Brooke, a labour Councillor. He later became Lord Mayor of Stoke-on-Trent and was instrumental in helping my mother persuade the City Council to support the transport and subsequent accommodation of eight more children from Czechoslovakia. He had great influence on the City Council and with the local miners and pottery industry people. The City Council donated the £50 per child and provided the required guarantee up to the age of 18 by making available a house—number 10, in their Penkhull orphanage estate—to accommodate these eight Czech children.

The children were brother and sister Paul and Raja Strass, Ralph Strass, a cousin, two more brothers, Asaf and Reuben Auerbach (later Potocky), Peter Feldstein (later Kalina), Hanna Frankel and Fritz (Bedrich) Schwarzkopf. They were all accommodated in number 10 of the children's home and became known locally as "the Czech children." David and Josef Placek, whose parents were also old friends of my parents, came over in Kinder Transports but were allocated to foster parents on farms in Northumberland. Fritz and Lilo Kisch were also able to come to England. They were a young couple. Their children, Erika and Ruth, were born in Stoke-on-Trent. Fritz Kisch was with me, years later, when I got a national press scoop taking photos of an aircraft crash. My father's brother, my uncle Fritz "Bunne" Strasser, and his wife, Lotte, lived in London. They had two daughters, Alisa and Dorli. Fritz Strasser spent the war years working as an engineer in a war production factory.

Miriam Potocky, author of the recent book, "Where Is My Home", the title of the Czech national anthem, is a daughter of one of the Czech children, and now living in the United States. Through talking with one of the other children of the Czech children, I discovered that all the children involved who came to England with the help of my mother and the City of Stoke-on-Trent were children of long-standing friends of my parents.

All of the Czech children went back to Czechoslovakia when the war ended in 1945 to see if their parents had survived. Sadly, none of them found their parents. They were all victims of the Holocaust, murdered in Nazi concentration camps.

More of my parents' friends came to England just before the start of the war. How, and by which means, they managed to get out, I don't know. All I know is that they all surfaced in Stoke-on-Trent because my parents lived there. They all re-established themselves professionally in England and, in due course, when they all lived in Penkhull, resumed their once regular card games. They came from Teplice, where they and my parents had led a typically comfortable middle-class life. They were all professional people, and their children played at each others' houses. The parents met regularly at the same reserved table at a restaurant behind the local theatre, and the men played cards. There were Hans and Ella Dasch who had two children, Hugo and Lisa. He was a children's doctor and, naturally, my doctor. There were Motte and Lotte Moutner who had a daughter, Ruth. He was a well-known lawyer in the town. Then there were Alf and Emma Fried who had two daughters, Helen and Hanna. He was the manager of a family wholesale hardware company. I was told that I said I wanted to marry Helen at the age of six!

My father got involved with an organisation called the Workers Educational Association (WEA), which provided adult education tutors for many subjects. Through that connection, he befriended Stephen Swingler and his wife Anne, both WEA tutors who had come to the area from London to lecture. I don't know why, but they came to live with us. Stephen later was called up to join the Army and Anne stayed on for some time with us. He was very pro-Czech. He quickly became a Captain and spent leaves with us. Later, he stood as a Labour candidate for Newcastle-under-Lyme in the parliamentary election and won, becoming an MP. Later still, he became transport minister in Harold Wilson's government.

When my father got firmly established in his job, we moved from Waterloo Road, which was quite a poor area, to Penkhull which was a nicer area.

Later, an Anglo-Czech friendship club was formed. We got Czech national costumes and did Czech folk performances, musical dances and singing at the club and for local audiences in working men's clubs and schools. Reuben Auerbach played the accordion and Ralph Strass the violin. Some just played a comb covered in tracing paper. I was part of the dancing group. My parents were involved as well.

On the 28th of July 1947 my parents became British by naturalisation. As I was at that time still under 21, I automatically was included and became British also.

My parents lived in Penkhull, a suburb of Stoke-on-Trent, until they died. My mother died in 1953 and my father in 1959. They are buried in the Carmountside cemetery there.

❖ 6 ❖
War and Education

MEANWHILE IN THE GERMAN-OCCUPIED PROTECTORATE of Bohemia and Moravia, SS Obergruppenfuehrer Rheinhard Heydrich took over as governor. He became known as the Butcher of Prague.

In 1942, Operation Anthropoid was mounted with the support of exiled Czech President Benes. Seven members of the Czech army were trained in the UK and dropped by parachute in Bohemia with the task of assassinating Heydrich. They stayed undercover for about three weeks and followed his daily movements. On 24th of May 1942, they ambushed him in his open staff car and wounded him. He died in a hospital on 4th of June.

The Germans started taking hostages and applying their particularly persuasive techniques to find those responsible for the assassination and those who were hiding them. They were unsuccessful, so they went to a mining village north of Prague called Lidice and announced that unless the perpetrators of the assassination surrendered or were given away, Lidice would be razed to the ground. All 173 men of the village were lined up and shot. The women were taken to Ravensbruck concentration camp in Germany. Children were taken to Germany to be Germanised. Finally, the seven Czech soldiers were cornered in the cellar of the St. Cyril Church in Prague where they put up a great fight but were eventually killed.

This was in 1942, and news of this massacre came to the UK to my town of Stoke-on-Trent, which was, like Lidice, a mining town. My father and Dr. Barnett Stross, who was friendly to the local Czech refugees, started a fund to rebuild Lidice after the war. This was called the "Lidice Shall Live" fund. They raised internationally a huge amount of money, enough to achieve the goal. A new village of Lidice was built next to the land where the razed village had been. The land of the original Lidice now has a rose garden and memorial sculptures to remind posterity of the atrocities of the Nazi regime. It is well worth a visit and has a museum next door with a chronicle of the tragic events that took place there.

To continue with my life in Stoke-on-Trent, I was transferred to Hanley High School. I never excelled at academic subjects. I was more mechanically minded, so I had a very short stay at Hanley High. I was soon transferred to the Junior Technical School in Burslem, which concentrated on science, arithmetic, chemistry and practical subjects like woodwork, metalwork, machine drawing and draftsmanship. The headmaster there was a Mr. Collinson, a quite stout man, a disciplinarian but very fair. He ruled the school sternly and used a leather machine belt to administer punishment on our posteriors when any of us committed a serious disciplinary offence. Proudly, I only felt the sting of the belt once during the years I was there. I've always been a quick learner. Once was enough.

This was war-time England. Although the school was only for boys, because many teachers were called up for the services, there were now lady teachers also in boys' schools. Mrs. Tucker was the mistress for English language and English literature. I had already achieved command of the English language early on, but she helped me perfect it. We had a very competitive spirit in our class, and I was always in the top four. We vied for first position in the different subjects. In those days, schoolboys in England called themselves by their surnames and never used their first names. The three competitors with me for the first four places were Doncaster, Lockett and Brindley. Besides these very good competitive friendships, I had another friend there called Reynolds who lived very near to us. His father was a disabled decorator of fancy pottery figures and worked from home. Reynolds was seriously into chemistry as a hobby, so we did a lot of home experiments which sometimes were quite dangerous. We had some minor disasters.

Other teachers at the technical school were Mr. Mills, who

taught chemistry, and Mr. Taylor, who taught metal work. Mr. Cooksey taught woodworking, and Mr. Thomas taught algebra and trigonometry. Mr. Howell taught machine drawing. Another Mr. Taylor taught geography, and he also was a good magician, so we often had practical demonstrations of magic during our lessons. Mr. Taylor was also a keen photographer, and years later when I had a photographic retail shop, he became a very good customer of mine.

I walked nearly a mile from home to the school and back every day. The school was near the football ground of the then quite famous Port Vale team. The more famous team in Stoke-on-Trent was, and still is, the Stoke City Team. It was the starting ground of Stanley Matthews, a well-known football player who would subsequently become Sir Stanley Matthews. He holds the record for never having had a yellow or red card for foul play held up against him in his entire career.

I also became a Boy Scout while going to the Junior Technical School in Burslem. I joined the troop that was known as the Second Hanley YMCA Troop. As you would expect, I went in for many proficiency badges, soon became a second with one stripe, then a patrol leader with two stripes, and finally the troop leader with three stripes. There was a very good permanent scout camp just outside Stoke-on-Trent, for which the land had been donated by the Copeland family, who owned the Spode china factory. It was called Kibblestone and was available for all Scout troops in the area. I regularly spent weekends there in tents with my Scout troop, enjoying many scouting activities and finishing with sing-songs around the campfire in the evenings. They also had a small swimming pool there, and for many years I held the long distance swimming record in it. The Scout leader in Stoke-on-Trent was C. Marshal Amor, and he also ran the Kibblestone Scout camp together with Arnold Edge, another great voluntary Scout leader.

Although I got very good schooling, exam results, and technical qualifications, this did not qualify me for University entrance. Therefore, I continued to the North Staffordshire Technical College, where I matriculated externally for the University of London.

This entitled me to go to University College, London, for a degree course.

While studying at the North Staffordshire Technical College, we had to take turns volunteering for fire watching at night-time, when the buildings were unoccupied. People nowadays don't have any idea what that means. It was part of the Civil Defence in those days. You could be subject to raids from German bombers virtually anywhere in England during the war. The Germans often dropped incendiary bombs to start fires rather than dropping explosive bombs. Most public buildings had teams of fire watchers who had buckets of sand and long-armed shovels. If the Germans dropped incendiary bombs on the building, we could quickly douse them with a stirrup pump and ensure that they didn't set the building on fire. This was a weekly, night-time duty. While we were waiting for the air raid sirens, which were always the first alarm, we played table tennis and cards. I had a good social life because of that. We had incendiary bombs only once in the time I lived there, and I wasn't fire watching the night it happened.

While I was in the technical College and before I went to university, I filled in the time by working at the Victoria Heating and Ventilating Company in Cobridge, a local sheet metal works that manufactured galvanised sheet ventilation equipment for the local pottery industry. This sheet metal works was run by two brothers known as Shufflebottom. One was the owner and the other, Joe, was the practical manager. I worked in the drawing office, using my experience from junior technical school. Most of the contracts were for custom-designed installations. My job entailed going out to factories that wanted ventilation and dust extraction equipment, measuring for these installations and then making working drawings. I thought at that stage that the graffiti in men's toilets was really quite vulgar, but when I went to these different factories to measure for the ventilating equipment, I also had to go to ladies' toilets. I found that the graffiti there was a lot worse!

In September 1943, at age 16, I started at University College, London, which had been evacuated to Swansea on the Gower peninsula of South Wales because of the wartime bombing in London. I spent a year there, the first of a three-year civil engineering degree course. My accommodation was a study/bedroom in student lodgings arranged with local landladies, and I lived in a house owned by a Mrs. Davis, along with four other first-year undergraduates. I also had the opportunity there to join the uniformed Civil Defence, still voluntary, and was made a dispatch rider and given a motorbike. If anything, I probably spent too much time on that and not enough time on study. Swansea was bombed quite a bit, and its town centre was rebuilt after the war.

❖ 7 ❖

Joining the War

I WAS NOW APPROACHING AN age and a time when I thought that I should be doing something more for the war effort. So after one year at university, in the summer of 1944, I decided to volunteer to join the army. Because I was of Czech nationality, I went to the recruiting office that was part of the Czech embassy in London—the embassy of the Czech government in exile in England. Fourteen days later, even though I was only 17, I was in the Czech Independent Armoured Brigade of the British Army.

I was issued a uniform, rifle, gas mask, tin helmet and everything that is necessary to change you from a civilian to a wartime army recruit. Amazingly I still remember my Czech army number which was T3777. Basic infantry training included marching, rifle drill, shooting practise, hand grenade throwing, long back-pack hikes and bayonet practise on hanging straw-filled bags. I trained in a seaside town in the south of England called Leigh-on-Sea, which is near Southend on the Thames estuary. It was impressed upon us how important it was to keep our rifle barrel cleaned and oiled. We had daily inspections.

Before the war, the Czech Army was a compulsory service army with very low pay. From 1934, mandatory service was two years. In Britain, mandatory service only started at the beginning of the war, but it stayed that way until well after the end of the war, until it went back again to a voluntary professional army the way it is now. The U.S. Army had a feature, even in wartime, we could never understand and that was selective enlistment, where a local draft board decided whether you should or shouldn't be called up. Another difference was that the Czech army was a citizen army.

It was your duty, and what happened to you, nobody could care about. In the U.S. Army, more than any army that I know of, you still retained much of your civilian status and privileges. In other words, your pay was relatively high—better than in any other army—and the quality of your equipment and your uniforms was superb. The British army was somewhere between the two. One of the benchmarks of the American army was the standard of meals. The normal canteen food that you got in the Czech army was mass-produced rubbish. The food in the British army was much better but nothing like the high quality of the U.S. Army. The food I used to get when later attached to the American army was better than a lot of civilians got.

Between the three armies, however, the chain of command is similar. When we were in infantry training, they told us that the sergeants who trained us were never sent with us to the front, because since you hated them so much you might shoot them in the back. If they were going with you to war, towards the end of training they suddenly became your best buddies to be sure you wouldn't shoot them on the battlefield.

At the end of the day, the army is there to defend the nation from potential attack. There's a huge difference between behaviour in an army in peace time and in war time. As you see in films about the U.S. Army, they instil an esprit de corps in you. In peacetime, it is all theoretical. In wartime, it is real because you have to depend on one other. There is a much stronger bond with your fellow soldiers in wartime.

During my basic training in Leigh-on-Sea, the area had been considered susceptible to German invasion or attack. So, the Ministry of Defence acquired all the seafront houses by compulsion for the duration of the war. The part of the Czech Independent Armoured Brigade that was still in training was billeted in those seaside houses. We had a field hospital and one house that was converted to a military prison. It was part of every recruit's duty to stand guard there—two hours on and four hours off in a 24-hour shift.

The unit I was in consisted of people who had joined in different ways to become part of the Czech Brigade. There were some soldiers there who were in the Czech army before the war, left in frustration over the country's failure to fight the Germans, wandered all over the place to France and joined the French Foreign Legion just to be back in an army again. They came to England from the Legion. That is probably the best, toughest military in the world. They were experienced soldiers. Then there were innocents like me along with other ex-students from England, having led a relatively sheltered life. We also had people who escaped the eastern way through Poland and Russia and somehow came to England. The one thing we had in common was we were all patriotic Czechs. But that is about all we had in common.

On completion of our training, we were sent across the channel to join the rest of the brigade. This was the end of 1944, long after the Normandy D-Day landings on 6th of June 1944. We were taken by train from Leigh-on-Sea, Southend, to Harwich. A standard sea crossing from there to the Hook of Holland normally takes two to three hours. We were embarked on this ship below decks and didn't come on deck until three days later because the ship, for some reason, stopped in mid-channel for two and a half days. That's where I learned to play poker. We just sat there and played cards, waiting in the Channel.

On arrival we were transported to Ostende, which is on the border of Belgium and France and billeted overnight in a Catholic convent. The main thing that sticks in my mind after so many years is that we were told, in no uncertain terms, that because we were in a convent and had to use their toilets, we must make sure that we put the seats back down after use.

From there, I knew we were going to the area of Dunkirk. This was, at that stage of the war, a German-held enclave. The German unit there had flooded the surrounding canals and made them into a virtual moat. It was not considered worthwhile to capture the place, and the Czech Independent Armoured Brigade was given the job of encircling it and just holding them in as virtual prisoners. We fired heavy artillery and used tanks for patrol reconnaissance to hold them in place. We did this from about October or November 1944 until the end of the war in May 1945. The French seaside town of Dunkirk was famous at the beginning of the war because the British Expeditionary Force was evacuated from there at the fall of France in thousands of little boats.

My little unit was in a village called Herzele and accommodated in a large French chateau. The lady owner was still living there, but we took over the whole chateau except for one small apartment for her. At first we slept on the floor, and then we built wooden bunks. Standard Czech Army practise was to make palliasses to sleep on, which were sackcloth filled with a little straw. The army took advantage of my motorcycle capability that I had acquired in the Civil Defence in Swansea, and I was made the unit dispatch rider. My unit in this village was quite a distance away from brigade headquarters in St. Omer. My daily journey was to take messages and bring orders from the brigade HQ to my company. It allowed me to see the countryside.

That was the situation until VE Day on 8th of May 1945, when we were told that the transfer of the whole brigade to Czechoslovakia was imminent. Apparently it was thought that there would be too much active recrimination if we went into Dunkirk, having contained the Germans there for many months. So the job of taking all the Germans in Dunkirk as prisoners of war was given to a Canadian division, while we were dispatched home to Czechoslovakia.

8

Crossing Germany

ON VE DAY, 8TH OF May 1945, the German enclave Kommandant Vice-Admiral Friedrich Frisius had still not surrendered, allegedly because he was not given orders to do so by his superior officers. His superior officers had already signed the surrender of the German forces in the west to Field Marshal Bernard Montgomery on May 4 at Lueneburg Heath in Northern Germany.

On May 9, I and five other dispatch riders from the brigade escorted a convoy of about 60 army vehicles of all sorts back to Czechoslovakia across Germany, which had just been occupied. I rode from Dunkirk to our destination in the mountain border region of West Bohemia. The journey was long and tortuous, though interesting. It was a very hot and dusty May. My face and exposed arms were sunburned, and I was covered in dust. The journey took us through Germany, which had just been fought in, and on about the second or third day we crossed the river Rhine in Cologne. The town had been absolutely flattened by bombing. The only thing that was standing up like a beacon in the middle of the town was the famous cathedral. By some miracle it was only very slightly damaged.

All the bridges were down, and the British army had built temporary Bailey bridges across. We crossed the Rhine on these army bridges. I suppose that because we were not priority traffic, we were kept off main roads and crossed Germany to Czechoslovakia on secondary roads. We had also been given orders that if a lorry (truck) was disabled for whatever reason and unable to continue, an armed dispatch rider had to stay with it. However, if a dispatch rider's motorbike went unserviceable, it was just to be loaded onto a lorry and the rest carried on. There was still a sense of danger, and no one was to be left on the road alone. We were also given instructions that there was to be no fraternisation with the Germans. Under those instructions, we crossed Germany.

We got to Czechoslovakia six days later. We started off as six dispatch riders, and we finished up with two—me and one other. Two were killed on the way. Further down the road, another one was smashed between lorries. The fourth one had an accident and the other motorbikes went unserviceable. We used their bits and pieces to keep our two motorbikes going. Happily, I finished that journey in one piece, and my motorbike finished it in a serviceable condition. It was a BSA 350cc bike, and there is a picture of it in this book.

On arrival at our destination near Susice, we had reports of shooting still going on there. It was now seven or eight days after VE Day, and armed conflict was supposed to have ended. The vehicles of our convoy were formed into a huge square with an armoured scout car in each corner. In the centre of this, we set up camp for the next few days. Regular guards with machine guns protected the camp. It reminded me of the wild west when the same was done with the covered wagon trains. Isolated parties of German soldiers were shooting at us. They were escaping from being captured by the Russians, preferring instead to surrender to the Americans or British. They were crossing Czechoslovakia to try to achieve that, hiding in the dense forests there during the daytime and travelling at night-time. They attacked farms, often killing farmers and stealing their possessions—particularly food, clothing and money to get to the West.

We were given the job of clearing the dense forests of these armed German soldiers. We combed the area by making a chain of soldiers two metres apart with rifles at the ready. We got scratched and damaged our uniforms as we went through and captured quite a number of Germans. At the time, the Supreme Allied Commander, General Eisenhower, had issued an order that, after a certain number of days—I can't remember how many—following the signing of unconditional surrender, any armed soldier who had not surrendered was to be treated as a bandit and could be shot on sight if they resisted arrest. That happened to a few of them.

In our off-duty time, we went out fishing and shooting rabbits. One day, two soldiers from my unit told me that they went out rabbit shooting, and when they started shooting, three German soldiers stood up from behind a little hill and surrendered to them with their hands up.

❖ 9 ❖

Searching for Ghosts

MY SMALL UNIT WAS NEXT billeted by a country pub which was an ideal location. The war was over now, and we were soldiers with no particular task. So we started making wooden beds again. We had our own cook house and latrines. We were a small, self-contained, tented unit with a sergeant in charge.

In Czechoslovakia each village usually has a tailor. We soldiers still had the standard-issue British battle dress uniform—ill-fitting and drab and not as nice as the American uniform of the day. I got the idea to let the village tailor remodel the jackets. It would still be the same uniform, but now it would have nice pleats in the back, open jacket-style lapels instead of closed necks, and would be made nicer with a tie. He did this for me and two of my friends, and then, of course, the whole unit had to have them. The local girls thought we all looked really smart in those somewhat nonstandard uniforms.

Here we were, billeted in the grounds of a pub in the lovely mountainous area of Bohemia, and then we learned of what exactly had gone on. We found that because of the Yalta Agreement, Czechoslovakia was to be in the Soviet sphere of influence. This was the term that the Russians used. In fact, the border of Czechoslovakia was to be part of the boundary of what later became the Iron Curtain. But we, part of the British army and the American army, had already gone beyond the border, and some units of the American Third Army got into Prague before the Russians did. Because of the Yalta Agreement, they withdrew and let the Russians officially liberate Prague. The demarcation line at that time was about halfway between Plzen and Prague. We were in the American zone. East of the demarcation line was the Russian zone.

I was still a dispatch rider and very anxious to find out whether any of my relatives and friends were still alive. The only way to do that was to cross over the demarcation line into the Russian zone. I had a motorbike, I was in uniform, and my sergeant kindly let me go, telling me to come back in seven days. Equipped with the usual "coinage" of the day—cigarettes—I rode to the demarcation line control post and showed the Russian guard my ration card from the NAAFI (the Navy Army and Air Force Institute), which was the British equivalent of the PX (Post Exchange). That and a few cigarettes made him quite happy to let a fellow Allied soldier pass his post, and I continued on the British army issued motorbike to Prague.

In Prague, I found that a lot of political prisoners and Jewish people had been taken to a concentration camp called Terezin (Theresienstadt in German). Terezin, an old fortress town, is about halfway between Prague and Teplice, the town in Northern Bohemia where I used to live. I arrived there less than three weeks after the end of the war. There were still a lot of very thin and haggard-looking people about, and I started chatting with them to see whether my grandparents on my mother's side had gone through there or if they remained. I also asked about my father's sister, who had stayed in Prague, and her daughter. I could get no information.

One thing about the Germans, even with their murderous ways, they were always sticklers on keeping records. They kept meticulous records on whoever was deported or put into the gas chambers. There were thousands of records, and I was able to establish that my grandparents had been in Terezin. But I couldn't establish whether they had died there or whether they had been taken to another concentration camp in the east, which is what happened to my auntie and her daughter. I then continued my motorbike journey further north to Teplice, but there was nobody there I recognised. I went to all the houses and flats we used to live in and also those of pre-war friends. After the seven days, I returned to my unit.

I am reminded of a quote from the proceedings at the Nuremberg Trials: "Having set up in occupied Czechoslovakia an insufferable regime of terrorism, the Hitlerites drove into German slavery many thousands of Czechoslovak citizens, showing no mercy even to children, who were sent to industrial plants, farms and mines."

The youth of Czechoslovakia were deprived of all opportunities for education. When, in 1942, a Czech delegation appealed to Reichsleiter Dr. Frank for permission to reopen the higher Czechoslovak educational institutions, he cynically replied, "Should the war be won by England, you will reopen your schools yourselves; should Germany win, then five-grade elementary schools will be enough for you."

In 1945, after the end of the war, the Czechs, understandably, decided that they didn't want those Germans who always wanted to be part of Germany to stay in the northern part of Czechoslovakia. The Czechs wanted their country to be completely Czech. They asked the German population to leave, and if they didn't leave, they "helped" them to leave. Many of the Germans did not want to leave, but back in 1938 they had wanted to be part of Germany. Now they were given that "privilege." Many houses were left empty, so Czechs were brought in to occupy them.

◈ 10 ◈

Farewell To an Arm

I STILL HAD THE USE of my motorbike, and we found that not too far from where we were billeted was the famous Czech factory of Zbrojovka, which was producing motorbikes and revolvers. I was laden with a huge number of cigarette packs for negotiating and given the job of acquiring some souvenir revolvers. I drove to the Zbrojovka factory and talked to a manager. They had just been liberated from years of German occupation—and I was part of the liberating army—so they wanted to show their gratitude. We also wanted to show our gratitude to them with our cigarettes, so we struck a deal. I came back with six just-off-the-production-line Czech revolvers in beautiful pigskin leather cases, complete with clips of ammunition. I was able to retain one of these souvenirs. The sergeant got another one. We played cards for the other four.

About four or five nights later, I was happily sleeping on my wooden bed. In the middle of the night this sergeant—his name was Marek—woke me up and he was waving the revolver that I got for him above me. He shouted, "Look at this you son of a bitch," swearing in the Czech equivalent, "This bloody gun you brought. Look, it's useless," and he started pulling the trigger, like playing Russian roulette. He was in an inebriated state and continued waving it around. He got on top of me, and the fourth chamber went off. Luckily, he was pointing it at the ceiling at the time. He just said, "Oh, oh, it's working now," and off he went. I was scared out of my wits.

The story of my souvenir revolver ends at the finish of my army career, when I was finally demobilised and came home to England. On the ship crossing the English Channel, there were regular loudspeaker announcements to returning military personnel saying, "This is a final warning! Anybody found with any arms or ammunition or grenades or any items of that nature will be severely punished. Revolvers are not allowed to be owned by civilians in England." They kept repeating this announcement, and I got really scared as to what would happen if they found the revolver on me. We were about mid-Channel when I decided it wasn't worth the risk. I took it off my belt and threw it overboard. It's probably still at the bottom of the Channel. I wonder if the other five are still in the possession of my former comrades.

◈ 11 ◈

Salute to the President

AFTER A WHILE, THE DEMARCATION line was moved west to the actual Czech border. All the Czech Brigade units were just inside the border of a now independent sovereign Czechoslovak Republic. We were handed back to the Czech Army command from the British Army Command. Consequently, we started getting our supplies from Czech sources rather than from the Americans or the British. Allocation of cigarettes and other NAAFI supplies also ceased. Our unit was told that we would be moved to standard pre-war Czech Army barracks in a town called Pardubice in Moravia.

Before that happened, we were using spit and polish to make our uniforms and vehicles look good because we were going to Prague to take part in the big victory parade on 30th of May 1945. This huge procession was well-organised and consisted of everyone involved in the liberation and subsequent victory. The Czech Independent Armoured Brigade took pride in being in that procession with its many British tanks and other vehicles. There were many bands and much flag waving. I proudly rode my BSA motorbike for the last time in front of the stand where the President of the republic, Eduard Benes, took the salute.

After the victory parade, we went directly to the Pardubice barracks. I realised that this was not what I had joined the Army for. We lived in old, probably pre-World War I, security-fenced-in barracks. We had awful food and military harassment for no reason at all. If you had just joined the army it was probably good for you, but when you had joined to help win the war and then came to that sort of peacetime situation, it just was not tolerable.

A friend and I decided it would be much nicer if we had a little apartment in town, living there until we were transferred to a holding camp for those waiting to be demobilised in the UK. Those of us who had joined up in England were entitled to be demobbed there. We found and rented a little apartment in the centre of the town. Our understanding sergeant counted us in rather than out at the nightly bed check and we went back every morning to the barracks to report for "duty." We just didn't sleep there. We stayed away when we got leave passes for weekends too. I took the opportunity to learn to dance at a very good dancing school in the town and met some charming local dancing partners.

Also we spent a lot of time taking away machine tools, lathes, power presses, milling machines, multiple drilling machines, injection machines, cranes and everything that was bolted down and everything that wasn't, from different factories in a wide area. We then spent days loading railway wagons full of these badly needed Czech machine tools to be taken to the Soviet Union. It is normal in wartime for the victor to take away some of the spoils of battle and booty and to take away reparations, as they are called, from a defeated enemy. But for an ally—which the Soviet Union was at that time—to take them away from the Czechs shocked me. From that moment on, I viewed everything that the Communists did with a great deal of scepticism. I realised at that stage the problems we were later going to have with the Russians.

The Captain in command of our unit—not the barracks—had a girlfriend in Prague, just under two hours away by car. He knew that I had an army driving licence for cars and trucks up to three tonnes. He had a jeep allocated to him for official duties, and every now and again I was enlisted to drive him to Prague to the Ministry of Defence. These trips mainly included a weekend, and he allowed me to stay in Prague and bring him back again at the end of the often extended weekend. I made quite a number of friends in Prague and practised the dancing I was learning in Pardubice.

Finally, the orders for my transfer to the holding camp in Plzen (Pilsen in German) arrived, and I joined the few other soldiers waiting to be demobbed in the UK. We still had no definite demob date. At least I was now out of the Pardubice barracks and in a camp in a town famous for the best beer in the world (of which all the other lager beers are mere copies). This beer is exported by its German name of "Pilsner Urquell" because its Czech name of "Plzensky Prazdroj" is unpronounceable by all but Slavs. "Prazdroj" literally translates to "Urquell" and means "fountainhead" in English.

◈ 12 ◈

Doors Open in Nuremberg

AS THE DATE FOR MY demob could still be a long time away, I asked for leave to go home to Stoke-on-Trent. I was given a pass, but the Czech Army was not in a position to give travel vouchers to use on Western European railways or any other comparable facilities. So I was just given a leave pass to allow me to be away from my unit for 14 days. It was easy in those days, for soldiers in uniform to hitchhike, so I hitchhiked across Europe mainly in military transport, got home and had a good stay there. My return journey to my unit was again by hitchhiking.

On the way back I had a night stop at an American Army transit camp in Nuernberg or Nuremberg as the name by which the trials were known. [I have chosen to use the American, and often British, spelling, rather than the original German spelling, for this autobiography.] This was a camp in the American Zone of Germany that was provided for any Allied army personnel in transit from A to B. In the evenings, one could go to a G.I. club. I went to this large G.I. club, and found that all the G.I.'s there were working in one capacity or another at the International Military Tribunal (IMT) in Nuremberg, the very famous war crimes court case of defendants from Hermann Goering and Rudolph Hess downward. After a few drinks we became friendly, and they asked me to come and have a look at the trials while I was there. They gave me a visitor pass, so the next morning I did just that. I spent the morning in the visitors' gallery looking down at the court room with two rows of the infamous defendants sitting there—Hermann Goering, Rudolf Hess, Joachim von Ribbentrop, Wilhelm Keitel, Ernst Kaltenbrunner, Alfred Rosenberg, Hans Frank, Wilhelm Frick, Julius Streicher,

Walther Funk and Hjalmar Schacht. In the back row were Karl Dönitz, Erich Raeder, Baldur von Schirach, Fritz Sauckel, Alfred Jodl, Franz von Papen, Arthur Seyss-Inquart, Albert Speer, Konstantin van Neurath and Hans Fritzsche.

I thought that, rather than spending my time doing nothing and waiting to be demobilised in a camp in Plzen, I could do something useful here. But how? I found out that there was a Czech War Crimes delegation there, so I knocked on the door of their three-office suite. A Captain Hochwald welcomed me in. I learned that the delegation consisted of himself, a General Ecer, a sergeant driver for the general's Tatra car, and a German girl typist.

I spoke Czech, German and English, and I said to him, "It seems to me that you are very understaffed here. Why don't you arrange a transfer for me to help you?" Luckily, he agreed and thought this was a splendid idea. He took me straight into the General's office. He too thought it a good idea, and there and then he wrote a letter to my commanding officer in Plzen. Four days later, I was attached to the American Army and working on war crimes matters with the Czech delegation. Because it was in the American zone of Germany, everybody who worked at the tribunal was automatically attached to the American army. I started my army career in the Czech army attached to the British army. Then, halfway through, I was in the genuine Czech army. Now I was in the Czech army attached to the American army.

In the Czech army, I was a lance corporal. When I got to Nuremberg, my rank was translated into the American equivalent rank of private first class (PFC). All the rubber stamps and things that I had made were "PFC Charles G. Strasser." After I had been in the Czech War Crimes delegation for a little while, General Ecer promoted me to sergeant, as this was deemed to be more appropriate to the duties I was performing. It came with a slight increase in pay too, so that was welcome. In the American army, a sergeant is denoted by three stripes. But in the Czech uniform, the equivalent rank is cetar (soft "c" and soft "r," as they both have hooks on them), which meant three round silver pips on your epaulettes.

I was granted all the benefits of an American G.I., including PX privileges and living accommodation. I had no expenses while

I lived in Nuremberg. Everything I wanted was provided, so anything I received from the Czech army was pocket money. All the social facilities were provided by the American army, including leave transportation. Any money that I had, I could therefore spend on films, beer and what have you. Interestingly enough, I acquired a taste for a drink that became my standard for a long time. It was the main drink that G.I.'s drank in those days—CC Coke, which stands for Canadian Club Whisky and Coca-Cola. I found that I could drink any quantity without it having any detrimental effects.

Whilst in Nuremberg, I was in G.I. billets. Most of the town had been bombed to smithereens, but there were still some houses standing that the American army had requisitioned. We lived in those and they were, in the typical American fashion, called Boys' Town. A favourite pastime in Boys' Town was playing poker at which I had already acquired some skill. I remember there was a G.I. with us of Native American ancestry. He always had a gun when playing poker and would not play poker without a gun on the table in front of him. He never used it though.

I was the only non-G.I. in Boys' Town. I met a lot of nice guys there. With one in particular I made a close friendship—a G.I. named Bob Mahon, who was from Baltimore, Maryland. We did a lot of things together, including trips to Prague in his army Jeep.

G.I. photographers from Army Public Relations were also based in Boys' Town, and that's how I became quite interested in photography.

From the time I was born, I was known as Gad Strasser. When I got to Nuremberg, everyone asked what this name "Gad" meant. Although I had lived with it happily, it seemed appropriate to get an English name. Bob Mahon suggested that I was a Charles. I agreed and accepted that as my new name from then on. However, I was slightly irritated by something that Americans do and English never do—using the word "Chuck" as a name for Charles. I had never heard of that before, and I certainly didn't like it. In England, if they don't want to say Charles, they usually say Charlie, and I don't like that either. So I am Charles and I don't like any of the variants thereof.

◆ 13 ◆

An Airborne Thrill—Almost

THE CREW CHIEF OF THE DC-3 allocated to the U.S. Chief Justice was also in Boys' Town. Apparently the chief justice did not like flying, so he never used it. We used it instead. That's where I got interested in flying. This was the most lavishly equipped DC3 I have ever seen; from memory it even had a piano in it. I got to sit in the right hand seat sometimes. We all happened to be interested in getting cameras, so whenever they did training flights in this aircraft to somewhere else in Germany, they loaded up with cigarettes and came back with cameras. That was all done in this American judge's aircraft. I'm sure he was never aware of that. The captain of the aircraft had a German girlfriend whom he took flying—also not within regulations.

The crew chief, who was in charge of the aircraft while it was on the ground, was always a master sergeant. He was also with us in Boys' Town, so we got on very well with him and his Captain and First Officer. They were officers and should have gone to officers' clubs, but they preferred to be with us. We would loan them sergeants' jackets, and they would come with us to the non-commissioned officers' clubs instead.

In those days, most G.I.'s were interested in going home with German cameras and other souvenirs. We were getting the standard American PX rations of cigarettes, so there was a good trade going on—a legitimate trade because of the PX allocations.

I had learned English in all the schools in England, and now I was thrown into an American language environment and had to learn that quite a lot of words have very different meanings between British English and American English. Our stationery supplies were drawn from a U.S. Army supply section. A lady Captain was in charge, and I went to her and gave her a list of the things I required. One of the items was a rubber. She said, "What? What is this?" I explained to her that when you write something with a pencil and it wasn't the right thing, you wanted to rub it out. "Oh," she said, "that's not a rubber, that's an eraser." She said, "Don't you know what a rubber is?" I said no. I learned that it was a contraceptive, a condom. Apparently one of the alternative uses of a condom in the U.S. Army, besides its traditional use, was as a rubber band to tie around the bottom of your trousers and then turn them down over your Army boots. You used new ones every time you did that instead of using rubber bands. That was quite an embarrassing first incident. Then of course I learned things, like a pavement was a sidewalk, a boot was a trunk, a bonnet was a hood, a lift was an elevator. There were many more possibilities for misunderstandings between the two types of English.

I stayed in Nuremberg with the Czech War Crimes Delegation, performing various duties of war crimes investigations including having pictures of the court proceedings printed for the press. S.S. people in our custody would be transferred to the countries where they committed their crimes and transport and guards for the journey were arranged. Whenever we got a report of a sighting of Martin Bormann, who was Hitler's number two, we passed on the information and started looking for him.

The many searches for Bormann were not successful. However, a skeleton identified by dental records as Bormann's was discovered in West Berlin in 1972. In 1999 a DNA test confirmed the identification. At first it had been thought that he was killed by Soviet troops not long after leaving the bunker. If so, he would have been the only top Nazi leader (the others being Adolf Hitler, Heinrich Himmler, Joseph Goebbels and Hermann Göring) killed by enemy fire; the other four committed suicide. But the presence of glass fragments in the teeth suggest that Bormann, too, probably killed himself with cyanide.

On one mission, I was asked to take a war crimes documents bag, similar to a diplomatic bag, to the British War Crimes Commission in London. This bag had a handcuff on it so you wouldn't get it taken away from you. I had the key, and the bag was handcuffed to my wrist. I got on a DC-3 to London with about six or seven other servicemen. It was a straight-forward, army-issue DC-3 with bucket seats along each side. We took off from Nuremberg Airport and were just crossing the French coast of the English Channel when the crew chief master sergeant came out of the cockpit and went back to the tail end of the plane. He grabbed some parachutes and put one in front of each of us. Civilian planes didn't carry parachutes, but all the military planes did. So there we were each with a parachute.

He said, "We have a problem, guys. There's a fire in the cockpit. These are parachutes for you. Don't worry about it yet, but I might tell you to use them."

Off he went back into the cockpit and closed the door behind him. We looked at each other, and nobody said anything. Going through my mind was how I'd been impressed as to the importance of these documents that I was carrying handcuffed to my wrist. What do I do? Do I jump with this bag still handcuffed to my arm, or do I unlock it and forget about it? I really didn't know what to do. I was looking forward to the jump actually. The plane started climbing straight away, very sensibly to a lesser oxygen altitude, and it did a 180 degree turn to be back over land. Well, I don't know how long it actually was. It seemed a long time, but it was probably less than 10 minutes, before the crew chief came out and said, "Okay, stand down. We've put it out." Apparently, there had been a short circuit of some sort in the padding between the outer and the inner skin of the aircraft.

I never did have the opportunity to make a decision as to how to deal with the bag when jumping. I delivered the documents to the War Crimes Commission and then went on a short leave.

Back in Nuremberg, one day I was strolling through the town and saw some youths flourishing a swastika badge on a belt, even though they were banned. They were indoctrinated. It was just three lads who were wearing these swastika belts. I said to them in German, "You're not allowed to have the Nazi emblems any more. Take them off." They were about 15 to 17 years old—I suppose ex-Hitler-Jugend (Hitler-youths, a paramilitary group). They immediately did as I said. They had been trained to take orders. I confiscated the badges.

The International Military Tribunal court in Nuremberg consisted of a judge and alternate judges from the United States, Great Britain, France and the Soviet Union, with the British judge presiding. The prosecuting counsel of those four Allied powers had an army of interpreters because all the prisoners were German. It had to be translated into German for them and into those four languages for the judges as well. The translators were in the courtroom behind a glass screen, and they did a remarkable job of instantaneous translations.

The court building was connected to the prison by an underground passage, and the prisoners were then brought up directly to the defendants' box in the courtroom in a lift. Thus, they were never exposed to public view until appearing in court. There was an American Colonel Andrus who was in charge of the guards at the prison. They had their own insignia and white helmets. The prisoners were being looked at 24 hours a day through the windows in their cell doors.

The court proceedings started on 20th of November 1945, at 10 a.m. and finished with the verdicts on 30th of September 1946. Eleven of the 21 defendants were sentenced to death, and 10 were hanged in a hall adjacent to the court on 10th of October 1946. Some of them got life sentences, others got long-period sentences, and others were acquitted. The one who stayed in prison longest was Rudolph Hess, who was in Spandau prison in Berlin. He was guarded by the four occupying powers on a monthly rotation basis and eventually died in that prison.

I was there when Hermann Goering cheated the hangman by crunching a hidden cyanide capsule. Modern day theories speculate that Goering had befriended a U.S. Army lieutenant, stationed at the Nuremberg Trials, who had aided Goering in obtaining cyanide. The cyanide had most likely been hidden in Goering's personal effects that were confiscated by the Army.

In 2005, retired Army Private Herbert Lee Stivers claimed that he delivered "medicine" hidden inside a fountain pen to Goering from a German woman he had met and flirted with. Stivers served in the U.S. 1st Infantry Division's 26th Regiment, which formed the honour guard for the Nuremberg Trials. Stivers claims to have been unaware of what the "medicine" he delivered actually was until after Goering's death.

Three days after the trials finished, I went back to Plzen, and there were my orders for demobilisation. I got my discharge papers and proper travel orders to take me back to England to start my civilian life.

During that period, my interest in photography, cameras and flying started. Those interests greatly shaped my whole life.

◆ 14 ◆

My First Exposure

BACK IN ENGLAND AFTER FINALLY getting demobilised I was ready to begin "climbing the mountain". I went into the war a boy, and I came out a man. I just couldn't face going back to university, so in November 1946 I got a job as a sales assistant in a local photography shop. There was a huge shortage just after the war, with no new cameras and films hardly available, but I was interested in photography and second-hand cameras.

I worked for a man called John Martin who had a chemist shop including developing and printing works in Leek and had opened a photography shop and studio and D&P processing plant in Pall Mall in Hanley. I later found out that he was also a Rotarian. I was offered £10 a week, which was good money in those days.

The manager of the shop was Jack Dean. He was very knowledgeable on photographic equipment and taught me a lot. Many, many years later when he was out of a job and nobody would give him one, as he was already quite elderly, I gave him a job in my company. I was pleased to repay his helpfulness to me in my first job.

When I came out of the army I decided not to go back to live with my parents. Desiring to be independent I went to live in a country pub, the Lawton Arms near Alsager in the neighbouring county of Cheshire. Two of my friends, Murti Mehra and Krish Bambery, also lived there and attended the North Staffordshire Technical College. Murti, from India, and Krish, from Pakistan, became great friends. They were there studying ceramics as Stoke-on-Trent is the pottery centre of the UK and its college is very famous for teaching ceramics and mining engineering—both the main industries of the area at that time.

The first vehicle I bought when I got out of the army was a BSA motorbike. The second one I bought was a second-hand old Austin 7 Tourer, amazingly I still remember the number COE 732. I've been in love with open cars ever since. Murti, Krish and I decided to spend the 1947 summer holiday touring and camping in Europe. My car was too small to take the three of us and camping equipment, so I decided to build a tin trunk to attach to the back of the car and to then put the spare wheel on to the back of that. This would enable us to put our tents and equipment into this trunk. The best way to achieve this was to go back to my ex-boss at the Victoria Heating and Ventilating Company in Cobridge, the sheet metal works place I had worked at before the army, and ask if, keeping out of their way, I could use their machinery to make my trunk. I would pay for the metal and materials used. He said yes and I did that in my spare time.

While I was making the tin can trunk for the car, I was positioning a sheet of metal when somehow or other I accidentally caused the guillotine to come down. The guillotine cut the top of my finger to the bone, and it was bleeding profusely. They got me in the car and took me up to the local Heywood hospital. My nail was literally hanging loose from my finger and the doctor put a tourniquet on it to stop the bleeding. I shall never forget that day. There was the most attractive nurse helping this doctor. He said, "Well, it's only hanging by a thread, and we might as well pull it out." So he got the tweezers and pulled it out, and she had a sort of dish there to put it in, but somehow he dropped it, and it dropped in between her shoe and her black nylon stocking. The doctor stitched me back together, but my nail never grew back again in one piece. That is how I got that funny nail on the third finger of my right hand.

The trunk was finally finished in time and we started our holiday. Funny thing, we never did any camping because we found that it was much more comfortable to find the local hostel of the Youth Hostel Association and stay overnight there. Unfortunately, they had a regulation that you were only allowed to stay at a Youth

Hostel if you were hiking or bicycling, not travelling by car. So we would park the car a couple of streets away, get our rucksacks out and walk up to stay overnight at the Youth Hostel.

In the winter of 1946/1947, John Martin, as the listed local photographer, got a call from the picture editor of a national newspaper called The "Daily Herald". There was to be a parachute drop of canisters containing food from a Royal Air Force Halifax bomber on the Leek Moorlands. The people there had been isolated by heavy snow falls and drifts for the previous three weeks and were now allegedly starving. The Royal Air Force had agreed to drop food for them and also to take a photographer from The "Daily Herald" on board. They wanted a local photographer to go to the drop zone, which would be marked out with a cross according to instructions given over the BBC radio, and photograph the food drop from the ground.

John Martin couldn't carry out his local photographer duties because the only way you could get to those isolated places was by skiing, and he couldn't ski. He knew I had skied a lot in my youth in Czechoslovakia and so he came to me and asked if I could do the job.

I said, "Of course, but I haven't got any skis."

"Oh," he said, "A friend of mine, Mr. Podmore, has got skis. He'll lend them to you."

"Fine, and I'll go with my Czech friend, Fritz Kisch."

Fritz had a motorbike with side car and his own skis. I took my Leica camera, and John Martin provided the film. We went the day before to Leek, where John Martin had his other shop and his processing works as well. Just outside Leek we started coming up against roads blocked with the snow, so we parked Fritz's motorcycle combination and started skiing in the direction of the village of Onecote, where we were going to stay overnight and ski the next morning to the drop area.

Off we went, and the wind was still blowing and the snow was still falling, but it was no problem for experienced skiers. Suddenly Fritz said, "This is funny, what's this thing sticking out of the snow?" It was the top of a telegraph pole! That shows you how deep the snow drift was. We went a bit further and scraped down through the snow some more, and we were standing on top of an abandoned truck.

We got to the pub, The Jervis Arms, in the village, and they had plenty of room because nobody could get out there to them. They said, "What do you want for breakfast?"

I said, "I thought you were starving."

"No," they replied, "we have plenty of food."

"Then why are these guys dropping food here?" I asked.

He answered, "You know, someone at the BBC invented this.

Anyone who knows moorlands people would know that they always have twelve months of food—in the pantry, the pig sty, the hen cote or the shippon.

We stayed overnight, and the next morning, on 13th February 1947, we skied to Grindon, where some local farmers had made a cross in the snow. At the due time, we heard the noise of a Halifax bomber coming. We saw it circling. The next thing we knew, maybe 300 or 400 metres from us, the plane crashed into the snow. I've flown over terrain covered by snow, and all the contours of the land that you normally see, you lose when it's all white. The pilot, Squadron Leader Donald McIntyre, should have known by his altimeter where he was, but he must have been flying visually and flew right into the ground.

The wings broke off, and Fritz and I went forward. There were some farmers there, the ones who had laid out the cross. The plane's petrol tanks started exploding. One crew member was still alive, and we pulled him out. The farmers took him to a nearby farm, where he died. All six crew, including a Burslem man—Sergeant William Sherry—and two on-board press photographers, including the one from the "Daily Herald" died unnecessarily. The containers that they were supposed to have dropped fell out of the aircraft, and they opened on the ground and also broke up. You could see bags of Tate and Lyle sugar and other items.

I was taking pictures fast and furiously, and when I got to the end of the first 36, I said to Fritz, "Take that cassette down to John Martin's in Leek. I came here to take pictures of the food drop, but now I have even more important pictures that need to be reported as news." So Fritz skied down to Leek. I stayed and took more pictures. John Martin's people in the processing works developed the film, did large glossy prints of them and got "copyright" stamped on the back. We were not clever or experienced enough in those days to put on the back, "Reproduction fee x-pounds." We had an exclusive scoop, and everybody would have paid it. As a result, the papers paid John Martin whatever they wanted to pay.

The following day, every single national newspaper and the local "Evening Sentinel" paper carried my pictures—big half-page pictures on the front page. The money started coming in from every direction and, in the end, it amounted to about £200. John Martin was kind enough to give me half.

Later on when I became a professional photographer, I got myself a police press pass and started taking pictures for the press. Ever since then, I have never been without a camera ready for my next scoop. If that would happen to me again, I know the procedure now. One of the most dramatic and most reproduced pictures is in the book.

Almost every year, on the anniversary of that day, not to commemorate the crash but to write about the severe winters that there used to be, the "Evening Sentinel" again publishes my picture taken in 1947. When in 2004 they reproduced it again without acknowledging me as the photographer, I sent them a bill for the reproduction fee. They paid the invoice, and I got paid for a picture after 57 years.

After the crash, there was a Royal Air Force inquiry, and I was asked to give testimony. In those days, they never published the results as to whose fault it was and why. It was, no doubt, put down to pilot error, and the flight should have never taken place. The whole effort was misconceived. It wasn't necessary. In 1999, the local branch of the Royal Air Force Association—made up of ex-Air Force people in the Leek area—decided to erect a commemorative cairn in the position where the Halifax had crashed. They invited me to the unveiling ceremony on 28th September 1999 at which the Lord Lieutenant of the county unveiled the cairn. There was also a Royal Air Force fly-past. A Hercules flew overhead at precisely the time that the unveiling took place. It was quite an honour for me to be invited to participate. I also met the son of

Squadron Leader McIntyre and some of the other relatives of the crew who perished on that day. I had flown over especially from Jersey and brought some of my pictures mounted on a peg board. Since the Royal Air Force Association was interested in them, I donated the pictures to the Leek branch.

That was the most memorable event in my working career with John Martin. After the Halifax episode, I was allowed to take photographs at weddings. Most photographers book more weddings than they can do themselves and then employ freelance photographers to cover the ones that are overbooked. Whenever they booked too many for themselves, I got the first opportunity. I started taking wedding photographs, and that stood me in good stead because later on, when I bought the professional photographic business in Newcastle, wedding photography was one of my main and lucrative sources of income.

◆ 15 ◆

Cameras—Not Made But Assembled

IN THOSE DAYS THERE WERE only second-hand cameras to be had because, of course, there were no imports from Germany throughout the war. Any cameras made in Germany during the war were made purely for the German armed forces. The situation in Britain at the beginning of the war was that the Army and the Air Force were so short of cameras the War Office advertised in the national newspapers for the public to give or sell their German-made cameras to the government. There was no maker of precision cameras in the UK before the war.

Cameras, like cars, are made not assembled. If you don't have a subcontracting industry, you can't make them. A camera subcontracting industry is needed for two main components—the shutter and the lens. We did have some good lens makers in the UK, but none were for mass-produced lenses. More importantly, there was no shutter industry. The timing mechanism is critical for the shutter. It enables variable and accurate speeds from one second to 1/1000 of a second, to control the length of exposure of the film to light. There were two types of shutters—a between-the-lens type of shutter, which was part of the lens mount, or a focal plane shutter. Cameras like Leica, Contax and Exakta, all had focal plane shutters that were immediately in front of the focal plane of the film. That gave the advantage of lens interchangeability and also higher shutter speeds.

Being able to change lenses enabled interchangeable single lens reflex cameras to be made. On these, because the focal plane shutter, when closed, protected the film from light, you could build in a mirror to reflect the image to a full screen viewfinder on top of the camera. The mirror would go up and down during the time that the shutter was required to be open for the pre-selected exposure time. Most mass produced cameras, at that time, had shutters that were incorporated into the lens components. There were two factories in Germany producing shutters and none in the UK. There were also factories in the United States, Russia and Japan producing shutters of that sort. So if you didn't have a shutter industry, you could not mass produce cameras, unless you imported shutters from one of those countries.

Because of this lack in the UK, the government tried desperately after the war to build up a British camera industry. All the German patents were thrown open at the end of the war, so any British manufacturer who wanted to make cameras in the UK could use German patents. The government paid for and encouraged delegations to go to Germany to see and learn how cameras are made. They gave subsidies to people, and there were about half a dozen factories in the UK that started making UK-made cameras.

A lot of aircraft parts manufacturers, when aircraft were no longer built in large quantities, started looking into the camera industry. The government encouraged them to start making cameras, and a lot of them tried by making copies of German cameras. Unfortunately, none of them stayed the course.

The British industry was trying to sell copies of old cameras and just couldn't succeed. Among all the brave attempts by British camera makers, there was one, K.G. Corfield, designer and maker of the Periflex, who stayed in the market longer than most of the other British firms because he did have some innovative capability. The factory, not far from my office in the Wolverhampton area, was opened by a man called Ken Corfield. He was an entrepreneur and a very highly skilled engineer. The Corfield Periflex had a periscope like a submarine. Through this inverted periscope, when pushed down, you looked, viewed and focused the image from behind the lens. It was a clever design, and he succeeded in selling quite a lot with good marketing. He then moved the factory to Northern Ireland and was bought out by Guinness, the beer brewer. They lost interest in it, and he moved away. Apparently they started making beer bottle tops there instead.

Several others had a go at making cameras, but none of them succeeded. They all came out with models, but none of them stayed on the market, because once import restrictions were lifted, and the German industry started again, they were not making cameras from old patents; they were making new designs. So the fact that old German patents were open was no advantage.

Later, the same thing would happen to the German industry when the Japanese came. In the new century, the industry changed radically and became ultimately a digital industry. The traditional camera makers were slow to change, and electronic home entertainment makers like Sony and Panasonic came into the field and started distributing their cameras through non-photo outlets. Although an entirely new market was created and huge quantities were sold, so many new companies entered the field from all over the Far East that overproduction resulted in the market not being able to absorb it. Prices tumbled, and traditional margins, which had not been that good anyway, as in my early days in the industry, just became unworkable. More about this later.

The mechanisms used to make a shutter consist of little gear trains. These were at that time used, not only in cameras, but also as timing devices in shells and in bombs, when it was still in the mechanical age. Now, of course, we are in the electronic age, and timing is done digitally. Because, after the First World War, the British government wanted to build up the industry in the UK, they put the highest protective import duty in the British tariff on cameras and shutters. In fact, it was called a Key Industry Duty and was 50% on any camera or shutter being imported from anywhere.

It is a fact that the Germans were the main camera making nation before the war and became that again after the war, because they had a subcontracting industry of shutter manufacturers. One in Munich called Deckel made Compur shutters, and one in the Black Forest called Gauthier made Prontor shutters.

There were many lens manufacturers like Schneider of Kreuznach, Steinheil of Munich, Isco of Goettingen and quite a number of others. The Carl Zeiss optical factories in Jena were in what became Eastern Germany after the war, and there were a lot of fights between the Eastern and the Western German Zeiss factories on trademark rights.

We didn't have enough cameras during the war, and we certainly didn't have any cameras afterwards until we started importing again from Germany. So any retailer in Britain in the immediate post war years could only exist by buying and selling second hand equipment. There was hardly any film being made other than for military use, including that film which was made for aircraft cameras. Eastman Kodak made most of those in the States, and we used it in the Royal Air Force. Those films, instead of being small roll films like 120 and 620 size, were five and a quarter inches wide, long rolls of film without backing paper. So immediately after the war, an industry sprang up in the UK to buy this ex-Royal Air Force film and cut it up for spooling onto the popular 120 and 620 sizes. When you brought your film in to be developed, the backing paper and spool that normally would be thrown away was recycled many times and then sold as ex-RAF film. This business ceased when a plentiful supply of normal film became available.

After I'd been with John Martin for nearly a year, I decided I wanted to start my own business. The plane crash was on 13th of February 1947. About six months later, in August of 1947, I was in business on my own at the age 20.

⬥ 16 ⬥
On the Climbing of Mountains

THERE WAS, IN THE NEIGHBOURING town of Newcastle-under-Lyme, a photographer by the name of William Parton, who had been established at 19 Hassell Street as W. Parton since 1894. Newcastle is best described as a dormitory town for Stoke-on-Trent. It is right next door. You can not tell where the one town starts and the other one finishes. A lot of the owners and managers in the pottery industry live in Newcastle. (There are many Newcastles in England.) Newcastle-under-Lyme has a town shopping centre and a high-class residential area. This W. Parton business was not in the main street of the town but just off it, opposite to what used to be a haymarket when William Parton first started the business. He was more or less the only photographer in Newcastle-under-Lyme, which had a population of about 60,000 people.

Parton took photographs of every mayor of the town for display in the town hall. He took these pictures, in the fashion of the time, in a sepia colour. The picture appears in shades of brown, as opposed to greyscale, as in a black-and-white image. Anybody who wanted a baby photograph gave him the job. He was the established photographer in the town, so of course he did weddings. He used to go to the weddings on a very old 1920s style motorbike carrying a big wooden tripod and big wooden plate camera on his back until apparently he had an accident one day and fell off. This motorbike was put upstairs in the building among all his collection of glass plates and he never used it again.

In mid 1947, I went to see William Parton and told him it was time he retired and I would like to buy his business. He threw me out.

But, as so many times in my life, fate was kind, and three weeks later—I had of course left my card—his daughter telephoned me and said "If you're still interested, my father and I would like to see you."

He wanted £350 for the business, including the building, which had a very old established photography studio and darkroom on the first floor and all his negatives, which were all on glass plates. I didn't have £350. I did have a motorbike, and it was insured by a broker named Lawrence Mercer. I went to him and told him I needed £350 and that I would pay it back within two years. I told him I didn't have any collateral security but I would promise him that as long as I stayed in business he would have all my insurance business. He wrote a cheque for the full amount there and then without any written agreement.

I gave notice to John Martin and bought Parton's business. I was not yet 21, which was the age of being able to do legal transactions. I think the whole thing was wrapped up in 14 days and I moved in. I've never worked for anybody else since. I've always been the boss. It was my aim to climb mountains and not necessarily make a lot of money but a lot of achievements—to get to the top of whatever I went in for. And that was the start of the journey.

John Martin wished me well, and when I started importing cameras, he became a good customer. He was a very nice man, a gentleman in every way. A very good photographer, he became one of the first Associates of the Royal Photographic Society in the Stoke-on-Trent area. He did a lot of commercial photography for the pottery industry for advertising and publicity. He had a very good business and was a man of immense integrity and a very good Rotarian as well.

William Parton was an old-style photographer. He had a specially built north light studio and took all his studio photographs by natural light. He also had an upholstered triangular "thing" for baby photographs. If they couldn't stand up or sit down even, he just wedged the baby into this "thing," and they couldn't move. It was fantastic. I used that right up until I quit the studio photography business.

After I bought the Parton business, I paid the loan back to the broker much quicker than in two years—in all a worthwhile transaction from which all parties benefited, and Lawrence Mercer certainly did handsomely with all the company insurance I placed with him from then until 1980.

❖ 17 ❖

Setting Up Shop

HAVING BOUGHT THE BUSINESS FROM W. Parton, I traded as "Charles G. Strasser, Newcastle Studios." At the time, I was still living at the Lawton Arms. When I bought the Parton building, I felt that I should live on the premises, so that is where I moved to and worked in this small photography studio that had a shop downstairs as well. I progressively expanded from just being a professional photographer doing studio and wedding photography to retailing photographic equipment and processing film for other people and about 60 chemists and photography shops in the area.

There was a perfectly good room above the Parton shop. It had, literally, tons of old glass plates of pictures Parton had taken of weddings and studio sittings for the past 50 years. I had the local rubbish and waste disposal people come to take it away and dump it wherever they dumped those things. They came, and it took them two days to clear the room of all the glass plates. Buried under the glass plates was the aforementioned 1920s motorbike Parton had used as transportation to weddings and the like. I had no idea of the value of it. They asked me what to do with it. I told them to take it away, and they did. It was probably worth a fortune. But I just wanted that room cleared.

I decorated the room and made it into a bedroom. It was next door to the waiting room for the studio. Upstairs also had the darkroom for processing and printing. Downstairs was the shop, and at the back of it was a toilet and a sink. It was not a proper bathroom, but I was a single young man of 20. I didn't need more than that. I bought a bed and lived there.

I shall never forget one episode. Customers would be directed to the waiting room to await their studio sitting. When I was ready, I would collect them and take the picture of the baby or whoever in the studio. One day, it was about 5 p.m., the receptionist downstairs shouted up to the darkroom, "Mr. Strasser, you've got a customer in the waiting room. Don't forget!" The receptionist left, and I forgot all about this lady. I went out. I didn't have eating facilities on the premises, so I went to a restaurant and locked the place up. I locked this woman in the shop. She was still there when I came back around 7 p.m. I would have thought that she would have the sense to be concerned. But she just said, "I'm still waiting for you. I thought you were very busy."

I took on another member of staff, a lady, to be the shop manageress and shop assistant. When you've got a photographic retail shop, you must have a facility for developing and printing customers' films. So you have two options—you either do it yourself or you send it out to a wholesale photo-finishing firm. That was now leading to the next stage. I decided to do our own developing and printing on the same premises and employed girls in the back, which we had converted for this.

I took pictures of weddings throughout the North Staffordshire area. That is how I got to know the area really well. When we started developing and printing films for chemists and photographic dealers all over the area, I first started collecting and delivering films myself on a motorbike. I probably know that local area inside out, every little street and every shortcut. A postman just delivers in his little local area; I knew the whole area, all the churches and the shops.

I decided, after a little while, we might as well start buying and selling second-hand photographic equipment as I had done at John Martin's. We cleared the room downstairs and made it into a proper retail shop and photography business. Now we had a shop going, and I started to employ more people. I never, ever, employed people until I had first created the need for more staff. I never wanted to be in the situation of having to lay people off, and we never did lay anyone off. (Except for imposed government measures in the years 1968/69)

As far as the photographic retail shop was concerned, customers came to me because I was a professional photographer. They came to me for advice about what to buy rather than going to a chemist as they knew that I was better qualified to give advice. At that stage my only competitor in Newcastle-under-Lyme was a photographic department within a chemist shop. All worked well, and I had very loyal staff.

The developing and printing business, a very seasonal business at that time, grew and we took on many girls for the processing, darkroom, printing and finishing work. I started to instil a family spirit and organised staff outings and social events in which I also participated and this continued even when we stopped the photofinishing and redeployed staff to the importing side.

I started then what I continued to do even later and that was mainly to take youngsters straight from school and to train them. In that way, they learned to do it my way, which worked better than taking them from other employers where they might have already got into bad habits. When we first started doing the developing and printing, we really just had a specialised interviewing procedure to find people who had common sense, enthusiasm and intelligence rather than academic credentials. Not having academic qualifications myself, that never played a big role in people we hired.

That even applied later with salesmen because we wanted to teach them how to sell our way, rather than somebody else's way. We liked applicants with photographic knowledge but not ones that had already been representatives for our competitors. We based a lot on competitive spirit and incentives and competitions within a sales force. A new salesman first came to head office and had a week's training. Then he would go out with an existing salesman for a week. Then we let him loose on his own. But we still called them back, usually every two months, to the head office to get new marketing information and an injection of enthusiasm. I knew from experience that when a salesman goes into a shop the first thing, after all the pleasantries, that a buyer always says is "What's new?" You have to have something new every time—not necessarily a new product but it could be a new marketing scheme for that product or new way of advertising it. A salesman can't always come up with something new, so he needs to come back to the head office and get updated. Marketing and good communications with your staff are very important.

◈ 18 ◈

Meeting My Match

IT WAS DURING THIS TIME that I met my future wife, Maureen Jane Lees, through my friends, Murti and Krish, who were members of a Co-op youth club in Stoke. I went with them one evening to go dancing at the club. At the door was a most attractive young lady, and they introduced us. She took my money with a smile, and we went in to the dancing, partying and socialising. It was a very nice evening. When she finished taking the money, because she had been friendly with my friends, she joined us, and we started chatting. She was a very capable young lady in addition to her good looks and lovely demeanour. She had been friends with my friends for some time. I went there on another occasion, because it was a nice club and she was a lovely girl. We became very friendly, and chemistry developed between us.

She told me that we could only be friends because she was spoken for and engaged to a Second Lieutenant in the British army whom she had met locally while he was training in Trentham Gardens, a huge Italian garden with a lake a mile long, just south of Newcastle-under-Lyme. It had an open air swimming pool, a huge dance hall and was the focal point for many mystery tours, from the whole of the Midlands, where you booked and paid your money but didn't know where the coach was going to take you. They invariably finished up in this Trentham Gardens. During the war, part of it was converted as an officer training camp with Nissen huts on the grounds. The huge dance hall part of the gardens was converted and used as a cheque clearing centre for all UK banks, which had been evacuated from London. So a lot of bank staff worked in that area, and a lot of officers were trained in the camp. Maureen had met this young officer there, but he had subsequently been posted somewhere else. We decided at first that it was fine to be just friends. Maureen was then a secretary and personal assistant to Dr. Green, the Director of the British Ceramic Research Association. It was a very good job. She was a very competent secretary, a very fast shorthand typist and also helped me by putting that knowledge at my disposal.

Soon, Maureen and I became more than just friends, and we started courting. We went out together on my motorbike and on car trips. Then, we decided that we would get married. She must have, I suppose, sent the usual "Dear John" letter to this young army officer to whom she was engaged. I never met him, but she told me I was infinitely more interesting than he was!

Maureen didn't leave her secretarial job for quite a while after our marriage. When she wasn't working, we went out and did speculative photography in dance halls and clubs. We took pictures of people dancing, and they could come and see the pictures at my shop. In those days, not many people had cameras, and film was difficult to get. Speculative photography was a good business. I did very little commercial photography: I just dealt with people.

With the business going well, Maureen and I got married on 8th of October 1949. We didn't have enough money to buy a house. As a matter of personal policy I did not believe in renting for my private home, other than for holiday accommodation, and have never done so. In those days you could get 95 percent loans from building societies, particularly the local building society. We found a very low priced house known as Montrose, which is a resort town in northeast Scotland. Our Montrose was located in a not-so-nice area at the end of Pitgreen Lane in Wolstanton. It was a small, semi-detached, two-bedroom house. We didn't have enough money to furnish more than just one living room and one bedroom because all the money that came into the business was used to expand the business. As it so happened, the house was on top of a little hill overlooking the valley containing the Shelton Iron and Steel Works, a steel smelting plant as well as a steel rolling plant. This industrial site wasn't a very nice view.

Maureen's father, Arthur Lees, was a foreman in the plant there and lived very near in Kelvin Street, Maybank, with Maureen's mother, Gladys Lees, and her younger brother, Geoffrey. Early in his life, Geoffrey emigrated permanently to Argentina, where he worked for a British meat packing company. He later transferred into the educational field and became a teacher at the British School in Buenos Aires, later becoming its headmaster. He married a girl named Edna, and they had two children, John and Elizabeth. I visited him just before he died five years ago in March 2002 in Buenos Aires. Edna had predeceased him.

As our financial position got better, Maureen and I began to talk about starting a family. We decided to improve on our Montrose house at Pitgreen Lane and sell it. Our next house was in a much better area in Trentham, which is part of the City of Stoke-on-Trent. It was a detached house at the top end of Allerton Road in Trentham. We decided to call our second house Montrose as well. Indeed, we kept the name of Montrose even for our third and final house in England. (It wasn't just to save the cost of the nameplate for the house; it was just a name we liked.)

In our new house on Allerton Road, we started our family. We stayed here a couple of years and then moved to Parkway, a bigger house, still in Trentham. We had more garden space in that house, and we placed two children's wooden Wendy playhouses side by side in the garden next to the swings. We lived close to a huge gardens and park where there was plenty of space for rural walks and, in the gardens, even playing facilities.

My eldest daughter, Suzanne, was born on 7th of December 1953, in the City General Hospital in Stoke-on-Trent. Dianne, my younger daughter, was born on 19th of March 1956, at the same hospital. Both were born under a well-known local gynaecologist, Mr. Burton. Maureen stopped work and became a full-time mother and housewife. By then, my business life had changed dramatically from being a photographer to having built up a company with overseas connections. It took me on visits abroad and to bigger customers in the United Kingdom. Of necessity, I spent a fair amount of time away from home. However, I always made it a point to spend family holidays together, and we usually went abroad to France, Italy and elsewhere in Europe on holidays. As currency restrictions eased and the children got older we became more adventurous and holidayed in the Caribbean and the U.S.

When the wholesale photo-finishing started, I commenced trading as "North Staffs Photographic Services." (We also used that name when we started importing in 1950.) We outgrew the premises at 19 Hassell Street when we started the wholesale processing side, and needed more space. Luckily, two doors away in a little lane called Balls Yard, there was an empty old furniture warehouse that we took over. We changed the name from North Staffs Photographic Services in Balls Yard to "Photopia Ltd.". We changed from a non-limited company to a limited company. Its trademark name was Photopia because of the concept that it was the Utopia of Photography. In the beginning we were wholesaling only UK made products and in particular some simple cameras made in Birmingham, not far away from us, by Coronet and some films from Dufay. We put the D&P processing in there and subsequently put the importing and wholesaling side in there too. Later we outgrew that and again needed more space, and I found another building in Hempstalls Lane, still in Newcastle-under-Lyme. It was a four storey building that had been used as a fustian mill.

An estate agent, Syd Whalley, also a member of the Newcastle-under-Lyme Rotary club, had bought this building and he couldn't sell it. He then had the idea of taking out some floors and converting it into a coach or bus wash place. As I was looking for a building I bought it from him. The top floor was beyond repair and the building had a sloping roof, so I just took that off and surfaced the floor with asphalt and made that into the flat roof. Now we had a three storey building, much bigger than we needed but good for expansion. Later on, we needed even more space than that.

❖ 19 ❖

"I'd Like To Be Your Sole Agent in the UK"

EARLY IN 1949 ON OUR first holiday trip to Europe, Maureen and I went to Switzerland in the firm's first vehicle, a blue Austin A40 pickup. In those days there was still a severe shortage of foreign currency and severe exchange controls were in existence in the UK. You could only take about £35 per holiday per year out of the country.

I learned at that stage, that there was a limit to one's progress if one did everything oneself. So the aim was to expand. I also realised that an industry involved in distribution, buying and selling, had a better profit potential than a manufacturing one and was less labour intensive. So that was my ultimate aim, to get into non-manufacturing and non-processing situations, where the skill of marketing could enhance one's opportunities.

On the way back from Switzerland, we stopped in a town in Germany called Wiesbaden. I went into a local photographic dealer there. I told him that I was a photo dealer from England and would be interested to see how cameras are made. "Is there a camera manufacturer in this town?" He said there's one up at 172 Dotzheimer Strasse, and so I immediately went there.

The factory, called Gebrueder (Brothers) Wirgin, was owned by a Jewish family before the war, making cameras called Wirgin. When we got to the factory, the name plate didn't read "Wirgin," it read "Adox." Hitler had taken the factory away from them and gave it to a German firm called Adox, the fourth-largest German film manufacturer. When Maureen and I visited the factory, the

Wirgin brothers had just been given the factory back, and I met a Dr. Max Wirgin who had, together with the family, spent the war years in the United States. The camera being produced under the Adox brand which they had designed before the war was now getting back its brand name of Edinex. They were turning out 35mm cameras, quite advanced for the day, and they were back in production.

Dr. Wirgin showed me around and, when we were done with the tour, I said, "I'd like to be your sole agent in the UK."

Looking me over he said, "You know, you've got no experience in importing or anything of that nature. In any case importing of cameras from Germany into the UK is not allowed."

"Yes," I agreed. "That's true at the moment, but sooner or later that's going to have to change. Then we could be the first to start importing and the first on the market because we've made arrangements now."

Seeing his resistance weaken I continued, "You've got nothing to lose. Give me the agency on the basis of six months from the time of importation into the UK being allowed. If I do a good job, we carry on together, and if I don't, you find someone else."

We shook hands on that mutually beneficial understanding, which was to last for many years until the firm went under through the fierce competition from Japanese camera makers. (Later on, in most of my negotiations, I did have agency contracts but always kept them very simple. I came to the conclusion that such a contract is only good as long as the people who signed it retain respect for each other and as long as it is mutually beneficial.)

So I returned home with an agency for a German camera firm, and I was not yet 22. I was wholesaling some UK made products, but only to a limited number of customers in my immediate area—not on a national basis. I was a nobody, and now I had an agency for an established German camera maker. At the moment, I couldn't make any money from it. But I prepared for it. After our handshake, we stayed in touch.

◆ 20 ◆

Every Lock Has a Key

I WAS NOW VERY INTERESTED to deal with government departments to find out exactly when it would be possible to import and what the procedures would be. I had to look for some means of selling these cameras, to make arrangements before importing became possible. As it happened I was lucky. It only took another four months after making my deal with Dr. Wirgin before the Board of Trade announced the arrangements for camera imports from Germany. An import licence would be required, known as open general licence (OGL), which meant you did not have to apply for it each time.

However, cameras were restricted to being in value no higher than £5-10s-0d CIF, which means Cost plus Insurance and Freight. There are two main ways to import—Free on Board (FOB), which means all the shipping and other expenses have to be paid by the buyer, or CIF and it lands at the UK port and everything is paid for up to that stage by the vendor. The regulation was that you couldn't go over the £5-10s-0d maximum CIF basis, and from that point on I learned that it was much easier for costing purposes to get every supplier to quote on a CIF basis. The vendor was in a much better position to get shipping costs and to calculate what the freight and insurance cost would be. It was not always possible with Japanese suppliers because they preferred FOB basis.

I immediately phoned Henry Wirgin, who was already installed at that time in Wiesbaden, and I gave him the good news. I told him we were ready to go on the announced commencement date of the OGL, and I asked him to send me a price list of everything he had available under £5-10s-0d CIF.

He laughed, "We only have one that cheap, a very simple 35mm camera, lever wind, with a four-speed shutter and a Cassar or Isconar lens."

"Fine. How many can you supply?"

"How many can you buy?"

I said "How about 100 in the first shipment."

"Very well but aren't you aiming a bit too high?"

I was convinced that the market had been starved for the last seven years and the dealers would snap them up quickly. But we'd have to start advertising. I'd already investigated that as well, with the main magazine at that time, the "Amateur Photographer".

The commencement day came along, and he sent the shipment from Frankfurt to Manchester Airport. Thus we became the first company to import a German-made 35mm camera into the UK after the war, and this was an important step on the start of my success story. The pent-up demand was so great because, during the whole of the wartime period, there were no new cameras in the shops. Camera demand was absolutely fantastic and initially, instead of having to sell them, we just had to allocate them.

I started going around selling to photographic dealer outlets all over the UK and opening accounts. There were just three of us in the whole of the company, besides all the staff in the wholesale photofinishing developing and printing side, my wife, Maureen, myself, and a girl in the office doing invoicing and packing.

When I had first met Dr. Max Wirgin, I put all my cards on the table and told him that I would need a bit of help from him to start with, because I had no money. So he gave me 30 days to pay, which was fairly easy to get in Europe. (It was almost impossible to get later on from the Japanese. They wanted a Letter of Credit and would not do business with you if you did not have one. Before a bank would issue a Letter of Credit you virtually had to have the backing of that amount of money in the account.) Because dealers were hungry for cameras, they readily agreed to pay me promptly for their allocations.

When I went to pick up the first shipment I had already arranged a sale to a dealer, "Robinson of Sale", in a suburb of Manchester, whose shop was on my way back from Manchester Airport to Newcastle. He was quite an astute photographic dealer and he regularly advertised in the "Amateur Photographer" magazine. He agreed to take 25 cameras from my first shipment.

A small but very marketing-oriented one-shop dealer in Station Road, Edgware called Dixons was also a regular advertiser in the "Amateur Photographer". This shop was run by a Stanley Kalms. Later when I called on Dixons I would fly in my plane into Elstree, the nearest airfield, and usually be picked up by Stanley. The business had actually been started by his father, who was a professional photographer. Stanley Kalms came into it and commenced retailing photographic equipment. He started about the same time as I did. By the time I started importing, he had four shops, and a central office and warehouse in Edgware. His lieutenants in the founding marketing team were Ernie Shenton and Ray Cooke. They always wanted at least half of my shipments. So Dixons of Edgware and Robinsons of Sales initially took three-quarters of every shipment sold before we started selling to other dealers.

Naturally, Stanley Kalms and I became good friends to the extent that we spent some family holidays together. He built up the Dixons business and went public—just before I did—with a London Stock Exchange listing on 9th July 1962, with an issued and fully paid share capital of £200,000. From there, he forged ahead with expansions and takeovers to a company employing 40,000 people in 14 countries of Europe and a profit of £1 million per day. He is undoubtedly the most successful retailer in the UK and was knighted in the Queen's Honours list to become Sir Stanley. In 2003, he was made a life peer to become Lord Kalms of Edgware, and he sits in the House of Lords. He handed over the reins of the Dixons Group in 2002. Our friendship has endured to the present day, despite his having been a tough business negotiator.

Back at the start of the government quotas, when Wirgin and I were working out our deal, I read all government regulations very carefully. I also learned how to challenge the government's interpretation. I never accepted things at face value. In the regulations, it said that camera accessories such as range finders and exposure meters could be imported regardless of value and without a quantity limitation. I did not have an agency for either of these accessories at that stage. But I had an idea.

So I called Henry Wirgin and said, "You also make a camera with a built-in range finder. How much is that camera?"

"Oh," he says, "that's £7."

"That's fine." I replied. "Can you take the range finder out and then put the top of the camera back on again. Put the range finder into a separate housing and send the two completely separate items and invoice them separately? I'll set up an assembly line here to put them back together again."

It was perfectly legal, as there were no import restriction on range finders as accessories. He agreed that it was a very good idea and started shipping.

Now we have got two models to sell, one which nobody else believed was importable. By then, my competitors had started importing cameras for £5-10s-0d but no one could believe it was possible to bring in cameras with built-in range finders. Such cameras couldn't possibly be made for £5-10s-0d. We set up an assembly line at our end. We took the range finder out of the temporary housing, built it into the camera, and screwed it all back together again—a normal factory assembly process. We had to collimate it as well, so we bought a collimator. That was the beginning of our after-sales service department. We did the same assembly exercise with built-in exposure meter models, and that gave us further models without competition.

Later on, we bought very sophisticated electronic testing equipment for shutter speeds, flash synchronisation, etc., but the collimator was our first entry into quality control of our products. More cameras in the hands of users meant more after-sales service, so we hired a full-time skilled camera mechanic, Hans Lehmann, an ex-German Luftwaffe prisoner of war who had stayed in England and was employed by K.G. Corfield in Wolverhampton. We brought in these cameras, and they were a huge success. Wirgin also developed new smarter models and changed brand names—from Edinex first to Edina and then to its final name of Edixa. The import restriction maximum value was increased to £7 CIF and later was lifted altogether. The Wirgin factory did extremely well in exports particularly to the United States and the UK but also all over the world. Mr. Otto Helfricht, a new works manager, came on board. He had fled from East Germany and had been one of the original engineers who had developed the Exakta single lens reflex camera. He developed a single lens reflex camera for Wirgin because consumer demand was starting to change toward more sophisticated models. Also, photographers wanted to see a large, full picture, which was possible in a single lens reflex camera, instead of the usual small see-through viewfinders.

◆ 21 ◆

Expanding

WIRGIN WAS THE FIRST BUT, over time, we built up the importing business with many other agencies. First we had just one salesman doing the whole country, and as we grew, we added more. We built up to seven and split up the UK into population density areas.

I discovered that in any retail situation, a shop manager or buyer will give a salesman only a limited amount of his time, knowingly or unknowingly. After that the buyer has exhausted his attention span amidst the many other pressing demands on his time. I wanted more time facing each customer, so I started new companies with new sales forces so that one salesman would go in, and then at another time another one from another company would get new attention and a new time span from the same buyer. By the time we finished, we had four different sales companies for photo products and one for audio and one for watches.

It was a difficult but an interesting time. We could sell all the cameras we were able to import in the first few years of our business. So to make up for this when only cameras were on quota, I had to find lots and lots of photographic accessories like exposure meters, range finders, flashguns, tripods, enlargers, projectors and screens and all sorts of things. If you look at our catalogues from those early days, they had cameras in the early pages, but by far the greater part of the catalogue was accessories because these we could import without restriction and then our marketing ability started to perform.

When I first started, I did a lot of the selling for the company myself and then when we started advertising I brought in one salesman called Stanley Kramer. He was the first person I employed from outside the area.

It was important to choose the right people, who could accept the responsibility, and now it was the question of how to remunerate them. There were basically three different choices at that time. We always differentiated between representatives and salesmen. I didn't like the term "representative". Establishment firms like Kodak employed "representatives". They paid them a fixed salary, which was medium. They had the security of employment at that time, and they probably had some sales targets, but they were, in the main, selling consumable items like films and paper and chemicals. They were taking orders rather than selling.

You then had, at the other end of the scale, people who were super salesmen and preferred to work purely on commission. They felt they could make a lot of money that way. They had a lot of confidence in their own abilities but, of course, that also meant that if they were ill or sick, they wouldn't be earning.

I chose the middle course of paying a basic salary and a commission. The basic salary, which was guaranteed, you could hardly live on. But if you were a good salesman, you could live well on the total income. With the commission percentage then agreed and fixed, I always promised that even if he earned more money than I did, the commission rate would not be changed. In all the years I've been in business, I've never varied from that, although I know other companies have. I would never say to a salesman that he earned too much just because he was making more than I was. If the salesman is earning more than I am, he's helping the company to earn a lot as well. Many companies who have different commission systems, when they saw that their salesmen were earning too much money, started cutting back on their commissions. I thought that was terrible. We never, ever did that, and we had two salesmen who, on occasion, earned more than I did as a result of their commission earnings. That was fine with me.

To the best of my knowledge, I never took salesmen from other companies in the same field as we were in. The only time we hired a salesman from our competitors was when we had employed him previously and he came back to us. We generally hired from the retail side of the business because we wanted them to have some photographic knowledge. Then we would train them in our ways and procedures. Many of them stayed on the road a long time or transferred to other jobs in the company. A number of the successful ones left and started their own businesses and did extremely well in them, either on the retail side or in promotional companies and so on. Most of them will tell you that the lessons they learned while they were employed by me stood them in good stead for a long time.

When I began importing and distributing on a national scale, we quickly outgrew the Balls Yard building. We then moved to the Hempstalls Lane building, which I had remodelled from four storeys to three storeys and extensively refurbished with internal partitions to create offices, the warehouse and a canteen, all to accommodate the import and distribution business. From then on we concentrated on importing and distributing. At that stage, I sold the 19 Hassell Street building and stopped professional photography and retailing. From that point our operations could be defined as 1) sourcing suitable products at the right price, 2) reaching suitable exclusivity 3) purchasing them, 4) marketing them well to create a strong demand, 5) selling them and 6) giving a good after sales service.

I decided that if you can get an item that is a consumable like films, processing chemicals or flashbulbs then the potential was much bigger than with an item like a camera which you buy once in a blue moon. So I was looking for consumable items. We were starting to build up a UK customer base very quickly, because initially we found we hardly had to sell. Dealers would call up and say, "Please can we have . . . " Later on that changed and we had to sell and give sale discounts and invent ways to entice them to buy. There had been a shortage for years. These were the first German cameras to come in. Until everybody else woke up to this situation, I had a four month clear run which was amazing.

I was looking for a consumable item. An obscure German man called Kissling had invented what he called a Kissling Flash Button to use instead of much more expensive glass flashbulbs. The early way to use flash in photography was with flash powder on a metal tray. The next step was magnesium strips, and then somebody invented the flash bulb, which was really a controlled amount of magnesium contained in a glass bulb. Mr. Kissling decided that flash bulbs were too expensive and too big, so he went back to the flash powder days and made little cardboard containers about the size of a tap washer, filled it with a controlled amount of flash powder, and sealed it with a litmus paper on the top. Sticking out of the base was a silver paper coated card foot which could be inserted into a flashgun made for these flash buttons, and this could either be fired manually or by synchronising to a camera shutter. You could put it into the camera accessory shoe just like a flashgun for bulbs. The light output of the Kissling Flash Buttons was about the same, and it performed the same purpose as the flash bulb but at about one-quarter the cost. It was a great idea, and I started importing and marketing them and got some good editorial write-ups on their performance. Indeed, we sold them to the extent that Phillips and Osram, the two major flashbulb manufacturers, started getting quite worried about this and kept on reducing the price of their flash bulbs to the point where it killed the flash button business. Again, it was something new, most dealers stocked them and it fulfilled a function for a time, so that was the second agency.

❖ 22 ❖

Quotas, Quotas

AS NOTED EARLIER, BECAUSE OF the maximum £5-10s-0d CIF import restriction, we were limited to just the one camera model or its variation. The quota first came into being in about 1950 and stayed at £5-10s-0d until 1957. Then a quota was established of £100,000 per annum for cameras over £5-10s-0d CIF for all imports, not just for my company. Therefore it became necessary to appeal for as large a percentage of the £100,000 as possible. We certainly got a very good share of the total quota. Then it wasn't until 1959 that the basic value per camera importable without restriction was increased to £7 CIF. Finally in 1960, the quotas were removed altogether. There was no quota as long as the cameras came from what at that time was referred to as a "relaxation area." That virtually meant Europe except for the Eastern bloc countries and the Far East. So at that time when the quotas were finished and there was no basic price limitation, cost didn't come into it, and you could bring in as many cameras of any value that you wanted from the relaxation area.

In 1957 a quota for cameras from Japan was introduced which, believe it or not, amounted to only £15,000 for the whole country. I could only import from Japan my allocation of the £15,000. Then, in 1960, there was a quota brought in for the Soviet Union of £165,000 and for East Germany of £82,000. It was some time after that, that all the import restrictions were lifted.

Each year you had to make sure that your portion of any quota was not reduced and hopefully that it was increased. There was one civil servant in the Board of Trade whose sole decision it was how to allocate these things. You could just hope that you presented a good case and awaited the next allocation.

As more new German manufacturers started, they were also trying to exert pressure, through their association in Germany, to also get a share of the quota. Really the only answer was to get the total quotas increased. But, the main reason for quotas was still the protection of the British industry. When that fell by the wayside, the government was desperately short of foreign exchange and wanted to discourage imports of any sort. Later on when the allocation of the ridiculous, pitifully small quota came for the imports from Japan, the same civil servant decided, for some reason or other, that he would give a quota for lenses to a retailer. Up to that time, quotas or allocations of imports were only given to bona fide importers. Of course, this retailer started advertising Japanese lenses, and the whole industry—both importers and other retailers—was up in arms about it. The civil servant then got moved sideways and, after that, we never had any more problems.

So it was all very orderly marketing, and even the Japanese, when they came into the picture, vowed that they would keep to orderly marketing. They did try their best, although later on, because of overproduction, orderly marketing went out of the window. However, the main reason for that was that in 1964, Ted Heath, the then President of the Board of Trade, abolished retail price maintenance (RPM). From then on, it was illegal for an importer or manufacturer to fix the final selling price of any commodity. There were some exemptions to that, for instance books, which for a long time could still be sold at fixed retail prices. The photographic industry tried very hard to gain exemption from this law because of the necessity of providing after-sales service and the need to maintain trained personnel at the retail level. We didn't succeed—and I'm speaking now for the Photographic Importers Association—so price cutting started. A retailer doesn't reduce prices totally out of his own pocket. He starts pressure on the wholesaler, the distributor and the importer to get extra margins, higher than his competitor, so he can cut prices even more. Generally speaking, therefore, any price advantage given to the end user came out of the pocket of the importer and the distributor.

In 1968/69, import restrictions had been removed but we were faced by yet another restriction on free trade and that was a Purchase Tax (PT). At that stage there was no Value Added Tax (VAT) but a Purchase Tax which was increased in 1969 to 50 percent. That was a huge barrier to sales. In 1970, the government increased it further to 55 percent. Additionally, we suffered all sorts of import levies and duty deposits which were introduced in the days of the Wilson government when there were a lot of currency problems creating sterling instabilities. They tried to restrict imports and to make it as difficult as possible to bring cameras and other commodities in. We were already paying a 50 percent Key Industry Duty, as I explained earlier. On top of that, we were paying a purchase tax of 55 percent. Also the government decided on a devaluation of the pound which resulted in our paying 16% more for all our imports. Then we were also paying an import deposit of another 50% which was an interest free loan to the government, not to speak about taxation on the company's profits which that year were almost non existent. So we were paying a lot of money to the government, without any thanks for all the extra work involved. For a full list of these government impositions, published in my Chairman's statement to shareholders in the 1969 accounts, see Appendix B.

In 1971, the Purchase Tax finally started coming down, first to 45 percent, and then progressively it came down to 25 percent in 1975 in preparation for the change over to a Value Added Tax in 1975. This was a multi-rate complex VAT. The rate depended on whether the items were considered luxury or essential goods—a very complicated tax structure with lots of anomalies. It still is to this day. It resulted in a lot of in-fighting as to which group a particular item fell into, whether a high tax rate, low tax rate or no tax rate type of commodity. Clearly, a lot depended on interpretation. I did a lot of negotiations on behalf of the Photographic Importers Association with taxation authorities, mainly Customs and Excise, to determine classification for VAT. This often resulted in ridiculous situations. For instance, it became beneficial to split a camera from its ERC (ever ready case), previously always sold together, because cameras fell into the highest tax group and leather cases in the lowest. If sold together, then the higher tax rate would apply. You could still sell them together, but they had to be listed, ordered and invoiced separately. There were many anomalies, and not only in our industry.

In 1972, we had a situation where certain goods coming from developing countries got a preferential tariff. For instance, if you could find a maker from Korea, which was quite an up and coming technical product sourcing country, then on certain types of products you could bring them in on a lower rate of duty than if the same goods came from Japan. That was another incentive not only to start chasing low labour cost countries but also the developing countries as a source of supply. Some goods from developing countries got a preferential duty rate of zero percent, but usually there was a limiting quota, so it was always a race to get part of it before it was exhausted. Usually, the quota was administered by the exporting developing country who issued a certificate to that effect.

⋄ 23 ⋄

Agencies and Products

OUR FIRST AGENCY WAS WIRGIN in Wiesbaden, and we kept that association for many years, until their demise. We kept 99% of the agencies.

The only agency we ever lost was one that I decided to give up, and that was for the Soviet camera industry.

The second agency we acquired after Wirgin was the Kissling Flash Buttons, and the third was a company called Wateler, which made a very good range of accessories like rangefinders, flashguns, cine lighting later on, and small bits and pieces like lens dusting brushes. They had a very good range of accessories, and we built up a very good relationship to the extent that the owner, Edmund Wateler, sent his son, Heinz, over to England for six months to learn English and our marketing methods.

Later, we took on the products of a very famous Swedish company called GEPE, founded by Goran Pettersson. They produced purely plastic moulded products, in the main, cine reels of all different film sizes like 8mm, Super 8, 16mm as well as plastic reel cans for them. Their main line was thin and super thin slide frames in many formats, mainly designed for bulk use in hospitals and government departments, police, etc., who used machine mounting of the transparencies. This was a very interesting business because it was a consumable item bought in bulk by large-scale users. Then, besides having the quite expensive machines for large scale users, they also brought out little popular hand operated machines for cutting the film and mounting in GEPE frames. They undoubtedly became the leaders in that field and still are today, although the use of slide films nowadays is very limited.

Then I found a factory making metal box cameras in Northern Germany. They made them under our brand of Photopia, and this was the very first of many of our own brand products. The name of the factory was Vredeborch run by a Mr. Krause. After the box cameras, they redesigned a stylish, very simple camera, taking 120 film, which we sold under their brand name of Felica.

Coming back to the quotas, the quotas were allocated not only on the basis of the UK importer, but for the German factory as well. So the German Manufacturers Association gave the Board of Trade a list of all their members for whom they wanted part of the UK quota. So if I got another agency for cameras, I could have more quota. That's how I got the Vredeborch agency. We sold their cameras to the limitation of the quota given without any problems at all. I always required exclusive agencies.

I then found in West Berlin—a very unlikely source—a maker of enlargers. The company name was Dunco, and because West Berlin was an enclave of the three Allied powers within Eastern Germany, we had to fly everything out. Well, when the Russian blockade was on, the Berlin Air Lift was used to bring in food and clothing and even coal by air. Because of the disadvantage of being in Berlin, having to fly everything out, the government gave a 4 percent exporting subsidy to companies that were making goods of different types in Berlin. So we got a 4 percent price advantage when we imported these enlargers. They were considered accessories, even though they had lenses on them and could be brought in without any quota restrictions or value restrictions. So that was a good agency. This firm was basically a sheet metal working company and all their enlargers were made of sheet metal. In those days, there were no such things as colour prints. When colour started, everything was done on colour transparencies. They also made metal transparency storage boxes, slide storage boxes. Most other storage boxes were made from wood or plastic. We imported a good quantity of those and did good business with them.

Both Wirgin and Dunco were using Steinheil lenses on their cameras and on their enlargers. Steinheil was a very famous, old-established German lens manufacturer. I went to see them in Munich and met a Mr. Pete Schicks and got the sole agency for their lenses. We began with their enlarging lenses, but then they also started making interchangeable lenses for single lens reflex cameras. It was a good agency.

Pete Schicks later left Steinheil and went to Liechtenstein to start a factory making a revolutionary type of cine camera with a motor drive in the handle. It was called the Carena. The money for the factory was provided by Prince Franz Josef II, ruler of Liechtenstein. This venture produced fantastic cameras with excellent lenses and excellent results but, despite good sales, they were apparently losing money hand over fist all the time. They never could make it profitable. I was told that every time they needed a new influx of capital, the prince just went down into the cellars of his castle and brought out another old master and sold it. It provided the money to keep the production of his cameras going.

I did not just sign agreements with my suppliers. I had very good personal relationships with all of them—bosses and their staff, and my staff with their staff also. With Wirgin, the man I met first when I was coming back from Switzerland was Dr. Max Wirgin. Then his brother, Henry Wirgin, took over. Their export manager was Mr. Pyrlik. Their chief factory manager, a brilliant engineer who had worked in Eastern Germany and came across, was Mr. Helfricht. With the Kissling agency the name was from a Mr. Kissling, the inventor. Dunco in Berlin was a Mr. Dunco, believe it not.

Then we got another accessory firm agency specialising mainly in plastic moulding products, like viewers, slide viewers, flashguns, slide frames, all sorts of things. This was a company called Ariosa, run by a Mr. Armin Sauer. Of all the first German firms we dealt with, only Mr. Sauer and Ariosa, since renamed Unomat, and Dunco have survived. Wirgin is no longer there. Kissling is no longer there. Wateler is no longer there. Regula is no longer there. Steinheil is no longer there. Carena is no longer there. Unomat changed to mainly making electronic flash guns. Dunco is making world-class professional enlargers with aluminium castings instead of from sheet metal.

❖ 24 ❖

Diversification

THE LAST CHAPTER FEATURED FIRMS that I had got the first agency for in the UK. Now we come to some firms where I got the agency because the previous one didn't do a sufficiently good job or they went out of business.

We had a gap in the range for some real quality gadget bags, designed specifically with movable clips and partitions so that you could lay it out for your particular camera outfit. Our next product range, then, consisted of some very deluxe gadget bags to hold cameras and their accessories—separate lenses, filters and films. They were made in Germany from fine pigskin leather lined with chamois leather under the name of Omnica. They helped round off our assortment. The agency was previously held by Corfield and became available, and I got it. We started selling those, and then we started going also into the professional equipment field.

Dunco stopped making the two amateur enlargers, and we were looking for more enlargers to replace them. So I flew to Bolzano, Italy, to negotiate with Durst, which is now a famous international firm. Back then, they were just getting into the exporting of their enlargers. They were also making a couple of quite cheap cameras that they had designed themselves but which didn't last long in terms of acceptability by the market. But they did make superb precision enlargers both for amateurs and also large ones for professional use.

Newspapers and press photographers in those days didn't use 35mm cameras. They used 5x4 inch cameras like the Speed Graphic or 6x6 cm Rolleiflexes and Hasselblads. You always saw the press photographers with these big cameras and flashguns with flash bulbs on the side. (Electronic flashguns had not yet been invented). They had to have enlargers for those, and many used Durst enlargers. The Durst agency also gave us the basis for starting a professional equipment division, selling through specialist professional dealers to commercial, industrial, medical, forensic, press and studio photographers and to hospitals, processing laboratories, newspapers and government departments.

When we took on this Durst Agency, a salesman couldn't carry such big equipment around with him in a suitcase as he could with camera samples. First of all, we attended lots of exhibitions where we showed these to professional photographers. It was then that I bought a second-hand bus that had seen the end of its life transporting passengers, and we converted this into a mobile showroom with shelves in the back where the seats used to be. Wherever we stopped, people could, by invitation, come and view. We also took this mobile showroom to conferences and exhibitions, so we had our own exhibition stand in our own coach instead of having to be inside a building.

The very first time I drove this converted bus myself from Newcastle to a professional photographers' conference and exhibition somewhere in the South of England, it broke down halfway there. I had some salesmen with me and my advertising director, John Battison. We had quite an interesting time because the bus needed a spare part which was made in the factory in Coventry that had to be got overnight. Then, the garage owner who did the work wouldn't start on it until he got paid first. Although we had to spend the night parked outside this garage, we still made it to the exhibition in time. It became quite a legend in the industry that we had an old bus converted into a showroom for photographic and graphic arts equipment use.

So we now had a very nice range of equipment. Then Wirgin, my very first agency, decided that they were going upmarket with a single lens reflex camera designed by this Mr. Helfricht. In fact, it was the first West German-produced single lens reflex camera. There were two produced in East Germany—one called the Exakta, using 35mm film, and the other one was the Praktica, using 127 size film and later also a 35mm model.

The feature and advantage of a single lens reflex camera was that it could use interchangeable lenses from wide angle to telephoto. It also had a 45-degree mirror, which went out of the way during the exposure and allowed you to see the actual size image you would get on the film directly through the lens in the waist level viewfinder. Later on, they put in a pentaprism so you could look at eye level through the pentaprism viewfinder, through the mirror, directly at the object that you were photographing and still get the full size image in the viewfinder.

That started a new era. First the East Germans, then the West Germans, and later the Japanese, all started making 35mm single lens reflex cameras and many lenses and accessories for them. This became a major business segment for us both with the Wirgin Edixa Reflex and simpler Edixaflex and later with the various Minolta single lens reflex models. The achievement of Wirgin, having brought out the very first West German reflex camera—and we distributed it—should not be forgotten. Wirgin was also the first West German maker to produce a 35mm stereo camera, a camera with two lenses that produced two transparency pictures at the same time. If you looked at it in a stereo viewer, which also had two lenses, you saw the picture in true three dimensional stereo. Fantastic, but it was too cumbersome to use and too cumbersome to process. You also had to mount the results in a special double slide. It was a fashion fad that didn't last very long. It was okay while it lasted. Because production capacity was all used on the Edixa Reflex and Edixaflex, Wirgin phased out his lower-priced 35mm cameras, which we started on, and also phased out the Edixa stereo camera.

As mentioned before, when a salesman goes into a shop, he's always got to bring out something new. So we went in with the Edixa reflex camera and the Edixaflex, but we now no longer had a low-priced 35mm camera. In the Black Forest of Germany, there was a camera factory called Regula Werk King. The name of their 35mm cameras was Regula, and the name of the owner family was

King. Their son-in-law, Willie Bauser, was in charge of sales. He had had a previous UK importer. I flew to see him and got the agency, the sole agency for that camera range. He was the one who later produced the Mastra camera, my first own brand 35mm camera. The factory was situated in the lovely spa town of Bad Liebenzell. I loved going there. They produced the cameras and later also extended the range into producing electronic flash guns when that technology came online.

To fill a gap for cine cameras and projectors I obtained the prestigious agency of the German firm, Bauer, a wholly owned subsidiary of Bosch.

Rather than getting a whole range of things, I started also looking for just particular items to fill gaps in our range. Our first import from the United States was an enlarger timer from the Industrial Timer Corporation in Centerbrook, Connecticut, called the Time-o-Light, which we sold as an accessory to the enlargers.

One day I was reading in one of the American magazines that, instead of using liquid chemicals to process film, which took a long time and special equipment, even in the dark room, somebody in the United States had invented a system which used the processing chemicals in a gelatin form, a jelly form. It was called Sigel, and it was made by a processing laboratory in Ann Arbor, Michigan. So I flew over and looked at it. It looked like an interesting product. We did what I thought was a good marketing job on it, and it just didn't go, probably because people did not want to abandon their trusted wet processing method. Unfortunately, it turned out to be one of our failures, and we had to drop it.

The other items we imported from the United States were Da-lite screens, both tri-pod and wall-mounted types, from the Da-Lite Screen Company in Warsaw, Indiana. Cine and slide projector screens displayed to advantage the colour cine films and transparencies, and these came in a glass beaded surface or a plain white surface or even a silver surface and were made in huge quantities in the United States at very attractive prices, despite the shipping costs to Europe. I got the agency and met up with their very extrovert boss who always insisted on doing something I'd never come across before—having breakfast business meetings. We did good business, but different companies have different cultures, and this guy went out of his way to make promises and held out possibilities of support which just never materialised. Although we did good business, we could not do it on a long-term basis because the support, although promised, just didn't happen.

❖ 25 ❖

Moving into London

NEWCASTLE-UNDER-LYME IS ROUGHLY HALFWAY UP England, between Birmingham and Manchester. It is extremely well-situated, from a distribution point of view, because the port of Liverpool is an hour and a half away and Manchester airport less than an hour away. However, most of our competitors in the photographic import distribution industry were situated in or very close around London, and the London dealers could call to their warehouses to collect supplies. We found that a lot of dealers in those days were living on a "sell an item and replace it" basis and not ordering good quantities. This applied mainly to the dealers in the London area, but they formed a good percentage of the nation's dealers.

In 1956, just before changing our name to Photopia, we opened a London office still called North Staffs Photographic Services, which was at 36, Wardour Street, on the first floor. It was the London office showroom and service counter, where retailers could come and pick up supplies. Our very modest office was in the Soho district, a seedy place in the West End of London. In fact, our little showroom was above a Durex shop, Durex being the most famous brand of condoms in the UK—always a source of amusement that caused many ribald comments.

We were at a crossroads because we wanted to encourage people to order in decent quantities rather than the sell-and-replace method like our competitors. If customers had to wait for deliveries, they were forced to do so, but the London dealers could call on our competitors, the distributors based in and around the London area and pick up items on a daily basis. A lot of them employed messengers to do just that so they did not need to hold big stocks.

Whilst, really, I did not want to trade on that sort of a high-overhead basis, we were forced into having that London office, and we were forced, eventually, to trade in the same way.

I advertised for a London office manager and had a good application from a young retail salesman who was working at that time at Wallace Heaton Ltd., which was a well-known photographic retailer in New Bond Street in London. They had many royal warrants as suppliers of photographic equipment to the Queen and to many members of the Royal family and had been retained by them over many years. This young salesman by the name of Peter Gorton joined us and stayed for many years. He did leave us once but came back again. He left for a short while to go to Germany to learn German and work for a photographic accessory company there. His knowledge of German helped him in his career progress and helped the company also. But, with us, he started as manager of the London office. He wanted to be a salesman on the road, so he took over one of the territories when we got to the stage of dividing the country into seven areas. He then came back to the head office in Newcastle as my personal assistant, then he became export manager and then purchasing director.

With our Wardour Street office we competed on a level basis with our distributor competitors in the London area. When we advertised we also gave the address not only of our Head Office but also that of our London office, so we had quite a number of amateur photographers calling on the London office wanting to look at and then find out where they could buy our products. I had made it a very strong rule that we would never compete with our dealers and would never sell any of our items direct to consumers. So when people came and said they wanted to buy an Edinex, or later, an Edixa camera, we wanted to make sure that they bought that item—one of our cameras—when they went to a dealer, rather than being persuaded by a dealer to buy something else because the dealer didn't have the camera in stock.

We made an arrangement with a dealer by the name of B. Bennett and Sons, just around the corner from Wardour Street in Cranbourne Street by Leicester Square. The deal was that he would always have our products in stock, and we would send customers round to them. This worked extremely well. As aforementioned, once they sold a camera, they would immediately send a messenger to replace that camera, so basically they usually had one for display in the window, one inside the shop and one reserve stock that was replaced when they sold one of the other stock items.

One of the salesmen working in that shop was a young man called Michael Hanson, and his aim was to become a salesman for a distributor. At the end of the first Photofair exhibition in London, I offered him a job as salesman, and he turned out to be one of the best. He had also worked together with Peter Gorton at Wallace Heaton before he went to Bennetts. I could see that he was very enthusiastic and would become an excellent salesman. He too stayed with the company for many years, although he left twice to go to Hanimex, one of my competitors, but he came back again. He started as a salesman and then progressed to special products division sales manager some years later. When he finally left for the last time, he went again to Hanimex and then left them to start his own company. He got the Tasco binocular agency for the UK—a quite famous international brand—and he built it up to be a huge success, getting other products and later sold out successfully to a public company.

Now back to the point of opening the London office. We then started a sales force, dividing the country up into seven geographic areas, not based on size but on population density. Some areas were huge, like Wales, where the country is mainly mountains and lots of sheep but very few towns with photographic dealers. Then we had very small areas like the centre of London. Some salesmen had a lot of travelling to do between calls, and others did not.

Dividing the country into population density areas should have, theoretically, produced the same turnover for each area. But, of course, that's pure theory. In practise, the salesman who got the London sales area still did better than any other because London gets more tourists and visitors than any other area. So the London salesman's job was always a prize job.

We built up and grew and started more companies and had more sales. In 1965, we moved from our first floor offices in Wardour Street to a ground floor showroom—still modest, but at least it was on the ground floor with a shop window in Noel Street, but still in Soho. We stayed there for a year, and then, after what I call the "Japanese camera era" had started, I found a wonderful duplex -partly ground floor, partly a first floor—showroom in Regent Street, one of the main shopping streets in the West End of London. We had already obtained the Minolta agency and the Durst professional enlarger agency. That was an ideal showroom for our London office.

In 1968, besides the London office, and with my experience of the Channel Islands, I decided to open a Jersey office. My Southwest UK sales man since 1963, Tim Knight, single at the time, jumped at the offered opportunity to go and live on Jersey and become its manager/salesman. We found suitable premises on the top end of St. Helier. We took a lease on the ground floor and basement of White Lodge in Wellington Road and were the only UK photo distributor to have its own office and warehouse in the Channel Islands. Tim got married in Jersey and served the company well for 31 years.

⟡ 26 ⟡
Computerisation

WHEN NORTH STAFFS PHOTOGRAPHIC SERVICES started importing, the invoicing and bookkeeping systems had to be changed, because we were now getting many new customers from other parts of the country. We had to make sure that all the products that left our premises were accompanied by delivery notes, the customer invoiced, and then a record kept ensuring that we got payment in due course. It was traditional in those days (and still is) to send out a statement, besides the invoices, at the end of each month that showed all the purchases made during the month, the invoice numbers, any payments that had been made during the same period, the balance owing and the terms of credit.

When we started, we were in the days of manual typewriters, and then we progressed to electric typewriters. The classic became the IBM "golf ball" typewriter where, instead of individual type holders, all the different letters were on a ball that went from side to side and up and down and produced crisp, beautiful letters and invoices.

This became too slow as we grew, so our next step was to switch to a Bradma, a metal plate embossing system. Permanent metal plates were embossed with the name of the product, its catalogue number and its prices. You could have up to five different prices for one product, because the person operating the invoicing machine could select which one of the five lines on that embossed metal plate was actually selected for printing when she pulled down the lever on the invoicing machine. Once the correct embossing plate had been made for that product, you never needed to check any of the information thereon again, and it was a simple matter of having one plate for every product in a cabinet with a rack of small pigeonhole spaces in it. On the protruding front of each plate the product name was also shown, so the girl just looked up, pulled the plate, selected the quantity, pressed on the lever, and put the plate back. Then, she took another plate down for another product and with an electric adding machine she totalled all the individual lines on the invoice to get a final total. It was revolutionary in those days but, in looking back, so primitive by today's standards.

We stayed on that system for a number of years. Each invoice still had to be double-checked for accuracy, and each total still had to be entered into a ledger, which by that time we had partially automated by using National Cash Register or Burroughs electric bookkeeping machines. Those were machines that picked up the last total, added the new total, and kept a ledger card and statement which was sent at the end of the month to the customer.

Slowly but surely, a revolution came with computerisation. In the UK, it started with machines that used punched cards and were really just fast information sorting and storing machines. One of the first companies to use and develop these in a big commercial way was the Lyons Tea Company, which also owned the famous Lyons Corner Houses in London. For obvious reasons, they called their computer Leo. They found that their in-house use was so successful that they founded a separate computer company to commercialise their systems.

That was how a company called ICL (International Computers, Limited) was formed. One of their factories and offices in Kidsgrove was only some 15 miles away from our head office. Together with Barclays Bank, who happened to be our bankers also, they formed a company called Baric. They were in the business of providing a complete computer service to companies who would use their big mainframe computer. These had terminals to that mainframe in their own offices, whatever distance away. All the standard programmes were on their computers, and all our information was in their computers. When we started on this system, we just had two terminals, but it was a revolution because this was our first taste of computerisation. It didn't require putting up a mainframe in our own offices, so there was no capital expenditure involved at all. We just bought time on their computer but had the convenience of having 24-hour access to it on the terminals in our own premises.

That worked extremely well, and we had a long term contract with them. Suddenly, one day we got a letter out of the blue saying, "Sorry to inform you, but we've now decided that we are no longer in a position to accommodate terminals into our mainframe computer, and in three months' time, we are pulling the plug on you."

While this came as a shock, it was yet another challenge or problem to be overcome. Sooner or later, we would have to have our own in-house computer anyway. My basic belief was that I wanted to be in control of our own information and data and do as much in-house as possible, as we had already done with other things like photography and printing. So we did our best, having been given this ultimatum. We negotiated an extension of their stated period, which they did not want to do, but they said they would be helpful in programming whichever computer we decided to buy. I also negotiated that they would have to pay us compensation for non-fulfilment of the time period of the contract. The computer we got and the programming of it was paid for by the compensation obtained for cutting us off from their service.

How does one go about choosing a computer without having any experience of mainframes? At that time, the phrase "Personal Computer" or PC had never been heard of. Also there were not all that many computers of a small enough size to be affordable or appropriate to the size of our business. We narrowed it down from six available to two that would be of interest, and we went to see them. I gave the job of the changeover to Rupert Cartlidge, my Assistant Managing Director, because he was first class on administrative things of this nature. Rupert and I also had to learn conversion to computing quickly to ensure we had that skill at Board level.

After Rupert travelled to the United States to see it in operation, the computer we chose was an American-made computer (most of them were in those days). Strangely, it was made by the Singer sewing machine company. It was a Singer System 10 and was an excellent computer. It lasted until I left the company in 1980. As all mainframe computers did in those days, it needed a special room with double entry doors and an air-lock, because it had to be kept at a particular temperature and humidity. Yet the computer memory and interchangeable hard disc memory was less than you would get on the average laptop computer today! The hard discs were huge multi-layer discs which one had to insert into huge openings under the lid on top of the computer.

So we had a Singer System 10 computer with requisite terminals to it and ultra fast delivery, but we had no programmes. Computers, programmes and operating systems in those days were totally separate things. So we enlisted the help of Baric who through their sister company, ICL, sub-contracted another company to help us to write the necessary software for our particular application. Not being a manufacturing business but an import distribution business, we wrote a dedicated specification. We then got the systems analysts in to give us what we needed in terms of stock control, invoice production, sales ledger, purchase ledger, budget control, payroll, management reports and accounts, all written in such a way that the different reports could be printed for different departments and to give us monthly up to date management accounts. That was no mean task.

Because of the time limitation, we literally worked day and night and weekends to get the job finished in time. Furthermore, it was recommended practise and normal for when people changed systems to run the old and the new system in parallel. You never start a new system without teething problems and, however well-prepared, things always come to light which you never thought of or forgot to consider at the planning stage. We did not have this luxury. From the day they pulled the plug, we had to be ready to go live, and we did.

Such was our acquired expertise of distribution requirements, in terms of automation and computerisation which we used in the programming, that for years later we still saw our programmes or the modules within our programmes being used in the ICL computer packages they sold to other people. (ICL grew to a very big size and was later bought out by Fujitsu in Japan. They in turn also did an agreement with Siemens, a very large German computer company, and became Fujitsu-Siemens. They are now one of the biggest operators in Europe.)

We were then the first in the photographic industry to be completely computerised. We knew from our competitors that some companies much larger than ourselves had huge costly and lengthy problems when they started computerising. We will always remember the dictum that I had put to my board that you should never ever leave the programming, and particularly the system analysing, to pure computer buffs or computer experts. It is essential that at least one board member of any company going in for computerisation should be aware of everything to do with computers and become a computer expert himself so he cannot be led down the wrong avenues by false advice and cost the company a lot of money.

◈ 27 ◈

Part of the Establishment

SOME OF THE ESTABLISHED GERMAN camera makers like Agfa had their British agents from before the war. Other British distributors got agencies for famous pre-war German camera makers like Zeiss and Voigtlaender. I considered these distributors to be the establishment. The famous British firm, Johnsons of Hendon, was a very old established chemical manufacturer which can trace its business origin back to a goldsmith named Richard Wight who established his business in 1743 in Maiden Lane, in the City of London. They made photographic chemicals and were also one of the big photographic distributors of British-made professional plate cameras before the war. After the war, as I had the Wirgin Agency for Edinex, later Edixa cameras, so they became agents for the famous German camera maker Voigtlaender. They had a camera called the Vito, which became a competitor of mine. They started employing a German by the name of Reuter to look after the import side of their business. They were part of the establishment. Ironically after many management and ownership changes, they amalgamated with Photopia after I left, and it is now Johnsons Photopia. The passage of time changes many things.

I suppose you could say I became part of the establishment when my application for membership in the British Photographic Importers Association (BPIA) was accepted. I don't know whether, initially, I really wanted to join. When I found that some of their actions were affecting me detrimentally, as with most associations or clubs, I decided that it was much easier to fight for change from the inside rather than from the outside. Then I decided to join.

Representing the BPIA I eventually achieved an increase in the total quota amount by emphasising that the demand was there that could not be satisfied. I went to London to the Board of Trade. I went a lot to all government departments, and they would always listen. In my experience government departments in the UK will always give you an interview opportunity and will always listen and will generally hear what you have to say. However it is important, always in life, to make sure that one talks to the right person—a person capable of making decisions. I always found out first who the person was who made decisions.

But I have never made bribes in my life because, first of all, my principles and moral values wouldn't allow it and, secondly, it really doesn't work in Britain with people in authority. Throughout my whole photographic industry career, despite what I heard went on in terms of sending expensive gifts to buyers by my competitors to get bigger shares of their business, I have never, ever, made any gifts to any buyer. Any sales incentives that were available from my company were published and open and transparent and available to anybody. Similarly, I would never dream of offering some sort of an incentive to get a bigger share of the quota. I don't think it would have worked anyway.

I would take any of my customers out for a meal to discuss business and solicit orders—either the proprietor, the owner of the store, or the buyer for the stores if it's a multiple like Dixons or Boots. But I would never do more than that. I could offer them discounts. That was open to everybody and would be to the benefit of the company and not the buyer.

At the end of it all, I felt that the government's motivation for having quotas existed for two reasons: First, that they were desperately short of foreign currency after the war. Second, they wanted to encourage a British industry in the change over from war production to peacetime output. They wanted to protect British industry, and they wanted to build up a camera industry in the UK. They could not do it if suddenly there was a flood of German cameras. So the first consideration was to protect British industry and to try and build up a camera industry. They didn't realise, at first, that it simply couldn't be done.

In the school uniform of Bury Grammar school circa 1940 (chapter 4).

The "Czech Children" with the house (inset bottom left) generously provided by the City of Stoke-on-Trent at their Children's Home in Penkhull, circa 1939, just before the Second World War started. First row from left to right, Lisa Dasch. 2nd row Petr Feldstein (later Kalina), Hanna Frankel, Ralph Strass, Asaf Auerbach, Raja Strass, Paul Strass. Top row, Reuben Auerbach (later Potocky), my mother, Fritz Schwarzkopf. Reuben, Ralph and Paul later joined and fought with the Czech Independent Armoured Brigade of the British army, as I did (chapter 5).

Despatch rider Private Charles Strasser of the Czech Independent Armoured Brigade having arrived in Susice, Czechoslovakia after taking a convoy from Dunkirk, France across occupied Germany in May 1945 (chapter 8).

A-1

Just 18 in my specially tailored army uniform jacket by the side of a river in the mountains of western Bohemia (chapter 9).

Stephen Swingler MP and his wife, Anne, on the day he won the Newcastle-under-Lyme constituency for Labour in the first post war Labour Government. They had lived with us for some time during the war when he was a WEA lecturer in North Staffs (chapter 5).

My very first car—after motorbikes. A second-hand Austin 7 Tourer, registration COE 732, and the predecessor of many open-air convertibles. This is the one to which I added a self-fabricated trunk for our first post-war European tour. Circa 1948 (chapter 14).

Somewhere in Europe on a holiday with Krish Bambury and Murti Mehra, two students of Ceramics at the North Staffs Technical College from Pakistan and India, circa 1947–48 (chapter 14).

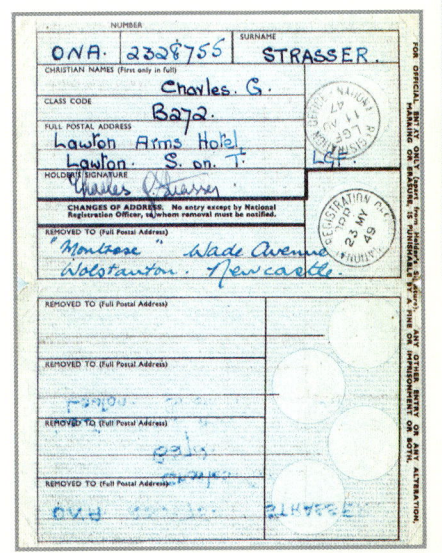

In view of the current debate on the introduction of Identity Cards, everyone had one during the war and until they were abolished in the early 1950s. Here is a copy of mine issued by the local office of the National Registration Office and written by hand, long before computers.

Presentation of Honorary Membership to the oldest photographer in Staffordshire by me, whilst Chairman of the Society of Staffordshire Photographers and in the presence of the Lord Mayor of Stoke-on-Trent and members. Behind me is member Ernest Warrillow MBE MA, for many years a photographer on the "Evening Sentinel" and a famous local historian and author whose photographic collection was donated to Keele University (chapter 83).

A-3

Awarding Honorary Membership of the Society of Staffordshire Photographers, at one of its annual dinners, to William Parton from whom I had bought his photographic studio many years before (chapter 83).

June 2006, in front of the basalt plaque erected in Etruria Park by the Society of Staffordshire Photographers in memory of Tom Wedgwood, son of Josiah and a pioneer inventor of the photographic process (chapter 83).

My installation as Chairman of the North Staffs Branch of the Incorporated Sales Managers Association (later Chartered Institute of Marketing) by Robert Copeland. Group also includes Gordon Baldwin, Peter Tunstill, Bill Parry and Gilbert Beswick (chapter 81).

At the 1965 theme ball—Arabian nights—of the North Staffs branch of the Incorporated Sales Managers Association, the MC, Bill Storey. I was chairman and Lord Stafford the President (chapter 81).

Another dinner of the North Staffs branch of the Incorporated Sales Managers Association under my chairmanship, from left to right, Maureen and Charles Strasser, Lord Stafford the President and the National Chairman and his lady (chapter 81).

All smiles for my friend the comedian Harry Worth, who came as the guest of the annual ball of the North Staffs Branch of the Incorporated Sales Managers Association, during the year of Chairman Roy Blurton. Group on the left includes Maureen and Charles Strasser and Yvonne and Rupert Cartlidge (chapter 81).

A picture of me used on my first photographic visiting card, circa 1948 (chapter 17).

Ten pin bowler in action!

Fashionably dressed for the 1950s with trilby hat and scarf and the ever present small "pippo" pipe.

I was a member of the "Gormless" club, a very exclusive Potteries monthly luncheon club with only eight members. It held an annual pancake tossing competition on Pancake Tuesday, and the picture shows my "turn" looked on by member Bill Watson, the then Chief Constable of Stoke-on-Trent (1964).

An experiment in change of hairstyle, lasted less than a year, circa 1969.

Guest of Honour at a Photographic Dealer Association national dinner in London, delivering a "State of the Trade" speech.

Charles, you have a trunk call from Thailand!

On the stand put up for the Press in front of the Brandenburg gate on the day in 1989 when the Berlin Wall came down after 28 years. Three hours later it happened and you could drive through for the first time since the blockade started in 1961.

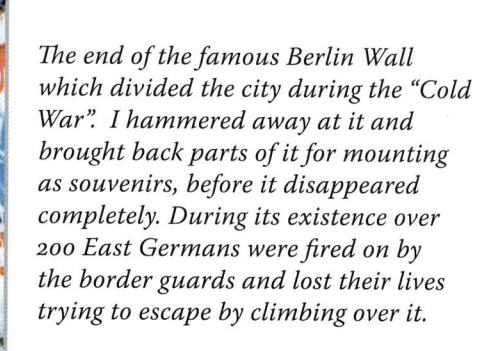

The end of the famous Berlin Wall which divided the city during the "Cold War". I hammered away at it and brought back parts of it for mounting as souvenirs, before it disappeared completely. During its existence over 200 East Germans were fired on by the border guards and lost their lives trying to escape by climbing over it.

On Wenceslas Square in Prague in the summer, looking up to the National Museum, on one of several return visits after my 44 years absence during the communist regime, circa 1992.

From the age of 60, I decided to celebrate only every 5th birthday, this seems to have slowed down aging. Here cutting the 65th birthday cake in 1992 at the ex-Photopian party held at Keele University.

I try out the chair that Hermann Goering sat in for the duration of the Nuremberg Trials. Immediately behind is the door of the lift which led through a passage direct to the prison. He cheated the gallows with a smuggled cyanide pill. This picture was taken during an IFFR fly-in and tour of the town and court buildings in May 2003 (chapter 12).

Photograph taken professionally by Peter Trenchard FBIPP AMPA in Jersey, circa 1987.

In Cancun a kiss from my favourite lady dolphin "Lissy".

June 2006, in front of the building that was the Junior Technical School in Burslem, which I attended in 1941–42 (chapter 6).

June 2006, standing in front of the home of my parents at 94 Trentham Road, Penkhull, where first my mother and then my father died.

With Josiah Wedgwood, the famous potter, outside the Wedgwood factory in Barleston, Stoke-on-Trent, in June 2006.

A dinner for the two trustees of the UK Strasser Foundation, June 2006 at the Moat House Hotel in Etruria. Left to right Charles, Alan Booth, my publisher Wade Keller, and Tony Bell.

Unveiling of plaque at the opening of the "Strasser suite" of lecture rooms at Keele University on the 3rd of December, 1993, in the presence of Vice Chancellor Prof. Brian Fender CMG MA (PhD Lond) and County Councillor Elsie Ashley OBE JP (chapter 86).

The "infamous" Secretary General of the United Nations Kurt Waldheim, with HRH Princess Margaret. Chancellor of Keele University after he had received his honorary degree (chapter 86).

On a visit to Keele University in June 2006 with Vice Chancellor Janet Finch CBE DL AcSS and Secretary/Registrar Simon Morris BA FBIFM (chapter 86).

In the "Strasser lecture suite" at Keele University on a visit in June 2006 (chapter 86).

By the commemorative plaque of the Battle of Jersey which took place on the 6th of January 1781 in the Royal Square of St. Helier (chapter 56).

June 2006, beside the grave of famous Victorian actress and friend of many, Lillie Langtry, The Jersey Lily, in St. Saviour's Cemetery in Jersey. She was born just opposite in the old rectory (chapter 56).

2006 wintering in the paradise of Marco Island, Florida (chapter 87).

In front of the Judge Jolly Bridge on Marco Island in 2006 with my friend and publisher Rotarian Wade Keller (chapter 87).

Recent picture—at peace with the past—rooted in the present —contemplating the future.

The Jersey St. John Ambulance Appeals Committee with a recently purchased additional ambulance. I am now the only male member of this energetic committee.

In top hat and tails with my OBE just after its presentation on the steps of Buckingham Palace.

The actual letter received from the Lieutenant Governor of Jersey, His Excellency General Sir Michael Wilkes KCB CBE congratulating me on the award of the OBE.

Continuation of letter from previous page.

> Think of no one who deserves it more than you do. All Jersey will, I know be delighted.
>
> With very warmest best wishes,
>
> Yours sincerely
>
> Michael Wilkes

Charles G. Strasser SB.St.J. M.Sc. FCIM.

The Cottage, Anse Port
St. Martin, JERSEY. JE3 6DI
Channel Islands. (Via U.K.)

Phone +44 (0)1534 851681 Fax +44 (0)1534 854559
GSM mobile 0979716969 e-mail strasser@bt.net

His Excellency General Sir Michael Wilkes, K.C.B., C.B.E.
Government House
Jersey JE2 7GH

16 June 2000

Dear Sir Michael,

Thank you for your hand delivered letter of congratulations on the award of the OBE in the Birthday Honours List.

Your beautifully written letter and the sentiments expressed therein really touched me. I only wish my handwriting was easily readable, then I would not have to resort to this mechanically produced letter of appreciation.

Since coming to England in 1939, as a child refugee from Czechoslovakia, I have received only warm hospitality and kindness. It has been my privilege to have been accepted as a member of the British community, its fine traditions and way of life, for which I am eternally grateful. My aim has at all times therefore been to make every effort to put back into that community, which I became an integral part of, voluntary and charitable service in many forms.

The honour of this national award is truly treasured.

Yours sincerely
Charles Strasser

My reply to above letter.

NEWS — JERSEY EVENING POST • FRIDAY 15 DECEMBER 2000

Rotarian's day at the Palace

BY PAULA THELWELL

ROTARIAN Charles Strasser was at Buckingham Palace last week to receive the insignia of Officer of the Order of the British Empire from the Queen.

Mr Strasser, a founder member of Rotary de la Manche, is pictured (right) with Beefeaters outside the Palace. He was accompanied to the investiture by his daughters, Sue Falloon and Dianne Mousley.

He was made an OBE in the Queen's Birthday Honours List in June for services to the community in his former home, Staffordshire, and in Jersey.

Colours

Mr Strasser said he was delighted to see three women who had worked for him years ago in Stoke outside Buckingham Palace. Sporting green and yellow balloons, the colours of his former company, they had travelled to London to see their former employer.

Mr Strasser said after receiving his honour that he had a short chat with the Queen who remarked on his association with Keele University. Mr Strasser told her it was an honour to receive his OBE from her, as he had come to the UK as a small child as a refugee from the former Czechoslovakia.

After the investiture he had lunch at the Ritz with his daughters before seeing a West End Show.

'It made a fantastic day, probably the most exciting day of my life,' said Mr Strasser.

A half-page press cutting dated 15th December, 2000, from the "Jersey Evening Post" about my investiture with the OBE at Buckingham Palace.

A-16

28

Going Public

WE WENT PUBLIC WITH PHOTOPIA International on 19th November 1962, with an issued and fully paid share capital of £250,000. Before we went public, our advisers said we needed long-term agreements—a minimum of five years with important suppliers. Fortunately, everybody was prepared to help us and signed five-year auto renewal agreements.

In those days, you could only apply for a listing on the London Stock Exchange when you reached an annual profit of £100,000, which is nothing today, but it was a lot of money in those days. In 1962, we had just reached that, so as soon as we could, we got a listing. When we published our annual profit figures, which you have to do from the previous five years, we showed a figure of £9,800 for 1958, £21,700 for 1959, £89,000 for 1960, £76,000 for 1961 and £100,006 in 1962. When we reached the necessary figure and went public, Stanley Kalms threw a party for me in a Kensington restaurant in London. He and his wife Pam and Maureen and I had a memorable evening together. We celebrated having reached that stage in our climbing the mountain.

Interestingly enough, I was running in parallel with Stanley Kalms. He was one of my major customers through Dixons Photographic Limited. Stanley took over his father's photographic studio business and started retailing in Edgware, so his start was very similar to mine. He went public with Dixons on 9th July 1962. At that stage, they had 16 retail shops. From the record, in the previous 10 years he increased from quite low annual profit figures, until he started his growth in 1959 at £24,000, in 1960, £30,000, in 1961, £77,000 and then in 1962, £160,000. He and I had always been on a parallel course of expansion, but he came to the point where not only did he overtake me but he developed into a huge conglomerate company having bought out many of his competitors and, coincidentally, my customers in the process.

Before we went public, nobody except me had any equity in the company. I had a board of three directors. They were directors of the operating companies and, on listing, also of the group holding company. The whole board also participated in incentive schemes in addition to their directors' fees and salaries. For everywhere in the company where it was possible to have incentives, we instigated suitable ones. When we went public I made available a small percentage of my shares to be allocated to directors and all staff, who had been with the company for three years, based on salary levels and length of service.

The procedure for going public is quite an interesting and very investigative process. You have to get independent auditors and solicitors who are experienced in that field to draft all the offer documents. You have to appoint stockbrokers who become stockbrokers to the company and will facilitate the trading in your shares. Many meetings were held to prepare this offer document. My guiding light in this was my local accountant in Stoke-on-Trent, Arthur Snow, who had a very high reputation in this field and had connections in the city. He was most helpful to me in preparing the way. The offer document for going public is published after scrutiny by lawyers, accountants and stockbrokers, after every "i" is dotted and every "t" crossed and it has been checked and double checked and investigated. On a small issue like ours, it was generally placed by the stockbrokers. They would say to this pension fund or that large investor, "There's a new issue coming, we are placing it, do you want any shares? How many do you want?"

We made a number of trips to London. Our introduction company was a company called Gresham Trust Limited. They also became our registrars and transfer office. Our bankers were Martins Bank Ltd., (later taken over by Barclays Bank) in Newcastle-under-Lyme. Our stockbrokers were Colgrave and Co. in the city of London. The solicitors were my long-established local solicitor in Newcastle-under-Lyme, Robertson, Worthington & Brodie, but

I always dealt with Jock Brodie, who became a close friend. The Stock Exchange also required a London firm of solicitors experienced in listings, so we appointed one of the big five called Richards, Butler & Co. The auditors to the issue were my local accountant A. B. Snow, Wood & Co. of which the senior partner was Arthur Snow. The independent accountants reporting to Gresham Trust Ltd., were Peat, Marwick, Mitchell & Co., a well-known name internationally. Later, when Arthur Snow's son, Geoffrey, joined me from his father's practise to become my finance Director in Photopia International, we used Peat, Marwick, Mitchell & Co. as our company auditors every year.

This offer document, which I've included as Appendix A, shows the history of the company, including the premises both rented and owned as assets of the company. It shows the management and employees and any contracts with directors that were in existence. We had to make a comment on the working capital, the profits and prospects and dividend policy. Then we enclosed the accountant's reports done jointly by Snow, Wood & Co. and Peat, Marwick & Mitchell. They signed the reports for the satisfaction of the Stock Exchange.

To get all this done, we had several meetings in London. One of these I remember particularly well. Arthur Snow and I came by train from Stoke-on-Trent to London and then by taxi from Euston station to the offices of Gresham Trust for one of these meetings. Arthur directed the taxi driver to take me past Carey Street and past the Old Bailey court building. Carey Street is the street where bankruptcies are notified and registered. It's a long street with offices of liquidators and bankruptcy experts. In England, there's a saying: "Be careful you don't go down Carey Street." It's well-known as being the gloom and doom of failed business ventures—sometimes innocuously failed business ventures where people have gone beyond the limit of their capabilities, not necessarily fraudulently. The Old Bailey is the high court where people who are not always honest in their business dealings finally get their just desserts. It's a famous domed building with the lady of justice towering above London holding the Scales of Justice.

Arthur had the cab driver stop here and, in his inimitable style, he said, "Now, Charles, I want you always to be able to sleep at night, and the only way you are going to do that is if you are always 100% honest in all your dealings, whether taxation matters or any other matters. I know you are an honest person, but these are the landmarks for people who are not. These two streets are not for you."

Arthur Snow was a great accountant. Until your business gets to a certain size, you can prepare your own accounts, but it's much better to have an accountant, and there are lots of them available. When I started my business, I went to the local practise of accountants run by a Mr. Goodwin. He did the annual accounts for me for the first few years, but he was too slow. If you want to learn from the previous year, it's no good waiting for another year to see the actual accounts. In the early days, I was not sophisticated enough to have management accounts. In later years—and certainly when we became a public company, having to publish our financial results twice a year—we needed budgetary control and regular monthly management accounts to see how we were doing.

Of necessity we agreed to part with Mr. Goodwin. Arthur Snow had a relatively small practise, and it was considered an honour to be taken on as a client by him. I had to make an appointment to be interviewed. It wasn't just a case of "I'd like you to be my accountant." I went for the interview and, as it turned out, he was happy to be my accountant. His son, Geoffrey, was articled to become an accountant at Peat, Marwick in London. When he came back, he went into his father's practise with a view to ultimately take it over, but I made him an offer, which he accepted, to be the finance Director of Photopia International Ltd. He stayed with the company and ultimately helped in the negotiations, 12 years later, when we ceased having a listing on the London Stock Exchange because a London-based public holding company made an offer which was accepted by all the shareholders. (Even at that stage, I was still a majority shareholder holding more than 50% in shares.)

At our London meetings, the person representing Gresham Trust most of the time was a very experienced financial adviser named Norman Baldock. The very knowledgeable and astute solicitors from Richards Butler were Malcolm Farrer-Brown and Pat

Grundy. From Colegrave was John Colegrave, later Stuart Holtorp, and from Peat, Marwick it was John Grenside, who later became the senior partner and whom, years later, I "bumped into" in Tokyo and we had dinner together. This was also our London team for the final signing at the offices of Gresham Trust. All the directors, Arthur Snow, Jock Brodie and my wife, Maureen, accompanied me to London, where we stayed overnight.

I took up the position, in the now public company, of Chairman and Managing Director. Rupert Cartlidge was my Assistant Managing Director, John Battison was my Advertising Director, and Jeffrey Pickford my Shipping Director. Cyril Smith was the Company Secretary. All of these had been with me for some time. One of the financial newspapers, the "Financial Times", published our going public. The writer must have done some research because it read that at the time of our listing, we were the youngest public company board having a listing on the London Stock Exchange. Our average age of 32 was younger than any other public board in the UK at that time.

To give all employees who had been with the company over two years, a "thank you" for loyal service and an incentive for capital gain and dividend income in the future, I gave them, from my own shareholding, a quantity of shares based on length of service and salary level.

We started a new life which, in practical terms, was no different except that now we had a responsibility to, as it turned out, 900 shareholders. Nine hundred individuals or companies took up the placing of our shares. Previously, we had one shareholder. Fifteen years later, we were absorbed into another public company, and we were back to one shareholder, which was that public company. But those 15 years were exciting years. We showed growth most of the time except during the years 1968/69 of the Harold Wilson government, when we had severe restrictions in terms of import controls and increased taxation for companies and for individuals.

In one year there was a situation where (with all the additional personal taxes) if you were in a high earning field, your tax liability could add up to more than 100 percent. That was not a good climate, not one that I was happy to live in. And, it might be noted, that regardless of the amount of tax we sent to the British Treasury, not once did we receive even a thank-you card. Oh, well!

In 1969, we just barely made a profit. We went down from a profit of £140,000 in 1968 to £12,000 in 1969. In 1970, the following year, it was only £41,000. It took us until 1971 to get back to where we had been in 1968 with a profit of £139,000. Then, in 1972, that went up to £209,000; in 1973 to £415,000; in 1974 to £578,000; and in 1975 to £690,000. That more or less stayed steady in 1976 with £628,000 and increased again in 1977, our final year as a public company, to £778,000. Although we increased again in the next three years, it was no longer necessary for us to publish annual reports and accounts as we were then a subsidiary of a public company. They showed our results in their consolidated accounts. (In the three years that I stayed on as Managing Director before I moved to Jersey in November 1980, we still increased on those figures from 1977. In fact, we reached the million pound annual profit mark in the year ended December 1978. Indeed, in those three years during which I no longer held any equity in the company, we produced a profit well in excess of the amount Central and Sheerwood had paid for the company.)

The public company has four groups of people to satisfy. Sometimes it's a difficult decision which of those four should take priority. You have your shareholders to consider; otherwise you wouldn't be a public company. You have your staff to consider, otherwise you couldn't operate. The other two groups are your suppliers and customers. Theoretically, each is as important as the others because, like a car with four wheels, each is essential if you want to move forward.

While we were a public company, the original 900 shareholders changed some but not a lot. Stock exchange rules were that any holder of more than 5 percent of the shares in any public company had to disclose who they were. As disclosed in the last report and accounts, we had one pension fund that had more than 5 percent of the shares. Once a month the registrars would send for me to sign new share certificates for the shareholders that had changed. So I could see who all the shareholders were, except in the case of nominee names. Interestingly enough, I discovered one of our shareholders was Dom Mintoff, the then prime minister of Malta. I don't know why I stored that name in my memory, but it came in handy two or three years later when we did a Mediterranean fly-about with friends of mine, Gordon and Mary Johnson, from Newcastle-under-Lyme.

We were flying from Sicily to Malta—quite a long sea crossing. When the Italian air traffic controller handed me over to the Maltese Air Traffic Controllers, he said, "Oh, by the way, we have no aviation fuel. What are your intentions?" We had already gone more than halfway, and I elected to continue. So we landed, booked a hotel, and I went back to the airport. I just couldn't believe that an international airport like Malta didn't have any fuel. It was true. The Shell people couldn't help me. None of the people there, including the airport authority, could do anything. I did not have enough to safely get back to somewhere where I could refuel. This was in the days when the Libyans were very influential in what Malta did and didn't do. Malta had fallen out with the United Kingdom authorities and the Libyans apparently just did not give them enough fuel.

Stuck in this position, I suddenly remembered that Prime Minister Dom Mintoff was a shareholder in my company. So I thought, "Go to the top." I phoned up his office. Speaking to one of the secretaries I introduced myself and explained the predicament. I impressed upon her that it wasn't safe for me to take off from Malta and that I had tried everything to get fuel. Could shareholder Don help me please to get some necessary assistance?

I was told that the only people at the airport who got fuel were the military. I told her I only needed a very small amount. She said, "Call me back in an hour."

An hour later she said, "If you'll be at the airport by your plane at such and such a time, a military tanker will draw up and give you a small measured amount of fuel to get you safely off the island and to your closest destination." They came through. It was quite a chance to remember that the Prime Minister of Malta was a very small shareholder in the company. I don't know why he ever bought any shares in my company, but there you are. I suppose it was just another investment for him and a stroke of luck for me.

A public company has to publish complete financial statements every year. The annual report contains the full and detailed audited accounts, all the facts about the company as required by the Stock Exchange, the chairman's report, interesting information about the company for shareholders and the progress of the company and its products. We always had our annual general meeting at the British Pottery Manufacturers Federation (BPMF) Club in Stoke-on-Trent. A few financial writers and interested people from the city came to our annual general meetings. We always provided a lunch for them at the club. The annual general meeting of any public company, if things go well, is like a one-act play. The procedure is totally prescribed, by Stock Exchange rules, as to what you can say. You mustn't give any advantage to any particular shareholder. All of that is procedurally laid down. The chairman is expected to give a subsequent events report on the progress of the company from the closing date of the reports to the time of the annual general meeting. Our annual general meeting took no more than about 15 minutes because no one asked any questions. So, everybody was happy with what we did for them in terms of return on their investment.

The advantage to me of going public was that I got the money for the 25 percent of my shareholding that I sold. The company also got better facilities for growth. In terms of capital facilities, when we went to the bank, it was much easier to get loans because we had a status. It was also much easier because the shares were quoted on a daily basis, and when I did finally come to sell, there was an established value for the business. Then, it was up to somebody, in our case a London holding company, to say, "Okay, the value of your shares is considered to be the right price by the public at X pounds per share, we're offering you 10% or 20% more than that." You didn't have to back it up with business value. So that was easy at that stage. On the other side, there were more accounting fees, stock exchange fees, listing fees, you name it.

Mind you, by that time, we had already acquired all the agencies. It would have been a plus being a public company and trying to get those agencies, but we already had them. In the final analysis, and I'm a strong believer in this, no matter what it says on your business card, it is you as a person that counts—the image you create and the impression you give, initially and over the years, the trust that you have created. A good reputation takes a long time to build but only seconds to destroy.

It's very important that your word is your bond, which is the motto of the London Stock Exchange. In every society, there are bad eggs. But you must be able to trust the majority of people. We always had a very good relationship with all our suppliers and all our customers, and it was all built up on trust and mutual respect.

⋄ 29 ⋄

Buying Groups

AS A RESULT OF ALL these quotas and competitive pressures on one dealer trying to beat another dealer in terms of the lowest price at which he could advertise and sell his cameras, there was a situation where the big dealers or multiple dealers like Dixons and Boots bought volume of goods or quantities of goods and exerted pressure to get better prices because they bought in large quantities. Even though they had higher operating costs, they were able to sell at lower prices than the small dealer. The small dealer couldn't just sit back and relax.

There were one or two quite clever wholesalers and dealers who started saying, "Hey, let's get together a group of dealers and we can then buy in quantity instead of each dealer buying separately in his own name. We will form a buying group, and then we can go to the suppliers and request the same terms as Dixons or Boots. Then, we will distribute to our members, and they can compete on pricing."

It worked for a time. It saved the distributor money in selling, invoicing and dispatching 100 cameras to one address in a bulk consignment rather than to 100 addresses, and that reflected in the volume discount. The dealers then had what were purely buying groups; they still advertised under their own names and continued to do business under their own names. Then another enterprising dealer came along, even more marketing orientated and clever, and said, "We don't just want buying groups, we need selling groups." So, having bought the goods at an advantageous price, they also wanted to advertise the fact that they had done so, and the only way they would do that—because it's too expensive for 100 dealers to place 100 advertisements—was to give that group a brand name and logo, and they became members of that selling group. Then that group would advertise under its name and logo the specially priced products available from it and list the names and addresses of its members. In this way, the member dealers still kept their own individual retail identity, but they were members of a marketing group. They could put the group's name and logo on their shop fascia in their particular town if they wanted to. That worked well for some time but, in any of these buying and selling groups, you've got to have strong leadership and strong management. A lot of them ran for some time, but then there were disagreements among the highly individualistic dealers in the groups who then thought, "Hey, I sell a lot more cameras than my competitor in another town. Why should we both get the same discount, and why should we both warrant the same size little space in the group mass media advertising?" So, one by one, the groups went overboard in the end, and a lot of dealers went by the wayside because they just couldn't keep up with the strong competition.

When duties finally came down because of the UK joining EFTA (European Free Trade Association), the forerunner of the EC (European Community, later the European Union), we got a gradual reduction in duty from the crazy 50% to nothing if it was manufactured in the EC. Then we only had a common external tariff, so cameras coming from Japan paid a duty but only the duty that was applicable to imports into the EC. So that led to a differentiation in costs but, despite that, the Japanese makers became so strong that ultimately the German industry just could not cope with the competition and they all, one by one, foundered and went bankrupt or just went out of business. That happened to all my camera suppliers from Germany. Fortunately, this did not happen until I'd set up a separate company called Japanese Cameras Ltd., and by that time had got good agencies from the Far East and I was able to switch most of our sourcing and purchasing activities to the Far East.

Slowly, even the European manufacturers realised they couldn't compete any longer with lower labour cost countries. Companies like Bosch, Franke and Heidecke, famous for their Rollei cameras, started transferring manufacturing plants to other countries like Singapore and Malaysia. Rollei started a huge factory in Singapore with German management and German engineering and a huge investment. I went to see their factory once while I was in Singapore. Initially, it seemed to go quite well. Long-term, they didn't succeed because really at the end of the day it was the Far Eastern management mentality of mass production, their system of finance, their system of engineering, their work ethic. I really don't know of any camera manufacturer from Europe who succeeded in manufacturing in the Far East other than having goods made under their own name by existing factories over there. When that situation arose, there were a lot of technical co-operation agreements. For example, Leitz, the German maker of the famous Leica camera, because they were left behind when the electronic and the chip revolution came along, did a technical tie up with Minolta under which Minolta made a lot of the electronic components for Leica cameras in their factories in Japan. They were still assembled in Germany, but they had a lot of interchange know-how which, in the main, was bringing Japanese electronic technology to Leitz. Minolta did make one Leitz camera in Japan, and it was marketed in the East under the Minolta brand and in the West under the Leica brand.

I was very active in various negotiations with government, in the first instance for my own company and then as a committee member of the British Photographic Importers Association (BPIA). Initially, I wasn't a member of the establishment. So, in the beginning, I fought all the battles regarding quotas and taxation for Photopia Ltd. Then I became a member of the BPIA and whenever it became a matter of common interest in the photographic importing industry, I was asked to use my negotiating skills and do it on behalf of all importers, which I did.

❖ 30 ❖

Clip-O-Matic

THERE WERE LOTS OF DIFFERENT slide films on the market. Kodak gave people the option to receive their slides in cardboard mounts or as transparency film. They never went into transparency frames, not even for multiple users. People needed their transparencies framed to protect them. You could get dust on them and dust, of course, would be magnified on your screen. They would tend to get out of focus on the screen because they were not held taut in the cardboard frame, and they could curve, particularly at different temperatures. As soon as you put your slide between the lamp and the lens on your slide projector, the temperature would change faster and, if it was unprotected, it would buckle and go out of focus. You virtually had to put them—if you did it seriously—into frames.

We then found two solutions and started making them for the first time in the United Kingdom. In fact, it was in a plastic injection factory owned by Gerhard Schuller, a friend of mine who lived in the same town. I said to him, "Why don't we make some transparency frames?" So, we sat down and designed two types. We designed the standard type with glass in them, and we put those into plastic boxes. They were called Photopia transparency frames, and we sold millions of them. These frames protected your transparencies and held them better when put into a slide projector. This was before the days of colour prints. The only way you could produce results in colour was by a colour reversal process. When you sent the film to Kodak after you'd taken your pictures, you got your film of colour transparencies back usually in cardboard mounts or as uncut film. To protect your transparency film, you would take it out of the cardboard mount and put it between the two pieces of glass and then put it into a plastic frame.

We then decided that, instead of taking this transparency out of the cardboard holder and putting it into two pieces of glass and putting it back into the plastic covers, why not keep it in the cardboard frame—because, by that time, transparent plastic technology had already advanced quite a bit—cut the four corners off, and mould two highly transparent pieces of plastic the same size as the cardboard mount and clip them together over the mount at the four corners? You protected the colour transparency, and you've got a slide ready to put into your slide projector. These were still Photopia transparency frames, but we called them Clip-o-Matic because you clipped them together, having cut off the corners. We also included a template to cut off the four corners on the mount and also a pair of Photopia scissors to do it with, all nicely packed as a kit for 20 slides in a colourful display box.

We also took out a patent on this labour-saving way of making a slide. It was much cheaper because it was just mass-produced pieces of plastic with no assembly required, as with glass. It was a real winner, and we kept selling it until colour prints came along and transparencies gradually were superseded, except for medical, forensic and educational use. So that was our first locally-made product under our name.

One day we discovered that our Clip-o-Matic frame had been copied and was suddenly appearing on the market. It was made at another factory not far away from us in Wolverhampton, a factory that made the Corfield Periflex camera. It was exactly the same thing as our patented frame, and I had to stop him from making it. He agreed to cease production and sales. We had quite a fight about it, but it never got to court, although it nearly did. When Ken Corfield and I met 20 years later at one of the Photokina exhibitions in Cologne, we both laughed about the episode.

It's been my philosophy to avoid court cases at all costs because, at the end of the day, the only people who profit from them are the lawyers, and it wastes far too much management time to engage in that sort of unnecessary activity. Indeed, for the whole of my business career, I only ever had one contentious matter that ended up as a court case. This was in the High Court in London over a Japanese-made cine camera, a Super-8 camera, supplied through an American company who had paid for the tooling, had the worldwide rights on it and called it the Vernon cine camera. The camera unfortunately had a design fault in that some films would bunch like a concertina and then when bunched would stop instead of going through the film gate. We had to credit dealers and take all these cameras back again. Our American supplier was not prepared to help, and the only way we could get compensation from them was to take them to court, which we did. Indeed, it was a High Court case in London and lasted five days with a Queen's Counsel on each side. Representing us was Kenneth Jupp QC, later to become knighted and a High Court Judge. I was in the witness box for a whole day. Because we had a lot of expert advice and witnesses on our side, we won the case and recovered all our costs.

◈ 31 ◈
Terminating the Soviet Agency

EVENTUALLY, I GOT THE CHANCE to take on the agency for the entire Soviet camera industry. This was an interesting exercise, completely in contrast to all our previous experience. We never knew where the factories were or which product came from which factory, because the whole business of exporting for different industries was carried out by different state export organisations. The one that looked after all the camera manufacturers and photographic and optical equipment in general was called Mashpriborintorg.

I went to Moscow and got the agency after lengthy negotiations. I realised that the cameras could only sell if the prices were crazy low, because although the product was made very solidly, in terms of design and technical features, it was at least five years behind the times compared to products made in Germany. The prices were interesting, and we took on the agency and brought in cameras like a twin-lens reflex called the Lubitel and 35mm cameras like the Zorki and Fed and others.

That relationship, as opposed to any other country's, never was on a personal basis because we were dealing all the time with bureaucrats, which I'd never been used to before. Everything that was promised was honoured. Contractually, you could rely on it. The big problem was that nobody would make decisions. When I went to a camera factory in Germany and we wanted to have a psychological price level to fit in the market place, you could negotiate and somehow find a compromise price. With the Russians, they would listen, but nobody could make a decision, basically because of the system. If they made the right decision, there was no benefit for the guy who had made it. If he made a wrong decision, he could finish in Siberia. So there was nobody making decisions and I think that some of the things must have gone through the hierarchy, right up to whoever was the President of the country at the time. That was one problem.

The other problem was that everything had to be done according to the Soviet five-year plan. So for example we might want cameras early in the year so they would be in the shops ready for the summer photographic season. But if their five-year plan said cameras will be exported to the UK in September, there was no way you could budge them from that. We worked well together for about two years, and then their methods were just unacceptable and could lead to an early grey hair situation. I decided to drop the agency, and a company called Technical and Optical Equipment Ltd., took it on. In a comment about this in a German magazine the translation read "Optically and Technically limited company took on the agency."

Dealing with Soviets at that time had some interesting side issues because the Trade Delegation of the Soviet Embassy in London was the contact point with Mashpriborintorg in Moscow. Whenever somebody came from the Trade Delegation to visit us in Newcastle, they had to get special permission because there was a tit-for-tat arrangement between the British and the Soviets, and I believe it applied to the Americans as well, that diplomats could only freely move within the radius of 25 miles from the respective capitals. They readily got this permission, but in advance of these people coming—it had to be planned well in advance to get these permissions—we always got a visit from the local Police Superintendent of the Special Branch to find out what this was all about and if there was any unusual requests which might involve national security or anything of that nature and would we please let them know. Nothing like that ever happened. It was a pure trading relationship—very correct but frustrating.

During the two years I had the Soviet camera agency I made several business trips to Moscow. The initial experience was interesting. While I was there on a business trip, I also did some sightseeing. During the whole of my stay, an Intourist young lady was allocated to me to ensure that I only saw things that I was intended to see. She did a good job in trying to show me Moscow, and we made conversation. The thing that struck me most of all, although they have beautiful buildings and a particularly beautiful underground Metro system, I noticed that all their buses and trolley buses were filthy. I was used to seeing them regularly cleaned in the Western World. So I made a quite innocent remark about this, and she took great offence at this, believing that I was insulting them, the Soviet Union. I really had to explain that we probably had automatic washing machines, car-wash type of machines for our buses, and that it was just a big contrast for me to see this there.

I had a couple of good visits. Invariably, the people from Mashpriborintorg would host a meal in the evening with much vodka drinking and many toasts to the peoples of the world, peace in the world, and all their usual type of Communist-inspired toasts. I had been warned about this beforehand, and given the advice that in order to keep up with their vodka drinking capacity without ill effect, it was a good idea to drink a half a pint of milk beforehand. Also before the toast have a piece of their black rye bread with a very thick amount of butter on it and caviar. I would then down their vodka, as is expected of you, in one gulp. It seemed to work, because usually about midnight they would suggest going to a local place or in the underground and look at all the stations, one by one. We did that, and a lot of late nights were spent in Moscow in that way. In the end, however, we gave up that agency and spent our time on other things.

Many years later I returned to Moscow with my Jersey Rotary Club after the fall of the Iron Curtain and collapse of the Soviet Union. It was a totally different Moscow from that which I had experienced in the Soviet era.

⟡ 32 ⟡

Photokina Exhibitions

THERE WERE TWO TYPES OF exhibitions we went to—those that we attended as buyers and those where we exhibited as sellers. There were exhibitions in the United Kingdom, and then there were international ones overseas. Some exhibitions were held at exhibition centres built especially for the purpose and then there were travelling exhibitions held in hotels.

The first exhibition I ever attended was the Photokina exhibition in Cologne which started in 1950 and was held at the huge fairgrounds of Cologne from the 6th to the 14th of May. For the first few years, the Photokina was an annual exhibition. Then in 1954 started a two-year cycle until 1960, when it became a three-year exhibition held in 1963 and then in 1966. From 1968 to the present day, it went back to a two-year cycle. Up to the year 2006, there have been 29 Photokinas, and I have attended every one of them—mainly as a buyer, but in those years when we had agencies which included territory in Europe, we also exhibited our products at the Photokinas and other exhibitions. The Photokina became a tradition. They became and still are the largest imaging equipment exhibitions of their type in the world.

As described in chapter 8, I went through war-devastated Cologne a few days after VE-Day in 1945. By the time of the first Photokina exhibition in 1950 quite a bit of the town had been rebuilt. Since then the exhibition was sometimes held in the spring, sometimes in the autumn, depending on whether the chemical and film segment of the industry were strong, or the optical equipment makers within the photographic industry were stronger, because their seasons were not the same.

The Photokina exhibition in Cologne was always a good place for sourcing products and meeting new potential suppliers. In the early days they were exhibitions of photographic equipment purely for German manufacturers. Considering that it was only five years after the Second World War had ended, it was a very brave showing of the resurrection and regeneration of the German photographic industry back to its pre-war dominant world position. Trade visitors from anywhere in the world were welcome. As the industry changed, so did the nature of the exhibits and the exhibitors.

When the Japanese came into the field of photography, they were not allowed into Photokinas at first. But when they became a force in the world market, the Germans had no alternative but to let them in. It is on record that in 1956, Olympus, a Japanese camera maker, was the first Japanese exhibitor. They were given very poor spots in these massive exhibition halls. Koeln Messe, the organiser of the exhibition, has 23 huge exhibition halls on unbelievably large exhibition grounds. In the early days, the Japanese were usually pushed to the very end of the exhibition grounds. Ironically, that has changed radically. Now, there are hardly any German camera manufacturers left, and the Japanese are in the best positions.

Japanese manufacturers are now no longer exclusively camera manufacturers but also manufacturers of imaging equipment. This includes all the digital still camera makers from Panasonic to Sony and digital media makers like Fuji. It even extends to mobile phone manufacturers, because their phones now include the capability of taking pictures. Computer companies such as Epson and HP have also come into the imaging field because they make not only digital cameras but digital colour printers for the home.

At Photokinas, my purchasing manager, advertising director, and I always made a point of going one day earlier before these exhibitions opened. Because I had a Press pass, we could get in anywhere. At a few exhibitions, we had a stand as well, so we had exhibitor privileges. Lots of exhibitors were still hammering away and building up their stands.

I always took along salesmen and sometimes we made going to Photokina an incentive prize in sales competitions. Most of the time, particularly in the early days, we took most of the salesmen, because it was a very educational trip for them and very advantageous for them to be able to talk about the new items they had seen when they later called on their retail customers in the UK.

Exhibitions are usually a fantastic source not only of information, but also of misinformation, otherwise known as rumours. Just to see how quickly they can circulate, I would start such a rumour myself by telling a particular piece of information about a company or product to anybody who was willing to listen and then seeing how many hours, or in some cases even minutes, it would take for the story to come back to me from somebody else, probably having been the rounds of the whole exhibition in the meantime. On one such occasion at Photokina, I would say that a particular camera agency had just changed from XYZ Company to ABC Company and that this could cause them a huge loss in turnover. In my case, the information I started round was correct, but sometimes a lot of that sort of tittle-tattle was pure invention.

Most of the time, I would fly there in my own aircraft and take along staff to fill the capacity of the aircraft. Others came by ferry, train or other transportation. We would pre-book and stay at the same hotel. Besides sourcing new suppliers and new items, and seeing UK customers, we also had a good time in the evenings. I used the opportunity to entertain staff that had come along. Cologne is a famous exhibition city and, therefore, has lots of entertainment facilities, including many good restaurants and watering holes.

One evening we finished up in a Cellar Bar Club which boasted a telephone on every numbered table. If you saw somebody you wanted to talk to at another table, you could phone them. As you might imagine, telephones were constantly ringing, particularly as the evening progressed. We all descended into this bar with lots of drinks and music and, as is my custom whenever I sit down at a table in a restaurant or bar, I take off my shoes to feel comfortable. When it came time to go home, I looked under the table and I couldn't find my shoes. I used the table's telephone to see whether anyone of my staff had accidentally moved them, but nobody admitted to having done so. It was past midnight, and there was no alternative but to go back to the hotel in stockinged feet. Lo and behold, when I got up next morning, my shoes were outside my bedroom door. I did not expect any of my colleagues to own up to this prank, but I have my strong suspicions as to the perpetrator of this act, which did contribute to the amusement of the evening.

In Cologne we all made use of meeting our colleagues from the industry in the UK, and there was a particular pub by the side of the Rhine which, through our habits, became the British pub. When people had finished meetings or dining in the evening, that's where they usually met, both inside and outside. There was always a huge crowd there exchanging the latest news and happenings in the UK industry.

At another early Photokina, I had a good night with Ken Corfield, owner of K.G. Corfield of Wolverhampton—one of the few British camera manufacturers, having designed and manufactured the Corfield Periflex. Allen Wood was with us. Allen Wood was the publishing director of "Amateur Photographer", the main photographic magazine wherein all manufacturers, distributors and mail-order retailers advertised. We were looking for yet another venue at about 1 a.m. and, for some reason, decided to go to the railway station buffet. Unfortunately, the ladies there were just mopping up the place for closing and, in an effort to accelerate their cleanup so they could open up again and serve us, the three of us got their mops and helped to clean the floors at the station restaurant in Cologne. Every time we met in the future, the memory caused renewed amusement.

The Photokina is still a huge exhibition, but it has changed out of all recognition in character. Besides showing equipment and materials, it is also a cultural show since there are many galleries of pictures from all over the world taken by press, professional and amateur photographers from their national exhibitions and brought for exhibition in Cologne.

From the year 2000, the Photokina organisers have invited me to be their guest and treated me as a VIP. They collect me in a large Mercedes from the airport, give me honorary status in terms of entry to the exhibition, and give me use of their VIP lounges and tickets for all the social functions. The same limousine collects me every day from the hotel and takes me to the show, and then does the same again in reverse at the end of the day, taking me back to the airport at the end of the visit. That very nice treatment has persuaded me to continue going to the Photokinas, although I have no business connection with the trade anymore. It is still nice to see old friends and to keep up to date with revolutionary developments. The Koeln Messe people tell me that they believe that I am one of only two people left in the industry who can say they have attended every Photokina since the first one in 1950.

❖ 33 ❖
British and Other Exhibitions

PHOTOGRAPHIC EXHIBITIONS IN THE UNITED Kingdom were held, quite modestly in the early post-war years, in places like the Royal Horticultural Hall in London. As the industry grew, the "Photofair" was transferred to Earl's Court and to Olympia.

Naturally, as one of the leading distributors, we participated in all the UK exhibitions and always very carefully chose the position of our stand because to my mind, position within an exhibition is much more important than the design of the stand itself. Since the exhibitions were always for both the trade and the public, we had to design our stand in such a way that the dealers could come onto the stand but the public had to be served across the counters without being able to come onto the stand.

We were the first company in the photographic industry to dress all our salesmen and staff in company blazers to have them smart-looking and identified with the company. I designed a heraldic badge for Photopia which we had beautifully embroidered and sewed onto our blazer pockets. Green and yellow were always the company colours. I still always write everything in green. The top left corner of the heraldic blazer badge depicted a castle because our company was based in Newcastle. The top right had three balls, because initially the company started in Balls Yard. They were the three balls that you usually find outside a pawnbroker. The bottom left had two range finders, and the bottom right a camera representing the products that we were selling. The badge was bisected with a green field in the centre with our trademark of Photopia. Everyone was issued their correct size, and we asked them to wear white shirts and yellow ties under the green blazers. Many years later, after I had already left the company, one of my transport drivers found one of these badges. He stitched the badge onto a white baseball cap and gave it to me at one of our company reunion dinners.

In the early days when we were selling purely German-made products, we provided snacks for our dealers in the form of German Frankfurters with German mustard, German rolls and German drinks. This attracted all our customers not to miss our stand. While they were there getting a bite to eat, our salesmen were more than happy to take their orders for our products, particularly for the new items which we always kept back to announce and show at exhibitions.

One of the important things in the technological industry is always to have something new to show, whether at an exhibition or even when a salesman goes into a shop. For us, exhibitions were always more than just self-financing. As that was not the case with all exhibitors, over the years the UK exhibitions fizzled out through lack of support from exhibitors. I suppose it also fizzled out through lack of the required attendance from the public, who could see all the latest equipment in their own town shop.

As far as shows for the retail trade were concerned, we still wanted to carry on, so we decided to take the exhibition to them. We picked out about 12 regions and had a travelling exhibition with a visit to a different hotel every day—and quite a number of miles between them at times. Later, as the range of merchandise grew, we had an interval of a day between each one to be able to properly set up our merchandise displays. Staff from the office, particularly the advertising and public relations people, would set up the exhibition, and the local area salesmen would attend because they were the ones who knew the retailers in their patch. I always made a point of going to all these exhibitions. Quite a number of dealers would come for that reason.

After a couple of years of our own company exhibitions, the BPIA also decided on having a travelling exhibition, and they used our experience as a template. So we joined the BPIA's travelling exhibition and gave up our own. Although distributors in the industry were always fiercely competitive with me and each other, it was a relatively small industry, so everybody knew everybody. Although you were competing, you met in the BPIA meetings and also at exhibitions and social functions. There was also an understanding between the different credit controllers of the different photographic distributors. If you had a customer who was persistently slow in paying or becoming a credit risk, there was a network to warn each other of potential bankruptcies and the like. If there was such a case, you would stop credit first and then inform your competitors.

As we moved into the audio and electronic field, I also attended the specialist exhibitions for those industries like the Audio and Hi-fi exhibitions that alternated between Düsseldorf and Berlin. When we were selling the projection equipment from our Yugoslav factory, we also took a stand in Didacta, which were exhibitions for educational equipment.

Then I started going to the American exhibitions organised by the Photographic Manufacturers Association (PMA), as it was first called, and later the Photographic Marketing Association. The first one of these, in March 1960, was in St. Louis on the Mississippi River, and it was my first visit to the United States. I went with my good customer and, by then, friend, Stanley Kalms, the boss of Dixons. We flew together and had to get out and clear Customs and Immigration at New York Idlewild Airport, as it was called in those days. Now it is John F. Kennedy Airport.

While at the airport, I turned to Stanley and took a picture of him and said to him, "We'd better have a record of the second coming of Christopher Columbus, since this is our first visit to these shores." I had just finished taking the picture when there was a heavy hand on my shoulder.

I turned round to see a uniformed New York police officer who said, "Don't you know this is a restricted area, buddy, and it's forbidden to take photographs here? I'll have to confiscate your camera."

Luckily, Stanley had a very quick mind. He took the camera out of my hands, opened the back of it, and said to the policeman, "There, I've exposed the film. Now there are no restricted views in here anymore." He closed the back of the camera. The police officer went away, and I didn't lose my camera.

We then travelled on to St. Louis and went to our first American-style convention and exhibition, which had a very interesting well-attended opening session in a huge auditorium. We were given what we thought was very typical U.S. sales hype. The mayor of the city and the organisers of the exhibition were there to welcome the crowd.

There was a preacher from Oklahoma, a Dr. William H. Alexander, who had come to the exhibition to be a guest speaker, and among many other things which I've long forgotten, he told a joke which I have used myself on several occasions since. Being a preacher himself, he told the story of a preacher who went to a very small country church and, unfortunately, only one local farm yokel turned up. But he decided, nevertheless, to go ahead with the full service. As is usual at the end of the service, he went to the church door to shake hands with the congregation. He said to his only attendee, "Hello and what did you think of my sermon?"

This yokel said, "Well, I'm only a country yokel, but when I go out to the field to feed the cows and only one turns up, I sure don't give her the whole load of hay."

In St. Louis, I experienced for the first time a practical example of the difference of the laws in different states of the United States. One side of the Mississippi River is in the state of Missouri, and on the other side is Illinois. At that time, one side was "dry" at certain times, and you could drink on the other side. Therefore, there is always a movement of people going across the bridge from one state to the other to further their alcoholic behaviour.

I also sourced one or two American products on that visit. Notably, I took up a connection with an American projection screen manufacturer who made both white and glass-beaded screens, both to hang on a wall and also, which was more popular at that time, on a tripod to fold and erect wherever required.

I've been to several PMA shows since in different towns of the United States.

◈ 34 ◈

Photokina Leads to Cokin

AT ONE OF THE PHOTOKINA Exhibitions, I saw that there was a French firm from Paris, who had never exhibited before, preparing their stand to announce a quite revolutionary type of filter to put in front of your lens to give you different effects. People had filters for years that were round and screwed into the front of the lens. But this Frenchman had invented a plastic holder which you screwed into the front of the lens and then you could slide in up to three different square plastic filters which could be just a single colour or graduated so you could have a different filter colour for the sky and for the foreground and different graduated effects.

Jean Coquin, a French professional photographer, invented it. His company's name, and the filter's name, was Cokin. (You can imagine some people mispronounced it and came up with some interesting variations of that name.) I thought this product had great potential. So when the fair officially opened the next morning, it was my first port of call. I met Jean Coquin and his suave, English-speaking sales and export manager, Marc Heintz. We liked the product.

I told them, "You need a good agent in the UK. We are a good agent in the UK. We have a sales force, we have many dealers. Your new product has a huge potential. When can you ship?"

"Oh," he says, "We've been keeping this quiet. We've been manufacturing for the last six months. Nobody has known anything about it until this exhibition. We can ship immediately."

This was such a revolutionary idea that I just wanted to check with some of my salesmen and potential customers and with some

British photographic press reporters present at the Photokina. I told Marc Heintz I wanted an option on this agency. They gave me until the next morning. All day long I kept bringing people to his stand—the press, customers, my sales people. All but one thought it was a great idea. One person said it would never catch on: "How can you expect people to buy a piece of cheap plastic and put it in front of a very expensive camera?" That's basically what it was. But he was selling the sizzle, as I always told my salesmen, and that's the important thing. You don't sell the sausage, you sell the sizzle. Jean Coquin was an expert professional photographer, and he produced specimen pictures without his filter and then with his filter. He got 60 different types of filters to produce different results. That's what the imaginative concept of this filter system was. So we signed. I got the agency, and I placed the order. We were his first export agent and customer.

Years later, Marc Heintz told me that my opening order was 10 times what he had anticipated to start off with. Cokin was a huge success, and we kept that agency until after I'd left the company. We had a wonderful relationship. It was a European product, so there was no duty on it. Cokin came out first with a standard range. He realised that you constantly have to have some innovation and new product, so he brought out new, different filters always showing the "sizzle" of the picture taken without his filter and then with. He also added a new type of holder in professional sizes for larger cameras. We did some fantastic advertising with which he was tremendously pleased.

Such was Coquin's success that Cokin filters were used by most famous professional photographers all over the world. In the UK Lord Lichfield, a cousin of the Queen, was an ardent professional user and was pleased to endorse the product. I went to his studio a number of times.

In the end, he got Minolta to be his United States agent, and it was a worldwide success. I started him off on the day he opened at that one Photokina.

Due to a change in camera fashions, it became necessary for Cokin to restructure. On account of French law it was impossible to reduce the work force, and Cokin went into liquidation. Marc Heintz bid for the company to the receiver and got it. Jean Coquin retired.

When video cameras and digital cameras came in, a radical adaptation to the new market was required. With small digital cameras, you couldn't screw in the standard filter holder in front of it. So they came out with a magnetic holder which allowed you to just put the filter in front of the lens. Not all the cameras were made from metal, so for non-metal ones he also made little self-adhesive stickers to hold the filter on. He's kept up to date with it and is still doing well.

When I finally left Photopia in 1980, I acted as a consultant for Cokin for about three or four years. Since he was in the business of attaching things in front of a lens, I developed for him—with the help of a Japanese factory I had been importing from—a ring flash unit, a round-the-lens electronic flash. It had four tiltable flashes in a circle around the lens, and it was particularly good for close-up photography, like dental photography. I developed it from the drawing board, made prototypes and then made the final product. I had it made in Japan under the Cokin brand and shipped to them direct.

◆ 35 ◆

Paul Plus and More

REALISING AS I DID THAT the manager of a single shop or buyer for a group, is only prepared either consciously or unconsciously to give a certain amount of time to a salesman, I decided the best way to get more time was to form a completely separate company and start a new sales force. In the main, as opposed to having agencies and selling under their brands, a useful reason for having a separate sales force was to sell things under the new company's brand name.

We also wanted to segregate our export activity for the group of products for which we had exclusivity or made under our own brand name for Europe. By doing this, it could also become a separate cost centre. So I started looking for a new name.

One day, I was passing a branch of a chain of supermarkets in the local area called Victor Value. I thought, "Hey, this comes off the tongue very easily and gives the impression that the products they were selling were good value and had something extra." So I sat down and thought we needed something like that where the two-worded name for the company had the same first letter as in Victor Value. I thought, first of all, we must have something that suggests good value and I thought "Plus" would be a good thing. That gives an impression that it has something extra. So I tried to come up with another word to combine with Plus that comes off the tongue easily and I coined Paul Plus.

We applied to the Registrar of Companies in London to register Paul Plus Ltd., and the man there asked, "Why do you want to register that?" "Well," I said, "it's the name of my favourite uncle." He accepted that. We registered Paul Plus Ltd. as a company and also a number of derivatives such as Plus, Pluscanar, Plustron, Plusjector as trademarks. Also, so as to make it look truly separate from Photopia, we used a different address. We did the same later with Japanese Cameras Ltd. With his permission, of course, we used the address of my solicitor in Newcastle. So the address of Paul Plus Ltd., instead of being Hempstalls Lane, became 29, King Street.

We recruited a new sales force, and we got new products from mainly existing suppliers but under our brand name. We brought out a catalogue, we sent out mailings, and it went well.

At that time there was a big market for slide projectors, starting with very simple types and then developing into automatic ones. At first, you just had a little slide carrier that slid in and out, and it was manual. Then, people came out with cassette types. Then came rotary magazines. Initially, the big operators in that market were Braun in Germany, with their Paximat projectors, Gnome in the UK, Argus in the United States, and Hanimex in Australia, who became an international name.

I found a firm called Vega in Ljubljana, Yugoslavia. They were making optical projection equipment of all sorts, and they had a little 150 watt metal die-cast manual projector that was as simple as it could be. I could see a big market in this for people who just did the occasional transparencies and wanted to show them to friends or at a party. If this projector could be bought at the right price to sell for less than £10 in the UK, an important price break point, it could be a mass-selling winner. I flew over to Ljubljana and got the right price and also the agency for their other products for the whole of Western Europe. Being a maker in a communist country, they lacked a management structure that could keep quality control as a prime requirement. Like all communist run enterprises they lacked incentives. We found that we had to teach them a lot in terms of electrical safety and even how to make sure that the name decals were stuck on straight all the time, and things like that. We designed new decals and a new box for them and rewrote the instruction book. We taught them a lot, and, in the end, we started selling this projector through Paul Plus Ltd. under our brand of Plusjector 150.

I then got Boots interested in the Plusjector 150. They were, at that time, buying Hanimex Projectors. Boots tested our slide projector. They had then, and probably still have now, the best quality control department of any retail organisation in the United Kingdom. They were extremely fussy, and to continue to do business with them, you had to comply with quite stringent requirements, not only of electrical safety but even things like dust specks in the projection lens or minor blemishes. It really was a case of sooner or later having to put in our own quality control department to check everything before it was delivered to them.

Boots checked out our Plusjector, a 150 Watt slide projector. They were happy with it, and we got our first very good bulk order. We redesigned the decal and the box and made it a Boots Projector. Boots was a company of over 1,000 shops, and we sold a lot of projectors to them under their brand. It stayed in their range for quite a time. That was the start of sourcing for them in all sorts of different fields like binoculars, cameras and accessories, which we did. This really was the start of our long-lasting relationship with Boots, sourcing their own label items in different parts of the world.

Sourcing for Boots was a tremendous business. It started getting so big that if we lost it, it would seriously affect us. So I decided to make it a company policy that no single customer could be more than 20 percent of our total sales turnover. We could do something about 20 percent if we lost it, but if it got bigger than that, it could cause serious problems. For example, if we did just a £5,000,000 turnover, no single customer was allowed to spend more than £1,000,000 with us. But of course we didn't want to stop their business at that point, so that meant if they approached the £1,000,000 limit, we had to increase our sales to other customers to ensure that they would still stay below the 20 percent of the business. So every time their purchases got bigger, the rest of our sales efforts had to get better, or our product range had to increase so that the principle of no one customer being more than 20 percent of our sales was preserved.

Boots started to become a very big customer and started to get to a position where they were going to be a more than 20 percent participant of our total group sales volume. Their business increased, and we had to increase the rest of our sales to accommodate the 20 percent, and so I looked for even more products for ourselves and for them. That came at a time when the industry was changing from being a mechanical/optical industry to becoming an electronic/optical industry—not digital yet, but, instead of using mechanical shutters, using electronic shutters, building electronic printed circuit boards and later flexible printed circuits into cameras. The technology was moving really fast. Consequently, we had to retrain all our service department people from being mechanical and optical engineers into electronic engineers.

Now that we could service electronics, we figured, why not extend our range to include pure electronic products like microwave ovens, radios, cassette players, tape players? We stuck to the same principle that we already had established with Paul Plus Ltd., and did everything under our own brand name only. We built up a very successful range of electronic equipment under our Plustron brand and started another company called Plustronics Ltd., and another sales force. In the process, we educated a lot of now famous names in the Far Eastern electronics industry who had not got a clue of electrical safety as expected in the UK and Europe.

For instance, I went to Samsung in Korea, which is now said to be a more recognised name even than Sony in terms of perception of brand name recognition. They were a big conglomerate in Korea and serviced the Asian market. They were making television sets in one of their factories at that time when I was first shown around.

It was a green field factory. In other words, it started virtually from scratch, being built in a field. It was integrated to start from making glass from silica for the television tubes, and then they made the cathode ray tubes and they built them into the sets, which hundreds of nimble-fingered girls assembled on the long production line. It looked like a mile down to the other end of the factory. At the end of the line, after being automatically put into cardboard boxes, they were then loaded into containers to be shipped.

They'd got that down to a T, but they were just starting on making microwaves, the era of the microwave oven having just begun. I thought that would be a good product for us, so I asked how many do we need to order for them to make it under our brand. It wasn't that great a quantity, so we started. I told them they'd have to airfreight a pre-production sample to the UK for testing, to make sure that it passes British standard BS415 for electrical safety requirements. They sent us a sample, and it failed. We worked with them to change this and that, and they sent more samples. By that stage, we had already got our own QA (quality assurance) department within the company because we were going into an area now which could potentially be much more dangerous than selling cameras, where you can't get electrical shocks. We wanted to make sure that everything was 110% safe, and I wanted to keep out of the courts as well. It took quite a time. They sent an engineer over and I think we sent our QA manager over as well. In the end, we got there.

Once we got it right, we started shipping them, and then we got Boots interested as well. We now had a new company called Plustronics conceived from Paul Plus but with an electronic connotation. Plustronics had everything under its own label and a new sales force. We were only partly facing the same customers but mainly starting now to go into what is called in the UK the "brown goods sector." Things like refrigerators and washing machines are called "white goods." Things like radios and tape recorders are "brown goods". Some shops sell both. Some sell only one or the other. We opened lots of new accounts and thus added the extra sales we needed. It was the right product at the right price at the right time, and we had good marketing to sell it. Samsung became a big source for us only in terms of microwave ovens.

If you really wanted to be profitable, in those days, you couldn't do it unless you employed a lot of sales people and grew in size and, in my view, you couldn't do it if you were in manufacturing. I'm sure a lot of people made money out of manufacturing, but there were a lot more people in retail and distribution who made a lot more. In both import and distribution, to achieve the right profit margin, you have to do very careful calculation, taking the base price landed in the UK, or the FOB price, if that was the way that it was quoted, and adding on your shipping costs. Then adding on your duties and then adding a percentage figure for your gross margin, which needed to cover all your overheads and your projected net profit.

Everything the company did was always done on forward budgeting—both in terms of target sales volumes and target margins—and our costing was done on the basis of, at the end of the day, showing a 10% net profit for our shareholders. Not many companies in the distribution field can do that today, but in those days they could. If you look at the history of our annual reports as a public company, we achieved that most of the time, except in the years when the government, under Harold Wilson, had put huge increases in taxation, import duties, purchase tax, import deposits, personal taxation, thereby reducing the buying power of our customers so everything in the economy was really stagnant. We never made a loss in our whole history, but that financial year, 1968/69, we almost did because the overhead was just so great.

Plustronics also had some wonderful portable television sets for which we coined the advertising phrase "unputdownables." I sourced these from the Orion group run by its chief Mr. Otake, whom I found in Kobe near Osaka in Japan. He had factories in Japan, Korea and Taiwan, at that time and, much later, all over the world, including Wales. He produced some items under his own brand of Orion, but, at that time, mainly under buyers' brands. I designed these little "unputdownable" 5-inch and 7-inch black and white and colour television sets with him on the back of a cigarette packet in a geisha house. He acted like and imagined himself to be a real Samurai warrior. His underlings were always at his beck and call. He ran the most efficient operation, as he had to, in that type of industry. We would design a product on a piece of paper in the evening, and then next morning he would have drawings ready for engineering. By the next day, he would have a wooden mock up of it. We would improve or approve that and then it was subject to a final working sample, and off we would go. Orion is still going strong with eight factories and is now one of the major makers of TVs and videos in the world, producing for 11 of the world's major brands.

The success of our business was sourcing, getting along with people, and providing service. But marketing is the most important part. Anybody can buy, but you have to be able to sell it as well. You still come back to having the right product at the right price at the right time and then having the right people to sell it and backing it with meaningful, sizzling advertising. Most of that we did in-house, even to the extent that we were one of the first companies in our industry to have its own printing press. We were one of the first in our industry to computerise. We were also among the first to have a fax machine long before they became common. To use a fax machine, you needed to have two people. At that stage there were very few people we could fax, but our advertising agency put a fax machine in to communicate quicker and to approve layouts quicker. They were the only people we could fax with for quite some time. It wasn't even called a fax machine in those days. It was a facsimile machine. It was a complicated thing and took a long time before it caught on.

So we did most things in-house. We had a very good advertising department and our own photography department. We did our own pictures for the catalogues, leaflets, and press releases. When we got really big, we started using advertising agencies and let them tender for our account. They had to submit plans of their proposals, and we would make a short list and choose one. Usually, we stayed with an advertising agency for three to five years, and then we would need new ideas. Even then, we still did all our press releases, all our house magazines, dealer bulletins and some leaflets.

We grew steadily to the time when I left, at which point we employed 160 people. That's quite a responsibility. But I still kept to the basic concept never to employ more people until we had shown that we really needed them and could keep them busy on a full time long term basis. In other words, the existing staff worked harder until it just became too much, and then we employed more people. This was to make sure that we would never have to lay anybody off, and we never did, except in 1968/69 when Harold Wilson's draconian measures made importing and trading almost impossible, nor did we ever put anybody on short time.

Initially, we used only the photographic enthusiast magazines for our advertising. We then went to national newspapers like the Daily Express and the Sunday papers and the Sunday supplements. We tried some local radio. We did a lot of dealer co-operative advertising. We laid down a plan that we would pay a dealer up to 50 percent of his advertising cost if he featured our product in his ad on a solus basis, and we laid down what solus meant in terms of space in his advertisements. This was a benefit to both companies and worked well. In the end, we spent a fair amount of our advertising budget on co-operative advertising.

❖ 36 ❖

A Road Not Taken

JACK HANNES WAS A FRIEND of mine who later also became a competitor in the UK. His company name comes from HAN-nes, IM-port, EX-port, thus, Hanimex. He started importing in the same small way that I did, but in Australia. He also started manufacturing there and built an international company with a big slide projector business.

In 1968/69, when things got really tough in the UK, both our companies were affected by the drastic measures of the government and my companies made only a very small profit that year and his made a small loss. So we got together and started discussions about a possible merger of our companies. I was going to look after the Western Hemisphere and he was going to look after the Eastern Hemisphere, including the Pacific. We agreed that it would be a good move for both parties. We were both public companies and therefore had to go through prescribed procedures of checking each other's financial situation even though we both had published audited accounts.

To facilitate the merger we opened our books to Hanimex. Also Geoffrey Snow, then a partner in A.B. Snow, Wood & Co. our auditors, later my Finance Director, flew out in February 1970 via Hong Kong where I met him and we continued to the Hanimex Sydney Head Office to look at their operation.

Independent advisers were employed and after lengthy telexes flowing both ways, final terms were agreed. A completion meeting was arranged for 28th of April 1970 at offices of Gresham Trust in London. Half way through this meeting, quite unexpectedly, Jack Hannes aborted the deal. Apparently Hanimex discovered that they could not complete the proposed merger because doing so would breach one of the loan conditions in their Articles of Association. It more than surprised us that this problem had not been foreseen by them. We had lawyers and accountants all set and had spent quite large sums of money and management time. I didn't speak to Jack Hannes for years.

Fate probably decreed that the deal was not to be and within a short time trading conditions improved and we continued our growth on our own.

After I had moved to Jersey in 1980 we started exchanging Christmas cards again and also met when the Rotary International convention was held in Brisbane in June 2003.

Jack certainly was one of the great larger than life characters in the world's photographic industry. Sadly he passed away while skiing in Switzerland on 31st of January 2005.

… 37 …

The Auctioneer's Hammer

EVERY COMPANY THAT RATES AS a manufacturer or distributor has a problem with end of line merchandise, ex-salesmen's samples, shop-soiled merchandise, goods which have been used for a demonstration or goods that are scratched or imperfect in some way. My company was no different in that respect. The answer I found for this problem was unique in our industry. We accumulated this type of merchandise which we were unable to sell in the normal way and held an auction once a year. Since we were a company selling only to retailers, the attendance at these auctions had to be limited to the same retailers to whom we normally sold new goods.

We accumulated the goods up for auction in a special room which we called the "Discontinued Goods Room". Then we invited dealers to come on a specific Sunday to our head office for the auction. We had no shortage of dealers coming to bid and buy nor of staff volunteering for this duty, because it was always great fun. Naturally, I was the auctioneer, and I was on my feet with the auctioneer's hammer usually from 10:30 in the morning when we started until about 5 in the afternoon, when we had sold the last lot and emptied our room of all the goods. We turned these goods from virtually no value into a very good amount of turnover.

It was a highly organised day. The dealers would come and sit down in our canteen where we held this auction, and throughout the day we provided them with tea, coffee and snacks. Some of our office girls came to perform that duty. Then people from the sales staff in the office and the warehouse brought the goods out and held them up for the dealers to see. I would then ask for bids.

It never ceased to amaze me how auction fever infects even

solid, conservative retailers. Although I always started the bidding at less than half the trade price for the goods, the dealers themselves would, in their enthusiasm to outbid each other, sometimes go up to a higher figure than they would pay for that item if they bought it new from us through our salesman. On several occasions, I really could not let them outbid each other to such an extent. I stopped and told them they could buy the same goods brand new at that price, and I started the bidding again. When they bought something at the auction, not only did they have to pay before they left the premises, but they had to take all the goods which they'd bought away with them on that day as well. We did make exceptions to that if they bought a lot. We would store it for them until they could come to collect it the following week.

Of course, my description of the goods invariably was quite flowery, and humour was the order of the day. So everybody went away happy with their purchases and had a good day's entertainment on top of that. It goes to show that a good transaction is one where everybody concerned benefits.

◆ 38 ◆

The Japanese Market Opens

IN THE MID-1950S, IT BECAME possible to import cameras from Japan, and that was the next radical change in the worldwide photographic industry.

During the 1950/53 Korean War, American press and Army photographers who were covering the war discovered how good Japanese lenses were. That brought Japan to the attention of the industry. Before that, they had never been internationally recognised. Suddenly everybody wanted to become an importer. Imports started to the United States first, and then Europe became interested. The usual bureaucratic control of imports started. The Board of Trade decided that the import of cameras from Japan had to be controlled, and an annual quota was set and made available to applicants.

Before importation from Japan was permitted, I had already gone there so we would be ready. The first time I visited Japan, I signed a sole agency agreement with Minolta. Although they had a number of factories, they still had their head office in a large, old building that had been used as a school in Osaka. They were not a sophisticated international company at that stage. By that time, I was a member of the British Photographic Importers Association. I also became Chairman of the Japanese section. I had become a member of the establishment.

The Minolta company was then a very small, unknown but long-established camera firm called Chiyoda Kogaku Seiko KK, which produced cameras under the brand name of Minolta. Mr. Kazuo Tashima, known to all as "KT", started the company in 1928. When I came into the picture in the 1950s, he was still the President of the company. He started the company by importing two German camera technicians who helped him start the factory in the Osaka region of Japan known as the Kansai region. They made the usual bellows cameras and also had just started to make a through-the-lens twin reflex camera before the Second World War.

Generally speaking, most Japanese cameras in those days were copies of German models of different makers. The making of cameras is usually an assembly industry dependent on suppliers of lenses and suppliers of shutters. A new national camera industry starts off by being a copying type of industry; that's how it started in Russia, and that's how it started in China. The Japanese were astute enough to carry on a lot of research and development and bring out, in due course, their own new models with advanced technologies.

Many of these companies that are now big names in Japan did not have their own export departments. Minolta had no experience exporting their products and, like other companies, they employed one of the big Japanese trading and import-export companies like Mitsubishi, Mitsui and C. Itoh. In the case of Minolta, they employed a trading company by the name of Kanematsu, which has offices all over the world including Hamburg, from where I started importing. All the stocks and everything for Europe were shipped first from Japan to Hamburg, and we drew from there.

Japanese Cameras Ltd., the company I formed to import from Japan, was the agent for Minolta cameras from 1954 to 1980. It was a very successful 26-year relationship and I have a certificate signed by "KT" to show his appreciation hanging in my study.

The initial cameras imported were the Minolta Autocord which is a twin-lens reflex—very much on the lines of the German Rolleiflex and Rolleicord—and two 35mm cameras which were the starter models. They later made very sophisticated Single Lens Reflex cameras with electronic content, the Minolta SR-1 and Minolta SR-3. Then they produced several advanced 35mm cameras and little sub-miniature cameras—the Minolta 16 which was made in a number of models. Because of quota limitations, we were once again in a situation where initially we didn't have to sell the product, but purely allocate it to hungry dealers. Once we established

Japanese Cameras Ltd., which had a separate address at 50 Piccadilly, Tunstall, Stoke-on-Trent, we recruited yet another sales force of seven salesmen. We, therefore, got yet another opportunity to sell to the same dealers but under another guise.

❖ 39 ❖

Doing Business, Japanese Style

THE SELLING OF JAPANESE-MADE CAMERAS (not only Minolta) initially met with quite a bit of resistance because of the experience of British prisoners-of-war in Japanese hands. A number of dealers said they would not touch anything made in Japan. In time, however, there were very few of them left because, if they wanted to stay in the photographic industry, they ultimately had no alternative but to sell what became the leading technological products in the world.

I started visiting Japan annually. Besides visiting Minolta in Osaka, I also did a lot of sourcing in Tokyo. On my first trips to Japan, I stayed at the Imperial Hotel, just off the famous Ginza, which seemed to be the chosen headquarters of the world's photographic buyers. The buyers also seemed to go in the quiet period after Christmas and New Year during January and February. I regularly met many international buyers during that time. Later, when the Okura Hotel was built, everybody migrated there. The Okura was a first-class hotel providing excellent commercial services, which is very important for doing business in the East.

The system is quite interesting in Japan. My previous experience in Germany and Europe was that you went to visit the particular manufacturer at his office or factory, whether you were sourcing and looking for merchandise or as an existing customer. In Japan, people came to your hotel room, except when we had made an exclusive arrangement like I had done with Minolta. Then, all the business was done in their offices and visits made to their factories. Otherwise, with smaller companies and because of the difficulty of getting around Tokyo, everybody came to the hotel by appointment. If business resulted from that meeting and one wanted to see the factories as I invariably wanted to do, then they would come and collect you and take you by car or sometimes by long distance train if it was outside Tokyo.

The Japanese had a most sophisticated commercial intelligence system. They knew when buyers came to their airport in Tokyo, which countries they had come from and which hotel they were staying at. I don't know if they got the information from luggage labels or from passenger lists, but as soon as you checked into your hotel room, your telephone would start ringing with callers saying, "I'm Mr. ABC from XYZ company, and we have a fantastic product which I would like to come and show you to sell in England." So you drew up a schedule of appointments, and your hotel room became your office. Sometimes it felt like a prison cell because you would do between eight and 10 of these potential buying interviews every day. You had to be equipped with the traditionally required minimum of 200 visiting cards. Every time you meet somebody for business in Japan, it's a ritual to exchange visiting cards. For foreigners, who are called gaijin ("outside person"), you had visiting cards printed in your native language on one side and in Japanese characters on the flip side. All the airlines flying the Japanese route in those days had a supply source of free visiting cards if you used their airline. In exchange you also acquired a collection of visiting cards with correctly spelled names and full addresses. It was a very useful system.

Often, these hotel visitors came in pairs. They presented their products and prices. Another unique thing is that people would come to you and say they represented a particular company and they would have samples from that company, but they weren't representatives of that company; they were freelance entrepreneurs who bought some of that company's product to show you. If they could persuade you to buy, they would go back to that company, and say, "I have a buyer here from England, and I've been able get him interested and I've sold him on your products. Can I bring him to you?" In most cases they would readily do that, and the man who introduced me made a commission on any sales that resulted from his efforts. Of course, if it was from a larger company, that would tend to increase the price. So one tried always to make a direct contact and therefore, if it came to a stage of actual business, one would insist on seeing the company and the factory and meeting the real factory people. Nevertheless, a lot of these smaller firms who had interesting products didn't have export departments and couldn't speak English. So these little entrepreneurs did perform a service because they did all the negotiations and in a lot of cases even afterwards did a lot of the export arrangements and documentation. One had to get used to that and be able to sort out the wheat from the chaff, as it were.

Another circumstance that was quite different, and had to be accepted because it was part of their culture, is that the politeness of the Japanese prevented them from saying an outright "no," as we would do if something was not acceptable. I'm told that before the war, there was no word in the Japanese language for "no" and that General MacArthur, when he brought the American post-war administration to Japan, invented a Japanese word for it. They still loathe using it, but at least there is a word for "no" which is used by foreigners but very rarely by the Japanese themselves.

Because of this, one had to predetermine—particularly in price negotiations with new suppliers—whether the price that they finally accepted in negotiations was realistic or not and whether they could produce the product for that price. If they couldn't, you just couldn't tell. They would say, "Yes, yes," and you gave them an order, and shipment just would never materialise. One got quite a lot of experience evaluating production costs in Japan and seeing what was and was not feasible.

The other method was to start one's own intelligence system. Because they couldn't say no, I learned to ask them whether or not they had done business with the U.S. or the UK on their particular product. If they had I'd say, "Well, let's have a look at an invoice to a customer in the U.S." They would bring you the invoice showing to whom they had sold their product, and then you could establish a base price—usually a rather good one because if they had sold to a big U.S. company, it probably got the best possible price. In this way, you could also see if that product had previously been sold to the UK and to which competitor. Japanese companies, and later all Far East suppliers, invariably quoted and dealt only in U.S. dollars for exports to any part of the world. We had to build into our costing a risk factor for the exchange conversion rate into UK pounds.

◈ 40 ◈

When Things Don't Go As Planned

THE INITIAL FLIGHTS TO JAPAN were quite a chore because this was before the polar route and before flights across the Soviet Union were allowed. There were only two ways to get to Japan. One was what we called the southern route, which went through southern Europe, the Middle East, India, Hong Kong or Singapore and then to Japan. This was a wearying journey which usually was in a propeller-driven aircraft in four hour stages. We would land in four-hour stages. Some passengers departed, and new passengers came on. Many, many hours later we arrived quite tired in Japan. The second route, usually used for the return journey, was across the Pacific, the United States and the Atlantic. Because going round the world in this direction involved crossing the international dateline, you gain a day, and you could have a day's stopover in Hawaii without using up a day. After a hectic buying trip in the Far East, a two to three day rest and recreation on the way back ensured getting back to the office ready to tackle the accumulated work and the processing of the deals done. Good stopovers were in Thailand going west and in Hawaii or San Francisco going east.

Later, the whole method of transportation changed when the polar route was opened from Europe to Japan. You flew to the North Pole and then slid down to Japan on the other side of the globe. There was a refuelling stop in Anchorage, Alaska. The route was first pioneered by the SAS (Scandinavian Airline System). KLM (Royal Dutch Airlines), which was the airline we used to airfreight our Japanese products to the UK, was the second to go on that route. At Anchorage, SAS handled the flights, and we went into the terminal there while they refuelled. We usually had an hour or an hour and a half there to do duty free shopping. You could then also come back that way. It was a quick way to get to Japan.

Much later, the Soviet Union allowed aircraft to fly over their territory. Then that became the quickest route, flying over Siberia to Japan. I've got quite a number of North Pole crossing certificates from KLM that always had to be signed by the captain of the aircraft. In those days, navigation equipment, even on airlines, was not as sophisticated as it is now. Compasses go hopelessly wrong the nearer you get to the North Pole. So the DC-7 aircraft that they used in those days had an astrodome built into the cockpit roof. They would carry a navigating officer as well as the pilot, first officer and engineer. The navigator would shoot the stars with a sextant to navigate, just like you did on a ship. Later, when jets were introduced, more sophisticated inertia navigation systems replaced the astrodome, the navigator and the flight engineer. Two crew aircraft became the norm. Being interested in flying, I did quite a lot of riding in the cockpit in those days, which was allowed and encouraged.

One year I went to Japan in a DC-8, and the transit in Anchorage became quite interesting. I had as always pre-arranged many appointments and also visits to Minolta in Japan. We landed in Anchorage as usual and went into the terminal building to be confronted with the announcement, "Sorry, folks, we've discovered in one of the engines that every single blade has been broken, and we cannot continue the flight to Tokyo. There will be a flight delay of two or three days. We are arranging transport to the Hilton hotel downtown and accommodation there for you." They thought the cause was that we had picked up a little bit of chain from the snow plough on the runway upon landing. Arrangements were made to have a new engine flown up from Amsterdam and fitted. Of course, the passengers didn't like that. I had to send telexes to reschedule all my appointments. I didn't like it, but KLM didn't have any traffic rights from Anchorage, which meant no other companies who were going through Anchorage could pick up KLM passengers. They tried every means to get us to Tokyo quicker. There was no way, so we had to wait for this new engine to be flown up and fitted.

In the meantime, they put us up at the Hilton. They were extremely generous and told us to charge everything to KLM. It was quite funny, because in London a passenger who was an export salesman for English cloth suitings boarded the plane and sat by me. He was already very merry on drink and continued taking advantage of the free drink service. He clearly was an experienced bar inhabitant. When we reached the Hilton and he heard that everything was on KLM, he invited all the locals in the bar to have a drink with him, and he just signed all the bills "KLM". Not surprisingly, therefore, the next day came an announcement from KLM: "This is getting a little bit out of hand. From now on, there is a limit of X number of drinks per passenger per day." It was still a generous figure but not enough to invite all the locals to be guests of KLM.

During our enforced stay at Anchorage, there was a London professor who was going to Tokyo to give a lecture. Clearly, he was going to miss his lecture. He went absolutely wild and insisted they must get him to Tokyo somehow or other and if necessary get the United States Government involved to get him picked up with a military plane. In the end, he had no alternative but to wait with the rest of us. The next day, KLM arranged a coach and took those of us who wanted to out into the mountains around Anchorage to go skiing. I'd always been a very keen skier from my early days in Czechoslovakia, so I looked forward to this and made the best of it. The professor, who thought skiing was too dangerous, came with us but stayed at the base camp hotel. When we came back at the end of the day from skiing, he was missing. Apparently he'd gone out in the snow and skidded onto a rock and broke his arm. He was taken to the hospital in Anchorage. He had his arm put in plaster and in a sling. The lesson—if something is provided for you, take advantage of it and don't stay behind.

The next day I rented a Hertz car and did some sightseeing around Anchorage on my own and did some window shopping in the town centre. People in those days had an idea that Alaska was really an uncivilised country of Eskimos. I discovered they even had parking meters, which at that time we did not have in England. When I got back from window shopping, I had a parking ticket stuck on the car because I'd overstayed on the meter. As I didn't want to pay it, I went to the local police station. It turned out that the desk sergeant had been in the United States Army and had trained near Stoke-on-Trent, my hometown. We started chatting about his experiences in wartime England, and he was kind enough to waive the fine.

Besides the very busy civil airport in Anchorage, there is also the biggest sea plane airport in the world right next door. The only way to get to remote areas of Alaska is by float equipped aircraft. Also not all that far away is the huge American Air Base of Elmendorf.

In a few days the engine was changed, and we flew on to Tokyo and carried on with our business. Sometimes things go according to plan, sometimes not, and you've always got to have a second option if it doesn't go to plan. There's no point in losing your temper, because it doesn't get you anywhere at all.

41

Japanese Agencies

I ALWAYS APPLIED TO GET Japanese agencies just for the United Kingdom and the Channel Islands, because at that stage we had no experience of selling in Europe. So I went to Japanese manufacturers and told them we were an experienced importer and that we had been importing from Germany. They were keen to use importers who had already got German agencies, as that was a sign that you are established and accepted by the photographic retail trade. A few of my competitors also got Japanese agencies. Some importers, like Johnsons of Hendon, didn't want to know anything about Japanese products. They were big distributors of German products: they had the Voigtlaender agency. One Mr. Reuter there just did not want to know anything about Japanese products at all, and they never touched them.

The initial trips to Japan resulted in getting quite a few new agencies selling the products under the maker's name and also sourcing for our other companies under their brand names of Plus and later Plustronics.

Our main agency was Minolta, but we needed also lower priced cameras and more accessories. We had a very low-priced camera made called the Pal M-4. It was branded under another of our registered trademarks of Pal, which we used for Japanese Cameras Ltd. We had a relationship with one of the biggest electronic flash gun manufacturers in Japan called Kako. I got the agency for a cine film editor and photographic accessory maker called Minette and quite a number of gadgets like exposure meters, gadget bags and tripods. We then started importing binoculars from Japan, which became a very big business. Japanese binocular manufacturing was, back then, a cottage industry, even for the most famous makes. Casting the basic aluminium parts is done in one factory, the lenses are ground in another, and the leather covers were made in a third. The exporter—the company putting its brand name on the binoculars—would arrange to collect all these different components and take them out into the country where the farming community would assemble them into the finished product. They were then collected, tested, packed and boxed according to the brand name they were to be sold under. It turned out to be a very successful business.

From the start, the Japanese government was extremely interested in preserving the good name of the photographic industry. In 1951 the engraving of cameras with "Made in occupied Japan" ceased. In 1953, they founded the Japanese Camera Inspection Institute (JCII) as a semi-government agency. It's first head was a prominent member of the Diet, Kinji Moriyama, and on his death his wife, Mayomi Moriyama, also a prominent member of the Diet and later Minister of Justice, took over. The institute had the task of inspecting every camera that was exported to anywhere in the world. They financed this by sticking on a little gold decal that said "Inspected by the JCII," when the inspection was finished. The manufacturer had to pay so much per thousand labels or per thousand cameras inspected. Later, that changed when the quality had reached a certain standard. They licensed larger manufacturers for self-inspection, and only the small manufacturers still had to take 200 cameras at a time to be inspected in Tokyo. This impressed consumers everywhere because this was the first time they were able to buy cameras and other optical equipment that had a government seal of approval.

Minolta added more still and cine camera models and many accessories. Their recognition by the world as a brand leader came with the camera called the Minolta Himatic-7, an extremely sophisticated 35mm automatic camera. The Japanese in general were good in automatic exposure and automatic focus technology. NASA chose this particular normal-production camera, and it was the first hand-held camera in space. It was carried by Col. John Glenn on 20th February 1962, when he was the first American to orbit the earth in the Friendship 7 Mercury spacecraft. That helped sales quite a bit and helped raise the brand image of Minolta. John Glenn was invited to visit the Minolta factory in Japan where the Himatic 7 camera was made, and he became a friend of Minolta. He also visited Minolta's lens factory.

It has always been my aim to sell a Minolta planetarium. A planetarium is a live simulation of the sky at night. You sit inside a domed building and see all the planets, the stars and their movements. There are audio presentations and educational programmes that discuss the constellations, etc. There are very few makers of planetariums in the world. One is made by Zeiss in Germany and another one is made by Minolta in Japan. Being the agent for Minolta, my ambition was always to sell one. Minolta themselves had sold one through their Finnish agent to a city northwest of Helsinki called Tampere. I got to know about the launching of this planetarium in Tampere and got in touch with a public entertainment company in the UK, whom I thought should be interested in it. They said they were interested, and in April of 1969 I flew two of their directors to Tampere for the opening. I wined them and dined them and they were very impressed, but it never did get a sale.

There was a fashion trend movement started by a company called Olympus to make half frame cameras. Instead of getting 36 pictures from a 35mm cassette, you could take 72 pictures on each one which would reduce the cost of your photography. Minolta had to keep up with the fashion trends, so they also came out with a half frame camera. They were looking for a name for it, and I suggested they should call it the Minoltina which would suggest it was small and it came off the tongue well. They accepted that suggestion, and in Sam Kusumoto's book (see the "Luck With Minolta" chapter) he mentions that the name came from me. They also then called one of their smaller cine cameras Minoltina.

Their research and development went into other related optical and electronic fields and they have quite a number of patents for which they will be paid royalties and licence fees. In the changeover period from mechanical/optical to electronic/optical they formed a technical co-operation agreement with Leitz in Germany who were the makers of the famous Leica cameras. It seemed quite a one-way agreement because Minolta possessed a lot more electronic technology than Leitz. Minolta made quite a number of electronic components for the Leica camera and shipped them to Germany. They then developed a non-reflex 35mm camera which was sold in Europe under the Leica name and in other parts of the world under the Minolta name.

Japanese Cameras Ltd. with the Minolta range became our top selling company in the group. Whenever there was a sales vacancy in Japanese Cameras Ltd., salesmen from the other companies, which they considered to be junior companies, always applied for that position. It had the best earning potential and was the most prestigious company for which to work. They were all part of the same group, and all the salesmen were on the same basic salary and percentage commission terms. But because of the volume of business at Japanese Cameras Ltd., salesmen there could earn more.

Minolta was one of only two camera factories in Japan that actually smelted their own glass for lenses. They had a completely vertically integrated manufacturing programme for their cameras with an optical glass factory near Kobe, the port town of Osaka—a very mountainous, clean-air region. The optical glass itself has to be smelted into the mouldings for grinding, polishing, coating, assembling and fitting, and this was all done at the factory. The highest mountain in the area was called Mount Rokko, so Minolta called their brand name lenses Rokkor lenses. We made use of this unique feature when advertising Rokkor lenses in the UK I noticed that Rokkor is a palindrome—it is spelled the same forward and backward. We claimed this is a unique lens, just as unique as a palindrome. As very few people knew what a palindrome was and had to look it up to see what the advertisement was all about, this teasing advertising was a great attention getter.

As aforementioned, all of the Japanese industry, from cameras to motorbikes and cars, was started by first making copies of existing products. Then they spent a lot of money on research and development to produce their own technology, allowing them to overtake the industries they had copied. In many cases, the copied industries could not then compete, and they went out of business.

When it came to promoting and selling their products overseas, the Japanese didn't do well in countries where they didn't understand the culture. The secret of their global success was that they usually picked good people in those countries and let them do whatever they felt was best to get the brand known and increase sales. In the case of Minolta, even after 26 years, when they decided to come to the UK themselves, they still employed local experts in marketing to run that side of their companies. They brought their own people in from Japan to do the administrative management work and the liaison with Japan. The marketing success of Japanese products is primarily the quality of the product and their technologically advanced status. But it is also in no small measure due to the skills of local experts' marketing.

◈ 42 ◈

Minolta and the Great KT

DURING OUR 26 YEARS OF holding the Minolta exclusive agency and distribution in the United Kingdom and the Channel Islands we obviously formed a very close working and also a personal relationship.

It all started with Kazuo Tashima, (KT), founder and chairman of the Minolta Camera Company. Tashima, who at one time was also president of the Japan Camera Industry Association, established the Japan-German Camera Company in 1928, by employing two engineers from Germany to help produce small cameras. In 1937, he reorganised and renamed the company Chiyoda Kogaku Seiko, the predecessor of Minolta Camera Company, which came into being in 1962.

Mr. Sandow was export manager in Osaka, but initially we dealt with the Hamburg office of their export house Kanematsu, led by Mr. Yoshioka and Mr. Tanaka and supported by two Minolta men, Mr. Fujii, later replaced by Koji Kusumoto.

Minolta then established their own export department in Osaka where I first met the charismatic Sam Kusumoto (brother of Koji). Sam became a great friend of mine and reached great heights within Minolta. When I first went to Japan in the early 1950s, he had just joined Minolta, as a University graduate, in the Export Department at the Osaka headquarters. From 1954 to 1958, he was a sales representative in New York City, founding almost single handedly what was to become the giant US subsidiary, the Minolta Corporation. Then, he was moved back to Osaka in 1959, where he became a sales planning manager until 1960. He then was promoted to Director of the Export Division in 1960 and stayed so until 1969, when he became President of the Minolta Corporation in the United States until 1995. From 1996 to 1998, he was Chairman of that corporation in the U.S. From 1999 to the present, Sam has been Chairman Emeritus of Minolta Corporation and later of Konica-Minolta, after the companies merged. He wrote a book called *My Bridge to America: Discovering the New World for Minolta*, and he became quite a famous ambassadorial figure for the Japanese in the United States. During a ceremony held at the Ministry of Foreign Affairs in Tokyo, the Emperor of Japan awarded Sam the Order of the Rising Sun. A little later, after Her Majesty the Queen awarded me the Officer of the Order of the British Empire, Sam and I congratulated each other.

Another University graduate who joined the export division in 1964, when Sam Kusumoto was its Director, and rose to even greater heights was Yoshikatsu Ota. He is now the big boss of Konica-Minolta. Ota-san, (Mr. Ota) was the first non-family member to take over from Minolta founder K. Tashima who had been followed by his son Henry. In 1968, he transferred to the Minolta GmbH, the German subsidiary responsible for European marketing in Ahrensburg near Hamburg. This was when our official business started with the European HQ under the supervision of Tim Nishimura. (Ota-san visited me in Stoke-on-Trent some time in 1969 or 1970.) In September of 1971, he returned to Osaka and was then responsible for photo exports other than for the United States and Europe.

Henry Tashima (son of KT) and Akio Miyabayashi succeeded Tim Nishimura and Ota-san in Hamburg soon after. In December 1972, Ota-san left the photography side and moved to the Business Machine Division, still responsible for exporting. In November 1975, he went back to Germany, this time to Hanover and opened a Business Machine Division there.

Later, in June 1995, he was promoted to senior executive director of the Business Machine Division. In June 1999, he was elected President and CEO of the Minolta Co. In January 2003, the merger of Konica and Minolta was announced. Ota-san was elected Director of Konica Minolta Holdings in June 2003. In August of that year, when the official merger took place, he was promoted to

Director and Executive Vice President of Konica Minolta Holdings. In October 2003, he was elected President and CEO of Konica Minolta Business Technologies Inc. Unfortunately, the photographic manufacturing side of the business, started by KT in 1928, came to an end when Konica Minolta announced ceasing production of all photo products in 2005. They were a casualty of the digital revolution.

Akio Miyabayashi was the boss of Minolta Europe from 1975 and besides regular contact with him, I also dealt with and had visits from Rick Kutani and Yasu Kada. Both Akio and Rick had been in Hamburg a long time and both married German girls and stayed in Europe after they retired from Minolta. Rick was in charge of Minolta UK when they took over from my company, Japanese Cameras Ltd, and I gave him his English first name. Besides Japanese, Akio speaks fluent English, German and French and lectures in any of those languages on marketing and other subjects. He has the same lecture circuit agent as Margaret Thatcher but told me although he gets excellent fees they are nowhere near as high as hers.

We had two Minolta technicians based with us in Newcastle— Mr. Maeda and Mr. Koyama.

It pays to have and maintain good relations with all people, even with competitors. You never know. One day you might be able to do each other favours. Everything always revolves and depends on people. The more people you know, the better your chances are that sooner or later you can benefit from their friendship or knowledge or know-how and they of yours.

◈ 43 ◈

A Spot in Piccadilly Circus

MY SALES MANAGERS, SALESMEN, AND I went to all Minolta European sales conferences which were held in different towns of Europe. Because of our excellent advertising and PR, we were usually held up as the "this is the way to do it" company. It was quite pleasing to be singled out. Besides having a prestige London show room in Regent Street and doing a lot of photographic press and national newspaper advertising, my aim always was to climb to the top of the mountain.

The top of the mountain in terms of advertising was to have a neon sign in Piccadilly Circus in London which is the centre of our world. It was like having neon signs in Times Square in New York, for the US market. Piccadilly Circus is full of neon signs of global brands. It is a huge roundabout with a statue of Eros and a fountain in the middle of it and traffic going all round it—quite a traffic hazard but all the tourists go there. Having signs in Piccadilly Circus was not just for marketing in the UK, but marketing internationally. That's why global companies seek to have a neon sign there. More than three quarters of the area was already full of neon signs. But on the southern side, above a very famous sports store in the Lillywhites building, there were no neon signs at all -apparently because they couldn't get planning permission. They were valuable spaces, but there were no signs on it.

I heard of a neon sign company that had the new technology of scrolling newscaster signs as in Times Square. This company had got planning permission to put up their sign there. So I contacted them and said, "You've got planning permission, but how about a huge neon sign above your newscaster to help draw attention to it." They rather liked the idea and quoted prices much higher than I anticipated. They then prepared some very nice neon sign drawings of the Minolta brand that had moving parts to it—lighting up and lighting down. I took the idea to Minolta and said, "This isn't just for the UK. You pay a major part of it because it really is an international sign."

"Oh!" they replied, "We haven't got any money and there's no provision in our budget for it."

So I said, "Well, this isn't going to come off in five minutes anyway. Make some provision in your next year's budget for it, and then we'll start." We came to an agreement. We paid too high a percentage of the annual rental, but we had the first photographic company neon sign in Piccadilly Circus for Minolta. Once it went up, everybody was pleased. It helped the brand image, and it helped make the job of selling cameras to retailers and then to the public much easier from then on. There is nothing in terms of visual advertising that can do more than to have a neon sign in Piccadilly Circus. This was the other big thing we did for Minolta which was quite unique and we'd reached the top of that mountain.

The 40ft. by 14ft. Minolta sign was ceremoniously switched on in 1966 and stayed up for some years. Then, whether due to the planning authority or the people who had the newscaster sign, the sign was taken down, and there is once again no neon sign on that side of Piccadilly Circus. While it was there, it was a Minolta camera exclusive. The biggest sign is still Coca-Cola, but Fuji films and cameras, Samsung, Sony, all the global companies have got huge signs there now.

I was the sole UK distributor for Minolta for 26 years, and during that time we built them up from a totally unknown brand to one of the leading brand names in its field. (We did have a lot of competition from other Japanese brands imported by other British importers and distributors.) In retrospect, getting the Minolta agency was a major factor in our development and growth. Minolta became a worldwide and well-known name. Even with Minolta, the photographic side became the smaller part of the business, and the copying machines and computer printers became far bigger than the camera side. Five years ago they could see that they had to get bigger quickly and the only way to do that was to amalgamate with another company in the same sort of situation. They decided to merge with a Japanese company called Konica, and they became Konica-Minolta. They always produced excellent quality products and in 2005, although they had some excellent digital cameras, they decided to pull out of the now non-profitable manufacturing of photographic products and concentrate only on the business machine side.

❖ 44 ❖

Finding Ricoh

EVERYBODY NEEDS SOME LUCK, BUT it is no substitute for hard work and a nose for where potentially to find success. When we started off with Minolta, we didn't really know them. When camera imports from Japan were first allowed, I wrote to many of the leading Japanese domestic camera manufacturers and Minolta was the quickest to react and to start talks with us. In retrospect, I was lucky to have acquired the Minolta agency. Minolta was also lucky to have found me. These things are always mutual.

We were their sole UK agent for 26 years but we never had more than initially one year, and later three or five year, contracts. Each one had to be renegotiated, and once the initial "honeymoon" period was over—when things were controlled by import quotas anyway—they wanted performance figures included in the agreement. I always loathed to include them because you could have a period of nationwide economic setbacks or even shortage of suitable models for the market and therefore you couldn't necessarily reach the stipulated turnover set in an agreement. This could be the end of an agency due to circumstances beyond our control. So I was always careful to stipulate escape clauses.

It became the fashion with Japanese camera makers to have their own companies in the different important export markets of the world. I don't think Minolta ever had an agent in the United States. It was such an important market that they started there themselves right from the beginning. In the UK the Olympus company was the first to form their own wholly-owned subsidiary and then one by one the others followed. In fact Minolta was one of the last, but clearly the writing was on the wall and hence, as explained elsewhere, I started looking for an alternative camera maker. It had to be one who was unlikely to want to form its own subsidiary in the United Kingdom.

One of the cultural habits of Japan is that they tend to follow the lead of somebody who discovers something. In this case, a Japanese company discovered it could do better business and make more profits if they had their own subsidiary in a particular country. They started the subsidiary, and other companies in the industry, said, "Hey, they seem to be successful, we must do the same." So in 1976, Minolta intimated that they too wanted to have their own Minolta UK Ltd. Having seen this happen with a lot of our competitors, I knew that sooner or later this was going to happen with Minolta. They gave due notice under our agreement and started their own company.

On my annual six-weeks' visit in January/February to the Far East, five years before Minolta gave notice, I had started to form a purely friendly relationship with a company called Ricoh. They were big in copying and printing machines and had a camera manufacturing subsidiary and facility. They had a range of single lens reflex cameras and 35mm cameras, not dissimilar from, but not as famous as Minolta. It's better to have something "not as famous" than to have nothing at all. I went and knocked on the door of the Ricoh head office, having received an introduction. It's very important to "open doors" in Japan. It is similar to what in England we would call the "old boy network".

I knew the people at the Japanese Camera Inspection Institute extremely well. On my annual trip, I always first paid a courtesy visit to the JCII to be welcomed by their Mr. Hibi, an expert and fount of knowledge on the photographic industry of Japan. They had a showroom there that displayed all the Japanese postwar cameras ever made, including current models before they received the final approval for export. It was possible to discover a new camera maker there that one had never heard of before. So I would go and see whether there was a possibility of business there. With the introduction of the Japanese Camera Inspection Institute, I went to see Ricoh. I knew they had an agent in the UK, but I thought maybe they could make a special model for me. Ricoh said,

"Well, Mr. Strasser, you're a very nice guy, but while you've got the Minolta agency, there's no way we can do business with each other. Come along, if ever that situation changes." I still went every year just to say "Hello".

After five years, the situation changed. By then, I knew the people there. I said, "Hey, on the 1st of January next year, we are not going to have a Minolta agency any more." On January 1, we had the Ricoh agency. Thus it was a seamless change. When I left the company they still had the Ricoh agency.

45

Subsidiaries

FOR MANY REASONS, WE ALWAYS kept the operating companies apart in the eyes of the public by having different addresses, different catalogues, and separate sales forces. There were certain things which were administratively easier to do as a group rather than as individual companies. For instance, after-sales service. We didn't want to have to print separate repair documents for each company. So instead of having all the names of the different operating companies on the document, which would have been confusing, we formed yet another company, called Interserve Ltd. This was our inter-group service company with one service department. Interserve Ltd., became a separate cost and profit centre. Over 80 percent of Interserve's work was warranty work for which there was no charge either to the dealers or consumers. The chargeable service carried out—the remaining 20 percent—produced enough profit to make it a profit centre. Most of the spare parts were supplied by the manufacturer of the goods, so we supplied the labour.

Later, we also decided that instead of having separate accounts departments with separate credit controllers, we would have another company called Consac Ltd., which did Consolidated Accounting for the group. In this case, because the invoices were produced by computer, they were produced for and sent out by the individual companies. But Consac sent out the statement at the end of the month on behalf of the companies. Instead of making separate cheques out to each of our different companies, the dealer only had to make one cheque out to Consac.

Then I had the idea that there could be certain benefits to doing some promotions as a group rather than as individual companies, although we still wanted to keep separate sales forces. For instance, I conceived a scheme called Interplan—inter-group sales planning—where we came out with a sales scheme in which, if a dealer did a certain amount of turnover, he could get retrospective, extra discounts. So for that we called in all the sales forces together and had a communal group conference and presented this Interplan idea.

I created a selling plan whereby any of the products ordered from any of our group companies would cumulatively help the dealer in reaching certain targets for which he would get those retrospective discounts. We would calculate all that on the computer, and we clearly had to make it fair. A small company with one shop out in the sticks somewhere couldn't compete in terms of reaching the same target as a company with six shops in major towns. So we took the group turnover for every dealer for the previous year and added a percentage, like 50 percent, to that. Then we told them if they reached their sales target—which was realistic because it was based on what they did the year before—then retrospective discounts would apply.

We published a "sizzling" document which I presented to the sales forces at a group conference. It was the first time we'd ever done that. By doing this, we gave them the enthusiasm to go out and sell the plan. The different sales forces were still competing with each other individually on merchandise, but as a group sales force they could benefit each other because the more the group sold, the more they would benefit. The Interplan was extremely successful mainly because we published the figures to the dealer, exactly what his target was, and how near he was to his target on each monthly statement. Then we gave him retrospective discounts in stages when he had reached his target or improved on it.

We were constantly on the lookout to buy other companies and competitors. We were unsuccessful in buying another company until Mayfair Photographic Ltd., came along. Mayfair had some good agencies and products and did quite well. It had changed hands from a very entrepreneurial importer, Freddy Weitzmann. He sold out at a good price to a company called Oxley Ltd. owned by a financier who, because of the peculiarities of the photographic trade, just didn't make a go of it and let it go into liquidation. It became a case of trying to preserve the agencies held by that company and negotiating with the liquidators. There was almost a set national figure that gave a purchase value to agreed tax losses. If you paid tax of, say, 30 percent and you could buy somebody else's tax losses at 15 percent, you paid 15 percent less tax on that amount of profit. There were strict rules as to what could be transferred in terms of tax losses. If you were in the same industry, you could do that. So we bought the company in 1967 for £40,000 including its available tax loss of £97,000 which we benefited from over the next three years. We quickly negotiated with the suppliers of the company, some of whom we already knew anyway because they were mainly Japanese suppliers.

We did not take over any of their salesmen. We started another catalogue series for this new company. The company was, among others, the agent of a Japanese camera manufacturer who made single lens reflex cameras under the brand name of Miranda. This was the first Japanese single lens reflex camera with an interchangeable viewfinder system that used a waist-level finder or a pentaprism finder. The Germans had already done it, namely Wirgin with the Edixa, my first agency ever, but this was the first Japanese company to do it. This and other agencies that we held onto proved valuable.

An American company owned the Miranda Camera Company, and it was one of the very few Japanese makers which had a non-resident ownership. It was a United States importer called American Import Corporation (AIC). They also had the agency for lenses made under the brand name of Soligor. They sold extremely well in the United States and it was also a good brand name internationally. They had interchangeable lenses for all the single lens reflex cameras by Nikon, Canon, Pentax, Minolta and all others then being made. We increased the sales for them tremendously in the UK. We didn't have an independent Japanese made interchangeable lens line, so Soligor fitted in extremely well.

An American of German origin and fluent in Japanese, Ralph Lowenstein, ran the Miranda and Soligor Tokyo office for AIC. We became very good friends. Unfortunately, that company later went into bankruptcy, and Ralph returned to the United States. He now lives in San Francisco. Whenever I went to Japan, I spent time with him. I even introduced him to his Japanese wife. I was importing my own brand of flash guns from Orient Denki, a very small electronic flashgun manufacturer in Tokyo. Uniquely at that time, this company had a female export manager named Kazue. I am not sure how it came about, but anyway I introduced the two to each other. They subsequently did business together and eventually got married and had two sons. It was a nice personal touch to our business.

Another business relationship in Japan which grew into a personal friendship was with Ted Yoshida who owned the Raynox factory and made cine projectors for us. In fact he is the only Japanese who invited me to his home where I also met his wife, Miyoko.

⋄ 46 ⋄

Expanding Beyond Japan

AS MY AND MY COMPANY'S electronic know-how increased and Japan slowly became a very expensive manufacturing country, my sourcing also extended to other countries. Generally speaking, buyers who chase good value merchandise tend to go for low labour cost countries. The next country, after the Japanese achieved a higher standard of living and workers earned more money, was Korea. After Korea, Taiwan followed and then Hong Kong. After that, it was partly Malaysia and Singapore and partly the Philippines. More recently, it became China. China will, in my opinion, become the dominant world manufacturing power. Most consumer items, even those under global brands, are made in China. A lot of the product made in China was originally Japanese technology. Even now, makers like Canon and many others have a factory in China because they just cannot make mass-produced electronic items competitively in Japan anymore.

When I went to the Far East for the first couple of times, I visited Japan only. Then I started going to South Korea from there. It was still the same business system. You booked a hotel room—always the Chosun in Seoul, at the time the only Western style hotel there—and eight to 10 people per day would come and see you. I started taking my purchasing manager and later purchasing director, Peter Gorton, with me. He would have a separate room, so we'd each see eight to 10 people per day. At the end of our trip, we'd exchange notes and see who we could do business with and what the comparable buying prices were.

We did quite a bit of business in Korea, producing initially under very primitive manufacturing conditions. We could see why their prices were low. We had gone into the electronics business then, besides just optical and photographic, so we got into tape recorders, microphones, wooden box speakers and the like. I bought some good quality speakers and wanted to see the factory. So I was taken there, and it was a shed full of quite young lads sitting there on little stools sandpapering these speaker boxes by hand to take off the rough edges before they went in for staining and varnishing. The conditions were primitive, badly illuminated and not ventilated. I wished I had not seen it. Frequently when we went to see factories in villages, they still had all the sewage flowing in little uncovered canals outside the houses. But, just as in early Japan, over a period of time these conditions improved tremendously. They started doing good export business, making profits, earning foreign currency and improving the working and living conditions. People used to go to work on bicycles. Then, they went to work on mopeds. Then, they went to work in cars. It's economic evolution. They started out-pricing themselves from the market, and then the whole thing would start over again in Taiwan, and it just keeps going.

Over time, we did business in all those countries. From Taiwan we bought electronic calculators with what were then known as LED digital models with little red almost illegible figures on them. It eventually progressed to LCD readouts, which we still have today. The first calculators sold in the UK for about £139. You can buy smaller, faster, more powerful LCD calculators now at Dixons or Boots for less than £2. We brought in the first handheld calculator from Minolta, with the Minolta brand name on it, although it wasn't made by Minolta but by a company called Sanyo. This was an eight-digit display that was extendable to 16 digits by pressing the second button. The display contained Nixie tubes, which preceded LED and LCD displays. Nixie tubes contained the 10 digits from 0 to 9, one above the other in inverted glass test tube tops. These were in a row, and the relevant digit in the stack lit up when you did your calculations. That sold at £139-19s-6d. We sold a fair number at what now appears to be a crazy price. As with all chip technology, which started first with transistors and then went to chips, we initially paid high prices. Then, as more research and development had been amortised and competition and mass marketing started, prices tumbled. Most importantly, when you start with a newer chip technology, maybe 60% of your production has to be thrown away because it is sub-standard. Then, as the yield improves, the prices of that chip come down dramatically as the throw-away factor is reduced.

We also started importing digital watches from Taiwan in a big way. We then started buying them from Singapore. Cameras and radios were next from those two countries. From Hong Kong we sourced radio cassette recorders and clock radios. I did one side trip to the Philippines because there was a small factory there making very low priced AM/FM battery operated radios which sold for about £3. We imported a substantial quantity.

Our Far East visits got longer as we started sourcing from all those different countries and companies. We got to the point where we were shipping huge quantities from different suppliers for our different companies, and very early on we decided to have our own in-house shipping department. Rather than using a broker for the shipping, the buying department would send the order to the supplier. Copies of it would go to the shipping department, and they would arrange which method of transport to use, ships or airlines. When the goods arrived in the UK, they would prepare all the Customs documentation in-house. All we used the shipping agent at the airport or the dock for was to do the actual physical clearance for us. Then, we'd send our lorry to pick up the goods or have the 40-foot container brought to our warehouse for unloading.

It was my policy to do as much as we could in-house. We printed our own advertising leaflets, press releases, house magazines, order forms, letter heads and report forms. That helped us remain competitive.

For shipments from the Far East, we used a method of transport known as "Sea/Air". It came across the Pacific to the United States by sea and then across the United States as ballast on mostly empty aircraft. Most of the internal U.S. air cargo traffic apparently goes from east to west, and a lot of the aircraft are empty when they return from west to east so you can get very good freight rates. It would then cross the Atlantic again by air, so that something that would take six to eight weeks by sea could be done in 21 days by Sea/Air or five to seven days by air. The method of transport you used depended on the value, weight and volume ratio of the product. We used Sea/Air a lot, and when it was totally by air, we always used KLM as our preferred airline. As a result, we did a lot of volume with them and negotiated very good rates. We also got quite a lot of free tickets to go to the Far East on sourcing and buying trips through that partnership.

❖ 47 ❖
Industry Revolutions

THROUGHOUT MY LIFE, I'VE SEEN many revolutions and changes in all sorts of fields where one had to keep up to date. It has always been my policy to investigate the latest labour-saving or technical improvements and innovations in terms of applications and presentation. Many companies who neglected doing this went under because they tried to stand still—something you can never do in the present fast-paced technology of the world.

One need only think of the radical changes in terms of making copies. How many people today remember something called carbon paper, which was a very thin paper coated with carbon? In the early days, the carbon came off on your fingers and made a terrible mess. Later on, they perfected it so it no longer did that. If you wanted three copies of something, you took three pieces of paper and two pieces of carbon paper and interweaved them. Then you put it into your typewriter or even into your handwritten copy board. When finished, you took out the carbon paper and either threw it away or used it again if it was a multi-use carbon paper. Today nobody uses carbon paper. So what's happened to all the carbon paper manufacturers? They have had to change. Then someone came along and invented an electrostatic copying machine called Xerox which produced copies by the thousands in a very short space of time. It revolutionised the copying and printing industry. We all use light bulbs today, but at the beginning of the last century people still used gas mantles in their light fittings; instead of electricity, they used gas. This necessitated huge storage cylinders in every town and miles of gas piping. The street lighting, which used gas as well, had to have men walking round them lighting each one individually every evening and putting them out again every morning. What happened to all the gas mantle manufacturers? They had to change, as we must all be ready to change.

In the photography industry, we started off with glass plates coated with light sensitive emulsion, which had to be loaded into plate holders and put in the back of a camera, and when the picture was ready to be taken the lens had to be shut. The cover of the plate holder had to be pulled out. The picture was then taken. You had to remember to push the plate holder cover back again, then take it to a dark room and hand develop the plate, and that became the negative. From that, a positive print in black and white was made.

Then someone came along and invented a material called celluloid, and we had celluloid-based films which were highly inflammable. Then somebody came along with a better, safer type of plastic base that still had to be coated with emulsions, and they started making roll films. That person was Mr. George Eastman, the founder of Kodak, who started his film business in Rochester, New York.

Then Oskar Barnack came along and thought that instead of having film on a spool with a backing paper and little red windows on the back of a camera where you could see the number of the picture that was in front of the lens at that particular time, he would have a cassette which would take the same size of film that was used in motion picture cameras in the cinematic industry. Barnack invented a camera called Leica in 1925 when the negative size of 24 x 36mm was first used. This became a world standard and has lasted to this day. Also, the film container used for the Leica, which is called a cassette, taking 35mm film, became the standard. The films were then made by Kodak, Agfa, Fuji and Ilford.

Then we come to another revolution in terms of cameras—from optical/mechanical to optical/electronic. They had always been the product of an optical/mechanical industry—optical for the lens and mechanical for the film advancement, the shutter and the iris. The shutter was used for different speeds thus controlling the length of the exposure. There was another mechanical device inside the lens for changing the aperture of the iris to give different depths of field.

That was in the days when, for electric and particularly audio and radio use, we were dependent on valves. These were huge in dimension. Therefore, any audio or sound equipment was of necessity also large. Then somebody came along and invented transistors, which took over. These didn't have the same heat problem, were smaller, and were easier to use in a manufacturing process because somebody else came along and invented printed circuit boards. Transistors could much more easily be positioned on a printed circuit board with other similar small components to produce a complete circuit as the name suggests.

Then somebody invented micro processors which were then built into integrated circuits and everything in all those different stages became smaller and smaller. That applied equally to computers and cameras. The camera industry changed from being an optical/mechanical industry to becoming an optical/electronic industry. But it was still using the traditional film material. That applied both to still cameras and cine or movie cameras. It enabled automatic focus and exposure and much more accurate controls all resulting in better pictures.

Then somebody found that the oxide tapes that people were using to record speech on tape recorders and dictation machines could also be used and adapted to put images on. This change took place first in the cinematic camera field, when video cameras came into play. These were huge to start off with and, as we know today, camcorders can be just the size of the palm of a hand.

As the basic recording material improved, somebody came along and after a lot of research and development brought out a digital image system for still cameras, again using an electromagnetic media for recording. We now have CDs, DVDs, SD digital, and flash cards etc. Over the years, all of these have increased their memory capacity without increasing their physical size.

In the period between 2002 and 2005, there was a rapid change from film cameras to digital cameras, and easy printing in colour from those cameras on a home computer.

Early in 2005, for instance, the Dixon Group—the largest retailer of imaging equipment—decided to stop completely the sale of traditional film cameras.

Almost everyone in the industry anticipated that digital photography would sooner or later become very popular, but no one thought this changeover would come as quickly as it did. Old established companies like Kodak were too slow in accepting this change. Going belatedly into the digital field, they incurred a great loss of millions of dollars as they caught up. Similarly affected, the world-famous German maker of films, Agfa, went into receivership in 2005. The revered Minolta company, with whom I had worked for 26 years as their UK agent, joined up with Konica to amalgamate their strengths and know how, but unfortunately they too left it too late and pulled out of the photo manufacturing side of the business completely in 2006. Kyocera/Yashica made a similar decision.

The whole marketing structure of the imaging industry has changed. Cameras, the sale of which used to be reserved exclusively to photographic dealers, are now sold in all sorts of outlets. A lot of the digital cameras are made by electronic equipment manufacturers who were not in the photographic trade when film cameras were being produced. A lot of their customers who were television, radio and sound equipment retailers are now selling digital cameras. In fact, they have become a commodity, and even supermarkets like Tesco sell them with groceries.

Looking back, I'm pleased I came into the photographic industry at a time when there was still room for an entrepreneur to build up a distribution business in the industry, during a very exciting time of change but still very much in a situation of orderly marketing. The present state of undoubted overproduction is leading to an impossible situation of not enabling manufacturers, distributors or retailers to make a sufficient margin to be able to re-invest into expanding their business. We have, therefore, a situation where only the very biggest global commercial companies will be able to survive in this class of business.

However, I believe that it is still possible, although more difficult, for an entrepreneur who has the ability to find or invent a unique product or a unique service to make a pot of gold. Take, for example, recent inventions like the Dyson vacuum cleaner. Who would have thought that a single unknown inventor could come along and revolutionise the global vacuum cleaner industry, an industry that was dominated by Hoover, a name synonymous with vacuum cleaners? A Briton, James Dyson, came along and invented a vacuum cleaner that didn't need bags to collect the dirt and thereby maintained its efficiency regardless of how much dirt it had picked up. He started making these in England with modern packaging and design and conquered the world in that industry.

Take again two Americans, Sergey Brin and Larry Page, Stanford University students in the heart of the Silicon Valley who thought up the concept and produced the PageRank algorithm, which was later incorporated into the Google search engine, a search engine for millions of computer users in the world. They had a unique product and beat the entire competing search engines to float as a public company with a capital value of billions of dollars.

Consider a young Swede by the name of Niklas Zennstroem, who found a way of harnessing computer transmission of data and adopting it to transmission of voice and pioneering the progress of VoIP (Voice over Internet Protocol). With superb marketing he built Skype up to over 100 million users in a period of less than four years and then sold it for over a billion dollars to eBay. And eBay is in itself a revolutionary concept of buying and selling over the Internet without going into a shop and, in particular, allowing the buying and selling of any commodity from any part of the world to another part of the world in a secure payment manner.

◈ 48 ◈

Making My Shares Bankable

DURING THE TIME THAT WE were a public company, I was still the major shareholder and waived my rights to dividends most of the time. The amounts waived were published in the accounts. This continued the policy I'd followed before we went public—to reinvest into the company, to take out only reasonable salaries and bonuses but not take all dividends. A lot of the income I would have derived from dividends would have been taken in taxes anyway. Over the years I was in business, I paid millions in taxes and, as I keep saying, never even got a thank you letter.

Waiving my rights to dividends and reinvesting in the company paid off. We were able to get a good share evaluation when we went public in 1962 and a reasonably good price when we finally sold to a holding company in London known as Central and Sheerwood Ltd. in 1977.

There were two reasons I accepted an offer to buy the company. One was that I was now getting to an age of about 50 and had always waived dividends, had never taken what one could call a large salary or bonuses. All my wealth creation was represented in pieces of paper called shares which had a value but there could be an economic slump the next year. There could be all sorts of reasons why the share price could drop, so I thought it was about time that I converted those pieces of paper into bankable money.

The other reason I accepted an offer to be bought out was very fully explained in my explanation letter to every employee in the Photopia International group of companies. That letter was dated 3rd of October 1977, and I quote, "The principle reason why, after extensive discussions, this offer has been accepted by us is one of the taxation system in the United Kingdom. If I, as a very substantial shareholder of Photopia International Ltd., were for some reason to die through accident or illness, my executors would have to sell all my shareholdings to meet the high capital transfer taxes. This would of necessity be a forced sale at probably disadvantageous prices to a possibly unwelcome buyer, who may not have the best interests of the company and its staff as his prime interest. To insure the best possible interests of the continued development and expansion of the company and to safeguard the terms of employment of our staff, it is better to freely choose our holding company partner now, and this is what we have done." Then I wrote, "We believe this step is in your long term interest also, that is, in the long term interest of the staff." I also made very sure that the vending agreement contained specific paragraphs to safeguard the development of the business and the protection of the future of all employees on terms and conditions of employment not less favourable than presently existing.

Central and Sheerwood Ltd., was a holding company which had a turnover in the previous year of 1976 of over £53 million and had interests covering engineering, printing and publishing and financial services. They were interested in Photopia International Ltd., to form the basis of a new sphere of interests to be further developed and expanded. Central and Sheerwood's boss and mentor was a gentleman by the name of Francis Singer. On the board were Sir Neil Shields and Nicholas Stacey. Their offer was a total cash offer and involved the payment of £2.546 million. At that stage, according to the document I still held shares in the company amounting to 52.75 percent of the company. Prescribed Stock Exchange procedures had to be gone through to get the agreement of all shareholders, but since I had the majority share, once I had decided to sell it was a foregone conclusion that the sale would proceed.

Nevertheless, all the documents—just as when we went public 15 years before—had to be approved. We had to get the approval of the Monopolies and Mergers Commission of the United Kingdom. The permission of the Stock Exchange had to be obtained as well. Also it was subject to acceptances of 90% of the shares held by the shareholders of Photopia International being received within the usual period, which was under the control of Central and Sheerwood. Once all that had taken place, we continued much as before but as a wholly owned subsidiary of Central and Sheerwood. They also appointed a very experienced company Chairman by the name of Leslie Thomas to be non-executive Chairman of the board. I stayed on as Managing Director while Thomas came once a month for board meetings. He was very happy with the way things were being run, so he simply chaired the board meetings, listened to our projected figures, and then went back to London.

A shareholder who purchased 400 shares in Photopia International Ltd. for £197.50 when we went public on 19th November 1962 and kept them until he accepted the offer from Central and Sheerwood Ltd. in November 1977 would have made a capital increase of £998.40 and received dividends amounting to £297.65, a total of £1,296.06. This represents a gain of £1,098.55 or 556.23% in 14 years: 39.73% per annum or 14.38% when compounded.

I had already bought a house in Jersey in June 1965, initially as a holiday home, but after the sale I finally decided to relocate to Jersey. Part of the reason was that I had paid that 30% tax on the sum of £1.3 million to the UK Treasury when I sold the company and wanted to protect my accumulated tax-paid wealth from further UK taxes. I moved to Jersey permanently because of the weather climate and also the tax climate, both of which were much better than in the UK. As long as you became a full-time resident in Jersey and could shake off UK domicile, which needed a year's staying in Jersey without going back to the UK, even for a funeral, you could be in a better tax situation. After a year, I achieved that. Jersey to this day doesn't have a capital gains tax or any death or estate duties, and the maximum personal or company tax is a 20% income tax. Income tax is the major tax in Jersey. That is why Jersey attracts the world's finance industry. All the major banks of the world have offices in Jersey. It is a respected off-shore finance centre with very strict controls which create international confidence in the Jersey finance industry and to prevent money laundering. Nowadays, even to open a private bank account in Jersey you have to go through very rigid procedures.

I never had any inclination to show wealth. I really didn't have wealth until I finally sold all my shares in the company in 1977. Before that, it was just paper, theoretical value. I wanted to retire at 50. I didn't quite manage it because I had to stay on another three years as part of our deal. On 20th November 1980, I officially retired at the age of 53.

◈ 49 ◈

The Captain Never Goes It Alone

I MUST ACKNOWLEDGE THE VERY important functions of the team in my organisation. Any successful entrepreneur, who is the instigator of ideas and innovations, can only put those into practise if he has a good team who can carry out his plans and dreams. I've been very fortunate in building such a team and have been rewarded with loyalty and long service from them. The top management consisted of what became the main board of directors of the public company Photopia International Limited, of which I was the Chairman and Managing Director.

- My Assistant Managing Director was Rupert Cartlidge, who started with me when I had one photographic retail shop. He became the manager of it and then progressed as the organisation grew. He was a first-class administrator and organiser. He did all the—what is now termed—human resources functions and therefore also interviewed, selected and engaged all staff. It was only in the case of higher level executive appointments that he built up a short list, and I came into the picture at the final selection. He was in charge of the day-to-day operations of the company.

- My Advertising Director was John Battison, who also started in the early years with me as a photographer and shop manager. John became a very effective Advertising Director, responsible for all the media buying, all design and managing of exhibition stands, both in the UK and other countries of Europe. He was responsible for all the in-house publications as well as all the different company catalogues, and he was an absolute master at his job.

- My Shipping Director was Jeffrey Pickford, who performed the vital task in our company specialising in imports and distribution. The logistics of liaising with overseas suppliers, shipping and Customs clearance and having everything at the right place at the right time is an essential task which Jeff performed to perfection. Before Jeff came to us, he worked for British Railways. He also grew with the organisation. Instead of using Customs agents at the ports and airports to do all the different form filling, we set up our own department with considerable knowledge of tariff headings, duty rates and procedures. We did everything in-house, which saved a considerable amount of money.

My colleagues Rupert Cartlidge, John Battison and Jeffrey Pickford were together with me the founding directors of the public company.

Our public company secretaries were: Cyril Smith, a J.P., who was the company accountant and secretary until 1971. He was then succeeded by Norman Watts, ACIS, then in 1973 by John Gibbs.

Geoffrey Snow, FCA, joined the firm in 1973 and became not only the accountant and company secretary but, having been the external auditor for the company, he also joined the main Board as Finance Director. Geoffrey was my inestimable right hand man in all financial and public company matters. His advice was invaluable.

Similarly, in 1972, David Morgan, who started many years before as a salesman and who had been Sales Director of the subsidiary companies, was elected to the main Board, in recognition of his successful leadership of the sales force.

All of the aforementioned remained on the main Board until we had the offer from Central and Sheerwood to acquire the shares of Photopia International. On completion, the listing on the London Stock Exchange of Photopia International as a separate public company ceased because it became a wholly-owned subsidiary of Central and Sheerwood.

Middle management—a very important part of the team—included:

David Coupe, who was the sales manager before David Morgan. David Morgan, mentioned above as a main Board director, came to join us as a salesman then left and rejoined us subsequently when David Coupe left us to progress his career elsewhere.

Peter Gorton, who successively and successfully fulfilled various functions. He started as a salesman. He was manager of the first London office, my personal assistant, purchasing manager and, finally, Purchasing Director of the subsidiaries. Peter took a one year sabbatical and went to Germany to learn German early in his career and this stood him in good stead in later years.

The manager of our service department was John Foden, who came to the company straight from school. As an apprentice, John Foden learned the camera mechanic trade from our then one and only service man, Hans Lehmann, and later service manager.

John Kirk, who was export manager. John sold all our own branded products and OEM products to customers all over Europe. He originally joined us at the age of 21 as a salesman in one of the subsidiaries, Paul Plus Ltd. He built up from scratch, with his inimitable flair, a very healthy turnover of the export department. He also travelled a lot with me to manufacturers of the products he sold.

The general office manager function—looking after the efficient running of the sales and administrative office—was in the hands of David Hire. He was ably assisted by the office supervisor, Anne Conyon (later Davies), who again came straight from school and they both gave many, many years of very loyal service.

I must not forget the effervescent David Shaw, who looked after internal and external public relations. He was a prolific writer who wrote many of the internal house magazines, the Minolta Club magazines, the sales bulletins and many of the catalogues. He handled the liaison with the media to ensure we got many favourable reviews of the equipment we sold. He too rose into the position without any previous training and took over that position from Jack Dean with whom I had worked when I first started as a photographic shop assistant at Martins in Hanley. Jack Dean was my manager there, and in his later years I gave him employment and he stayed until he really was unable to fulfil the functions. He decided to retire and hand over to David Shaw.

Phil Parker was the computer department manager who was in charge of all the company's data processing. He was also responsible for ensuring that we were able to deal with all incoming orders on the day they were received and start the ball rolling in the system of distribution.

Mike Vozza was our Quality Assurance manager and was responsible for checking incoming shipments and outgoing ones to OEM customers. He also advised potential suppliers of safety requirements and tested their samples until they satisfied our standards. His department and staff were located in a next door building.

Warehouse manager John Ward ensured proper control of both incoming and outgoing deliveries and ensured quality of packing and generally looked after the staff in the warehouses and the packing department.

My faithful, understanding, personal secretaries were kept extremely busy—particularly since I had a very strong rule that any letter, whether from the public, trade customers or anyone else that was addressed to me personally, would be replied to by me personally. My dictating machine was red hot, and I kept my secretaries busy all day. Whenever I needed information to be able suitably and correctly to reply to customers' letters, I always sent their letter to the relevant department head with my famous green ink annotation at the top, "Facts to CGS." Those facts had to be on my desk within hours so I could reply to the incoming letter the same day.

Over an extensive period, my secretaries were Christine Bengry (later Sutton), Margaret Ansell and Kath Hire. To help whenever needed and during holidays, a senior typist from the typing pool, Phyllis Bailey, took over the function of being my locum secretary.

The next in line—probably the most important of all, because nothing happens in this world until something is sold—were our salesmen. The first salesman that we ever had who was totally on a free-lance commission basis was Stanley Kramer. Some of the "five star" salesmen, in alphabetical but not chronological order and excluding those mentioned previously who rose to management positions, were; Roger Ailing, Alan Bethel, Max Blakeman, Barry Coates, Alan Bourne, John Cookman, Malcolm Douglas, George Duerden, Richard Fearns, Mike Gilmour, Mike Hanson, Ken Kitchener, Tim Knight, Fred Litchfield, Chris Mason, Chris Nichols, Ian Rosewell, Vic Rosewell, Arthur Sams, Mike Shailes, Mitch Thompson, David Uwins, Mike Wadsworth, Frank Wilkinson and Bill Wiper. Each one of these in their own way contributed not only in terms of sales but also to the very interesting and eventful regular sales conferences we had at head office.

We had three London offices. The first one was at 36, Wardour Street, which was above the Durex contraceptive shop. The next one was at 21, Noel Street, and the final one at 235, Regent Street. The latter was managed for a long time by Norman Whibley. Each office was better than the previous one, but they were all in the prestigious West End of London.

As a matter of record herewith is a "loyalty list" based on date of joining and length of service to the company and its successor. Those still with the successor company are indicated by *.

Name	Joined	Length of Service
Christine Sutton (Bengry)	1950, age 16	8
Anne Davies (Conyon)	1951, age 15	17
John Foden	1954, age 15	30
Phyllis Bayley	1955, age 15	43
David Hire	1955, age 20	34
Rupert Cartlidge	1955, age 23	28
John Battison	1955, age 24	25

Peter Gorton	1956, age 22	30
Mike Hanson	1957, age 21	16
David Morgan	1958, age 29	27
Jeffrey Pickford	1958, age 32	26
David Shaw	1959, age 19	19
David Coupe	1961, age 28	8
John Ward	1962, age 18	21
Alan Clark*	1963, age 15	44
Pauline Hancock*	1963, age 15	43
Tim Knight	1963, age 23	31
Kath Hire (Davis)	1963, age 15	12
Tom Valentine*	1967, age 16	39
John Kirk	1967, age 21	11
Keith Sanderson*	1970, age 16	36
Gerald Doyle*	1973, age 17	33
Geoffrey Snow	1973, age 35	11
Phil Parker	1973, age 26	6
David Harper*	1975, age 17	32
Robert O'Leary*	1975, age 16	17
Mike Vozza	1975, age 40	8
Glynis Otley*	1977, age 25	29
Linda Bossons*	1978, age 23	28
Peter Wood*	1978, age 27	28
Mark Simcock*	1979, age 16	26

Without wishing to lay claim to being a marriage broker, there were a number of marriages between staff at the company. I call it the Cupid list. They were:

> Kath Davis / David Hire
> Grace Edwards / Joe Howell
> Sheila Smith / Harry Ottolini
> Gwen Whitehead / Ian Salt
> Pam Bullock / Ray Lewis
> Judy Robinson / Alan Clarke
> Susan Hammersley / Chris Mason
> Christine Weaver / Colin Mullineaux

Susan Prendergast / David Harper
Florence Coleman / John Ward
Lorraine Reader / Ian Rosewell
Sylvia Joines / Mike Vozza
Janet Moore / Steve Watts
Sylvia Gavin / David Mansfield
Susan Smith / David Wilson
Anne Pepper / Philip Parker
Susan Rhead / Neil Walklate
Ann Doherty / Kim Smith
Keith Sanderson / Janet Powney / Pearl Long / Michelle Gibson

◈ 50 ◈
Ousted

ON THE 20TH OF NOVEMBER, 1980, three years after Central & Sheerwood took control of Photopia International, I transferred my domicile to Jersey. I still acted as an offshore consultant to the company based in their Jersey office.

After starting my first retail shop in Newcastle-under-Lyme, I advertised for a retail manager for my expanding business. Rupert Cartlidge who had worked in a picture framing shop in Hanley, next door to John Martin in Pall Mall, where I had worked, answered the advertisement and was hired. He started his business life history with me as a retail manager in my Newcastle shop. He then progressed with the growth of the company to ultimately become the Assistant Managing Director. He was the day-to-day administrative manager of the company. I concentrated on policy and sourcing, and he did the "hiring and firing." He interviewed salesmen within my policy that we didn't want to take salesmen from other competitive companies. In the main we wanted to have salesmen with photographic knowledge, who had worked retail behind the counter in some shop in the area of the country where we were looking for a salesman. He would do all the interviewing and choose the successful applicant, and I would then just see him for the final approval. (I am pleased that we did very little firing. Over the years, we had one or two cases of dishonesty, but no cases of redundancy except in the horror years of 1968/69.)

Rupert and I worked together for many years. He was a very able Number Two to me. He took full responsibility for running the company during my many absences overseas, although, we always stayed in touch. People always told me that a Number Two very rarely makes it to become a Number 1 in the same company. I didn't believe that, but it proved to be the case when Rupert became Number One with Photopia after I retired. He clearly tried his best to run the company in the pattern that I had set. Apparently, it just didn't work out. Central and Sheerwood came to me in Jersey and asked if I could find them a new Number One. They didn't want to get rid of Rupert Cartlidge. They wanted him to carry on in the function that he knew so well as a Number Two. I still had a lot of connections within the industry and was still acting as a consultant to the company. I gave the matter due consideration.

One young man had been in a management position with David Williams, one of my competitors. (David had come into the photographic industry and also started from scratch, but only later when the Japanese imports started.) This young man was Chris Coleman. I thought he could do this job as Number One. I phoned him and explained that I was acting on behalf of Central and Sheerwood in finding a Number One for Photopia International and that I thought he could do the job. I asked if he was interested. In case he was, I would recommend him and they would see him in London for a job interview. He said he was interested, they interviewed him and he got the job.

Less than six months after he started, I got a letter from him, in effect saying:

"Dear Charles, in the process of my re-organisation of the company, I have come to the conclusion that I no longer welcome your name on the letterhead as Life President or Honorary President. Also, I would no longer like to pay you the fee that was arranged for your consultancy services to the company. For a similar amount, I could probably avoid making two typists redundant. I hope that you will have understanding for this and look forward to hearing from you. Yours sincerely, Chris Coleman."

I could not believe it. My faith in human nature took quite a turn. This is a man whom I had recommended for the job, and one of the first things he did when he got the job was throw me out. I considered it below my dignity to reply to him. But I did write to the Chairman of Central and Sheerwood to acquaint him with the letter. I didn't know whether he was aware of it or not, but I told him that as far as I was concerned I had an agreement with the company to be a consultant, and if they wanted to give me notice under the terms of agreement that was fine. They had every right to do that and if they felt that my name did not any longer enhance the letterhead, then it was entirely up to them. They were exceedingly embarrassed and apologetic. Ultimately, I did get notice under the proper procedure under the agreement.

Talk about getting your just deserts, not very long after that I saw the demise of Chris Coleman's employment as the Managing Director of Photopia International. His services were dispensed with. (It is probably not appropriate in an autobiography or in a published book to go into too much detail as to why these services were dispensed with. I will therefore refrain from doing so.)

◈ 51 ◈

The Wheel Turns Full Circle

AFTER CHRIS COLEMAN TERMINATED MY consultancy agreement with my old company, I no longer had any legal or even moral ties to the company. I owed some loyalty to the people who were still there from my management time, but not to the company. Because in the industry my name was still associated with the company, I thought it prudent to advise some of my competitors and members of the British Photographic Importers Association, that I no longer had any connection with Photopia International and that if any of them wanted the benefit of my extensive experience, I would be prepared to consider offers for a consultancy to their firm. In response, I got three or four replies which showed interest. Out of those, I picked the reply from Johnsons of Hendon, which at that time was run by a young man by the name of David Vaughan. We formulated an agreement on a figure which was satisfactory to me, and we agreed on a plan of action to try and get new agencies. Naturally, he was also interested in acquiring some of the agencies which Photopia International held. Effectively, I was to do what I was good at and source new products and agencies for Johnsons of Hendon as I had previously done so successfully for the Photopia International group.

We rapidly came to the conclusion, from what we heard in the industry, that Photopia International and Central and Sheerwood were not doing well. I thought Central and Sheerwood might be interested in selling Photopia International. Before Johnsons of Hendon made a bid for the company to Central and Sheerwood, they had to be satisfied that the agencies held by Photopia International would transfer readily. Most agency agreements say that, should the ownership of the company change, then the supplier had the right to stop the agreement. David Vaughan and I travelled quickly to Germany, France and Holland where most of the Japanese manufacturers also had representation offices. I saw the people that I knew well, who were suppliers to Photopia International. At that stage, I thought it prudent not to bring David Vaughan into the picture, so he waited in the car while I saw the people concerned. In certain cases, once I'd established that they were prepared to change if another company took over with my recommendation, I introduced David to them. As a result of those trips we ascertained that most of the agencies would be happy to stay if Johnsons of Hendon were to take over.

I brought the two parties together—Central Sheerwood and Johnsons of Hendon. They came to an agreement, and David Vaughan took over Photopia International. Its status then changed once again from a subsidiary of a public company to be again part of a totally private company. As part of the rationalisation programme, David decided to close down his expensive London operation and move the whole of his company. He literally and physically amalgamated the two into my old head office building in Newcastle-under-Lyme. He also took over my old chair in my old office.

The wheel had turned full circle. The captain's chair was again occupied by an entrepreneur.

In a way, I had also ensured the future for my old company and its staff. The company name was changed to Johnsons Photopia Ltd. I stayed as a consultant with him for a number of years. Then, there really was no longer a need for my services, so they came to a natural end. David Vaughan and I are still friends and regularly have phone conversations. (In June 2006 he offered the company to three of its senior managers and a "Management Buy Out" was completed. Interestingly one of the three, David Harper, originally started with me as a trainee technician. As I had done before him, David Vaughan changed his shares into bankable money.)

So I had a home in Jersey, an office, a consultancy, a social life and still a lot of time on my hands. After having been in Jersey only a short while, people whom I knew in the industry, came and proposed that I should become their agent purely for the Channel Islands. They had realised it was a worthwhile territory. We had shown this to be the case when many years before I had decided, as the only British photographic distributor to do so, to open an office in Jersey to cover the Channel Islands.

I decided to form a new company in Jersey called Omnitec Ltd. My daughter, Suzanne, joined me for three years from 1981 and ably managed the whole of the administration, including later the property portfolio. I then got agencies just for the Channel Islands. I got the agency for Citizen Watches Ltd., the largest watch manufacturers in the world, for the Channel Islands. In the meantime, Citizen Watches of Japan had started their own UK subsidiary and were no longer serviced by the Photopia group. I got the Channel Island agency for Brother, a very large Japanese company, who at that time were the biggest sewing machine manufacturers in the world. They made them under many different brands. I got involved when Brother started making typewriters and computer printers. Later, they also produced labelling machines similar to Dymo. We built the Channel Island market for Brother to a tremendously good business, opening substantial dealer accounts and introducing them to government contracts.

My policy in Jersey was the same as it had been in the UK and that was to keep out of the retail side and be purely an importer and distributor for the Channel Islands. My policy in the UK had been to give the best possible pre-sale and after-sale service and to ensure that the staff were made constantly aware of the fact that their income derived entirely from satisfied customers. Therefore, the old adage that the customer is always right must be observed. This principle is even more important in a small community because if you lose a couple of customers in the UK, they can easily be replaced. They will not make a lot of difference to your turnover. That situation is quite different on a small island where two dealers cannot be replaced and probably form quite a percentage of your total business.

Soon after I started Omnitec, my old company, Photopia International Ltd., decided that they no longer wanted a local office or to hold stock there. So they changed the operation and made Tim

Knight a freelance agent for them. He therefore could also, at the same time, work for me as a freelance agent for the newly acquired agencies. Consequently, the tenancy of the office and warehouse at the White Lodge in Wellington Road, on the outskirts of St. Helier, changed from Photopia International to Omnitec Ltd. When the whole White Lodge building came on the market, I decided to buy it. Therefore, I actually took over as landlord. The building had offices on the ground floor and storage space in the basement, and the other three floors were converted into flats, which provided investment income.

Soon after, Tim Knight and I decided that although the availability of parking space at White Lodge was an asset, it was not as easy for people to come to see us as it would be if we had an office in town. A suitable first floor office and storage accommodation became available in Mulcaster Street, and we signed a lease for it and moved to this very central location. I found new tenants for the ground floor and basement at White Lodge. Now almost all of our Jersey customers could be reached by walking in St. Helier. Additionally, it was just a case of Tim Knight going maybe twice a month for a day trip to Guernsey and once every six months on the boat trip to the small islands of Alderney and Sark, to see our customers there.

The expansion of the business also made it obvious that we needed once again to computerise. Since it was a totally different type of operation, in both magnitude and application, to the Newcastle one, I started looking for a suitable package programme to install on the then emerging PC computers. No package was found which was ideal, but I found a development company in the London area who were very close to producing a suitable programme for use on a PC by small manufacturing, distribution and service companies. They agreed for me to have an input into the development of their package, which I spent some time on. Therefore when it was released, it fulfilled all our requirements. I took on the agency for selling that programme in the Channel Islands. This really brought me into the IT community and got me involved with the formation of the Jersey Computer Association (see chapter "Community Service: Clubs and Charities.").

To keep me out of mischief with all this time on my hands, I had made some property investments. Before I went to live in Jersey permanently in 1980, I had purchased a substantial corner block of residential accommodation over shops in a prominent site in St. Helier. Then I acquired other buildings and administered this whole portfolio within Burlington Services Ltd., from the Omnitec offices. That brought a useful regular income. Later it came to the point where, particularly with residential accommodation, the frequency of call-outs became unacceptable, and I decided to sell.

I decided to put all the properties on the market. They sold one by one. The large corner multi-storey apartment building was the last to be sold. It was sold to David Kirch, a well-known Jersey property developer who added it to his already extensive property holding in St Helier. With this sale I came out completely from the property investment business with a substantial capital gain.

Finally, in October 1989, Tim Knight bought my shares of Omnitec Ltd. and took over the running of the company. In effect we exchanged roles. He became the beneficial owner and Managing Director, and I became a freelance salesman for him so I could still have an interest in the industry.

Now I had even more time for travelling, and Maureen and I could spend more time together.

❖ 52 ❖

My Family

I WAS AWAY FROM HOME quite extensively. When we started importing, it was for visits to customers and meetings in London, usually not for more than two or three nights at a time. However, when we started importing from the Far East, it clearly was not possible to come home for weekends, and I was away for four or more weeks at a time. So, Maureen, my wife, virtually had the responsibilities of a father as well as a mother for our children. She did a tremendous job of bringing up two lovely girls.

My business travel did have its compensations. We had a good lifestyle and always had good holidays together which didn't stop until our daughters got married. Even after that, we had an extended family holiday in Aruba. At first our holidays were in the UK, then on the European continent, and later we went farther away to the Caribbean, the United States and even Brazil.

On one holiday, we took a cruise—our one and only—which took us on the P&O liner Canberra from Southampton down through the Bay of Biscay, past Portugal and the Strait of Gibraltar, along the coast of West Africa and down to Sierra Leone, where we turned around to go past the Canary Islands and Madeira and then back to Southampton. The weather was good for us, and we participated in most of the recreational activities provided on the boat as well as going on shore at every port of call and doing local tours there. I played a lot of poker in a poker school on board. It is alleged that I won enough money on those games to have paid for the trip, but there is absolutely no truth in that. I think my younger daughter invented that one. She, in turn, started to be interested in boys, and I remember one evening, when she went missing for a couple of hours and I searched for her all over the boat. I believe she may have had a crush on one of the ship's stewards.

The cruise was at a time, long before satellite communications and mobile phones, when the means of communication back to my office were poor to non-existent. Before the cruise, I had already had misgivings about being away for an extended period without daily contact with the office, which I had always maintained even when in the Far East. There was a ship's signal office where one could pass messages.

We all decided after the cruise that we enjoyed land-based holidays with the better flexibility of movement. Other holidays which we enjoyed were winter skiing holidays in Austria or Switzerland. Sue and Di were very fast learners when it came to skiing, and they gained their proficiency grades and enjoyed the pleasure of cross-country skiing and slope and slalom skiing. Sue became a better skier and often skied off chasing boys.

One of our greatest and I suppose most sentimental holidays with the family was to the Holy Land of Israel. We travelled extensively and visited all the Christian and Jewish holy sites. Naturally we visited the kibbutz where I was born and which is still thriving and we then rented a car and drove the long way south through the desert past the Dead Sea to the Red Sea resort of Eilat.

The first school our daughters went to, back in England, was the Lyme School in Newcastle. One year after they started there, they transferred to a school which took a larger age range called Edenhurst, which was run by Bill and Sylvia Copestick. Bill Copestick was a well-known headmaster, and his wife taught at the school. The girls stayed there and were very happy. Both of these schools were in the tradition of English schools where the children all wore school uniforms to make them all equal. It was a very good school with lots of parent participation and extra curricular activities like sports and plays, and we regularly participated in those events. We were active in ensuring the happiness of our girls at these schools.

Maureen and I came to a big decision as to whether to let them progress to local high schools or to send them to boarding schools. After a lot of discussion and taking advice, we decided their ultimate character-forming would be helped more by mixing with a larger circle of children of their age group. We wanted them to go to a well-known boarding school with an intake of children from other countries of all creeds and colours. We thought a good boarding school would shape them better for future life and give them early responsibility and training for accepting responsibility and decision-making from then on. We finally chose Cheltenham Ladies' College in Gloucestershire, which had an excellent reputation. They both did very well at this school. Although they both started at different times, they went to the same school house, Glenlee, at the boarding school.

Once the children had gone to boarding school, Maureen became more active in Rotary's Inner Wheel, which is a club for the wives, widows and partners of Rotarians. She made many friends there and joined in, with her usual enthusiasm, the many charitable activities of Inner Wheel. We also socialised quite a lot and had many parties at our house or at our friends' houses. During that time, we made use of babysitters when the children were still with us. Many of them were girls working for me in the company who were pleased to earn the extra money. Later, we had au pair girls from different countries in Europe all of whom stayed for quite a while as they enjoyed the lifestyle with us.

When they later went to boarding school, which was quite a distance from our home, we visited them for all exeat days or weekends on which parents were allowed to visit and take the children out of school for the day. So we took them out, usually to a restaurant of their choice at lunch time. Because there were many foreign students whose parents couldn't always make the long trip to visit their children, we often also took some of our daughters' friends from overseas with us. We discovered an excellent Indian restaurant in town of which we became regular customers. We always had a good time together.

Cheltenham is in a very beautiful part of England known as the Cotswolds, and we got to know it well on the many exeat travels. The nearest airfield, which used to be first Staverton then Gloucester-Cheltenham Airfield, is now called Gloucester International. It is halfway between Gloucester and Cheltenham and about 40 minutes' flying time away from my home airfield. It was much faster than going to see our daughters by car, but we also did that sometimes.

One particular lunch, we had a meal at the best hotel in Cheltenham, and I ordered a cold meat pie and the girls ordered their usual fish and chips. When it was served and I cut open my meat pie, there was a thick layer of mould—green and other colours—between the meat and the outer pastry crust. This so upset me that I have never eaten cold meat pies since. I showed my mould culture to the waiter and asked for the manager. He was most apologetic and of course said it had never happened before. I suggested to him that we ought to mark the occasion and instead of my making an unpleasant scene and reporting it to the local health inspector, it might be appropriate for him to make a charitable donation to the St. John Ambulance Brigade. I suggested a quite hefty amount, which he immediately agreed to and made out a cheque to the St. John Ambulance, which I presented to them on my return home. It was an unpleasant situation, but we made it into a win-win situation for everyone concerned.

Our connection to Jersey became stronger all the time. The house we had there was initially intended to be used as a holiday house. Once we bought it, Maureen and the children spent all the school holidays there, and I flew there for the weekends. By this time, I had my pilot's licence and an airplane, so the transfer of family or just me for weekends took place in whatever airplane I owned at that time. They all enjoyed flying—or at least they enjoyed it from an age when they were aware of it. We took Sue to Jersey when she was still in a carrycot. Sue and Dianne took on various summer holiday jobs in Jersey as they were growing up—jobs as varied as being the usual waitresses in cafes or even drive-ins to being air hostesses on the local Intra airline. One year, Sue was a hostess on a hydrofoil service between Jersey and France. This job involved meeting a lot of interesting people and being concerned with their safety and, also, she could practise her French.

At Cheltenham Ladies' College, our daughters both got the necessary A Levels which entitled them to university entrance. They both applied to go to Keele University, again at different times, and they were both accepted.

Most children who go to school in their home area try to go to a university away from home to start their adult life. In our case, both our children went away to boarding school at a much earlier age, and they both chose to come back to a local university. This had the added advantage of being able to come home and raid the fridge, get mother to do the laundry for them, and come away on trips with us whenever they pleased. They both did their four-year courses at Keele. Sue got a Bachelor of Arts degree in Sociology and Psychology, and Dianne got her BA degree in Law and History.

Sue then went on for a year of teachers' training at a college in Chichester and then got a job as a teacher not far from home in Market Drayton. After that, she—quite independently—applied and got a teaching post in Jersey, and she went to live in Jersey long before we went there on a permanent basis.

Dianne went for a one-year barrister training course in London together with Tim Mousley, her future husband, whom she met at Keele University. They started living together in accommodation they rented in London. I visited them in London once and asked if I could go to one of their lectures. This unusual parental request was met with, "Well, we've never seen anybody do this, but we'll try." Indeed, I went with them to a lecture that happened to be on forensic tests for prosecution of drivers who may have drunk too much to be safe on the roads. I enjoyed sitting in the back row of the huge lecture theatre and learned a lot of the definitions of alcohol content in blood and the rights of a citizen to refuse a blood test or breathalyser test and the consequences thereof.

Dianne and Tim got on well at the college. After having gone to the legal college in London for a year they both, as is required, went into pupillage in barristers' chambers. The standard procedure in the long early years before one can finally join chambers as a full fledged barrister was to go into what is known as pupillage with an established chamber. A chamber is a group of barristers. All barristers at whatever stage of their career are self-employed but form groups either in London or the provinces to share offices and the services of a clerk of the chambers who arranges the cases for them. Dianne and Tim both found pupillage places in different chambers. When they finished that, Tim obtained a tenancy in that chamber. Later, when he did most of his cases in the western circuit, they decided to live in that area and moved from London to West Tytherley. Dianne decided to go into commercial law and departed from chambers to go into industry. She found a job as a legal adviser to the Beecham Group. Later she changed to the Burton Group, whose head office was in the West End of London, and she stayed there until she started a family. Neither of my daughters came back to live at home after they graduated from university. Both later got married.

Dianne married Tim Mousley. They lived in London first and then later moved to Hampshire, which was the patch on which Tim's chamber did a lot of their work.

Sue married Chris Falloon, an air traffic controller at Jersey airport. They lived in a house underneath the extended centreline of runway 09 at the Jersey airport. Sue was also interested in flying. She got her Private Pilot's Licence and spent a lot of time at the Jersey Aero Club. It was through these activities that she had met Chris.

The Falloon family was based in Jersey, and the Mousley family was based in England. We regularly either went to England to visit the Mousleys or fetched them to stay with us in Jersey.

Unfortunately, neither marriage worked out, and they parted from their husbands.

❖ 53 ❖

My Grandchildren

MY TWO GRANDCHILDREN FROM SUE and Chris are Matthew John, born on 23rd of February 1984, and Amanda Jane, born on 14th of January 1986. My two granddaughters from Dianne and Tim are Hannah Elizabeth, born on 6th of April 1987, and Sarah Joanne, born on 25th of March 1992. When the grandchildren were growing up, we took much pleasure in entertaining them at home, having picnics together and going to many local events.

Matthew John Falloon, my eldest grandson—and the only boy among my grandchildren—was always a very active child interested in sporting activities. He was a great football enthusiast and all-round sportsman. He would dive off the highest piers in Jersey into the sea. He became addicted to riding moto-X bikes and participated in many racing events in Jersey. He is quite an open-air sporting enthusiast. He went to St. Peters School in Jersey and then transferred to the Victoria College Prep School. From there, he went to Victoria College proper. He found that he was not sufficiently interested in academic subjects and decided to transfer to a course at Highlands College—a more practical course in motor engineering. During holidays, he worked very successfully in the service departments at local garages.

However he soon decided, probably through peer pressure, that he wanted to earn a lot of money immediately, so he became an apprentice stone mason. Jersey has several famous products. One is the milk from Jersey cows, another is the Jersey Royal Potato, and the third is Jersey granite. Jersey has a lot of granite quarries, and many of the old Jersey buildings are built from this material. Even now a lot of walls and facings are done in granite. The dressing of the granite, making the stone fit just right next to the other one, is a very skilled occupation. It is a dying trade and one where a lot of money can be earned. So Matthew decided to take on an apprenticeship and in 2006 finished that and became a fully qualified skilled craftsman in that trade. I'm sure he will want to start his own company and hopefully follow in his grandfather's footsteps, who was also not all that strong in academic subjects in his school days.

Amanda Jane Falloon, a lovely young lady, was also a very lively youngster in her early years. She also went to St. Peter's School and had an interest in music and particularly in dancing. She went to dancing school and had a best friend named Hollie, from whom, almost like a twin, she could not be separated. They sat together at school through the years. They went to the same dancing school, and formed a dancing team and gave displays. Their relationship broke up later when they both went to university at Southampton, where Amanda decided towards the end of her first year that university was not her cup of tea either. She hated it in England. So she came back to Jersey and started looking for a job in computer design and graphics. As she was unable to find a trainee post in this field, she then started training to be a legal secretary in the second biggest law firm in Jersey and has now been promoted to that position. She is very happy and does a lot of partying and socialising.

Hannah Elizabeth Mousley, another attractive young lady, went to the village school in West Tytherley very close to where they lived. At an early age, she became interested in horses. Her mother, Dianne, at roughly the same age, was also interested in horses and, because she was busy studying, I said she couldn't have a horse of her own until she was 21. When she was 21, she no longer wanted a horse, because by that time she wasn't living in that sort of an area anymore. As a result of that, she wanted to ensure that her daughters were not treated in the same way, so she got interested in horses again, living in that sort of an area where you could easily stable them. Both she and Hannah, and later Sarah, became very involved and enthusiastic with anything to do with riding and competitive show jumping. As a very dedicated mother, Dianne transports the horses for both her daughters all over the country to participate in these events. She drives a seven and a half ton horse lorry with a very small living accommodation in the front. Hannah has done very well. In 2005, in a fierce nationwide competition, she got into the final 16 from the whole country that were selected for the Horse of the Year Show in December to be held in Olympia, London. The whole family went to see her perform there on 18th of December 2005. Although, she did not get a clear first round, we are all very proud of her. She went home with the satisfaction that she made it to Olympia which, in itself, was a great achievement. She continues her training with an international show jumper.

Sarah Joanne Mousley was born last, five years after Hannah. She is a very bright girl, and is very extroverted. She followed her sister to the village school in West Tytherley, and she then went to a private school, partly as an external pupil and partly as a boarder. She then transferred to quite a unique boarding school in the North of England called Queen Ethelburgha's. It is one of the few schools that has accommodation for horses so you can take your own horse and stable it at the school and ride it during non-academic times. She too has won quite a number of events at shows.

All my grandchildren have turned out to be happy with their lives, enjoying them, and are all still happy to join granddad for Christmas in Jersey. I am very proud of all of them and welcome their visits.

◆ 54 ◆

A Shadow Falls

A SAD SHADOW WAS CAST on our family life when, in 1981, Maureen was diagnosed with Alzheimer's disease. During her first tests at the hospital in Jersey, we thought she just had memory loss. I was present for one of the tests. She stayed in the hospital for observation for two or three days, and my friend, Jim Hollywood, conducted the test. Jim was a consultant psychologist. He asked her—what I thought at the time was a funny question—to subtract 4 from 100. I still have that vividly in my mind today. She couldn't do it. It was a most surprising and disturbing first clue. Resulting from these tests, they decided that a brain scan should be undertaken. We were in our first year in Jersey trying to shake off UK domicile. Part of that requirement is not to go back to the United Kingdom even for a day, not even for somebody's funeral. You must have a 12 months' residence in Jersey without any financial ties to the United Kingdom and without any visits to the United Kingdom to make sure that you would be clear of any potential taxation liabilities in the UK. Therefore, the doctors decided we should go to a well-known neurosurgeon in the well-equipped American Hospital in Paris, and it was arranged for us to do that.

We went there the following week, and she had colour scans of different sections of the brain. The professor then showed the results to me in private and gave me the dreadful news that she had Alzheimer's and that this would be progressive, either slowly or quickly. He told me she would have somewhere between three and ten years at the maximum to live and, towards the end, a life of poor quality. I could not possibly tell her this.

We went back to Jersey with that in mind and, in possession of this knowledge, the whole family made an effort to let her lead as normal a life as possible. This was particularly so when she was no longer able to do things for herself. I still took her on flying trips with the Flying Rotarians and let her enjoy as much as possible being with her friends.

Maureen's gradual degeneration came as a terrible shock to both Sue and Di. In about 1989-1990, even though we had a very good housekeeper/companion at the time, Tina Velosa, who was very dedicated to Maureen, the doctors decided that she had to have 24-hour nursing care. At that point, I arranged for her a good nursing home—Beauport Nursing Home in St. Brelade, Jersey—where I visited her daily. She finally passed away peacefully in her sleep on 7th of August 1992.

Her funeral was in a packed St. Martins Church, and we were honoured that the Bailiff of Jersey at the time, Sir Peter Crill, came to the funeral. She is now buried in a grave in St. Martins Parish Church Cemetery where, hopefully in the distant future, I have chosen to rejoin her, when my time comes to depart this earth for the big hangar in the sky.

Maureen was a lovely person, very friendly, very outgoing and had a lot of friends. Although in many Alzheimer's cases, people become aggressive to their nearest and dearest, that thankfully never happened with Maureen, though she did get to the point where she didn't recognise me. But she never lost her kindness in spirit. Maureen and I had a really wonderful life and partnership from the time I met her to her untimely death. I was very fortunate to have such an understanding partner because, as will be appreciated from my life pattern as described in this book, of necessity I had to be away a lot from home. She accepted that.

⟡ 55 ⟡

Dear Friends

PAUL AND IREEN O'BRIEN WERE two of our dear friends with whom Maureen and I enjoyed socialising. They had children roughly of our children's ages—daughter Jackie, and sons Mark and Justin. Paul was the Managing Director of his family firm, selling silica and sand and the like for industrial purposes. Through them, we also met his brother David, and his wife, Sheila. I had known her previously as the daughter of Reg and Lily Boorman, the managing director of the local BTH factory, which produced fractional horsepower motors for domestic equipment, and as a member of the Newcastle-under-Lyme Chamber of Trade. Our circle of friends met regularly and went to outside functions like balls, fancy dress and Christmas parties together. Maureen enjoyed cooking and regularly was the hostess at our house for such parties. Of these I remember one incident after which I was never allowed in the kitchen again. I was helping to make some sort of a pate in a blender, and I was stirring with a rubber and plastic spatula in the blender without switching it off. The spatula got ground into the pate and nobody noticed.

Unfortunately, Paul died tragically in a road accident.

Later, we made friends with Gordon and Mary Johnson. Gordon was initially a road builder. Later, when government restrictions started on capital developments such as roads, he changed to house and commercial building. Strangely enough, after we met at Rotary and made friends, it came to light that I had many, many years before, taken their wedding pictures. This turned into a very close friendship. The Johnson's had two children, Martyn and Elizabeth, again approximately the ages of our children. They both were active in Rotary—Gordon in regular Rotary and Mary in Inner Wheel. They also came with us on a lot of the Flying Rotarian fly-ins and fly-abouts. Unfortunately, Gordon died after a week's holiday with us in Jersey in September 2001.

On one of our many holidays with them, this time in Antigua, I gave up smoking. We were lying on a white, sandy beach with a cloudless, blue sky and an azure sea, and I was coughing with the little pipe I had almost permanently stuck in my mouth. Totally unpremeditated, I dug a hole in the sand and put in my pipe, my full tobacco pouch and even my gold lighter, and I never smoked again. I had never smoked cigarettes but only little cigarillos, Rio6 or Henri Winterman's, or my pipe filled with Clan aromatic tobacco. Not having something in my mouth was very difficult, so I took to chewing paper clips. Luckily I was able to stop this also after a couple of months, as I don't think it did my teeth any good. To stop smoking was one of the best decisions I ever made, and I don't believe I would still be here today had I not done it.

My family tree with my maternal grandparents and my paternal grandmother on the right and my father, my mother and me, on the bottom row, all circa 1929.

My mother as I remember her in Czechoslovakia before being parted from my parents in 1939 (chapter 3).

218 Waterloo Road, Cobridge, Burslem, Stoke-on-Trent, the terrace house on the left, my parents' first home in England where I later rejoined them. Also showing 216 next door, the home of Alderman Austin Brooks (chapter 5).

94 Trentham Road, Penkhull, Stoke-on-Trent, the second parental house in the Potteries from which I joined the army in 1944 (chapter 5).

A very young and beautiful Maureen, my future wife, just after I had met her (chapter 18).

My unpaid part-time helper Maureen with me in front of the 19 Hassell Street shop and studio, in 1948 where it all started (chapter 17).

Probably the first of my annual photographic Christmas cards in 1948, a year before Maureen and I got married.

The invitation to the wedding of Maureen Jane Lees to Charles G. Strasser (chapter 18).

Maureen and I on our wedding day the 8th October 1949 (chapter 18).

Our first marital home in 1949, a semi detached house at the end of Pitgreen Lane, Wolstanton (chapter 18).

Our last home "Montrose" in Parkway, Trentham where we had lived happily and brought up our young family, before we moved to Jersey in 1980 (chapter 18).

One of our early photographic Christmas cards, this one in the year of my beard which I grew and kept for 12 months as a bet. When it was ceremonially cut off I preserved it, to this day, in a picture frame.

Ditto, 58 different ones made and used annually to date.

Ditto, with Suzanne and Dianne in their "pony" years.

In a gondola in Venice on a family holiday with Stanley and Pamela Kalms, circa 1954 (chapter 20).

Steven and Richard Kalms with my daughters Sue and Di on a family holiday with the Kalms's in Italy, circa 1954 (chapter 20).

Our family group with Sue and Di in their teenage years, circa 1969.

Sue and Di, during University summer holidays, working as air hostesses for Intra Airways in Jersey.

A proud moment. My daughter Suzanne receiving her BA degree from the Chancellor of Keele University, HRH Princess Margaret (chapter 52).

. . . And proudly displaying it in her Keele University gown (chapter 52).

Another proud moment. My second daughter, Dianne, receiving her BA degree from the Chancellor of Keele University, HRH Princess Margaret (chapter 52).

Dianne after having received her BA degree from the Chancellor of Keele University, HRH Princess Margaret (chapter 52).

Giving away my elder daughter Sue on her wedding day, 7th May 1983.

Dianne's Wedding on the 4th April 1981.

Family picture outside Keele Hall at the University after receiving my Hon. Master of Science degree in 1979 (chapter 86).

Leaving our silver wedding party at the British Pottery Manufacturers Club in Stoke.

"The Cottage" on the coast at Anne Port, St. Martin, our home in Jersey in the Channel Islands (chapter 59).

My 4 grandchildren Matthew and Amanda Falloon and Hannah and Sarah Mousley taken in 1995.

With my 4 grandchildren, Hannah, Amanda, Sarah and Matthew, taken in 1999.

With my daughters Sue and Di in Jersey taken in 1999.

Outside Buckingham Palace, after the investiture, with my two daughters Dianne and Suzanne and holding the actual OBE medal (chapter 90).

Maureen's grave in the St. Martins Parish church cemetery in Jersey where I plan to rejoin her, hopefully in many years hence (chapter 54).

… 56 …

A Country of Choice: All about Jersey

WHENEVER MAUREEN AND I TRAVELLED the world, we always were asked where we came from. When we answered "Jersey," most people seemed perplexed as to where that is. People in the United States automatically jump to the conclusion that it is New Jersey. We then spoke our familiar refrain, "No, not New Jersey, Old Jersey—an island in the English Channel between England and France and nearer to France." Then, in an effort to help, we mentioned the world-famous Jersey cows, which quite a lot of people have heard of but still they don't know geographically from where they originate.

Many readers will already know of my long-standing devotion and praise of the island of Jersey all over the world and from many platforms. Most Jersey readers will be bored with this section. If they are, they can skip it and restart again when this historical brief has finished. Otherwise, they can continue reading and take delight in checking that I have my facts correct.

For the benefit of my non-Jersey readers, it may be appropriate to give some of the history of its status.

Jersey is an island that is nine miles by five miles in dimension and therefore 45 square miles in area. It is the largest of the Channel Islands, which comprise Jersey, Guernsey, Alderney and Sark. The populations are approximately 90,000, 58,000, 2,400 and 610, respectively. There are inter-island boat services and inter-island air services between Jersey, Guernsey and Alderney. These three have their own international airports. Each of these islands has its own government and its own laws. Alderney is part of the Bailiwick of Guernsey, although in certain local matters it has its own jurisdiction.

As in the UK, Jersey was occupied by the Romans, who named it Caesarea, from about 56 AD. After the collapse of the Roman Empire came the Dark Ages, which lasted until the arrival of the Vikings. In 911, Rollo took control of the French area around Caen. This was the beginning of the Duchy of Normandy. In 1033, Rollo's son, William Longsword, added the islands to the Dukedom of Normandy, and since then the inhabitants of Jersey have been answerable only to the Duke of Normandy and his successors, the British Sovereign.

Note this well: When Guillaume le b'tard, Duke of Normandy, conquered England in 1066, he became King William I of England as well as Duke of Normandy. Jerseymen were part of those forces. Therefore, Jersey men helped conquer England. Subsequently, King John lost the territory of Normandy to his cousin, Phillip II of France, but Jersey remained loyal to the English crown. Because of this loyalty, King John granted to the island certain rights and privileges in 1215, that enabled them to be virtually self-governing, subject only to royal assent and enactments through the Privy Council. Thankfully, these were written down and remain an important part of the island's constitution today.

In the English Civil War, the aristocracy of Jersey, not surprisingly, backed the crown. It was at this time that Guernsey went along with Cromwell, and there has been an enmity between the two islands ever since.

The last attempt by the French to take Jersey took place on 6th January 1781, in what became known as "The Battle of Jersey". A French volunteer force landed at La Rocque Battery on the south east coast under the cover of darkness. They made their way into the St. Helier town centre, where they established HQ in the States (government) Building in the Market Place (now the Royal Square). A party surprised the Lieutenant Governor, Moses Corbet, and forced him to sign a document ordering the regular garrison and militia to lay down their arms and surrender, under threat of the town being burnt. However, a militia officer, Captain Clement

Hemery, was able to alert Major Francis Peirson, who had command in the absence of the garrison's senior officers on Christmas leave. He chose to ignore the order and sent out instructions that other commanders should do the same.

When the leader of the French forces, Baron de Rullecourt, summoned the principal fortress, Elizabeth Castle, to surrender, the commander bluffed his way into procuring more time—allowing Peirson to dispatch more troops to increase the number of defenders—then opened fire on the French, driving them back, with the Castle's extensive and well sited batteries. Finally Peirson led the 95th, 78th and elements of the Jersey Militia against the main force in the Royal Square. Victory was achieved rapidly, though both Peirson and de Rullecourt were killed. After such a defeat, the French never attempted to invade again. The battle was a major embarrassment to the French government. The house where Peirson died, then a doctor's residence, still exists and is now the Peirson Pub. The statue of George II that stood there then is still in place.

A big jump now takes us to the German occupation from 1940-1945, when the islands were the only part of the British Isles occupied by the Germans. While there, the German forces, with slave labour, built a huge number of defensive positions as part of Hitler's Atlantic Wall.

Shortly after the D-Day Normandy invasions on 6th of June 1944, Allied forces were on the French coast opposite to and only 14 miles away from Jersey. For the whole of that period from June/July 1944 to the liberation of Jersey on 9th of May 1945, the local population was near starvation. The Red Cross ship Vega made several journeys carrying supplies and was a very welcome sight in those days.

There are to this day many reminders of the occupation in bunkers and other concrete buildings, which are practically impossible to remove. There are many tourist attractions in the form of occupation museums, including a German underground hospital built by slave labour. It was never completed and never used, so it is suitable as a museum piece and has recently been refurbished as the Jersey War Tunnels.

Many Jersey residents were offered the opportunity to leave the islands for the United Kingdom before the occupation started, and many men also left to join the British forces. The Germans made quite a lot of propaganda use of their occupation. There is a well-used picture of a bobby, a British uniformed policeman, with a German soldier in the centre of St. Helier. The Jersey police uniforms were identical to the British police uniforms.

In the post-war period, tourism grew, as did the export of agricultural products. The Jersey Royal potato and later flowers became additional sources of revenue. From 1960, a favourable taxation climate, the stable government and lack of party politics encouraged banking and finance to come to Jersey. They quickly became the main income earners for the island from 1970 and beyond, as Jersey has become highly respected in the world of offshore finance centres.

Undoubtedly, the most famous resident of Jersey was Lillie Langtry, popularly known even in the United States as the Jersey Lily. She was born in Jersey in 1853 and became a famous English actress and one of the first English women of elevated social rank to go on the stage. She made her debut at the Haymarket Theatre in 1881 after her diplomat husband had failed financially. She was never considered a great actress but was noted for her great beauty and for her affair with King Edward VII. There are many buildings, pubs and streets in Jersey named after her. When she died in 1929, she was buried in St. Saviour's Cemetery. Her grave is still a tourist attraction. She also spent some time in the United States. Those interested in her American connection might look up the name of Judge Roy Bean. He was a famous person in American folklore from Langtry, Texas. The description given to Lillie Langtry was that she was a courtesan.

At the time Lillie Langtry was born in Jersey, a Frenchman by the name of Victor Hugo took refuge in Jersey from 1852 to 1855 after being exiled from France. Victor Hugo was a famous French poet, dramatist and novelist, a leader in the romantic movement. Although his father was a general under Napoleon, Hugo opposed Napoleon III and was banished first to Brussels and then to Jersey and then Guernsey. He stayed in Guernsey until 1870. In 1870, he returned to Paris in triumph and was elected to the National Assembly and the Senate. Before he died in 1885, public veneration and acclaim marked his last years. He is most famous for two novels, "Les Miserables" and "The Hunchback of Notre Dame".

Lastly, Gerald Durrell, better known locally as Gerry, was a naturalist, zookeeper, author and television presenter. He is best known for founding the Durrell Wildlife Conservation Trust and the Jersey Zoo in 1958. He wrote a number of books based on his animal collecting expeditions, zoo keeping and conservation efforts. He died in 1995, and his widow, Lee, is still very active as Honorary Director of the Durrell Wildlife Conservation Trust, now known as Durrell.

In practical terms, the Jersey government has been able to maintain a very advantageous taxation system. There is no death or estate duty and no capital gains tax. The major source of revenue is income tax. But the highest level of that for companies and individuals is 20%, with individuals still having tax allowances which are offset before the 20% swings into operation.

The "independent" status covers all Jersey's activities and, besides taxation, it covers postal, telecommunications, health and education and all the other usual services provided by government. Basically income tax is the only tax. There are some very small stamp duties in relation to transfer of property. So far there is no purchase, value added, or sales tax. Although, in the latest financial proposals, there has been talk of a 3% goods and services tax to be introduced in 2008.

Property owners have to pay a fonciers rate to their local parish for the provision of local services like road maintenance and rubbish collection. The States of Jersey centrally run government services, and the 12 parishes, which are each run by an elected Connetable, provide local services. Each parish has a parish hall, a parish elementary school and a pub all usually situated in the same area. There is also a parish church and parish cemetery. So you can be hatched, matched and dispatched all in your own parish.

The following pertinent points are taken from the Jersey Constitution:

Sovereignty

1. Jersey is a Crown Dependency (as are the other Channel Islands and the Isle of Man) and not part of the United Kingdom. The United Kingdom comprises Great Britain (England, Wales and Scotland) and Northern Ireland. Geographically Jersey is both part of the British Isles and of the British Islands. Jersey has its own laws, judiciaries and executives. When England was conquered by the Normans in 1066, the Channel Isles became subject to whoever was on the English throne since they had already been annexed by Normandy in the tenth and eleventh century. When France regained Normandy in 1204 the Channel Islands remained under the jurisdiction of the English crown.

   For more information on the origins of self government see: www.statesassembly.gov.je/frame.asp

The Constitution

2. The Lieutenant Governor is appointed by the Crown and is the Queen's personal representative. He has traditionally been a senior member of Her Majesty's Armed Forces but this is likely to change in the future. He is also Commander-in-Chief of Jersey, and the Commander of the Armed Forces of the Crown in Jersey. Communication between Her Majesty's Government (through the Lord Chancellors Office) and Jersey is conducted through the Lieutenant Governor.

3. The Bailiff is President of both the States and of the Royal Court. The Deputy Bailiff assists him and is able to perform the same functions as the Bailiff when authorised so to do. They are both appointed by the Crown.

4. Other Crown appointees are the Dean of Jersey, the Attorney General and the Solicitor General.

The Legislature

5. The island legislature is the States of Jersey.

6. The States comprises the Bailiff, the Lieutenant Governor, the

Connetables of the twelve parishes, twelve Senators, twenty-nine Deputies, the Dean of Jersey, the Attorney General and the Solicitor General. Although they all have the right to speak in the Assembly, the right to vote is reserved for the fifty-three elected members consisting of the Senators, Connetables and the Deputies. Should it be necessary, the Bailiff has a casting vote.

7. The Senators are elected for a term of six years and have an Island mandate, six retiring in every third year.

8. The Connetables are elected for a term of three years by their Parish and serve in the States by virtue of the office they hold.

9. The Deputies have a Parish mandate, they are elected for a three year term.

10. Enactments passed by the States require the sanction of Her Majesty in Council except in specific instances.

11. The Council of Ministers is made up of a Chief Minister and nine other Ministers chosen by all States Members. Each Minister is legally and politically accountable for his/her area of government.

Elections

12. A General Election is held in Jersey every three years. Six of the twelve Senators are elected in October and all of the Deputies are elected in November.

Party Politics

13. Jersey politicians are independent of political parties, there is no party line for politicians to follow. Constituents expect their Deputy to represent their views in the States.

Official Language of the Courts

14. Debates in the States are conducted in English. Legislation is now drafted in English although French remains the official written language of the Courts. Contracts for property transactions have

historically been written in French but new legislation means that in future they will be written in English.

The Royal Court

15. Criminal and civil matters are both dealt with by the Royal Court which consists of the Bailiff (or Deputy Bailiff) and Jurats. There are twelve Jurats elected by an Electoral College. The Bailiff is the sole judge of law and it is he who determines whether costs should be awarded, and in what amount. The Jurats determine other matters. There is also a Court of Appeal with judges travelling over from England, in some instances video conferencing is used with the Appeal Judges in London conferring with people in Jersey.

The Magistrates Court

16. Minor criminal matters are dealt with by a Stipendiary Magistrate in the Magistrate's Court. In most cases it is the Centenier who brings the case to the Magistrate's Court, however in some circumstances a Prosecutor will bring the case instead of the Centenier, this is where the case is likely to proceed to the Royal Court or where more complex argument of law is required. This enables the Attorney General to be represented.

17. Petty Debts are also dealt with in the Magistrate's Court.

Parishes

18. Geographically Jersey is divided into twelve Parishes, each having its own municipality. Each parish has its Connetable, Centeniers, Vingteniers and other officers elected for a three year term of office. The Governing body in each parish is known as the Assembly of Principals (ratepayers).

Parish Hall / Town Hall enquiries

19. Enquiries are conducted by a Centenier who deals with very minor matters on the spot, penalties are limited to a maximum of £100 per offence. More serious matters are referred on to

either the Magistrates or Youth Court as appropriate where normally the Centenier will bring the case before the Magistrate.

**

On the parliamentary structure of the Bailiwick of Jersey, it is a British Crown Dependency loyal to Her Majesty the Queen and is part of the British Commonwealth. It pays the UK government for providing defence and foreign services. The Lieutenant Governor lives in and has offices and staff at Government House.

The government, which until very recently was a committee-based legislature with no prime minister or cabinet, has been considered not to be too efficient a form of government. In particular, there are problems of committees doing things on their own, without consideration of how it affects other functions of government. After a report known as the Clothier Report, a lot of changes have been recommended and accepted. As a result we now have a Chief Minister equivalent to a Prime Minister in the UK. We also have a similar division of responsibilities amongst the ministers of economic development, transport, finance, health, education and others. Hopefully this will lead to the more joined up form of government anticipated.

The laws in Jersey originated from Norman French law, and parts of it are still in Norman French. To be admitted to the Royal Court in Jersey, you have to be a member of the Jersey Bar and be a Jersey Advocate. You must also pass Jersey Bar examinations to qualify. A lot of the Jersey system is still based on voluntary service, so many of the parish officials and all the police—except the fully paid uniformed States Police Force—are voluntary. In the case of a car accident in the countryside, you can easily be interviewed by a Centenier, who could be a local farmer, who at his sole discretion can then order you to attend a meeting with him at the local parish hall on an evening to be decided by him. He will then decide whether to let you off, impose some sort of fine, or decide it is worthy of a court case.

Jersey's use of the British defence forces and the British Foreign Office is very practical, as it must save a lot of revenue not having to have an embassy in every country of the world and not having to maintain an army. Jersey does have a locally-manned Territorial Army unit of the British Army based in Jersey. Jersey also has its own currency, the Jersey pound. It is pegged at par value with the British pound. It is unique in that we still have a pound note, whereas the UK only has pound coins.

Jersey is not a member of the European Union but is, through its connection with the British Foreign Office, an associate member. So it has all the advantages and none of the disadvantages of such membership.

Because of its size, it has an immigration problem, which it tried to solve by limiting immigration through its housing laws. You can buy a house, but you cannot live in it without housing committee permission to do so. Permission is given only after 13 years of residence or if residence is required for an essential employee of either private industry or government service. For instance, if Jersey were to need an additional brain surgeon and there isn't one available in Jersey, then housing permission would be given usually on a three- or five-year limited contract basis.

The other qualifying paragraph in the housing law is for immigrants who are potentially very high contributors in tax or are famous. So with very low 20% tax in Jersey, one would have to be an extremely wealthy individual who is still earning high income to get qualification under this paragraph.

The last possibility to come to Jersey and get residential permission would be to marry a local resident.

So how do people come to live in Jersey? Well, there are a number of approved lodging houses where no residential qualification is required. One can stay in a hotel without qualification for a limited period. Every resident and qualified house-holder in Jersey is allowed to have up to five paying lodgers in his house. Other than that, you have to live under the aforementioned circumstances for 13 years before you get residential qualifications in your own right.

This may seem a rather harsh restriction for those wanting to live permanently in Jersey, but you have to remember its small size. The island does not want to become an island of high density high rise buildings like Hong Kong. For every new immigrant, you also need not only residential room but also hospital facilities, education, sewers, water and other provisions which in themselves need additional space and investment.

Over the years, the size and strengths of the agriculture and horticulture industries and even the tourism industry have been overtaken by the offshore finance industry. It now contributes well over 50% of the revenue intake of Jersey. By its nature, the finance industry is a high salary payer, and with the limited amount of labour available, Jersey has no unemployment worth speaking of. However, this has created a situation whereby none of the locals want to do the menial but very essential work like potato harvesting, hospital cleaning, garbage collection or waiting in restaurants. From the 1950s, Jersey attracted imported labour for these tasks. These jobs were filled first by Frenchmen who came from the surrounding French coastal areas, then Italians, and then Portuguese, mainly from the island of Madeira. In all those countries, when things got economically to a better standard of living, people no longer came to earn better money in Jersey. The latest intake is from Poland and Kenya. Besides still having about 10% of the population from Portugal, we now already have a population running to over 3,000 from Poland and quite a few from hotel and restaurant training schools in Kenya.

Two interesting facts about the position of Jersey in worldwide terms:

- Jersey has more telephone lines per capita than any other country in the world. That is probably due to the fact that it is so heavily populated by the finance industry, which makes very large use of telecommunications.

- Jersey has more cars per capita and also per square inch of road than anywhere else in the world. It is said that if all the cars in Jersey were on the road at the same time, nobody would be able to move. Jersey has 800 miles of road if you count every major and minor road. That is quite a lot in a 45 square-mile island.

The climate is listed in international reference books as being temperate with mild winters and warm summers. It usually has the best summer sunshine record in the British Isles. It is at the bottom end of the Gulf Stream, and that is why the weather is quite different from the more northerly England.

The winters, in comparison to other places in Europe, are certainly mild. It is unusual to have any snow. It falls for a couple of days every three or four years at the most. It usually finds the island unprepared for it, and the schools close for those days. It really would not justify the huge investment to pay for snow clearing and other measures for this rare occurrence. Despite the so-called mild winters, I found as I got older that the dampness in the winter combined with the cold temperatures were not as pleasant as in the other island I found in Florida called Marco Island, where one can swim through the winter in an outdoor pool or even the sea. Marco has a wonderful community spirit also and that is why, for the last five years, we have now spent the winter on Marco Island.

The many cultural activities in Jersey include a theatre, the Opera House, with a seating capacity of 700, and a well-supported Arts Centre, which has a 250-seat auditorium and a concert hall converted from a church building. There is an annual Battle of Flowers, which has been going since 1902, with breaks only for the wars. It is always on the second Thursday in August and as its centrepiece has a procession of themed floats decorated with local flowers. On the same day, there are fireworks and fly-pasts and all sorts of other carnival style activities.

Three times a year, air displays are given, usually including the famous Red Arrows. We have local food festivals with various themes, not to speak of the many tourist attractions like the Jersey Zoo, Lavender Farm, Jersey Maze, Underground Hospital, various museums, properties and castles administered by the Jersey Heritage Trust, many wonderful coastal and inland walks, and a vast choice of excellent restaurants.

Education in Jersey is available up to A level, and university entrance has to take place in the United Kingdom or in France. It is supported financially, depending on income of the parents, by the government education department. We have Highlands College for further adult education, which has courses ranging from cooking to building to car maintenance.

Because of Jersey's Norman origins, whenever a loyal toast is proposed to Her Majesty the Queen, as at the beginning of Rotary meetings, the toast as in England is to "Her Majesty the Queen." However in Jersey, usually one or two Jerseymen add to that, "Our Duke."

Having lived permanently in Jersey now for over 26 years and on a holiday basis another 15 years before that, I am often asked what I particularly like about Jersey and why I am so proud and patriotic about it. Originally, we chose it because of its climate for a holiday home. Later, we chose it additionally for its tax climate for our permanent residence. An island has a distinctive community spirit, and Jersey is particularly welcoming and friendly to new residents who are prepared to contribute in many ways to the traditions and activities of its community. I am happy and proud to have done that. We have had a wonderful life with its people, made many friends and participated in many of its unique activities. I have become a member of its clubs and societies and consider it now as my home. It is said that any place which is a country of choice is much more of a recommendation than a country of birth.

❖ 57 ❖

Learning To Fly

I GOT INTERESTED IN FLYING by the sheer astonishment that something so heavy could stay in the air. The first time I had an actual connection with it was when I was in the Czech Army attached to the American Army at the International Military Tribunal in Nuremberg. The crew chief of the DC-3 which had been allocated for use by the American Chief Justice, was billeted in Boys' Town with the rest of us. Since the judge didn't fly the plane at all, we did, and I got really hooked on flying.

When the time came and I had sufficient funds to be able to learn to fly, I did so. In March of 1955, I went to a grass airfield called Burnaston which had been used during the war for some flying training. It was the home of the Derby Aero Club and situated near to Derby. The airfield was halfway between Derby, the home of Rolls Royce aero engines, and Burton-on-Trent, the home of Bass Ale, then the best beer brewed in the United Kingdom. At that time I could only spare weekends, and I usually took Maureen, and Sue in a carry cot. It was most challenging and enjoyable. However, the first chief flying instructor (CFI) allocated to me was a man named Hustwaite who had been a DC-3 captain in the Royal Air Force. He was not cut out to be a flying instructor. He had no skill in instructing, no patience, and at the slightest mistake he snatched the stick out of your hand. Normally, students of medium intelligence should be able to go solo in a plane in anything between 7 and 10 hours. I had done 13, and I still had not soloed. He told me one day that I would never be able to fly and, because of him, I was at the point of giving up.

Luckily—yet another one of those moves of fate—he transferred his "skills" to an aero club in Blackpool, and a new CFI named Matt Mallory came in. Matt was as different as chalk from cheese. He was a laid-back Australian who had an excellent manner of teaching. He would never dream of snatching the stick from a student. Instead, when I made a mistake, he told me how to correct it. After one hour and five minutes of flying with him, he got out and sent me solo. It was the most thrilling time of my life. Suddenly, your instructor gets out of the aircraft after the flight that you've just made together, and he says, "Okay, you're on your own now. Do me one circuit as you've been taught to do it, and come down and we'll celebrate." That moment comes quite unexpectedly. I had been overdue for it, but having been told that I would never fly, it was good for Matt Mallory to inspire confidence in me.

I took off from the runway on my own for the first time, and it was a mixture of exhilaration and asking myself, "What the hell am I doing up here?!" You feel very alone, but you've been taught the procedures. You do your circuit, and you make a landing. Once you're back on the ground, your total confidence comes back for the future. Then you carry on with the rest of the flying training course, which includes air exercises and navigation, radio procedures, meteorology and air law. Then you get to the stage, usually in about 35 to 40 hours (nowadays the minimum is 45 hours), when you can take your flying exam and your written theory exam and then get your Private Pilot's Licence.

A circuit is a pattern of procedure for taking off from the designated runway, which is the runway facing into wind or the nearest direction facing into wind and making four 90 degree left turns, landing again on the same runway. On take off you climb up to 800 to 1000 feet, depending on the airfield. If it's the usual left-hand circuit, you turn left and then you do a crosswind leg to a distance you've been taught, usually a mile or so. Then you turn left, and that becomes the downwind leg. Along that downwind leg you do all your pre-landing checks and then you come to a position when you start to put one stage of flaps down to slow down and prepare for the landing. You start the descent and come to what's known as the base leg which is a left 90 degree turn again. You turn left when you are about to intercept the extended centre line of the landing runway, which is the one from which you've just taken off, and you are then on finals, the final part of the approach. You let down more flap and descend from there, usually at about 500 feet per minute. It all happens quite quickly, depending on the speed of the aircraft. Finally, when you're over the threshold, you reduce power completely and flare out and slowly let the aircraft meet the ground.

I learned to fly on Austers, which are known as tail dragger airplanes. Later I proceeded to more modern aircraft which are nose wheel aircraft. On that first solo circuit, I was in an Auster, which was an old British army artillery spotter plane with two seats in the front and a swivel seat in the back for the spotter. It was much more difficult to land than a nose wheel aircraft, because you actually stall it onto the runway. You have to get the aircraft into a level position so the three wheels, including the tail wheel, stall from a maximum of about a foot to six inches above the ground. You touch the ground, and that's a perfect landing. Then you taxi down the runway and taxi back, in my case, to the club house. That circuit procedure is followed in all Visual Flying Rules all over the world. There are radio procedures to be followed if the airfield has a tower. For landing, after cross country flights, you might get a straight-in approach already from a long way out, or they might clear you only up to a certain holding point.

I did my first solo on 24th of June 1955. Shortly thereafter, I flew my first flight away from the airfield. Up to that stage, the procedure at Derby was not to teach you any detailed map reading and in those days there was no radio navigation. It was all compass and map reading, recognition of ground landmarks, and comparing them on the map, which you carried in your lap. On 3rd of July 1955, in Auster registration G-AIBW, Matt Mallory told me to fly around the area—to Derby on the one side and to Burton-on-Trent on the other. He told me to never lose sight of any one of those three points, either the airport, Derby or Burton and to get myself oriented and practise flying on my own.

It was a gorgeous day, but when I got to the Derby area and started circling the town, all of a sudden there was a little cloud. In avoiding the cloud, I got into a situation where I no longer recognised what was below me compared to what was on my map. Matt had instilled confidence in me. He told me never to panic. He also said if I ever got lost, there were so many airfields, particularly military or ex-air force airfields that if I kept flying a straight heading, within 10 or 15 minutes I would come across an airfield and I could just make an emergency landing there. So I followed his advice, and it turned out to be good advice. Lo and behold, a few minutes later there was indeed a long runway. In those days everything was done visually, and every airfield had what was known as a signal square. This had markers on it to tell you which direction runway is in use in the form of a T and whether the airfield was in use or not. The signal square would also tell you whether they had a left hand or right hand circuit, among other things.

I flew over this airfield and there was the signal square with huge letters in white that read "WD." Those letters usually identified the name of the airfield, but at that time I didn't know that. I pondered what does WD mean? The most common use of WD in the United Kingdom at that time was "War Department." So I thought it was a military establishment of the War Department. I thought, gosh, they probably store the atom bomb here or something like that. Am I really going to try and land here and get into trouble? Then I thought it's much better to argue on the ground than to stay in the air and get lost again before finding somewhere else. I decided to land.

This was my first experience of landing on a hard runway because I'd learned to fly on a grass airfield. I came down with what I thought was a nice approach but it made a hell of a noise when I landed. I wasn't used to all that noise, and I thought I was bouncing too much. I did what I had been taught to do and overshot the runway. Back then, it was called an overshoot. Now, it's called a go-around. I did an overshoot, and the second time I was determined to stay down whether I bounced or not, and I did. I started taxiing off the runway. The whole place was deserted because it was a weekend. The airfield turned out to be a Royal Air Force airfield. The Air Force doesn't work weekends, so if anybody wants to start a war, they should always start it on a weekend. When I did finally spot an airman near a hedge, I taxied to him and I cut the engine.

I told him I was lost and asked him where this was. He said it was Royal Air Force Wymeswold.

I said "What do the letters on the signal square mean. Are they War Department?"

"No," he said, "It's the first and last letter of WymeswolD and that's normally how they designate them at military airfields."

I said, "Well, it's getting late in the day, and they'll be getting really worried at my own airfield. My wife is there, and they sent me off for just half an hour's flying, and now here I am."

So he took me to his Nissen hut and we tried to make an outside call, but the base exchange told him that only officers are allowed to make outside phone calls. I asked to speak to them, and I explained the situation. I asked if he would put me through to Derby Aero Club. He did, and they said, "Just stay there; we'll come over in another plane with another pilot and fetch you."

It was starting to get dark now. Immediately after I'd made this phone call, an air force fire engine and a jeep with air force military police pulled up. They told me I was not allowed to land there (it was a bit late for that) and that I'd have to come with them to the guard house and we'd have to file a report. I explained to them that people were coming for me, and I gave them my name and address. I told them if they wanted anything further, just to get in touch with me. If the person at the air field that you need help from is himself a pilot, you will always get help. One of the guys there seemed to have been a pilot and he said, "Okay, let him go." My second plane arrived carrying Matt Mallory, dropped him off and flew back. Matt took command of my plane to return to Derby.

We had great difficulty starting the engine because the Gypsy Major engine of the Auster doesn't like to start when it's warm. I had to hand swing the propeller. We got it going in the end and rather than taxi out to the runway, he just took off from that position using the taxiway. By the time we got back to our home airfield, the club members' cars had been organised to line the direction of the grass where we were supposed to land with headlights making an artificially illuminated runway. After we landed, I apologised profusely for using so much manpower and the trouble that I caused. But Matt Mallory was so laid back, he just said "Sooner or later every pilot gets lost. You just did it earlier than most. You'll just not be worried about it if it happens to you again. Or if you're in the air, you know that it's not the end of the world to be lost."

⬥ 58 ⬥

My First Wings

I GOT MY UK CIVIL Aviation Authority Private Pilot's Licence on 19th of August 1955, which means I've had a licence now for over 50 years. Once you get your Private Pilot's Licence, you are entitled to fly in Visual Meteorological Conditions and in daylight only, and you are also entitled for the first time to take passengers. My first passenger was my wife, Maureen. We did a one hour flight over the Potteries, my home area. Then, on the same day, I took up my father for a one hour and 45 minute cross country up to Barton near Manchester. I was enthusiastic on that day to have flown two hours and 45 minutes. Although at the beginning of this book I said I kept no diaries, by law I had to keep a pilot's log book. For this reason I can account for every minute of my over 50 years of flying, showing when, at what time and where I went and whom I carried.

My daughter Sue's first flight was on 23rd of May 1956, when she was just over 2. Then I started taking up friends. I took up my very good friends, Paul and Ireen O'Brien in June of 1956 and Ian and Pam Ramsbottom in August 1956. I got to the point of using the plane quite a bit, but every time I wanted to fly I still had to go the 30 odd miles to the Derby airfield and rent an aircraft. Eventually, I got to the point where I wanted my own aircraft. I started looking and found an Auster, which was the plane I had been used to. I found one advertised by a farmer in a place in Yorkshire called Sherburn in Elmet. I went up to have a look at it and, believe it or not, it was housed in a low-roofed pigsty that had two trenches for the wheels to go down into so it accommodated the aircraft.

The plane was in quite good condition, so I bought it, there and then, on 30th of March 1958. That was Auster Mark 5 registration G-ANRP. Now I had to transfer it from that pigsty back to Derby Aero Club. It was an aircraft which had a Direction Indicator in it, which I'd never been taught how to use. I didn't realise that you had to reset it every few minutes. When I'd flown for about 20 minutes I suddenly realised that the compass heading, the direction I was heading in, was totally different from the reading on this Direction Indicator. I was in a similar situation to the time before when I got lost, when what I read on the map no longer agreed with what was underneath me.

I thought, well, this is a strange aircraft, I'd better find out where I am. From the air, I found a big field that looked big enough to land in, and I just landed. In aviation terminology it is called a precautionary landing. A farmer approached, and I said, "Excuse me for landing in your field, but can you tell me where I am?" He showed me on my map where I was, a place called Harthill, and I then realised the short distance that I still had left to get back to Derby. He offered a cup of tea, which is traditional in England. After tea, I took off and completed the flight uneventfully. I soon learned how to use a Direction Indicator, and I became quite good at flying.

To show off my new aircraft, the following Sunday I flew to an airfield called Leicester East, about a 45 minute flight, where a good friend of mine, Reg Spears, was the chairman of the Leicester Aero Club. He was in the photo finishing business, so I'd known him also through the photographic trade. Later, he went into partnership with another friend, Sam Senett, in Jersey. He changed his abode to Jersey long before I did, so when I subsequently relocated to Jersey, I already had an old friend there.

I was happy with my Auster taildragger until I noticed an American-built aircraft called the Piper Tri-pacer in one of the aviation papers. It had a nose wheel and was much more equipped like a car and with better radio equipment. A Greek ship owner who was progressing to buy a twin engine aircraft had this aircraft for sale. Its registration was G-APXM. He was an anthropomorphist and had painted the words "Mother's Blessing" on both sides of the cowling of the engine. Although I never did have my mother's blessing, which he no doubt did, I kept it, for I thought it was quite a nice name. I began to use the aircraft for business and still for occasional pleasure. I suddenly got a whole list of people who were anxious to come with me for flights, including customers, friends and employees.

When I bought the Auster, I didn't want to do a 30 mile trip to Derby every time I wanted to use it. There was an old disused airfield on the outskirts of Stoke-on-Trent called Meir. During the war there had been an ordnance factory nearby making bomb sights, and this airfield was used for fitting those bomb sights to aircraft and then testing them there. It had a runway in horrible condition, but it was usable. The airfield was used only by gliders on weekends, so I applied to the City of Stoke-on-Trent and they gave permission to use it and to build a small hangar. I used the same building technique as the farmer had used to build a lower roof and two grooves to push the plane in backwards—a very simple breezeblock construction with a corrugated iron roof and concertina doors. I now happily transferred my operation to Meir, which was only three miles away from my home.

After I bought the Tri-Pacer, I found it wouldn't go in my hangar because it had a nose wheel, not a tail wheel like my Auster. Instead of the grooves, I now had to build a "shoe." My carpenter from work made a raised shoe so that when backing in and you came to the nose wheel, it would go up the little sloped shoe, which would put the tail down so that the tail would not hit the down-sloping roof. It was the opposite problem to the one with the Auster.

A little later another local pilot, Fred Holdcroft, also applied for permission from the city, and he also built a little hangar next to mine for his Piper Tri-Pacer. He was an electrical contractor who did a lot of work for me at Photopia. We now had two users at the airfield. Another user appeared from time to time who had a home built plane called "Fred". It was on a permit to fly. I became good friends with Fred Holdcroft and he at times came to Jersey Air Rallies with me. He also joined me as co-pilot in my plane when I got a twin and when we flew transplant kidneys for St. Johns Ambulance Air Wing.

I kept the Tri-Pacer until it became obvious that I really needed a twin engine aircraft to fly more seriously, and particularly more safely. A plane produced at that time, a Cessna Skymaster, had an unusual configuration in that instead of one engine on each wing, it had one engine in the front and one engine at the back between a twin boom tail. They advertised this as being much easier to fly because if you lost an engine, you would not have an asymmetric problem. They claimed that this plane was so good that you could lose your rear engine and not even notice. I was interested in this aircraft. A famous British TV quiz personality, Hughie Green, who was a pilot and was Canadian, had a Skymaster for sale, and he flew down to demonstrate it for me.

I flew a demonstration flight with Hughie Green in his Skymaster 336, N77072, which he had on the American register. I didn't buy it, although I was very impressed. Unfortunately for him, just at that time Cessna came out with a model 337 which had a retractable undercarriage and flew faster. I decided on that and bought it new on 25th of May 1966, from a guy called Ernie Crabtree who was the distributor for Cessna and whose company was based at Leeds/Bradford Airport. Its registration was G-ATNY. I always bought and owned my aircraft. In 1962, the status of my business changed to that of a public company, and we now had shareholders to be accountable to. Any journeys performed for the company on its business were charged at what a normal economy airfare would have been for the number of people carried.

◆ 59 ◆

Flying Brings Us To Jersey

MAUREEN AND I HAD BEEN to Jersey to participate in the famous Jersey International Air Rallies. Upon visiting the rallies, we fell in love with Jersey. We were looking for a holiday home somewhere, and the usual places British people looked for holiday homes at that time were the French Riviera, Spain or Majorca. I looked at all those places and came to the conclusion that they were too far away to be regularly used. When we started going to the Jersey Air Rallies, I realised the rallies were an hour and a half's flight away from Meir, my home airfield, and that the Jersey airfield was much more likely to be used regularly. Therefore, after our second air rally there, I gave instructions to a local estate agent in Jersey, John Rice of Rumsey and Rumsey, to look for a holiday house for me.

At every air rally we went to he showed us around some houses in Jersey. Sometimes I went with Maureen and sometimes I went with Fred Holdcroft. On the third time I'd gone with Fred, John Rice said, "I've got a house which I think you'll fall in love with or you'll tell me off for even showing it to you. It's the sort of house you either like or hate." We went and viewed it, and it was absolutely ideal—just what I was looking for. It had big rooms. You could swing a cat in the bedroom (not that I wanted to do that). I phoned up Maureen at home, and she got on the next British European Airways flight to Jersey. She viewed it, and we decided then to buy it. We bought it on 28th of June 1965. In those days it was still easy to buy and live in a house in Jersey, whereas now it's almost impossible unless you've got residential qualifications or fall into a special category in the housing law.

The house, which I still live in now, is called "The Cottage" at Anne Port. It's right by the sea on the east coast of Jersey facing the west coast of the French Cherbourg Peninsula, which is only fourteen and a half miles away. We can see the French coast from all our east-facing windows on most days and even the lights of the coastal houses at night time.

Once we owned the house and finally sold all my interests in Photopia, I gave away or sold the furniture in my house in Trentham, Stoke-on-Trent. We already had a furnished house in Jersey to move into permanently on 20th of November 1980. In the meantime, I'd already made a lot of friends, both personally and in Rotary in Jersey, so it was a very easy transition to what then became my "retirement" home.

The early Jersey International Air Rallies always took place on the first weekend of May. The Jersey Aero Club, then called the Channel Islands Aero Club, organised the rallies. I joined that club first as an overseas member and then as a life member when I relocated permanently to Jersey. Once I relocated my aircraft to Jersey, I became very active in the Jersey Aero Club and was elected to the committee and also later on became the Vice Chairman under its long-serving Chairman John Such.

A beneficial part of the club was its flying department, which had good training facilities and was a good school for prospective pilots. Anybody who learned to fly in Jersey had to fly over the water, "go foreign" and be able to communicate by radio because Jersey is in what is known as Class A airspace, which is very strictly controlled air space. It was therefore considered to be a very good basic training. My elder daughter, Sue, learned to fly there, and many future airline pilots started learning to fly at the Jersey Aero Club. The club now has a very nice club building and some hangars at Jersey Airport. The club's members represent quite a large percentage of the landing statistics at Jersey Airport. If it wasn't for the training and visiting General Aviation and club aircraft using the airport, the air traffic controllers would sit there for a long time each day twiddling their thumbs, because the commercial airline schedules are no longer as numerous as they used to be.

As I got more interested and involved in flying, I became a member of the Aircraft Owners and Pilots Association (AOPA), as most GA flyers should do. It is part of an international organisation representing the interests of General Aviation pilots. AOPA started in the U.S., and now has over 407,000 members there. There are national AOPA's in the different countries of the world. I was invited to join the Board and the executive committee of the UK branch. Once I'd been to a number of meetings, they asked me to become the chairman of the Channel Island Region to strengthen the AOPA activities in the Channel Islands. I formed a new region within the UK section because of our different status and political basis to that of the UK. Our laws, even aviation laws, are different in the Channel Islands, and our Air Navigation Orders are even different in Jersey and in Guernsey. Therefore, one has to negotiate separately with the authorities in the two islands.

The division amongst pilots is that those who fly for airlines and airline companies are called airline pilots. General Aviation pilots cover every other civilian aspect of flying. It includes private jets, even 737s, which are privately owned by companies and flown around by commercial pilots, right down to a pilot who flies only VFR on his Piper Cub. They are all embraced in the term General Aviation. AOPA, at the present time, represents all those owners and pilots. I have always contended in my little fiefdom that I really am not interested in representing people who own private jets and are not pilots themselves but have them flown by commercial pilots. They have their own organisations and are well-qualified to look after their interests themselves. What I'm looking after are the interests of pilots who fly their own aircraft, whether company aircraft or small aircraft. Generally speaking, they will—with the exception of a few who own jets and fly them themselves—be aircraft up to about three tonnes in weight.

They're not just recreational aircraft because, as I used to do, a lot of people owning these aircraft use them very extensively for their business purposes but they fly themselves. So owner pilots, recreational or business, is in essence what should be represented by AOPA. It's interesting to note that in the United States, which is the mother and the father of flying, since the Wright Brothers invented the first successful flying airplane, AOPA is a very strong organisation with its 407,000 general aviation pilot members. It therefore has tremendous lobbying powers. In the UK, we have nothing like that sort of representation because we don't have that number of pilots to draw into membership. However, the status and lobbying power of AOPA in the UK in terms of representing its members, vis-à-vis the various authorities like the Civil Aviation Authority and the Department for Transport, is also very good, although in a much smaller measure than in the United States.

To be able to fly in IMC (Instrument Meteorological Conditions) in controlled airspace one needs an Instrument Rating. In the USA nearly 50% of GA pilots have one. In the UK less that 2% of GA pilots do. I hold both UK CAA and US FAA instrument ratings. To represent the special interests of European Instrument Rated pilots, the PPL/IR Europe was formed and I am a founder member of this organisation.

I bought the Skymaster 337 and started using it seriously for business. We also acquired a supplier in Yugoslavia in a town called Ljubljana, so I flew there quite often with staff. This plane did good service. It had the two-engine feature of being safe, but it did have one drawback. Its single engine performance was not very good. Normally that doesn't matter, but if it has a single engine ceiling of 5,000 feet and you're going over the Alps, which are higher than that, if you lose an engine, there's no way out. I decided that I had to get a traditional twin engine that had de-icing equipment, turbocharged engines, fuel injection, and good single engine performance—as good as you can get on a light twin. The aircraft that filled that specification best was a Piper Seneca II. Piper names most of their aircraft after Indian Tribes. So a Piper Seneca II it was to be.

While I still had the 337, I participated in competitive rallies. I never went in for competitive racing but only competitive rallies. One was called the Irish Air Rally that terminated in a little airfield called Ballyfree. I entered it in June 1967 and again in June 1968. The second time I entered, it was called the Rothmans Irish Air Rally. It was sponsored by Rothmans, the cigarette company. The

C337 is a six-seater aircraft, and I took Maureen and my daughters, Sue, 14, and Di, 12, and two friends of ours, so we had all the seats filled. One of the means of gaining points, which were accumulated for assessment of your position in order of merit, was to fly the longest distance in the time given. When you registered for the air rally, you were given what your take-off time was, what time you had to be over a certain point on the Irish Sea coast before landing, and a time to land at Ballyfree. You had these two times to observe for points. It was essential to check which way the wind was blowing to see how, in the given time, you could achieve the longest distance. They calculated the time available on the normal airspeed, and aircraft were handicapped according to this.

I found out from the Met office the day before that it was likely to be a southerly wind on the next day, so we flew from Meir down to Oporto, the most western point in Portugal, and stayed the night there. Promptly at 7:15 the next morning, our allotted take-off time, we took off. I had already pre-arranged this, when we got there the night before, with the manager of the airport. He was very friendly. We told him we were in a competitive rally and that we needed to really take off on the dot of 7:15 in the morning. He also presented us with lots of bottles of the famous local Port because they were thrilled that somebody participating in an international rally had chosen to take off from there.

The direct line journey took us across the Bay of Biscay and over the Scilly Isles and across the Irish Sea—a long, long journey. Our arrival time was to be 12:15 p.m. The French air traffic controllers happened to be on strike, so we could get no assistance from them. It really was a case of going back to dead reckoning again. We were only two miles out when we got over the Isles of Scilly. When we got over the final point on the Irish Sea coast, the point where they timed your finishing of the journey, we were only 10 seconds out, so we got a lot of points for that. When later it was announced that I had won the rally and the Rothman's Trophy, it was much to the consternation of a professional female pilot named Sheila Black. She entered most competitive rallies, and she wanted to win everything that there was to be won. That year, she elected to start from

Switzerland and was badly advised as to the winds. She didn't take kindly to the fact that I got a beautiful silver cup from Rothmans and was interviewed on Irish TV. It was a great occasion.

In the plane with us, we had two plastic buckets and cleaning materials. Upon landing, Sue and Di did a spit and polish of the aircraft, and as a result we won the Concours d'Elegance as well.

◈ 60 ◈

Airfield Hopping

BECAUSE WE DID TRIPS TO Ljubljana in Yugoslavia, I decided to change my aircraft. In the meantime, the base we were using in Meir was due to be closed because it was going to be sold by the city of Stoke-on-Trent for housing. This happens to a lot of little-used airfields. I suggested to the city council, "That's fine, but once it was closed it would leave the whole of the County of Staffordshire with no airfield." However, there was another disused airfield in much better condition than Meir not far away called Seighford. I persuaded the city to make planning application to convert that into the "City of Stoke-on-Trent Airport". They were very enthusiastic about it, particularly Town Clerk, Harry Taylor. But, unfortunately, the airfield was not in their territory. It was in the County of Staffordshire territory, and Staffordshire was opposed to this plan. It went to a Ministry planning appeal. Of course, as always happens, the people living around the airfield were opposed to it. The NIMBY principle—Not In My Back Yard—had some of them come at me with pitch forks, and they punched cars and all sorts of things. It was quite a battle. There was a lot of publicity about it, and after months of waiting, the application was turned down.

There was one other airfield in Staffordshire, in Wolverhampton, where I'd also landed quite a number of times. It was also closing down, so now there was no airfield left in the County of Staffordshire. It was probably the only county without an airfield in the whole of the United Kingdom. We lost Meir and the new airfield didn't come off, so I had to change my base to East Midlands Airport, as it is now called. It was Castle Donington in those days. I made a deal with the local air taxi company called King

Aviation. At that stage I didn't yet have an Instrument Rating so the deal was that they would provide, when necessary, an instrument rated pilot to accompany me; they could use my aircraft when they were short of aircraft and I could use their aircraft when mine was unserviceable or being maintained. We had a good relationship at that airport, but it was some distance to get there.

In April of 1972, I changed base because of the new motorway that was built in Manchester. It was now much quicker for me to get to Manchester than to Castle Donington, so we changed operations to Manchester Airport. I made a similar deal with an air taxi company in Manchester called Northern Executive Aviation.

I bought a Seneca II on 28th of July 1977, and the first one I owned was registration G-BEVG. I then changed to another, better equipped one on 8th of April 1979, registration G-BFKO. As a result of a crash of that aircraft on 17th of November 1979, I bought on 2nd of April 1980, with the insurance money from that crash, a brand new Seneca II registration G-PLUS—my third Seneca II. I still have that plane. Some years ago, I changed to the American register, and the aircraft is now known as N37US. Additionally I have flown quite a number of different types, which I rented in different countries, for flyabouts with Rotary and on holiday.

In November 1971 Eurocontrol, a pan-European organisation controlling European airspace, introduced charges for using airspace at any level when filing or flying IFR (Instrument Flight Rules). Aircraft under all-up-weight of two tonnes were and are still exempt. A Piper Seneca weighs just a few kilos over this figure. Therefore since no physical change was involved I applied to the Civil Aviation Authority for re-registration of my Seneca II to 1,999 kilos.

I was informed that to do this I would have to provide a new manufacturer's operations manual showing this weight. It took me almost two years to persuade the Piper Aircraft Company to do this. They could not understand the European system for charging for the use of airspace or landing fees—neither of which prevailed in the U.S.A. With pressure from their UK distributor they finally provided the required manual.

Then the CAA said that in addition a major modification was

required and that a CAA charge would be, from memory, £500. In fact the "major mod" was a re-placarding of the panel with three changed speeds, a changed weight and balance calculator showing the new maximum weight of 1,999 kilos. I did all this, paid the CAA and obtained the new certificate. From that point I ceased being charged Eurocontrol fees. These by the way, have gone up annually and now are almost equal in amount to the fuel cost of the journey. Happy to have left that club! Once the type of aircraft has been accepted at the lower weight—every other Seneca owner could also join the club of under-two-tonnes-exempt aircraft.

Piper then saw the opportunity for increased sales in Europe and listed a conversion kit consisting of a new ops manual, a new plastic weight and balance calculator, three speed limiting decals for the panel and list this at about $250. So once again my initial efforts have ultimately hugely benefited many others.

In Appendix D I have included a list of all the aircraft I have flown.

◆ 61 ◆

Further Certification

I GOT MY BRITISH PRIVATE Pilot's Licence when I finished my flying training in 1955. Flying only in VFR conditions became too restrictive. I needed to get my Instrument Rating. The best way to achieve that was to go to a State in the United States with good weather and take a concentrated course. I could not spare working time and decided to combine my training with the rest of the family having a holiday. I chose Opa Locka, Florida, near Miami. It was a very good training school, and I took the whole family on a booked holiday in Miami. They went to the beach every day, and my daughter, Sue, drove me in a huge American rental car to the Opa Locka airport very early in the morning every day. She also fetched me very late in the evening. I started my concentrated instrument training flying course on 23rd of December 1972, and finished it on 31st of December 1972. During that time, I completed 16 hours of actual flying plus the intensive ground school, and I passed all the FAA tests.

With the American Instrument Rating, I was entitled to fly a British-registered aircraft in controlled airspace under Instrument Meteorological Conditions until about 1982. Then, the UK CAA decided that if you wanted to fly in British-controlled air space in a British-registered craft, you needed a British Instrument Rating. They still recognised the American Instrument Rating if you flew an American-registered aircraft in British-controlled airspace, as do all the U.S. airline captains who fly to England. But for some reason, they decided to change the law for any aircraft if it was on the British register.

Therefore, I faced the alternative of either putting my aircraft onto the American register or getting a UK CAA Instrument Rating in addition to my American FAA IR. Although I later put my aircraft on the American register, at that time I opted to go back to school and get the UK CAA Instrument Rating. It is well-known that once you've passed any kind of exam or test and were asked to pass it again many years later, you probably won't pass. You forget a lot of things which you wouldn't need in practical terms but which you need for examinations. So it was quite a tough job to get the British Instrument Rating, but I got it. Only about 2% of British private pilots have a UK CAA Instrument Rating because it's so difficult to get. It's tailored mainly for commercial and airline pilots, whereas the Americans, although the actual flying tests are very similar, tailor the written part of the test purely on instrument-related subjects and leave the commercial subjects to the tests for those licenses. For that reason, nearly 50% of American private pilots have instrument ratings. The American system is much safer because many more pilots get taught and tested on how to fly under Instrument Meteorological Conditions.

◈ 62 ◈
St. John Ambulance Air Wing

AROUND 1973, AN ORGANISATION CALLED St. John Ambulance Air Wing was formed and I became a member. St. John Ambulance is a well-known organisation. The uniformed volunteers provide first aid and ambulance duties and attend public events like car racing, horse racing, open air events, theatres and cinemas. They formed the Air Wing for the purpose of transporting human kidneys for transplant from donor hospitals to recipient hospitals.

In the early days, a human kidney had a limited "shelf life." It was usually thought to have a chance of a successful transplant if it wasn't out of a body for longer than six to eight hours. This required air transport, so St. John Ambulance Air Wing was formed based on using volunteer pilots from all over the UK. It started off on a very modest ad hoc basis. Besides volunteer pilots, they needed a good organisation to coordinate between the donor hospital, the national organ matching service based in Bristol, and the receiving hospital. The detailed kidney tissue requirements of those on the waiting list were on the database at Bristol. After receiving the matching criteria from the donor hospital, they searched on computers for the nearest match. The St. John Air Wing operations room, based at St. Margarets Hospital in Epping, had already come into the picture when a donor kidney became available, and they found a member pilot nearest to the donor hospital and put him on standby. They knew he would be required, but at that stage they didn't know where he was going to take the kidney. When the transplant matching service at Bristol had finished their search and the receiving hospital was known, the controller for that mission then made a second call to the standby pilot and told him where to fly the kidney. Then they started coordinating the flight arrangements with the airfields and air traffic control, informing them of the pending medical priority flight. In many cases, they had airfields opened at night. The St. John Air Wing transported most of the kidneys at night because during the day they could be put on a commercial plane.

I did my first kidney flight on 16th of June 1974. The kidney was available in Belfast, Northern Ireland. Because I happened to be the nearest volunteer pilot to Belfast, I flew from my base airport in Manchester to Belfast to pick up the kidney. From there, I flew it to Newcastle-on-Tyne, where the recipient patient was prepared and waiting for the operation. I had the traditional cup of tea there and flew back again to Manchester.

My second kidney flight was six months later in December of 1974. That time I flew from Manchester to Birmingham to pick up a kidney which was required for a recipient back in Belfast. So this time I took a kidney to Belfast rather than picking it up from there. Then it was back to Manchester.

I flew another kidney in April of 1976, interestingly enough, from Manchester to Amsterdam. This transplant service was not limited to the United Kingdom. There were other European countries with transplant organisations.

In April of 1978, I flew another one from Manchester to Belfast for pick up then to Birmingham for drop off and back to Manchester.

In September of 1978, I picked up a kidney in Belfast again and dropped it off at London Heathrow. It was the first and only time I ever landed at the busiest airfield in the United Kingdom—and at night time.

Most of these flights were with Fred Holdcroft as my co-pilot. He still had his own single engine Tri-Pacer, but we flew all these trips in my twin-engine Seneca II. Either the police, Securicor, or an ambulance service would bring the kidney to the airport of departure or to the airfield of pickup, and they would come directly to the aircraft to hand it over. They handed me just a brown cardboard carton labelled "Transplant—Urgent." The kidney was in dry ice inside the carton to preserve it. Immediately upon landing where the kidney was going, a police car would be sitting at the end of the runway, and they would take the parcel off you and deliver it to the recipient hospital—lights on, sirens blaring.

The coordinating team duty controller at Epping accomplished everything except the flying. It was very efficient. Air traffic control were part of the scheme, and because you didn't have time to do all the pre-flight planning that you would normally do for long distance flights, the air traffic controller did this and the weather planning. It was classed as a medical emergency flight, and they gave you radar assistance whenever required and were most helpful. In a number of cases people opened up airports in the night to receive these kidneys.

I was only one of several volunteers of this kidney transplant air wing service, and later I was made the Midland region controller. I tried, therefore, to get more pilots as volunteers to share the load. It's interesting to note that quite a number of kidneys were picked up in Belfast. This was at the time of the Northern Ireland problems, so some were trying to put two and two together and find out just where some of these kidneys came from. Kidneys could only be used for transplant if people had signed kidney donor cards beforehand or their relatives agreed to it at the time of the death. Furthermore, it was a rule of the St. John Air Wing that pilots would never be told the identity of the donor or the recipient nor if the outcome of the transplant was successful or not.

⬥ 63 ⬥

My Last St. John's Flight

DURING MY VOLUNTARY SERVICE TO the St. John Ambulance Air Wing, I flew eight kidneys to be transplanted. My last flight for the Air Wing took place on 17th of November 1979, and was in my second Seneca II, G-BFKO. On this occasion, I got a phone call at home at 11:30 p.m. and was told that there was a kidney which was available from Liverpool but they didn't know yet where it was to be taken. I immediately phoned up Fred Holdcroft at his home to also be on standby, and we got dressed and ready to go. It was a terribly foggy night.

We finally got the instructions that it was to be flown from Manchester, where the kidney would be delivered by police car, to the Royal Naval Air Station at Lee-on-Solent near Southampton, normally closed at night. It took us over an hour to get from home to my hangar at Manchester Airport. It would normally take only 35 minutes. When we got there, we couldn't get the plane started. It was a very cold November night. Fred called to the tower, they sent the fire engine, and we started the aircraft engines with a jump lead to the fire engine, as you would do with a car with a flat battery. We got the latest actual weather for Lee-on-Solent from Manchester tower, and it was given as good visibility of 10 kilometres and 2/8 cloud at 3,000 feet—that is VFR conditions. What they didn't tell us was that it was only estimated down there because they didn't have a Met officer on duty.

It already seemed strange because the rest of the country was covered in fog. Manchester was so foggy that when we were ready to taxi we had to radio the tower and ask if they could send the fire engine again to lead us onto the runway. Taxiway edge lights are always blue and not as easy to see as runway lights, which are bright white. The fire engine came across, and we followed it along the taxiway to the main runway and finally took off at 3:34 a.m. with a ground visibility of 250 metres. Once we had climbed out of the fog, we were in the clear and climbed to our cruising altitude of Flight Level 090 (9,000 feet). After take-off, Manchester Air Traffic Control confirmed that there had been no change in the good weather given us for our destination—no problems, gorgeous evening, nice flight. We got everything ready for the descent and approach.

We listened to the weather for UK airports on the Volmet frequency and realised that everywhere was fog bound and that if we didn't get into Lee-on-Solent, we would have to divert to the nearest reasonable weather airfield, which was in Dublin, Ireland. The weather we had been given for Lee-on-Solent gave us no cause for concern. If we couldn't get in there, the kidney would be wasted. The London Airways controller gave us descent and handed us over to the tower controller at Lee-on-Solent. He had come especially on duty to open the airfield, and he gave us the weather, which told us that we would break cloud at 2,500 feet with a visibility of five kilometres. He cleared us to descend to 3,000 feet to the LS non-directional beacon (NDB), which is positioned at the outer marker for the Instrument Landing System (ILS) at Lee-on-Solent. Later, he cleared us for an ILS approach for Runway 23. This is a published approach, and we got the approach plates with us with the procedures. They didn't have radar for vector positioning, but with the given weather, radar was not required. We should have been able to see the runway from five kilometres.

When we were cleared for the approach, we set it all up and double-checked frequencies and altimeters. My self imposed decision height limit was 500 feet. We intercepted the ILS localiser and glide path, got the undercarriage down, and everything set up for the landing. I stayed on instruments and Fred, as the co-pilot, shouted down every 100 feet from 1,000 feet—800 feet, 700 feet— and we got to 500 feet and didn't see the runway lights. Then it was full-throttle for an overshoot to Dublin. The tower controller asked, "What are your intentions?" I decided to give it one more try, and he cleared us to rejoin for the procedure. We ran through the same procedure again. We got down to my self imposed decision height limit of 300 feet this time and were already on full-throttle starting the overshoot. All of a sudden, at 290 feet with wheels down and already in a landing configuration, we crashed. It happened without any warning of any sort, and it's a miracle we both survived. The area that we crashed in was gorse land, and it tore the wheels and wings off. We came to rest in a few hundred metres' distance in a horizontal position. There was no fire. I'd switched all the switches off.

I asked Fred, "Are you all right?" He said, "Yes, I'm all right." There wasn't a scratch on either of us. I told him to get out as quick as he could. The front door was jammed, so we got out through the rear door and took the box with the kidney with us. We walked around the aircraft. It was so foggy we didn't see there was a road about 15 metres ahead of the crashed aircraft until a car slowly went by with headlights on. We then went to the side of this road and discussed what we should do. Fred suggested we stop one of the cars going by. It was about 5 a.m. The cars seldom passed, and nobody would stop for us. I wouldn't have stopped either for two strangers on the side of a remote country road with a brown paper parcel. About an hour later, a Post Office van came along and stopped because he'd got wire mesh protection around his windows. He asked, "What's your problem?" I said, "We've just crashed a plane, and we've got a kidney here which is desperately needed for a transplant in Portsmouth Hospital. Could you please give us a lift to the nearest police station?" He explained that it's against Post Office regulations to carry passengers but said he would drive to the nearest police station and get them to come to us. Ten minutes later, a police car came. The policeman told us there was another police car on its way. He said he'd take the kidney to the hospital and the second police car would take us to the police station. When we arrived at the police station, I asked to be shown on the wall map exactly where we had crashed. It was nine miles away from the airfield at Lee-on-Solent where we should have landed.

I phoned up Maureen and told her what had happened. I told

her she was likely to get some newspaper reporters phoning and not to worry, as Fred and I were both alright. They were going to take us to the Royal Naval Air Station to sleep it off. We had to stay there because the inspectors from the Accidents Investigation Branch were coming from London and we had to give a report on what happened.

Everything had gone wrong that night. After we got some sleep, the accident investigators interviewed us independently, presumably to see whether we would say the same thing. The forecast that we'd received for Lee-on-Solent was wind 010/07 visibility 10 kilometres and a cloud base of 2/8 stratocumulus at 3,000 feet, which is a lot more than you need for instrument landing. You could do that VFR. We took off from Manchester at 3:34 a.m., and the Manchester Air Traffic Controller telephoned our take-off time to Lee-on-Solent and then passed to me the updated actual weather which was "no significant change." I was, therefore, expecting a perfectly normal approach and landing. When I was handed over by London ATC to the Lee-on-Solent controller, he gave the actual weather as five kilometres with a 1/8 cloud base at 3,000 feet. Apparently, he had said five kilometres with an 8/8 cloud base at 2,500 feet but had not corrected my read back. Either way, there was still nothing to indicate that I should expect a marginal ILS.

The plane had the undercarriage ripped off, a wing severed, and both props bent. It was a write-off. It was transported to the RAF at Farnborough for further investigation to see whether the instruments had gone wrong and to determine the cause of the accident. They wanted to find out—and so did I.

First, we had completely wrong and misleading weather reports. It was then established that there was a ship in the docks at Southampton broadcasting on the same frequency that had been allocated to the LS non-directional beacon at the outer marker position of the ILS and the start point of the published procedure. So, on our second approach we were homing onto a ship instead of onto the NDB beacon. They also discovered that the ILS system at Lee-on-Solent was a very old type. There were only two of that type left in the whole of the UK, which have side beams as well as front and back beams. Normally, on an Instrument Landing System, you have little red warning flags appearing if you're not receiving a good signal either for the centre line localiser or the glide slope. The warning flags tell you whether it's operational or not. Any warning flag appearing would require an immediate abandoning of the approach. Well, we didn't get any warning flags. The reason was, after the false NDB indication, we were on a side beam instead of on a front beam. None of the communication between the Lee-on-Solent controller and me, which is normally always recorded, was available because the controller who had come on duty forgot to switch on that equipment!

They also decided that because we'd been working all day the day before, and then had this hassle with the weather and starting the plane at Manchester, we were therefore fatigued and not in top form mentally. As a result, one of their recommendations was that the St. John Air Wing operations manual should include a warning about the possible danger of pilot fatigue.

How did AIB establish how we got to be nine miles away from our intended point of landing? Our crash was just before 5 a.m. They put an advert in the local paper to ask anybody who was up at that time, and in the area of the crash, to report where they were and whether they heard or even saw the aircraft. Remarkably, six men did. They had been delivering milk and bread. From where these witnesses said they heard the aircraft, the investigators plotted the actual path of it. It seemed we had done the correct procedure but in the wrong position because of the false signals. The safety recommendations also included that airport NDBs near the coast should not be allocated frequencies used by shipping, and when pilots are given weather reports, it should be clearly indicated whether it is estimated rather than measured.

Her Majesty's Stationery Office published the report one and a half years later. It is available from the Department of Trade, Accident Investigation Branch, and is called "Piper PA-34 (Seneca II) G-BFKO report on the accident at Beaulieu Heath, Hampshire, on the 17th of November 1979." It is a very thorough report. They came to see me at my office several times, and everybody had an opportunity to comment on it before it was published. The body of the report confirms all the obvious things, such as the pilots being properly licensed in accordance with the requirements of the Air Navigation Order to carry out the flight.

After 20 pages of Inspector of Accidents C.C. Allen's report and detailed analysis from the Accident Investigations Branch of the Department of Trade, the investigation report finishes with the following findings and conclusions:

"Findings:

1. The pilots were properly licensed in accordance with the requirements of the Air Navigation Order to carry out the flight.

2. There is no evidence of pre-crash failure or malfunction of the aircraft, its engines or equipment, apart from the unserviceability of the transponder which had no bearing on the cause of the accident.

3. Both pilots were suffering from a significant degree of fatigue by the time they commenced their approach to Lee-on-Solent.

4. The commander was passed an estimate of the cloud base which was substantially too high. Had he known that the cloud base was actually about 500 feet, he might have carried out his first approach in a different manner and possibly landed from it.

    [In fact, I would have had I known that it was 500 feet. I wouldn't have done a self-service procedure. I would have asked before being handed over by London to Lee-on-Solent, whom I knew did not have radar, to vector (position) me onto the ILS, and then I would have been properly established. I got such a good weather report that I did not do that.]

5. Following an unsuccessful ILS approach the commander followed ADF indications to a position he thought to be the LS NDB (ILS outer marker), but was most probably an unidentified radio transmission close to Fawley. He commenced his second approach from this position.

6. During his second approach the commander followed false course indications in the back course region of the ILS. At the same time he followed what he believed to be valid glide path signals, down to the point of impact.

7. Glidepath signals may be received in the area between Fawley and the crash site which give a fluctuating 'fly down' or 'on glidepath' indication, though with the glidepath flag showing.

8. At the time of the accident, there was in the area, a steep refractive index gradient close to the surface. This may have been capable of enhancing the field strength of VHF transmission sufficiently to hold the glidepath flag clear.

9. The commander permitted the aircraft to descend below the decision height which he had established as being appropriate.

Cause:

The accident was caused by the commander permitting his aircraft to descend below his self-determined decision height without having established any visual reference.

Probably contributory factors were:

1. The state of fatigue of the crew at the time of the let-down, and the self-imposed pressure to complete the flight.

2. The passing of an incorrect cloud base to the commander.

3. An unidentified radio transmission from a source in the area of Fawley Refinery, on or near the frequency of the outer marker NDB, which misled the crew as to their position.

4. The commander following false ILS localiser and glidepath signals, presented without warning flags, in the back course region of the ILS."

The report's Safety Recommendations included the following: "It is recommended that:

1. The operations manual of the St. John Ambulance Air Wing should include a warning on the possible dangers of pilot fatigue.

2. At all aerodromes when pilots are given actual weather reports it should be clearly indicated when the cloud base is estimated rather than measured.

3. Further consideration be given to the possibility of allocating frequencies which are not used by shipping to NDBs situated near the coast."

As a result of the accident, all the local reporters came and did interviews, and the story hit all the local and national papers. As aforementioned, it is the policy of the St. John Ambulance Air

Wing that the pilot would never know who the donor or recipient of the kidney is, because they do not want you to be emotionally involved. Exceptionally, in this particular case, I got a letter from Mr. A. Polak, the Professor of Renal Medicine at St. Marys Hospital in Portsmouth and the consultant surgeon who was going to plumb the new kidney into the recipient in Portsmouth hospital. He wrote, "I'm writing to thank you for the help you gave us in obtaining a donor kidney for our patient, Mr. Robbins. In view of the risk you incurred and the losses you suffered on his behalf, I would like to tell you that the decision not to use the kidney was a very difficult one. It was based not only on the unavoidable delay in receiving the kidney and the matching tissues to us, but also of the last minute uncertainty about the grade of match between the kidney and the patient. This was all the more important because Mr. Robbins' body had rejected a previous kidney transplant in which the match was not perfect. May I thank you again most sincerely for your courageous efforts to help our patient. Yours sincerely."

I replied to his letter thanking him for the explanation because I was puzzled as to why the kidney had not been used, particularly considering conflicting newspaper reports.

Luckily, both Fred and I escaped without even a scratch. Surely, either the flying angels or St. John must have been watching over us.

◆ 64 ◆

The End of the Ambulance Air Wing

WE HAD A VERY FAMOUS pilot in St. John Ambulance Air Wing—a person by the name of Winston Churchill. Not Sir Winston but his grandson. He was an MP for the Manchester Davyhulme constituency from 1970 to 1997. As a volunteer pilot, he also did a number of kidney transplant missions usually together with his wife, Minnie, in their Piper Seneca. He once flew one to Hamburg, and when he came on the radio, they asked, "What is your aircraft type and the pilot's name?" He said, "Winston Churchill. I'm a medical priority pilot delivering a kidney." They thought he was joking. They didn't know that there was a grandson of Winston Churchill. Then they wanted to charge him a landing fee. Having volunteered to do a 970 mile round trip in six hours in his own airplane in bad weather to deliver two kidneys, he told them, "I've brought two fine British kidneys to save two German lives. If you think I am paying landing fees, you are mistaken." That led to quite a bit of newspaper publicity as well.

The St. John Ambulance Air Wing ceased shortly after that, not as a result of my crash but because the preservation techniques of kidneys vastly improved and it was no longer as urgent between bodies as it used to be. When preservation techniques improved, road transport sufficed. It carried on for a small length of time for heart transplants. However, in the case of heart transplants, the transplanting surgeon who puts it into the recipient always insists on being there to take it out of the donor. So it became completely different logistics. You had to leave from the airport of the recipient hospital, fly the surgeon team to the donor hospital, wait for him to take the heart out, and then take the team back again. The small aircraft we were using were no longer suitable for that. It became a pure charter operation of bigger air taxi aircraft.

St. John Ambulance Air Wing was a voluntary service, but pilots could claim for the petrol they used. I never did. All the airports I landed at waived landing fees for these missions as well. The co-operation you got from the airports was fantastic—not charging for landing, opening specially at night, air traffic control giving routing assistance, police and ambulance services delivering and collecting kidneys. It was just unfortunate that so many things went wrong on that one very foggy night.

Because of my service to the Air Wing, I was honoured when St. John made me a Serving Brother of St. John, which is a very high honour in that sphere.

# 65 …

The "Strasser Scheme" for AOPA

IN 1997, THE UK CIVIL Aviation Authority (CAA) published a review of General Aviation Fatal Accidents 1985 to 1994 under the title of CAA CAP667. Clearly this was of great interest and I bought it and read it from cover to cover and in particular its recommendation 9.2(c) which stated—"There were a number of fatal accidents where a timely diversion or precautionary landing could have avoided an accident. In the UK there is a 'culture' of pressing on and hoping for the best rather than accepting the inconvenience and cost of a diversion. This 'culture' needs to be changed, firstly by educating pilots and secondly by persuading Aerodrome owners that there should be no charge for emergency landings or diversions. *It is recommended that all Aerodrome owners be persuaded to adopt a policy that there should be no charges for emergency landings or diversions by general aviation aircraft."* Clearly such an important recommendation should have been acted upon and implemented by the CAA itself and failing them by the General Aviation Safety Council (GASCO). As neither of these bodies took any action and it seemed that no one was going to, I thought it too important a potential life saving recommendation to be just shelved. Accordingly, I started what became known as, the "Strasser Scheme" on behalf of the Aircraft Owners and Pilots Association (AOPA) UK, of which I was and still am a Director and also the Chairman of the Channel Island region. It was my aim to get all United Kingdom and Channel Islands' airports and airfields to agree to the CAA recommendation and to waive all charges in the case of emergency and precautionary diversion landings. I knew this was going to be a formidable task but I did not anticipate the number of letters and phone calls it would take to convince some of the airports of the merits of the scheme and to agree to participate, nor the length of time it would take to get to the present total.

For strategic reasons I did not approach the Director of Jersey airport first as I did not want to risk getting a "No" from him. So my first approach was to Guernsey airport, whose then Director Alan Bridle not only agreed to be the first to join, but was also kind enough to draft the abuse limiting conditions which he allowed me to use, and have since been accepted by the other participating airports. With that in hand I got Jersey airport to be the second to join and Cambridge was the third. At first it was hard going to persuade airports to join and after the first year I had only got 66 out of the potential 213 airports and airfields to join. I spent a lot of time and effort explaining the aim of the scheme, on the phone and in writing, to airport directors and in particular citing instances where GA pilots had even been charged over £200 for a precautionary landing. Gradually more and more airports joined and the breakthrough came when the British Airport Authority, BAA, agreed to join after I had written to the Chairman, having had refusals from the individual BAA airports (except for Southampton). I never intended to, nor did I, approach London Heathrow, London Gatwick and London City for obvious reasons. My next success was the Ministry of Defence who, after a lengthy process of my finding the correct decision making person, agreed to join the scheme initially for a 12 months trial period. They made the scheme permanent for all their 36 military airfields including all Royal Air Force, Royal Navy and Army airfields, as they had no reported abuse. We now have a situation where 193 airports and airfields have joined the scheme—none have left it. 17 have so far refused to join and 3 as mentioned above have not been approached. I have not yet given up on the hard core 17 and am particularly disappointed that Biggin Hill and Gloucestershire, both of which are considered GA airfields, have refused to join. I have also appealed to any AOPA member who has any influence with the 17 remaining airports, who think they can not afford the loss of revenue in exchange for this potentially life saving scheme, and told them that I would be grateful for their help in convincing them to join the other 193. The number of abuses is negligible and I think most GA pilots value the benefits of the scheme too much to risk damaging its integrity. I probably get involved in about six complaints from pilots and three from airports in a year and depending on the facts usually resolve the matter. The biggest remaining problem is the growing number of airports which insist on compulsory handling for GA and in those instances where the landing fee has been waived because the airport is a participant of the "Strasser Scheme", the handling agent has still insisted on collecting his sometimes very high charges.

For the many aviators among the readers of my book, I append (Appendix E) a copy of the last "Press Release" which lists by name all the 213 airports and airfields, both participating and non co-operating.

◈ 66 ◈
Fired Again!

THE AIRCRAFT OWNERS AND PILOTS Association (AOPA) is a worldwide organisation representing the interests of General Aviation (GA) pilots. These are generally defined as any aviation activity not covered by the airlines, charter companies and the military. It therefore includes everything from a privately owned Boeing Business Jet to a Piper Cub. In the USA, AOPA has over 407,000 members and as a result a huge lobbying clout. I have been a member of AOPA UK since my early flying days. When I came to live in Jersey permanently in 1980, I realised that despite the valuable work done by the Jersey Aero Club (JAC), of which I had also been first an overseas member and later a life member, that the interests of the owner or part owner of an aircraft were not adequately covered by it. I therefore considered forming a new CI (Channel Islands) affiliate of the worldwide AOPA. However it soon became clear that it would make more sense to use the existing Head Office organisation and resources of AOPA UK and I formed what was the first Region within the British Isles. Despite the board of AOPA UK trying to get other regions set up to follow the successful CI example, no volunteers emerged to take on this task and the CI is still the only region. The Board of AOPA UK appointed me as the Chairman of the CI Region and I was also nominated and elected to the Board of AOPA UK in September 1993. The late Graeme Le Quesne was, until his untimely death, my vice-chairman and his position was taken over by Mike Liston. I am indebted to both of them for invaluable advice and support.

The CI Region has now substantially more members per head

of population than the UK and a sufficient number to give us a strongly backed negotiation position.

Because in the UK and the CI the interests of large aircraft including jets, even though used privately, are specifically looked after by other organisations, I spend most of my time looking after aircraft of under three tonnes mainly used for recreational or private business purposes.

The Jersey Aero Club, the Guernsey Aero Club and the Alderney Aero Club are all "corporate" members of AOPA and use its well-known and approved syllabus for pilot training. In the vast majority of cases the interests of the Aero Clubs and AOPA CI coincide. However things which largely affect visiting GA pilots and their aircraft, such as landing and parking fees, need separate vigilance and negotiating with the appropriate authorities.

Each of the Islands has an airport. Jersey and Guernsey are constitutionally independent and Alderney Airport is administered by Guernsey. Both Jersey and Guernsey have their own aviation laws, defined in their own Air Navigation Order (ANO) and although both are modelled on the UK ANO they are amazingly proud of their differences. There is also the allocation of airspace. The large area of airspace encompassing the three islands and a large area to the North, South, East and West of them is known as the Channel Islands Control Zone and all of this massive area is what is known as Class A airspace—the most tightly controlled airspace in existence. In the UK only much smaller areas surrounding London and Manchester have Class A airspace. To complicate matters even further the CICZ, which is operated by Jersey Air Traffic Control (ATC), shuts down when Jersey airport closes, generally from 9:30pm to 7:00am and it then reverts to French airspace and control.

All my negotiations and suggestions to get changes made are therefore with the Jersey or Guernsey Airport Directors, the Chiefs of Customs and Immigration and Special Branch and of course the Aviation Manager of the fuel supply company and Tourism. Even little things and suggested improvements sometimes get a negative response and get accepted only after further discussion and sometimes extensive research and proof that they would benefit the authorities also.

A list of the AOPA CI negotiated benefits for GA aircraft is appended herewith:

- 5% discount on Shell Avgas 100LL fuel uplifted in Jersey or Guernsey on Fuel Supplies credit account. Subject to all aircraft part/owners being paid up AOPA members.

- Letter available from Jersey or Guernsey Customs, in English and French, for locally based aircraft, to confirm non-VAT status of Channel Islands in case of challenge by European Customs officers.

- ATC flight plans accepted by Jersey and Guernsey ATC by fax from Aero Club, home or office. Can be sent days in advance enabling sector or return plans to be put into the system locally.

- No Customs "General Declarations" or reporting required for Inter Island flights in to and from Jersey.

- Customs "General Declarations" accepted by fax for outbound or inbound flights (except that Immigration want to see non EU nationals). AOPA members, who have registered their details, need only give their names and state "see AOPA List" for Jersey or give their Guernsey allocated number for Guernsey, instead of filling in all the personal details each and every trip.

- In Jersey half ton breakpoints up to three tonnes for landing/approach fees for GA aircraft at £4 per half tonne. For locally based aircraft an annual contract based on 55 landings with "no charge" approaches available on prepayment at 15% discount. In Guernsey half ton breakpoints already exist and landing fees are already lower than in Jersey.

- In Jersey seven days free parking for visiting GA aircraft up to three tonnes and free airside transport to and from aircraft if parked other than in GA area.

- For all Islands, Jersey Met office provides route forecast service for locally departing aircraft and on phone request also by fax.

- Current duty free fuel concession constantly being monitored as it was nearly lost in Jersey and only prompt and resolute action by AOPA CI convinced the then President of Finance (Sen. Pierre Horsfall) to make a U-turn on his Budget proposal.

- All three Channel Islands airports will waive landing and, if applicable, parking and extension fees in case of a genuine aircraft or weather emergency leading to diversion or precautionary landing. Indeed scheme extended to 190 UK including all MOD airports.

- Jersey ATIS available by phone from anywhere in the world on +44(0)1534-498073.

- Airside/landside access for GA, through JAC, successfully negotiated with Customs, Immigration and Special Branch and implemented.

- "One stop" no charge handling for all GA under three tonnes at Jersey Aero Club under GARAFA (General Aviation Recreational Aircraft Friendly Airport) scheme.

- Taking action on behalf of individual members who felt aggrieved by decisions of officers of the airport authorities and in all cases achieving reversal or compromises to the members satisfaction.

- In view of our membership, both individual and corporate, being materially higher per population in the CI region than in the UK, we enjoy acceptance by both islands' Airport Authorities, Customs, Immigration,

Special Branch and Rescue services, as the representative organisation for General Aviation regarding all matters affecting GA.

Undoubtedly the main achievement was to get a new airside/landside exit/entry point at Jersey airport through the new JAC. Before this, all visiting GA pilots and their passengers were transported on arrival and again on departure from/to the then GA parking area to/from the main terminal building. When, because of the repositioning of the main taxiway, the JAC club building and hangars had also to be relocated, I could see the opportunity of doing away with this bus service and letting pilots and their passengers walk from the new GA parking area right next door to the new JAC buildings.

This obviously needed the agreement of all the airport authorities and parties involved. I knew my main difficulty would be the then Jersey Airport Director and so I went to see the Chief of Jersey Customs first. After explaining the plan in detail he agreed to it providing a live surveillance camera was installed in the JAC GA handling area and that they were given use of a curtained off room for potential interviews and of course they could still do random spot checks at any time.

The then Head of Immigration, who I thought might prove more difficult, also agreed, providing a General Declaration listing all occupant details was faxed to their airport duty officer. In both cases the arriving pilot and passengers were not to leave the airport for 10 minutes in case they were wanted to be seen by Customs or Immigration. The same also applied to Special Branch who came into the picture because of the anti-terrorism regulations.

Armed with these two important agreements I then went to the Jersey Airport Director, but only after I had also prepared a well researched 15 page report. This showed how my proposal was going to save the airport over £100,000 per annum, which they paid to Aviation Beauport, the local air taxi and charter Fixed Base Operator, for providing the minibus service and which would no longer be required. Clearly my report also suggested how this massive annual saving was to be apportioned. The results were 1). lower landing fees for GA aircraft up to three tonnes, both for visiting and locally based aircraft on contract, 2). seven days free parking also benefiting Tourism, 3). a fee to the JAC for the use of their premises for this purpose, 4). the provision of no charge handling of the visiting GA pilots and their passengers, 5). the provision of a micro bus for the occasional transport if visiting aircraft were parked other than in the GA parking area and the transportation of the rare non EU visitors to Immigration.

So as soon as the New JAC was built and put into operational use, my suggested and by now fully agreed procedures were adopted. They were confirmed by a memorandum of agreement which I drafted and which was signed by all participating authorities and parties.

In late April 2006 the JAC committee, to try and compensate for the continuing losses being made in the flying department decided, without any consultation, to increase the compulsory handling fee of £5 which they called a Facility Fee (FF) and which was instituted in the previous year despite my objections on behalf of AOPA. They now proposed to increase this FF from £5 to £10 for single engine aircraft and £20 for twins. These charges to be over and above the airport published landing charges. Additionally they also wanted to bring in another FF of an equal amount per day of parking. For an aircraft of between 1500 and 2000 Kg. paying a landing fee of £16, not competitive with nearly all surrounding French airfields, this would mean a total charge of £26 for a single or £36 for a twin staying just for one day, or £106 for a single and £176 for a same weight twin staying for seven days.

Doing my job as AOPA CI Chairman, I registered my objection on behalf of visiting GA aircraft and also mailed a bulletin to all AOPA CI Region members stating clearly what the JAC committee wanted to do. This also included their intention to acquire a ten year lease of the GA grass area and thereby accept all future liabilities, claims and maintenance responsibility and in return retain all the visiting GA aircraft airport landing charges but surrender the agreed fees the airport paid to them for the handling. When I obtained the accounts of the club I found that this would make them worse off! I concluded the bulletin by asking my members to let me have their views on all the issues and what action, if any, AOPA CI should now take. I received a large number of responses with all but one being against the JAC proposals. Many of the responders also sent copies of their response to the JAC chairman and committee.

It so happens that, earlier in the year, I had been invited by the JAC committee to be the "guest of honour" at the forthcoming annual Jersey International Air Rally. My portrait and a whole page detailing my many actions on behalf of GA, was in the Rally Programme brochure, which had been extensively distributed and I was looking forward to giving out the many prizes at the Rally dinner. Imagine my surprise when completely out of the blue I got an e-mail from the then Chairman of the JAC withdrawing the invitation to be their guest of honour and which read as follows: "The committee of the Jersey Aero Club considers that the adverse reaction received as a direct result of your distribution to AOPA members on the 12th of May, 2006, has damaged the relationship between yourself and the Club to an extent where it would be inappropriate that you attend the main function of the 2006 rally as their guest of honour, and withdraws its invitation".

I still went to the Rally dinner as I had done on many previous occasions and paid for my ticket. To show that I was not as small-minded and to treat the whole affair as quite farcical, I wore a specially made badge inscribed "I was fired" during the rally and at the dinner, much to the embarrassment of the JAC chairman and the amusement of the participants and local members.

Anyway, none of the JAC proposals, except for the £10 FF, have been implemented. I am still making great efforts to help the JAC obtain additional funding to allow them to reduce and ultimately wipe out the loss on the flying department. But I will always object to penalties imposed on visiting or local GA for the purpose of subsidising losses in other areas.

⋄ 67 ⋄

More Flying Adventures

WHENEVER I WENT ON HOLIDAYS or fly-abouts too distant to warrant taking my own plane I would rent an aircraft locally. Having both UK CAA and U.S. FAA licenses facilitated renting aircraft in different countries. Some countries, like Barbados, required you to get a local licence for the revenue, but they issue it—just a piece of paper—on the basis of the American or the British licence.

In December 1974, we travelled to the Bahamas for a Christmas holiday. I rented a Cessna 172 aircraft registration N7004G and went around island hopping from Oakes Field to Nassau to Freeport to Great Harbour Cay and then to Nassau and back to Oakes Field.

For Christmas 1979, we went on a family holiday to Barbados, and I hired a Cessna 182 there and did an island hopping tour to St. Vincent, Mustique and Martinique and back again to Barbados. The island of Mustique will be well-known to British readers because it's the island where Princess Margaret spent a lot of time. It has a very small air strip which slopes up at one end and gives you speed when you're taking off to help you avoid a mountain at the other end of the runway. It also slows you down if you get that far upon landing.

In 1980, I bought the Seneca II, which I still possess. On 12th of November 1980, I did the last flight from the United Kingdom to Jersey to transfer my domicile and residence.

Not that I ever wanted to fly commercially, but purely as an intellectual challenge and to get more aviation experience, I went to a place called Kennett, Missouri, in March of 1982 to train for, and get, my Federal Aviation Authority Commercial Pilots Licence.

We took a holiday in June, 1982, in Las Vegas where my late cousin, Norbert, lived. I rented a Cessna 182 there, which is an excellent aircraft. I flew around the Grand Canyon on that trip, taking off from North Las Vegas Airport and landing at Grand Canyon airport. That was the first time I came across the practical concept of density altitude, which applies when you go to an airfield at a high elevation, particularly combined with high temperatures and humidity. You need considerably more landing and take-off distance because you can get in a situation where an airfield is 4,000 or 5,000 feet high but the density altitude might be 7,000 or 8,000 feet for your landing/take-off distance calculation.

I used my aircraft to go to quite a number of exhibitions, like Photokina in Cologne and the Cebit in Hanover, an exhibition for computer hardware and software and including communications, mainly Information Technology.

Christmas 1983, we spent in Antigua in the Caribbean. There I hired both a single engine aircraft and Seneca twin aircraft to fly about at different times to different islands. These were both on the American register, so I was able to use my American pilot's licence. We flew to the islands of Montserrat, Dominique, Anguilla, and St. Maartens (which is half French and half Dutch) and to Pointe-a-Pitre, Guadeloupe.

About that time, I flew many business trips from Jersey to Paris, France, where I used an airfield west of Paris called Pontoise. I was a consultant to Cokin, the famous filter makers in Paris, started by Jean Coquin and Marc Heintz, for whom Photopia were the first agents in the UK. I acted as a consultant for them in designing an electronic flashgun which would fit into their filter system to go round the lens. It was a ring-type of electronic flash gun with swivelling sides which could be used for close-up photography, dental photography or photographing products for catalogues, etc. That went very successfully and meant that I had to fly a lot from Jersey to Paris.

Christmas and New Year, 1984 and 1985, we spent with my now-deceased cousin, Harry May, who lived in Port Charlotte, Florida. The nearest airport was Punta Gorda, and there I hired a Cessna 172 on different occasions. We did trips from there to the east coast of Florida to Titusville, which we used as a base to go and view the NASA Kennedy Space Centre. I also landed at Tampa International and the Apollo Beach airports during that time.

In July 1993, I took a trip to Prague to take part in an aviation exhibition at the airport. I bought a SkyMap for my plane. SkyMap was one of the early moving map displays based on a Global Positioning System (GPS). A company called Skyforce designed, invented and made it in Great Britain. Honeywell later took over Skyforce. I was so impressed with SkyMap I felt I could sell it, so I got non-exclusive selling rights for Skyforce products, which included not only the UK and the Channel Islands but also European sales.

Since I visited the Czech Republic on a number of occasions, I thought I would try selling SkyMap there and took part in an aviation exhibition. The Czech Air Force showed a lot of interest in the unit. Subsequently, on visits to Prague, I attended a number of meetings at the Czech Ministry of Defence with officers whom I only afterwards realised had no purchasing or executive powers but were just interested in new technology. It was an interesting exercise and one of the few occasions where, despite great effort, I just did not achieve any sales. It was a great lesson on how important it is to seek out the one person able to sign an order. On this trip in July 1993, after the exhibition, I also flew to a place called Kunovice, where I visited the factory of the Let Aircraft manufacturer. I gave a demonstration of the SkyMap unit, and then flew back to Jersey via Prague and Antwerp.

An interesting side note on my visits to the Czech Ministry of Defence in Prague was the nature of the office doors. They had one normal door and a second door which was a metal door with prison bars which could be locked. This was a feature left over from the communist era to enable the immediate imprisoning of officers suspected of dissident activity. On my second visit these doors were in the process of being removed.

In May 1994, I took part in an Irish rally at Kilkenny which quite a number of aircraft from Jersey had entered. We all came back via Wales and stopped the night at the North Wales airfield of Caernarfon, which was owned by a Jersey resident, aviator extraordinaire Mike Collett, whose wife, Miranda, learned to fly and got her private pilot's licence at the JAC and is now a British Airways 747 Captain. Mike owns Air Atlantic, which is based at Coventry airport which, at that time, he also owned. He also collects and owns classic aircraft quite a lot of which are on display at Coventry. We had a nice evening meal together and a day out with him at his airfield in Caernarfon and then all flew back to Jersey.

In June 1994, the annual Popular Flying Association (PFA) show took place at Cranfield where we exhibited our Navtor programme for the first time.

February 1995, we were in the Napa Valley, famous in California for its vineyards. In that time, I needed to do my FAA bi-annual— a test that is required to be taken every two years to keep your licence valid—so I rented a Cessna 172 at Napa Airfield and did both my flying and theoretical Bi-annual Flight Review (BFR). We flew over quite a lot of the countryside, seeing all the miles of neat rows of vines. This little airfield in the middle of nowhere had quite a large building on it because Japanese Airlines used it as a training base for their trainee airline pilots.

During that year, as indeed many other years, I did quite a lot of trips from Jersey to Southampton to collect my younger daughter, Dianne, and my two granddaughters, Hannah and Sarah.

In the very end of November 1995, I had a very eventful trip from Jersey via Nuremberg to Prague. I parked the aircraft there in the usual way. There was a lot of snow about, and even more fell and froze whilst I was in Prague. When I came back to the airport, the aircraft was covered with snow. It took me a good two hours to clear it sufficiently for it to be safe to fly. I asked for someone to help me taxi, because we were parked miles away from the terminal building. There was nobody available, so after starting the engines I commenced taxiing on my own. A few feet later, I heard a bang on the left-hand side and saw a piece of metal fly off the propeller. I immediately stopped the engines and went out to see what had happened. Some stupid person had left a big metal aircraft wheel chock just lying there. With everything covered in snow, I didn't see it. It shouldn't have been there. It should have been a clear area. It took the tip of one of the three blades of the propeller off altogether and bent another one. The danger when something like that happens is that it could damage the engine. Clearly, the aircraft was not in flying condition after that, and the propeller couldn't be repaired. It needed a new one, which meant ordering it from the United States. That was the end of that flight.

A new propeller was ordered. Luckily, one was available from stock. The insurance company agreed to pay for it. I did all the necessary form filling and reporting to the Czech Aviation Authorities because they wanted to carry out an investigation as to who had done what at what time. Then there was a delay to the propeller coming by Delta airlines because when it was ready to be shipped, there was snow in the United States and the particular flight it was supposed to be on didn't arrive in Prague. Finally, the propeller came.

Then I had to get it cleared through Czech Customs. Although it was going to be fitted and immediately exported, they still wanted all the import documentation done and the import duty paid. After a lot of research into their Czech Customs tariff and Czech Customs rule books, I found a paragraph which showed that duty was not payable for an instance of that sort and, confronted by that, they released it. One of my usual mechanics, Bob Dukes from Jersey, had flown over commercially to Prague. I managed to get the aircraft into a hangar so he wouldn't have to work in the icy cold outside. He took off the old propeller and fitted the new one. He had brought two new oil filters for the engine because we had to cut the old one in half to see that there were no metal particles in it and no shock damage to the engine. He did a tremendously quick and good job, and the following day the aircraft was ready to fly back.

I flight-planned back to Jersey and had only just been in the air for about 15 minutes—still inside Czech air space—when I noticed an engine running roughly. It was the other engine this time. The oil pressure stayed okay, so I nursed it along and diverted to Nuremberg. The engineers there found that one of the cylinders needed new rings in it. There was another three-day delay. So Bob Dukes, the Jersey mechanic who had done such a good job fitting the propeller, flew back commercially to Jersey, and I waited while the engineers in Nuremberg did what was necessary to the engine. Finally, and uneventfully, I flew back to Jersey. That was a long episode and in over 50 years of my flying the most complicated set of circumstances to get the aircraft back in the air that I've experienced.

Although the engineers in Nuremberg did such a good job on the engine to get me back to Jersey, when it came to the annual Certificate of Airworthiness inspection on the aircraft in May of 1996, we found that the engines, which have a maximum permitted life of 1,800 hours, had come to the end of their life. You either have to replace them with new engines or with reconditioned zero-hour engines. I decided at that time to refit with two new engines, and those are the ones I'm still using now.

My two daughters had never been to the Czech Republic or Czechoslovakia, as it was previously known, since they grew up during the time of the Communist Occupation. There had been no opportunity to show them my original home country. At last in 1996, I flew there with my younger daughter, Dianne, and my grandchildren, Hannah and Sarah. Starting in Jersey, I picked them up in Southampton, and we flew with a refuelling stop in Maastricht to Karlovy Vary which is the Czech name. Because that's so difficult to pronounce, most people use the German name of Karlsbad, which means "Charles's spa." It's a spa town in Northwest Bohemia used in the 1800's extensively by the European Royal families as a health cure spa. Many visitors still use it for that purpose today. After an overnight stay in the beautiful town, we rented a car and made a trip to Prague and other places I wanted to show them. We visited the village of Lidice, which the Germans had razed during the occupation. We visited Terezin, which was a concentration camp in Bohemia during the German occupation. Our tour, of course, included the flats and houses I lived in as a boy and the schools I went to both in Prague and in Teplice-Sanov (Teplitz-Schoenau) in Northern Bohemia, now renamed Teplice-Lazne. That was quite an event-packed, memorable trip lasting six days in May of 1996. My fellow travellers loved it.

On a sad occasion on 7th of August 1996, I flew to Coventry to attend the funeral in Stoke-on-Trent of my friend, Paul Strass.

He was one of the Czech children originally in the Penkhull Children's Home. He had served in the war in the Czech Independent Armoured Brigade as I had, but he went back to Czechoslovakia when he was demobilised. He started a family there. I never had any contact with him while he was there until the "Prague Spring of 1968" that lasted from January 5 to August 20 of that year. It was thought that a more liberal regime would come to pass in Czechoslovakia when Alexander Dubcek came to power. On August 20, the Soviet Union and its Warsaw Pact allies, except Romania, invaded Czechoslovakia and the liberal dreams failed. Paul Strass took the opportunity to leave and come back to England with his wife and children. For the second time he was a refugee. The first time was from potential problems with the Germans occupying the country and the second time from actual Communist domination. Maureen and I decided we would put them up in our house until they could find their feet and a job and earn some money and then find somewhere to live. Paul, his wife Franja, and their children lived with us for two or three months until he got quite a good job in a computer factory nearby.

In September we had a holiday trip to Florence in Italy. It was from Jersey to Limoges again, then to Cannes and from there to Florence.

At the end of May 1999, as I had done for many years, I ferried some children from an orphanage in France for a day out in Jersey. Several volunteer aircraft from the Jersey Aero Club participate. We fly empty to the French coast airfield of Granville and pick up the children and their teachers. They have a day out in Jersey and in the evening we fly them all back again. That gives them a really thrilling day out in another country.

I made an interesting day flight on 11th of August 1999, to experience the total solar eclipse. It only happens every 18 years. It's when the sun and the moon are aligned and the sky goes totally dark while the latter obscures the former. It was calculated that the nearest place from Jersey where it would be possible to experience this was in the French town of Rouen, which is just under an hour's flying time from Jersey. You're not allowed to look at the eclipse directly, so vendors were selling all sorts of polarised glasses.

I invited three Rotarians—David Beaugeard from the Rotary De La Manche Club as well as Brian Troy and Tony Allchurch from the Jersey Club—to come with me. We took a picnic, and like many others who flew in to Rouen especially to see this phenomenon, we just spread it on the grass of the airfield and waited for the passing phase. It was truly an amazing sight.

In April 2000, I had my first extended stay in Florida. I rented a Cessna 172 and flew from Naples to Key West to Ft. Myers Page Field and then to Boca Raton on the East Coast to visit Abe Fiegelson, an old friend who used to be the Minolta agent for Canada. Then I flew to Lakeland to attend "Sun and Fun", the second largest aviation show in the world. That was my first extended experience of Florida. I liked it very much and decided at some time in the future to do what we in fact later did and that is to winter in Florida.

On 16th of May 2000, my aircraft was re-christened and changed its name from G-PLUS, on the British Register, to N37US, on the American Register. Quite a lot of book work procedure had to be done. It had to be released from the British Register and accepted onto the American Register and a trust company had to be formed because only American citizens or American corporations can own American registered aircraft. There are attorneys and specialists who are able to form these American trusts, and the FAA fully accepts that the beneficial owner can be a non-American citizen but they must be able to enforce their regulations and be able to get at a trust or company or citizen of the United States. The registration letters on the side of the aircraft had to be repainted, and all the documentation had to comply with FAA regulations from then on. The flying regulations have to comply with the country where the aircraft is registered but also to the regulations of any country which that aircraft flies in or over.

Normally, in the air, when you talk with controllers after you've made the first contact and identified yourself with the full call sign, you only refer to yourself with the last two letters of your call sign. Therefore I selected the number N37US because it had the same last two letters as G-PLUS.

On 15th of September 2000, I did a direct, non-stop flight from

Jersey to Berlin Tempelhof Airport in three hours and 57 minutes. Berlin Tempelhof Airport is famous because it is a very unusual airfield, right in the middle of the city, with all the approaches right over all the houses until you get to the threshold. Hitler built it before the war. His famous German architect, Albert Speer, designed it. Speer also designed many government buildings and the famous Nazi parade ground for party rallies in Nuremberg. Templehof's famed massive Teutonic buildings survived the bombing almost completely and are still in use. It was also the airfield the Allies used to supply Berlin during the famous Berlin airlift in 1948/49 when everything had to be brought in by air to keep the city going. A lot of old Second World War aircraft like the Dakotas and DC-3s were used for that purpose on a massive scale of airlifting. Because it was in the city centre, it was the only airfield available.

Later in 2000, we flew more children for a day out. This time we did the trip the other way around with several aircraft from the Jersey Aero Club taking some children from a school for handicapped and children with learning difficulties from Jersey for a day out in Granville. On this occasion, rather than coming back, we stayed the day in Granville to bring them back to Jersey at the end of the day.

◆ 68 ◆

Combining Two Interests

MY MAIN INTERESTS, ASIDE FROM photography, were flying and computing, and it was a combination of these which led to the development of a useful flight planning programme for pilots. I got together with another Jersey pilot and computer programming expert, Richard Strudwick, an accomplished, self-taught programmer who had a photographic memory. When he went in for pilot's written examinations and got less than 100 percent, he was always disappointed. We initially developed a programme for our own use—something to make our own flight planning easier—without any commercial objective at that stage. However, as soon as we started showing some of our results to other pilots, while we still had it as a beta version, they wanted a copy of it. After we gave a few away, we realised we had a marketable item. With our piloting experience, my aviation and navigation experience (which at that stage was greater than his), and my marketing experience, we got together and developed a flight planning programme for the whole of Europe which I named "Navtor". These were the early days of home computers, and we wanted a programme that was going to be better than any existing manual or even homemade computer system.

We spent an extraordinary amount of time before we actually brought it to the market, and it was an instant success—so much so that it got interest from other European, non-English speaking countries. We translated all the instructions into different European languages, starting with French and German and then Italian. I even got it translated by a Flying Rotarian friend into Swedish for the Scandinavian market.

Prior to being able to use a computer for flight planning, a pilot had to get out a map and pin point the areas he wanted to fly over or to draw that up onto a paper flight plan, and then work out the actual course in degrees with a protractor. Then, he had to work out either still air time or, by putting in the wind factor, the length of time it would take to go from one point to another and what the arrival time at each point would be once the take-off time was known. All that had to be done by way of what was colloquially known as "dead reckoning." Nothing checked the accuracy of it.

What we did was to put every airport, every VOR beacon (directional beacon), every NDB (non-directional beacon), and things like compulsory reporting points and so on for the whole of Europe into a database—and that was a huge job. All the pilot had to do was to put into the computer the point of departure, the various points he wanted or was required to fly over, and the destination airport, and we would present him with a readymade, printed out flight plan with all that information accurately in it. Pilots could also put in wind speed and direction, and the Navtor flight plan would show the newly required heading to fly. We also built in a feature so when he put in his destination airport, he pressed a key and it would give him, onscreen, a choice of the nearest airports as alternates. Pressing another key would add the chosen alternate to his flight plan.

That was only the basic flight plan for the pilot to use. We went a step further and provided another report where it would show airports and beacons etc., at a chosen distance either side of this track. We defaulted to 15 miles either side of track, so it would make, if you like, a 30-mile "air road" for the pilot's journey. On a second printout, we would give all the frequencies of any airport that he was over-flying or any flight information service frequency that was applicable to that air road and any other frequencies and beacons—not necessarily the ones he'd chosen but other ones that were available in case the ones he'd chosen were not available. We then had another report which would give area navigation data, giving distance and bearing from beacons to his chosen ones and other waypoints on his route.

All these things which previously had to be done manually by drawing a line on the map and then measuring angles, were now done automatically by computer. This increased tremendously the speed as well as the accuracy. The standard flight plan that has to be filed with Air Traffic Control was another by-product of the programme. Airfields don't frequently move, but beacon and communication frequencies do change, so that information had to be updated on a weekly basis. We therefore made update programmes available. We then developed Navtor AOC, a more sophisticated programme for commercial operators like air taxi companies and charter companies who were under much stricter regulatory control by the Civil Aviation Authorities. This made provision for fuel used by sector, fuel reserve calculations, things of that nature, and that was approved by the CAA. Part of that approval was that the purchaser had to have a weekly update service from us to ensure that all the information was always accurate. That sold at a very much higher price than the normal programme for private pilots.

After we had spent hundreds of hours in development and testing, Navtor became a great business.

In those days, floppy discs were the state of the art. I had to update and make the current programme, copy it to floppy discs, put it in a nice, clear plastic case and dispatch it. The cost of the materials and the postage was negligible. Therefore, virtually the entire price we charged the consumer was clear profit. After we got rid of all the bugs and had become No. 1 in Europe for this programme, the activity lost its challenge. It became a very mundane operation, and all the joy of the challenge had gone. Both Richard and I wanted to sell, so I looked for someone to buy the company. We found another pilot in Jersey by the name of Ken Faulkner who was interested. Navtor was a limited company, so he bought 100% of the shares of the company, and it continued trading as before. Richard and I shared the profit from that transaction, and it was quite a nice figure by that time.

Unfortunately, although he paid a lot of money for it, Ken seemed to quickly lose enthusiasm and interest in it and ultimately just let it drift. In the meantime, a friendly competitor of Navtor had developed a similar but inferior flight planning programme called Navbox. Anything to do with Information Technology needs constant development all the time. Once we sold Navtor, he raced ahead and started putting in a map display within the programme so that you could just point to different waypoints on the map and it would do the flight plan from that, rather than you having to put in names or latitudes and longitudes. Later still, our competitor converted the map to a moving map display when coupled to a GPS antenna, and he overtook Navtor and is the undoubted leader in the field now.

I recognised the superiority of Navbox and that, coupled with the lack of support that was being given to Navtor, made me change to Navbox Pro-plan. I then found it so good that I arranged with Peter Mundy of Navbox that I would start recommending and selling his programme rather than the one that I had originally developed together with Richard Strudwick. I am now listed as Peter's Channel Island outlet and, because we don't have any sales or Value Added Tax in the Channel Islands, we have the advantage of being able to sell it cheaper.

◆ 69 ◆
Skylog

DURING THE TIME OF MARKETING Navtor, a programmer and pilot from England, Andrew Sowerby, approached me about a programme he was developing. To develop aviation programmes, you have to be a pilot in the first instance and a programmer in the second. He had started developing a programme to computerise a pilot's log book, an item that, by law, every pilot all over the world has to keep and enter into it every single flight he makes. This is quite a chore, as all the different types of flying have to be listed in separate columns and manually totalled. If you want to analyse your log book, it's quite a job, whereas if it is computerised, providing the programme is correctly written, many different reports can be tailored to suit the user's requirements. He thought that since I was already selling Navtor and helped to develop it, we could tag his computerised logbook onto that. We had to find a name for it and I suggested, since it was a log and was for activity in the sky, that the name SkyLog would be appropriate. I searched the trademark registers. Nobody had used that name before, so SkyLog it was. Similar to the Navtor experience, we soon found that we needed two versions, one for private pilots and another for professional pilots, which became SkyLog Pro.

Programming had already started taking into account the requirements as per the layout of the ubiquitous blue pilot's log book completed manually by pen ever since flying started. A pilot's logbook is required to be produced to the CAA when you apply for your Private Pilot's Licence to be issued. You have to show that you've gone through the course and completed the required number of hours. Then you have to send it again to the CAA if you are going in for any rating like an IMC or multi-engine rating—all of which have a requirement for a number of hours and evidence of which they want to see. Even more so, you need to log hours when you go in for your Commercial Pilot's Licence and your Airline Transport Pilot's licence where you get a frozen licence until you've reached a minimum number of hours and only then will they validate your frozen licence.

We hit a major snag early on when I went to the CAA and showed them our SkyLog programme for approval. They said, "No. We believe in the reliable manually written 'quill pen' method."

"Why," I asked them, "will you not accept a computerised version?"

"Ah, because people can cheat too much with computers, whereas if we have it in a handwritten book form, we can see where they have overwritten it or opaqued it out or rubbed it out."

I returned to Andrew and told him of the problem. If we have a computerised logbook that's not accepted by the CAA, it's not a marketable item. We had to overcome this. I told Andrew that as soon as we overcame that, they'd come up with something else that they didn't like, because basically they do not want to go away from the little blue logbooks. This was a Civil Aviation Authority which was dealing with modern computerised aircraft, but they wanted to keep the logbooks in the quill pen era.

We came up with the idea that the only way to overcome the first hurdle was to have an unalterable audit trail which would automatically produce any change that the user would make to any individual entry. It would ignore any entry that no change had been made to but put an asterisk against any entry in the log which had a change made to it and put that entry on an audit trail showing both the before and after alteration entry. It could be a legitimate date change or could be an alteration of hours as an afterthought but it was disclosed for the CAA. It wasn't all that difficult a programming job, so we did it. Back I went to the CAA and explained that whenever anybody sends you a printout from our SkyLog programme, with it they will get an audit trail and that will show the before and after of any entry that has been changed. The whole thing would be much better for the CAA too because they were having to manually check the additions of totals on each page of the submitted blue logbook. If they had a computer printout report, they would know that all the totals in there were correct. They wouldn't have to go through it again. I told them we could even provide them a programme, free of charge, so instead of the pilot having to send them a printout report, he just needed to send them a CD with his SkyLog reports on it. Our programme would give them a printout of the relevant part required for the certification of the particular rating.

They thought it might be a good idea, but then (as I had warned Andrew) they came up with some more perceived problems. Eventually, we did everything they required and one by one overcame all their objections. Then I asked them, "Now why can't you approve it?"

"Because we don't approve logbooks and, therefore, we can't approve computerised logbooks."

So I said, "Okay, maybe I'm using the wrong word here. Will you authorise the use of our programme for submission to you in support of applications for licenses and ratings?"

Finally they said, "Yes, we will accept SkyLog, considering that you've overcome all the problems but we still want to see the printouts and audit trails as hard copy."

They no longer had any basis for objecting to accepting the product that we got on the market. So we were now able to put into our advertising "SkyLog accepted by the CAA for licence and rating submission." For our marketing purposes, "approved" or "accepted" had the same meaning. From there onward, we were in business, and to the best of my knowledge and belief, our "acceptance" is still unique.

We started off with floppy disks but changed to CDs when that era started. Some people were still only capable of accepting floppies, so we had availability of both. We had two programmes, SkyLog and SkyLog Pro. The main difference between them was the professional pilot programme included duty hours, which a private pilot doesn't need. A professional pilot has a maximum number of duty hours per day, per week, per month, per year laid down by the Aviation Authority and these can also be a different number of hours for different airlines. These might be even stricter than the CAA or the FAA or any other authority. So the programme had to be written in such a way that the user could change the duty hours to those laid down by his employer. In any pilot's logbook, you have to show separately the night flying hours and the day flight hours, so we also built into the professional version a world database of airports and a programme which could work out on a long flight, let's say from Hong Kong to New York, which part of the flight was daytime and which part was night time. The pilot doesn't really know at what point it legally changes from a daylight to a night time flight, but our programme apportions it automatically using the airport database and the take-off and landing times.

These were big steps for the professional pilot. Pilots from airlines all over the world began using the professional version of SkyLog. Somewhat to our surprise, that version, although it's three times more expensive, sells in much higher quantities than the private pilot version. During the course of time and with the advent of PDAs, we've changed the programme so that both PDA operating versions can be used whether they are of the Palm type or the Microsoft Windows type. All versions do things like giving the pilot advance warning when his licence is expiring or that his medical needs renewing and, in the case of the professional version, that he's getting dangerously close to using up his permitted duty hours.

SkyLog is a product that I'm still involved with. But, again, it was getting mundane to do the actual making of floppy disks and CDs, so Andrew and I agreed that we'd bring a third party in to do this and also take over the marketing function. I found an ex-employee of mine and a keen pilot, Ian Rosewell, who is the Managing Director of a very successful promotional gift company. He is now the distributor of the SkyLog programmes, which initially we did as a direct marketing exercise. He now additionally supplies wholesale to pilot accessory shops. Andrew is still the development department, Ian is the sales department, and I'm the publisher of the programme. As is needed in the technology arena, we are still constantly developing and refining SkyLog. Airline pilots come up with new ideas and suggest them, and we accommodate them.

SkyLog doesn't need updates, but as we develop it we produce upgrades. For instance, you could synchronise it with information you gathered on a PDA and make it a better programme. We publish any changes made on the website, and users can buy an upgrade at half price. That too creates quite a nice business.

If you are interested in seeing the full details please go to www.skylog.co.uk or my website www.gtaviation.co.uk/skylog.

❖ 70 ❖

Rotary International

ROTARY WAS FOUNDED IN CHICAGO, Illinois, in 1905 by a local solicitor named Paul Harris. He and three of his friends rotated meetings in their respective offices, and that is how the name of Rotary came about. Their initial aim was—and this is frowned upon nowadays—to facilitate doing business amongst similarly minded business and professional people. The idea caught on, and the first main club was formed in Chicago and then spread rapidly in the United States. Shortly thereafter, the club spread to other countries. It came to the British Isles first in Dublin, Ireland, and then in London, England. Now approximately 1.2 million Rotarians belong to more than 32,000 clubs in more than 200 countries and geographical areas. It is the world's largest volunteer service organisation, a global network of community volunteers.

The concept of Rotary membership is based on being non-political, non-sectarian, non-religious, non-governmental, and accepting members of all colours, cultures, creeds and nationalities. When the movement started, it was purely a men's club and limited its membership to one member of one classification (profession) per club. It was thought to seek the best in each particular business or profession in the recruitment area of that club. Both those recruitment criteria have been relaxed now. Since a U.S. Supreme Court case, the admission of women was forced upon the movement and is now universally accepted. Similarly, the one member per classification has also been eased.

Rotary is a service organisation formed to do good for the local community, internationally, and generally. Its motto of "Service Above Self" suggests giving service both in manpower and in money, wherever it may be required. The meetings have to take place weekly, although the club I now belong to in Jersey is one of 11 clubs left still insisting on working under the old constitution where the weekly meeting was not a requirement. They meet every 14 days. A vote has to be taken annually to see whether they still want to continue on that basis. So far, the overwhelming majority of members of the Jersey club annually vote to keep the 14-day rotation of meetings.

Rotary Clubs have always been banned in totalitarian countries. Rotary did not exist in the Soviet Union, any Communist country, Nazi Germany, or in Franco's Spain. (It is only now just about to start in China.) Because of this, the Germans stopped the Rotary movement in Czechoslovakia—which had started in Prague in 1925—when they invaded the country in 1938. It was re-started after the Second World War in 1945 only to be stopped again by the Communists in 1948. After that, it was re-launched, hopefully forever, in 1990. There are now very few countries left in the world where Rotary is not accepted, so it is truly an international organisation. One of Rotary's aims is world understanding, and it's interesting to note that even in areas of tension like the Middle East, you still find Rotarians on opposing sides being friendly and welcoming to each other. That is what the Rotary movement is all about.

Rotary International has what it calls the Four-Way Test, which Rotarian Herbert J. Taylor (who later served as RI president) created in 1932. He created the test after being asked to take over a company facing bankruptcy. The test was created for employees to use in their business and professional lives. The Four-Way Test, which Rotary adopted in 1943, is one of the basic tenets of the Rotary movement, and it reads as follows:

"Of the things we think, say or do:

1. Is it the truth?
2. Is it fair to all concerned?
3. Will it build goodwill and better friendships?
4. Will it be beneficial to all concerned?"

The official Object of Rotary is as follows:

The Object of Rotary is to encourage and foster the ideal of service as a basis of worthy enterprise and, in particular, to encourage and foster:

- FIRST: The development of acquaintance as an opportunity for service;
- SECOND: High ethical standards in business and professions, the recognition of the worthiness of all useful occupations, and the dignifying of each Rotarian's occupation as an opportunity to serve society;
- THIRD: The application of the ideal of service in each Rotarian's personal, business, and community life;
- FOURTH: The advancement of international understanding, goodwill, and peace through a world fellowship of business and professional persons united in the ideal of service.

Just one example of the practical side of Rotary is the elimination of the dreadful disease of polio on a worldwide basis. For many years, Rotarians all over the world collected funds so that, together with the World Health Organisation, they could buy the necessary medications and organise the necessary camps in polio distribution centres for administration of the vaccines. These polio camps were generally in third world countries. The aim was to eradicate polio by the year 2000. By 2000, a great majority of countries had eliminated polio, but additional money was still needed because there were some pockets left. A new campaign for more money was started. There are now only three countries left with pockets of polio. It has been a massive $600 million collection and countless volunteer hours to help immunise over two billion children against polio. What a fantastic achievement!

Rotary Clubs are fully autonomous within the rules of procedure laid down by Rotary International. The world is divided into districts, and each Rotary district has a Governor. The Rotary International Board of Directors is based in Evanston, Illinois, and is in charge of continuing policy and, with staff, international financial management.

Each Rotary club has four main service committees.

The first is Membership Services Committee, which is an internal committee that looks after the running of the club, its future officers and its social activities. It also publishes the club bulletin and is one of the main executive committees of any Rotary Club.

People often think the next most important committee is the Community Service Committee, which organises charitable events. It also adopts roads to maintain, plants trees in barren areas and makes suggestions to local authorities about providing amenities.

The third committee is the Vocational Service Committee, which advocates good business standards. It also ensures that the youngsters who go into vocations are advised about opportunities, how to go about interview procedures and how to choose careers.

Last but not least (and to me the most important), is the International Service Committee, which helps communities in other countries with disasters, diseases and developing better facilities.

On a local level, Rotarians look for worthy causes in their own areas as well as disaster help overseas. If a club has a campaign to help build new classrooms in Africa, then the local Rotary club in that area is enlisted to make sure the money actually goes for the intended purpose. To facilitate this, Rotary has the largest charitable foundation in the world, the Rotary Foundation, which dispenses $95 million each year. Although this is administered from the head office in Evanston, Illinois, the beneficiaries or the need is usually identified by a local club. The foundation will then make matching grants towards such projects. The foundation is also the world's largest private provider of international education scholarships. It funds more than 1,000 students annually to study overseas and act as cultural ambassadors. Rotary also partners with eight prestigious universities around the globe to educate mid-career professionals in peace and conflict resolution.

❖ 71 ❖

Joining Rotary

I WAS INVITED TO JOIN the Rotary Club of Newcastle-under-Lyme, and when the invitation came, I was very pleased to accept. Because of my background, I have always been active on the International Service Committee from the time I joined to my later membership with Rotary Club of Jersey.

As explained in earlier chapters of this book, my first involvement with Rotary was at the age of 11 when I came in a Kinder Transport from Czechoslovakia to England in 1938. Rotarians Gilbert and Gladys Heywood of Bury in Lancashire "adopted" me. Gilbert Heywood's classification was a music shop proprietor. As part of their humanitarian and Rotary service, they agreed to take me into their home until I was at least 18. As it turned out, I was there for less than a year. I was one of the fortunate few from these children's transports whose parents were still able to escape before the Second World War started. I was reunited with them in 1939 and went to live with them.

My invitation to join the Newcastle-under-Lyme Rotary Club came when I was active as a committee member of the Newcastle-under-Lyme Chamber of Trade. There, I had met a men's clothing shop proprietor, Keith Saunders, who owned a shop by the name of Marsdens in Newcastle, and he put my name forward. In those days, the procedure was quite strict. You weren't allowed to know that you'd been nominated until a ballot had been taken amongst all members to see whether they would accept you as a member. Also, before nomination, you were asked to attend an information committee where the aims of Rotary were explained. It was a secret ballot, done on the black ball principle. If one black ball appeared in the voting basket, then the matter went no further and you were not told anything. I was accepted. Many years later, when I was the President of the club and had access to previous minutes, I found out that I had been nominated much earlier but had one black ball in the basket. I also found out, since he told me later, that the black ball came from a local photographic shop owner. Although I was not nominated as a photographic shop proprietor, he thought another member of a similar classification ought not to be a member of his club. This Rotarian, Jim Wain, became a very good friend and customer of mine in subsequent years. From a bulletin I received from the Newcastle-under-Lyme club, he is now the longest-serving member of the Newcastle club.

Now a member of Rotary, I immediately got interested in the International Service Committee. It wasn't long before I was elected chairman of this Committee. Keith Saunders and I remained friends until he retired and went to live in Bournemouth. He eventually became the President of the Newcastle Rotary in 1970/71. He handed over to me the Presidential chain of office the following year. I organised quite a number of international events. In particular, I pulled together non-British visitors and area residents and held evenings where they showed their national costumes and performed some cultural activities. We also used those opportunities to collect funds for international charities.

During my time in the Newcastle-under-Lyme club, I did a lot of international business travel. One of Rotary's privileges is, once you are a member of one club, you are automatically allowed to attend any other Rotary Club in the world. I made very extensive use of that privilege. Wherever I was in the world, I always made a point of going to a luncheon or evening meeting of the local club. I got to know many other Rotarians in this way.

Although all Rotary Clubs basically work to the same rules and goals, there are tremendous cultural differences between clubs in different countries. Time keeping especially reflects the culture of the country. A Japanese club will start exactly at the prescribed starting time and finish exactly at the prescribed finishing time— usually one hour later. But Spanish clubs never start at the prescribed time, and members will come to the meetings an hour after the published starting time. The end of the meeting could be at any time. The status of Rotarians in Japan is thought to be much higher than in the United States. Big, national corporation chairmen are driven to their Rotary Club meetings in company chauffer-driven limousines. Top corporate executives in Japan are usually quite old. The average age of Rotarians in Japan is much higher than in other countries, although that is starting to change. The main club in Tokyo, which has over 400 members, has a multi-language translation system for their meetings. You use a little transistor receiver on which you dial your language, and you get the speeches instantly translated. Some of these old company chairmen doze off during Rotary meetings—quite a common occurrence. At many Rotary Clubs in the United States, they sing a Rotary song at every meeting. At some clubs in Japan, they do so too, and you'll see these old company chairmen standing up there miming in English the Rotary Club songs. I thought this quite funny, as this singing is not practised in Europe.

I eventually became president of the Rotary Club of Newcastle-under-Lyme for 1971/72 having joined the club in 1964. The Rotary Club of Newcastle-under-Lyme also made me an honorary life member when I attended their charter anniversary in 2003 which was held at Keele University.

In 1980 when I left the UK to reside in Jersey I was able to continue my Rotary service by becoming a member of the Rotary Club of Jersey.

At the Presidential handover dinner of the Rotary Club of Jersey in 2006 I was presented with a certificate to celebrate my (over) 40 years of Rotary service. Additionally I received a certificate to show that a tree had been planted in my name in the Pestalozzi Village Rotary forest to mark the occasion.

❖ 72 ❖

Travelling the Rotary Connections

I MADE FRIENDS IN ALL the countries I visited because I always made a point of attending a local club meeting whether on business or on holiday. Often, the classification system was a great advantage. You could ask which member is the local photographic dealer, the local photographer, or the local photographic importer and then sit by somebody with a common interest. When I visited the main Rotary Club in Hawaii, I asked the same question and was introduced to the Hawaiian Islands regional manager for Kodak. He was wearing a white suit—a splendid-looking man. He asked me how long I was staying, and I said just another day. He put at my disposal a company chauffeur-driven car to show me around the island on the following day, which I gratefully accepted. On another occasion I was with my friends, the Johnsons, on holiday, this time in Mombasa. Gordon and I went to a meeting, and a local Rotarian invited us all to his house on Sunday and took us out on his boat. Friendships on an international basis started in that way. Similarly, when Rotarians came to Newcastle, or later to Jersey, we were happy to reciprocate and provide the same sort of facilities that were accorded to us by quite different Rotarians elsewhere. The Rotary movement is like a family; there is automatic connection of understanding. This is one of the great pleasures and benefits of Rotary.

When I transferred my residence from Newcastle to Jersey, I was invited to join the Rotary Club of Jersey. I was happy to accept. I had already, as was my privilege, attended Rotary Club meetings in Jersey during holidays, so I knew many of the local Rotarians and the transition was almost seamless. Once again, I took pleasure in accepting responsibility for many of the international-oriented events. Because I then had more time on my hands, I did quite a lot more than in the previous club. For a number of years I organised a fellowship visit to different countries in Europe, and this became a much looked forward to, pleasurable occasion every year, usually in February or March. I organised trips to places where Rotarians would not, at that time, normally go to on their own—Moscow, Vienna, Prague, Znojmo, Istanbul, and Berlin, all in days after the so-called Iron Curtain finally came down. I usually tried and often succeeded in arranging a visit to and a reception at the British Embassy. I tried to receive an official invitation for our members, particularly since Jersey doesn't have its own embassies around the world. As the British Foreign Office looks after the interests of Jersey in its embassies, I always took the opportunity to remind the ambassador or the commercial attaché or whoever hosted the reception, that it was part of their duty to look after the interests of Jersey. I also always presented them with a Jersey flag, which none of them previously had, to put into the office. The international fellowship part was a mandatory meeting with the local Rotary club which I prearranged and which invariably was most interesting and convivial. Then we usually did some sightseeing and cultural trips like visiting the Bolshoi Ballet in Moscow, a side trip to St. Petersburg, and all these were most memorable occasions.

Most trips, despite careful advance planning and meticulous detailed instructions to participants, had their "incidents" which remained as oft repeated permanent trip recollections. Probably the best remembered sequence was on the 1998 Moscow trip. The booking was done through a specialist Russian tour operator in London. My contact was a young Russian woman who also accompanied us to Moscow and back from St. Petersburg, handing us over to very capable local guides once we had arrived in those two cities. All the flights were with British Airways (BA) and were via London, where my friends, Gordon and Mary Johnson, also joined the trip. Russian visas had been obtained well before time. These were separate documents, as opposed to being stamped into the holder's passport. There were about 30 of us in the party, consisting of members from both the Jersey Rotary clubs and their wives. About one hour before the arrival time in Moscow, the wife of one Rotarian, who shall remain nameless but is well-known in both Rotary clubs, came to me and said, "Charles, we have a problem. We have left our visas at home."

I consulted the senior stewardess and our Russian speaking guide, who both told me that no one had ever succeeded in entering Russia without a visa. The normal procedure was for them to be put on the next plane back to anywhere in the UK. Quite coincidentally the BA Moscow station manager also happened to be on board. I persuaded him to get the Captain to radio ahead and get one of his staff to start negotiations with the immigration officers to try and make an exception and admit our unhappy couple. On arrival, they were whisked off to immigration with our Russian-speaking guide to assist.

The rest of us went through normally and waited for our luggage at the carousel. When it stopped, the only people whose luggage had come through were the Johnsons' who had boarded in London. Clearly, ours had not been transferred from the Jersey flight. So I had 28 people with only the travelling clothes they stood up in and the next aircraft from London not due for 24 hours. In that time, we were scheduled for the reception at the British Embassy and the festive fellowship meeting with the Moscow Kremlin Rotary club. So I negotiated with the BA station manager that he would sign the bill at the airport shop, and that's where we all went next, holding the coach arranged to take us to the hotel.

In the meantime, I was updated with reports about the progress of our visa-less couple. It looked quite hopeful, as the airport immigration had submitted the matter for a decision to the Russian Foreign Ministry in town. Well, the scene in the airport shop was hilarious. Everyone went for toiletries and then underwear and shirts. The only ladies knickers available were big Russian sizes and would take two of our ladies! The faster shoppers started checking out, and the rouble totals started mounting up to the point where the shop manager consulted British Airways to make sure that the signed bills would be met. The BA station manager, wisely, had gone home, and his number two came up and just in time stopped some of us who were in jeans and no jackets from buying trousers and jackets. He made the ridiculous suggestion that the coach into town should stop at a clothes hire shop and we should hire the necessary items from there. I refused this offer and told him a substantial claim would follow. I then learned that no answer had yet been received from the Russian Foreign Ministry. As it was time for the airport immigration man handling the case to go home, he closed the office and British Airways had to put them on the next plane home. I will leave you to surmise what happened to their non arrived luggage.

Our huge central hotel, right on the corner of Red Square, had four entrances. Too late, we realised that the one we had been dropped off at by the coach, was for much lower grades of room. We all had to reassemble and find another entrance. By the time our luggage caught up with us, we had been to the aforementioned functions and the ballet in our jeans and Russian shirts and the ladies in their oversized knickers. Despite that, we had a great trip.

I was delegated to make the claim on BA on behalf of everyone rather than doing it individually. I was able to get a free return ticket for each person to anywhere on the BA European network and no deductions for the Moscow airport shop purchases.

The overnight train trip to St. Petersburg was an exciting adventure. Boarding time was not until after midnight, so I arranged an evening meal in a Moscow cellar night club. We got a room for the remaining party of 28 and drank the health of all absent friends many times to the music of a gipsy band whose hands had to be crossed with more than silver. We were all told to lock ourselves in the sleeper compartments on the train and not to open the door to anyone until the train stopped in St. Petersburg. We all arrived safely and spent the day visiting the renowned State Hermitage museum and other sites.

When the Iron Curtain finally came down, it was possible for Rotary clubs to be formed again in Czechoslovakia. So, I persuaded the Rotary Club of Jersey to adopt and help with the formation of a Rotary Club in Czechoslovakia. Rotary International allocated to us the interim Rotary Club of Znojmo which is in southern Moravia just north of the Austrian border—in distance nearer to Vienna than to Prague. I took up contact. At that time, one of the main problems of the formation of Rotary Clubs was that the people who were keen to become Rotarians just had no money to be able to pay the levies required by Rotary. So one of the many duties required of a supporting club was to help financially with membership fees and other items and also to review and help with Rotary procedures. In fact, the Rotary Club of Geras-Waldviertel in an Austrian town just across the border nominated one of their members, a local pharmacist by the name of Winfried Leisser who went to their weekly meetings and guided them in Rotary procedures. We, the Rotary Club of Jersey, provided the backup and financial wherewithal. We also did a fellowship visit when about 20 Rotarians from Jersey visited Znojmo. Znojmo is also known as the gherkin capital of the world because the area grows small cucumbers that are made into gherkins (the Americans call them dill pickles). It also has many vineyards. On another occasion we were there for their wine harvest festival.

Jersey Rotarians have problems pronouncing Znojmo, so I had to teach them. It's not a very large town; it has a population of 37,000, but is growing. We made good friends there and flew to visit them first. A number of us flew commercially to attend their charter meeting when their club was officially given the charter to become the Rotary Club of Znojmo. We took them a number of presents including a President's chain of office and gavel. The son of a Rotarian, David Reynolds, carried a special cake with a Rotary wheel on top, all the way from Jersey. Peter Marek, of Czech origin himself, kindly made the cake. At the time, he was the head chef at the L'Horizon Hotel in Jersey.

We stayed in Znojmo for some time. We had a civic reception and brought the greetings to their Mayor from our Rotary District Governor and also from Sir Peter Crill, Bailiff of Jersey, who sent one of his special medallions. We left with them an invitation to come and visit us in Jersey. Not only did they accept that invitation, but every member of their club with their spouses wanted to come. Again they had no money to do that, so we funded their journey to Jersey and home-hosted them. For most of them, it was their first experience of the West, and they had a really good time. When we saw them off on the boat, back to St. Malo where they got their coach back to Czechoslovakia, we started a Mexican wave on the shoreline and they did the Mexican wave from the boat. This signalled some very good friendships had been made. To this day, there is still an exchange of young people between the two communities.

For the activities I led to foster the formation of the Rotary Club of Znojmo to when they finally got their charter, they made me an honorary member of that club.

◆ 73 ◆

The Flying Rotarians

THE INTERNATIONAL FELLOWSHIP OF FLYING Rotarians (IFFR) is one of many recreational fellowships within Rotary. It is open to any Rotarian interested in aviation, but most of its members are General Aviation or professional pilots. The world is divided into the Flying Rotarian regions of Europe, the United States, the Far East and Australasia. Each of those regions is further subdivided into sections. Europe is subdivided into the Scandinavian, Iberian, French, German/Austrian, United Kingdom, Swiss and Italian sections. The United States has northern, central, southern, western and eastern subdivisions. Each one of those sections has its own President and organised fly-ins so everybody can meet for long weekends. These are usually organised at a small airfield by a local Flying Rotarian who knows the area and are purely social fellowship occasions with an interesting sight-seeing programme. Usually, 10 to 30 aircraft will attend a fly-in. In most instances, the local Rotary Club arranges a joint meeting. It is true Rotary fellowship.

Wherever I visit a Rotary Club, I give a little talk on the Flying Rotarians and other fellowships. I then ask if there is anybody in that club who has an interest in aviation or, better still, is a private or professional pilot. In this way I have recruited a countless number of new members for IFFR. When I went to stay for the winter on Marco Island and attended the Marco Island Rotary club, I did the same there. I found that there were four members there who had pilot's licenses, had previously held pilots licenses, or were interested in aviation through their spouses. I was able to make four new members. Since then, I've discovered another pilot, and hopefully Marco Rotary will then have five Flying Rotarians. It's one of the aims of IFFR to find pilots so members with another common interest besides Rotary can join this fellowship. In practical terms it means that they can take part in fly-ins and fly-abouts and get an annual directory of members. If they fly to most parts of the world, the directory enables them to find a Flying Rotarian there to make contact with. In the Jersey Rotary club, we have several Flying Rotarians. When the last Lieutenant Governor, Air Chief Marshal Sir John Cheshire, KBE, CB, came to Jersey and visited the Rotary Club of Jersey, he was made, as is a tradition, an honorary member of the club. I took the opportunity of making him an honorary member of the Flying Rotarians as well. He proudly wore the Rotary Badge with wings, the special insignia of IFFR, on Rotarian occasions in Jersey.

I'm proud that my Jersey Rotary Club provided two World Presidents of the Flying Rotarians—me in 1986 through 1988 followed by Rotarian Graeme Le Quesne, a pharmacist, who was elected World President in 1999 through 2001. I thought we were unique, but there is a Rotary Club in Dallas, which has also provided two World Presidents.

Each year at the Rotary International Convention, to which all Rotarians are entitled to go, the Flying Rotarians meet for their annual general meeting, their annual dinner dance and to fly about together in that area for some days after the convention. Many Flying Rotarians attend the Rotary International Conventions, not mainly for the convention, but because of the opportunities to meet and enjoy the fellowship of Flying Rotarians from all over the world. I have attended 17 Rotary International Conventions in the following towns and countries:

    1982–Dallas, Texas, USA
    1984–Birmingham, England
    1987–Munich, Germany
    1988–Philadelphia, Pennsylvania, USA
    1990–Portland, Oregon, USA
    1992–Orlando, Florida, USA
    1993–Melbourne, Victoria, Australia
    1995–Nice, France

1996–Calgary, Alberta, Canada
1997–Glasgow, Scotland
1998–Indianapolis, Indiana, USA
1999–Singapore, Singapore
2001–San Antonio, Texas, USA
2002–Barcelona, Spain
2003–Brisbane, Queensland, Australia
2005–Chicago, Illinois
2006–Copenhagen/Malmo, Denmark/Sweden

In all of those, since 1987, we've either had a pre-convention or a post-convention fly-about. In 1999 since Singapore is not large enough for a fly-about, we flew commercially to Darwin in Australia and did it from there.

1987—Munich, Germany

The convention was in Munich during my term as IFFR World President. Four Flying Rotarians flew across the Atlantic to Jersey in their own single engine aircraft from the United States. They did not have enough fuel to do it in one hop; they did it via Newfoundland, Greenland, Iceland, North of Scotland and down to Jersey. Their arrival in Jersey was a great occasion.

Other Flying Rotarians joined us at the pre-convention get together in Jersey, and we all then flew together to Munich. On the way, I overheard an air traffic controller who was quite puzzled about all these private aircraft suddenly flying in his airspace to Munich. He asked what's going on. We explained to him that we were all flying to a Rotary International Convention in Munich.

In June 1986, a year ahead of the Munich RI convention I made plans for hotel accommodation for the IFFR members. There was a Swiss section fly-in near Lake Geneva at an airfield called Sion, and on the return from there, with Rotarian Ron Piggot, I stopped over in Munich to find a hotel for the following year's convention for the Flying Rotarians. The big fly-in to Munich, under my IFFR World Presidency, became the first Rotary International Convention where the Flying Rotarians were able to stay in one hotel, resulting in a lot of good fellowship. I had set a pattern which others tried to follow at IR conventions. The hotel I had found was on the outskirts of Munich and was in a brewery the owner of which was also a Rotarian, so we had it made. We also held our annual dinner there and I was most surprised during the evenings proceedings to be presented with a Paul Harris Fellowship award for services to IFFR. It was the first time in my life that I was speechless.

1988—Philadelphia, Pennsylvania, USA

Three of us from the Jersey Rotary Club—Graeme Le Quesne, David Reynolds and I—planned to visit, before the convention, our twinned club in New Jersey. They arranged to pick us up on arrival at Newark in a helicopter! We stopped over in New Jersey, and visited Flying Rotarian Dan Nalven and his Rotarian wife Barbara. Dan kindly flew us in his Cessna 210, from his local airport in Westchester, on a low level trip. It was a most exciting trip down the Hudson River, around the Statue of Liberty, and back up again to Westchester.

1990—Portland, Oregon, USA

We arranged to fly together with one of the first, if not the first, lady Flying Rotarian, Marlyn McClaskey. She had a Piper PA32, and we flew with her from her home airfield near San Francisco up to Oregon for the convention. During that time, we had a most interesting visit, organised by a Flying Rotarian, round the Boeing factory in Seattle watching B747's being built.

1992—Orlando, Florida, USA

The post-convention trip with the Flying Rotarians was to Pensacola, the U.S. Navy Air Base on the Florida panhandle. They didn't want us to land there, so we landed at a small airfield just inside Alabama on the gulf shore. I had rented a Cessna 182RG aircraft at Merritt Island, Florida for that trip. Our annual dinner was on the deck of a simulated aircraft carrier in the Naval base.

1993—Melbourne, Victoria, Australia

A very memorable Rotary fly-about was after the Melbourne RI Convention in Australia. I was fortunate enough to be able to rent exactly the same plane that I own, a Piper Seneca II registration

VH-IED. This trip lasted from 24th of May 1993, to 5th of June 1993, and took us from Melbourne to Mildura to Leigh Creek to Coober Peddy which is the opal center of the world. More opals are mined there than anywhere else in the world and everything, even the hotel, is underground. Then we flew to Uluru, the aboriginal name for the famous Ayers Rock. Of course we flew several times in the mandatory figure 8 around the big rock. Then we finally landed in Alice Springs, our destination. We stayed three days, and on the way back we went to a really nicely-named airport called Oodnadatta, then to the famous mining town of Broken Hill, then to Bendigo and back to Melbourne.

That was an interesting trip because for quite a large area it was over what was called the Australian Outback where for hundreds of miles you see nothing at all. Before we were allowed to take the trip, I went on a half-day survival course. We also had to take with us survival gear, plenty of water, an axe, a shotgun and signalling equipment. The signalling equipment consisted of mirrors. We were told that such is the Australian rescue service that, providing you filed your flight plan properly, giving a time after which, if they hadn't heard from you, they should start searching for you, they guaranteed to find you within 48 hours. You just had to survive that long.

1995—Nice, France

In June 1995, we took another Flying Rotarian trip to the Mediterranean, this time with Gordon and Mary Johnson as passengers. We went from Jersey to Limoges, which is the pottery centre of France. From there, we went to Cannes. When I came to do the pre-landing checks there, we didn't get the three green lights even though the activating lever was down. We possibly had an undercarriage problem. We flew past the tower and they told us they couldn't see any wheels down. We then let them down with the emergency lever, which, on a Seneca, works on a gravity system and the next time we flew low past the tower they could see the wheels down. They can tell that they are down, but can't tell whether they are locked or not, so it's still nice to do a very soft landing in case they are not locked. We landed without a problem.

All the times I've had undercarriage problems, either the lamps or a micro switch contact was not working. Thankfully, I've never done a belly landing or a collapsed-undercarriage landing.

From Cannes, we went on to the island of Elba, famous because Napoleon was exiled there. We visited a lot of Napoleonic historical spots, museums and the house where he lived. From there, we went on to Alghero, then Bastia and then back through Perigueux, France, which is famous for French foie gras, a delicacy produced from goose liver. To get more and more goose liver, they force feed the geese by stuffing food down their throats. Many people think it's very cruel, but they still eat it.

1996—Calgary, Alberta, Canada

This post convention fly-about was to be to Alaska and back. Gordon and Mary Johnson were to be our passengers. We had pre-booked a rental aircraft. However when I went to inspect it, I found it to be in such a poor condition and without supporting maintenance paperwork that I refused to take it. No second choice was available. So we saw all the other participating aircraft off and decided to do our own thing. We rented a four-wheel drive car and planned a trip to Vancouver over the Rocky Mountains taking in Banff, Lake Louise and Whistler on the way. When we got to Vancouver and had done our sight-seeing there, I thought there might be a cheap Air Alaska flight and we could join up for a couple of days with our Flying Rotarian party. So I phoned the airline call centre and asked if they had any specials to Anchorage. The agent asked me how many in our party. He then offered a buddy fare where one person pays the full fare and any other additional ones pay only $50 return. However he said we don't fly from Vancouver only from Seattle. We decided to go and drove across the Canadian/US border, picking up the reserved tickets at a travel agent on the way, left the car at a Holiday Inn where we were going to stay on our return, took their courtesy car to the airport and made it to our original fly-about destination. Everyone was surprised to see us. What a great experience.

1997—Glasgow, Scotland

The post-convention fly-about was to one of the Scottish islands called Stornoway. Our journey took us from Jersey to Coventry to Prestwick to Stornoway to Inverness to Aberdeen to Edinburgh to Southampton and back to Jersey. In Stornaway airport they told us that we had been the biggest group of aircraft that had arrived there since the second world war. Local Rotarian Norman Macleod had arranged the programme which included a tour of the island and everyone digging their own block of peat. The day finished off with a typical Scottish Ceilidh (pronounced Kalee). The food was stupendous, the drinks kept flowing and the dancing was wild. On that occasion, we gave a lift to American Flying Rotarians Marlyn and Larry McClaskey, as they sometimes gave us a lift in their aircraft in the U.S. We sometimes fly with other Rotarians or I simply rent an aircraft and fly it myself.

1998—Indianapolis, Indiana, USA

This gave the opportunity for the McClaskeys, who we had given lifts to after the Glasgow convention, to let us be their passengers. Instead of us flying to Indianapolis commercially, the McClaskeys invited us to stay with them near San Francisco and fly with them in their aircraft halfway across the United States to go to the convention. We flew commercially to San Francisco and then flew with Marlyn and Larry from Petaluma, their home airfield in California, to Cedar City, Utah, to the Grand Canyon in Arizona and from there to Colorado Springs. There, we disembarked from their aircraft. Marlyn and Larry flew on to see some friends before the convention, and we stayed at the home of Flying Rotarian Don Bymaster, who lived in Colorado Springs.

We then flew with Don Bymaster and his wife, Lorena, in their Mooney 203 aircraft from Colorado Springs to St. Joseph, Missouri, and then to Mount Comfort, Indiana, which was near the convention. I then attended the convention, the usual IFFR dinner dance, and the annual general meeting. After the convention, I rented a Piper PA32 Lance and piloted this for the post convention fly-about. That took us from Mount Comfort to Muncie to Dayton and Moraine, Ohio, to Mackinac Island, Michigan, which is near the Canadian border. From there, we did a day trip on a train across the border into Canada.

We then flew to Chipawa County Airport and from there to Oshkosh, which is famous for the biggest aviation show in the world. This wasn't on at the time we were there but, nevertheless, we still got the feel of it. It's a huge airfield, and for the first time ever I stayed in a motel for aircraft as well as for cars. You taxied your aircraft right up to the building and left it in front of the bedroom as you would with a car. You took your cases out of the aircraft into the air motel—an unusual experience, possibly one you could only have in the United States.

From there we flew to Meigs Field in Chicago, which is on the lake front. Meigs is famous because it is the default airfield on the Microsoft Flight Simulator programme. Millions of people have bought the programme, and the airfield that came up first was Meigs. That is, until Mayor Richard M. Daley one night surreptitiously had the runway dug up and closed it down permanently. I've tried to land there several times on the computer, never very properly, but I had no problem landing there in an actual aircraft. It was the most thrilling experience to make your approach right alongside the level of the Chicago city skyscrapers. That's where we gave the aircraft back to the rental company and went sightseeing in Chicago. We also visited Evanston, the headquarters of Rotary International again, before flying home.

1999—Singapore, Singapore

Singapore is not a country that you can do a fly-about in because it only has one airfield and its territory is indeed very small. So the IFFR committee decided we would attend the convention as normal Rotarians and then fly commercially to Darwin in Northern Australia. We would all rent aircraft there, except the Australian Flying Rotarians, who had their own planes. I rented a Cessna 210NT, a high wing plane, ideal for sight-seeing.

The Australian section had organised a great fly-about in Northern and Northwestern Australia that took us from Darwin to Kununurra to a small airfield called Drisdale River. That was a private ranch type of air strip in the middle of nowhere. Their nearest neighbour was 150 miles away. Small aircraft land there, so the air strip has a small restaurant and gift shop for that purpose. The children of the proprietor and the workers do their learning on the radio. If they need medical aid, they call on the radio for the flying doctor. Interesting to note, they use helicopters for herding. They have a lot of cattle on this huge, many thousand-acre ranch, and when they want to sell cattle, they herd them together with helicopters. Some countries use cowboys on horses; they use helicopters.

From Drisdale River, we went to Broom, a very famous place. It has many songs about it and is the Japanese pearl-diving centre. They use Japanese for pearl-diving off the coasts of Australia. In the cemetery, there's a special section for Japanese pearl divers who didn't make it home. From Broom, where we spent some days, we went to Hall's Creek and from there to Katherine and back to Darwin.

2001—San Antonio, Texas, USA

The post-convention trip was fantastic. I rented a Cessna 172SP, a very recently-made model for a change. It was extremely well-equipped navigation and avionics-wise, and we flew from San Antonio's Stinson airfield to Big Spring, Texas, Midland to Carlsbad, New Mexico. All these places we stayed overnight and the local Rotary Club entertained us. Carlsbad was particularly interesting because they have a cave inhabited by thousands of bats. There is one air vent where they come out at a certain time of the evening in a huge swarm, and they go on to whatever it is they do. It has become a tourist attraction. There was an amphitheatre around this air vent where the bats come out—a frightening thing to watch, but interesting nonetheless.

From there, we flew to Santa Fe and from there to a place called Farmington Four Corners Regional Airport. On the GPS, I inserted a mapping point and flew over Four Corners, the only point in the United States where four States all meet. They are Utah, Colorado, Arizona and New Mexico. Then we flew from there up to Bryce Canyon airfield where the altitude is 7,586 feet above sea level. The consideration of density altitude for landing and take-off distance came into being again, but it was no problem because the runway is 7,400 feet long. It was a fantastic place to be, to look down into the canyons. We did quite a bit of sightseeing by coach there as well. The journey back took us through Santa Fe, Amarillo and back to Stinson, Texas.

2002—Barcelona, Spain

Our Flying Rotarian friends from New York, Dan and Barbara Nalven, came to Jersey to be our passengers in my Seneca II N37US for that trip. We went from Jersey to San Sebastian in north eastern Spain for a tea and pee stop and to refuel. We flew from there to Sabadell, the nearest general aviation airfield to the convention in Barcelona. The post-convention fly-about started from Sabadell and went to Granada and from there to Seville and from there to Cascais, Portugal. During the Second World War, Cascais became a refuge for several kings and heads of European countries. With them came many other famous politicians, writers and actors. Important exiles include the Duke of Windsor, King Umberto of Italy, Princess Joanna of Italy, King Carol II of Romania, Prince Juan of Spain, Count Henri of France, some members of the Hapsburg family and Regent Horthy of Hungary.

Cascais has very unhappy memories for us because we lost an aircraft there. The crash caused the death of its pilot, my very good friend, Graham Le Quesne from the Jersey Rotary Club. That year, he was the World President of the Flying Rotarians.

Also in that unfortunate accident, his three passengers met their death. Graeme had run into bad weather after taking off from Cascais and decided to return. To the date of this book going to press, the Portuguese authorities have not yet published an accident investigation report, which normally in most countries comes out within about a year of the accident happening. We're now over four years away from that time.

The planned small destination airfield after Cascais was having bad weather, so I decided not to fly there and chose Lisbon instead, near the small airfield, because they were just above limits as far as weather was concerned. When we got closer, the broadcast weather had deteriorated, and I decided to divert. I went north, straight to an airfield called Santiago, which was back in Spain. There, we met up with a number of others who had also diverted there and heard about the overdue aircraft and then the terrible news about the crash. We ended the fly-about and went back to Jersey via San Sebastian, and from there Dan and Barbara went back to the United States.

2003—Brisbane, Queensland, Australia

Before the convention in Australia many of the IFFR participants met in New Zealand where a trip of both islands was arranged for us in a PBY Catalina amphibian flying boat. The post convention fly-about from 5th June to 14th June started at Brisbane's Archer Field where I rented a Cessna 172 VH-BYR and flew north to Roma and then to Longreach in Queensland. This is the airfield where Qantas (Queensland and Northern Territories Aerial Services) started and they have the Founders Outback Museum there now with an ex-service Qantas Boeing 747 on static display. If things go according to plan the first Boeing 707 used by Qantas will join it. We continued to Hughenden and Cairns where we did a couple of night stops. Then on to Hamilton Island on the Great Barrier Reef where we also stayed to enjoy the great outdoor activities. Then back to Brisbane via Gladstone.

2005—Chicago, Illinois

We had planned to do the post convention fly-about with Dan and Barbara Nalden. Unfortunately Barbara was due for an operation and they had to cancel. We could only get seats in another aircraft, a Cessna 337 with Fred and Chris Newman from Niagara Falls so we flew there commercially from Chicago and flew with them to Portland. Two days later we were all due to fly to the next stopover place, Groton–New London. There were about 22 IFFR aircraft on this fly-about. The weather at Groton was just above limits for an Instrument approach and those with an Instrument Rating decided to go. I went with Fred in his C337 N59N and we decided to fly it as a two crew operation with him flying on instruments and my monitoring him, counting down altitude and looking for the runway lights. They appeared just before we approached decision height and we landed safely and joined three other IFFR aircraft who had landed before us. When we arrived at the hotel we heard the that one of our aircraft had attempted the approach and having gone around for a second attempt, had crashed in the water short of the runway. Later we got the terrible news that two Flying Rotarians and their wives did not survive the accident. We held a service for them the next morning and although the others continued on the fly-about we decided not to and went to spend the balance of the time before the planned return to Jersey in Nassau. It has now been decided that in future fly-abouts no one would depart if the next destination airport was not able to accept VFR arrivals. Participants with Instrument ratings could file IFR plans for the journey but could not go unless everyone was able to go.

2006—Copenhagen, Denmark.

This was the handover, at the AGM (Annual General Meeting), of the IFFR World President's chain from Angus Clark of the UK section to Brian Souter of the New Zealand section. Angus, together with his Flying Rotarian wife Alisma, had done a tremendous job during his two-year stint and had probably visited more sections all over the world than any previous World President. The annual dinner was well attended and as usual I had been asked to MC the proceedings. I had also invited three members of the Marco Island Rotary Club who were attending the convention to join us for this function. They were President Linda Keutmann and incoming President Kelly Townsend and incoming President of the Marco breakfast club Mary Ann Kline.

For the post convention fly-about I had invited Marco Rotarian Wade Keller and his wife Sue to be my passengers. Because Wade is also my publisher of this book, on the way back I took them to my old abode in the Potteries and to Jersey. I started the trip in Jersey, overnighted in Eelde in northern Holland and then flew to Roskilde, the Copenhagen airfield, for the start of the fly-about. We then flew to Vestervick in Sweden near Stockholm where we left the planes and, after a city tour, all boarded a luxurious overnight ferry to Helsinki in Finland and returned on it the next night having done our sight-seeing during the day. The next leg took us to the mountain airfield of Fagerness in Norway where we stayed in a huge mountain hotel with lots of facilities including an evening meal of reindeer stew in a tepee complete with local entertainment. Our last port of call was a landing at Sindal in Denmark and then by coach to Skagen, the northernmost point in Denmark where the Baltic Sea turbulently meets the North Sea. The journey home was via Eelde and Coventry to Jersey. The Kellers enjoyed every minute and Sue took lots of photographs everywhere.

❖ 74 ❖

For the Love of Flying

IN 1978, WELL BEFORE ATTENDING my first Rotary International Convention, I participated in my first IFFR fly-about. From 23rd of June to 2nd of July 1978, we flew a very good IFFR fly-around the Mediterranean. Starting off in Manchester, we stopped over in Jersey, then flew to Cannes in France, where we had arranged to meet the other participants. There we met for the first time Rotarian John Ritchie and his wife Mary. They were the only ones on that trip who are still members of IFFR now. Indeed John filled brilliantly almost all offices in the UK section of IFFR. From there, it was to Ajaccio in Corsica, Olbia in Sardinia, Palermo in Sicily, Tunis in North Africa, Catania in Sicily, Pisa in Italy and then to Venice, Italy, before returning back to Manchester via Nice and Jersey. It was quite an extensive and very interesting fly-about. In Tunis many of us bartered for the traditional carpets varying in size according to space available in aircraft. Most of the 20 aircraft taking part flew VFR, but since I was instrument rated I did most of the legs filing an instrument flight plan. Therefore, I didn't necessarily follow the same route as some of the others. On the trip from Catania, I had flight planned non-stop to our next destination, Venice Lido.

When we flew into Italian airspace, the controller suddenly came on the air and said, "You cannot go on the next planned airway because we have military exercises."

So I said, "Well, can we change levels?"

He said, "No, you just can't go that way. What are your intentions?"

They're not really bothered. They're just sitting there in a very comfortable chair, while you are in the air with flight plan difficulties, and that particular route is now no longer available to you. This was in the days long before GPS when one could just press a "direct to" button and it would tell you what course to take. I realised that we would have to go a long way around to get to our destination and that I did not have sufficient fuel to do that. I decided we'd better ask to come down and re-fuel. I picked the nearest airfield to our position which was Pisa, famous for the Leaning Tower. I said to the controller that we want to divert to and refuel at Pisa. He said that wasn't possible because it was a military airfield, and again he asked what my intentions were. I said my intentions were to land there whatever sort of airport it was. He handed me over to the tower there, and we made a landing.

When we landed, we were welcomed by an armoured car with a machine gun mounted at the front. This car and several other military vehicles escorted us off the runway. We followed this convoy to a military area. The officer in charge asked me why we landed there. I told him his military exercises had prevented us from going the planned route and we now had to get some fuel, which I hoped they had for us. It turned out that, although the airfield was controlled by the military, it did have some civilian traffic at another part of the airfield.

The commanding officer arrived in a Jeep. He had "wings" on his uniform jacket, so I knew he was a pilot and therefore would be sympathetic. He was, but he still insisted on checking the fuel left in our tanks to see that we weren't lying and that we hadn't just landed to see the Leaning Tower of Pisa. Fuel was then provided at the civilian end of the airfield, and off we went and continued our flight to Venice Lido, where we joined the rest of the group. I did an extra unplanned landing on that particular trip.

That trip was the first European-organised Flying Rotarian fly-about. Rotarian Francis Willinger organised it. He was a very ardent Rotarian. He organised this fly-about brilliantly. Unfortunately, he died in an air crash a few years later. His club had organised flights for deprived children in the Swansea area, just to give them the new experience of flying. Fortunately, none of the children were hurt.

Because I liked and enjoyed that trip so much, we did another Mediterranean trip in June 1979 with my Rotarian friend, Gordon Johnson and his wife Mary. That was not a Rotary fly-about other than that there happened to be two Rotarians in my plane. That one took us from Manchester to Jersey to Cannes, France, to Catania, Sicily, to Malta, to Catania, Sicily, to Rome Ciampino, to Bordeaux, to Jersey and back to Manchester. It was on this trip in Malta that the obtaining of aviation fuel with the help of the Prime Minister of Malta took place which I mentioned in a previous chapter.

In June 1985, there was an IFFR fly-in to Venice. We flew from Jersey to take part in that and again landed at the little Venice Lido airfield. On the way, we landed at Nice and stayed with our Jersey Rotarian friends, Noel and Elizabeth Sayers at their home in Eze, which is near Nice. We then flew on and took them with us to Venice and also back to Jersey. When we got back to Jersey, the undercarriage wouldn't come down. It happens sometimes. On the Seneca if the hydraulic system fails, you've got an emergency back-up system that depends on good old gravity. When you pull a normally secured lever, the undercarriage drops down and locks. You still have to make sure that the wheels are down because they come down through the emergency system. Usually, what you are recommended to do is to fly low past the airport control tower so they can check from below and tell you that all three wheels are down. We landed without problems although, as at all airports when that happens, they did have fire engines standing by.

In June of l986, the German section of the Flying Rotarians organised a fly-in in the North Sea Islands known as the Friesian Islands, which are partly in Holland and partly in Germany. We flew from Jersey, had a stop over in Ostende, Belgium, and in Eelde, Holland, and then flew on to Borkum, which is one of these islands where we cleared German Customs. Then we flew on to the island of Juist, where the actual fly-in was held and where the first Rotarian chairman of the German section, Rotarian Theo Wupperman, sponsored a youth sport training home for deprived children from all over Germany. We spent a long weekend on this very nice island and then flew back to Jersey. The Friesian cattle are not quite as famous as the Jersey cattle, but the islands are known for their cattle.

Then, later in September of 1986, we flew all the way up to Norway where the Scandinavian section of the Flying Rotarians had their fly-in. We flew from Jersey up to Manchester to pick up our friends, Gordon and Mary Johnson, thence to Aberdeen in Scotland where we stayed overnight. The next day we flew across the long North Sea crossing, where for some of the time you are out of radio contact. Then on to Stavanger to clear Customs and from there to a little airfield at Hamar, which was where the chairman of the Scandinavian section had his home. On the way back, we stopped over in Oslo and back again via Stavanger for the North Sea crossing direct to Manchester and then to Jersey.

In November 1986, again with the Johnsons, we flew, commercially but still on a Rotarian occasion, to Mexico where Flying Rotarian Federico Compean had invited us to stay with him at his house in San Luis Potosi. Quite a number of American Flying Rotarians also flew in for that one. While there, we also flew, at great altitude and without oxygen, with Federico in his Cessna 210 to Puerto Vallarta. Also during this Mexican fly-in, on 20th of November 1986, in an air-conditioned Seneca II owned by a Californian Flying Rotarian Bob Langslet, we flew from San Luis Potosi to Monterrey, Mexico.

In June 1989, we did a Rotarian fly-in that the Italian section organised. We flew from Jersey to Limoges to Cannes to Venegono, North of Milan in Italy and back again via Cannes and Bordeaux.

In August of 1989, we did a trip to Denmark. That one was extremely well-organised by the Scandinavian section of IFFR, and it took us from Jersey to Hamburg to Odense where we spent a day, and visited the many reminders that it was the birthplace of Hans Christian Andersen and then to Billund where we stopped for the weekend. Billund is where the famous firm of LEGO produce their plastic bricks for children's building sets and where there is a huge exhibition of many items made with LEGO.

In February 1990, RIBI President Len Smith came to Jersey with our District Governor, and I gave them a flight round the northern French coast, Mont St. Michel and the Normandy landing beaches.

During a Photokina in Cologne, on 7th of October 1990, I was having dinner with my friend and ex-employee, Ian Rosewell. We discussed the fact that the reunification of East and West Germany had just been announced on the 3rd of October and it was therefore, presumably, possible to fly over what was East German airspace. We agreed to meet at Cologne airport the next morning. I arrived early in the morning only to find a note on my windshield, "See you in Berlin." As a result he was the first GA pilot to land in Berlin and I was the first GA light twin to land there. Previously East German airspace was limited to three air corridors, though restricted to British Airways, Air France and Pan Am. Flights to Berlin had been closed to General Aviation for 45 years. I still had to go through Customs in Berlin Schoenefeld in what had been East Berlin even though I had done an internal flight as they said they had not yet had any new instructions.

In April 1991, we had a holiday in St. Lucia in the Caribbean, which is the home of Flying Rotarian Peter Barnard. He had a Piper PA28 that he always readily rented to me. I did a lot of island flying there, and this particular year we flew to the island of St. Vincent.

Later in April 1991 I was able to fly to Prague for my first visit to Czechoslovakia in 43 years. By the end of the 1980s, the leader of the Soviet Union, Mikhail Gorbachev, had experimented with glasnost and perestroika. Emboldened Czech citizens demonstrated against the communist regime. One of the demonstration leaders was a well-known dissident, Vaclav Havel, who became the first President of the new Republic of Czechoslovakia in December, 1989. This was known as the "Velvet Revolution" and was later followed by the "Velvet Divorce" when Slovakia separated from the Czech Republic in 1993.

In January 1990, I wrote a personal letter to President Vaclav Havel, on my Rotary International letterhead, saying that after 42 years I wanted to return for a visit but was not going to do so without assurances on basic democratic freedoms. I wrote that I wanted freedom of speech, association and travel. I wanted everyone to be able to express their opinion without fear of arrest. I wanted everyone to be able and free to travel without cross-border hindrance. Finally, I wanted everyone to be able to enjoy freedom of association, such as the freedom to form Rotary Clubs, which had been banned under the periods of the Nazi occupation and the Communist domination.

I did not get a reply from President Havel, but it certainly seemed to have helped. Within a few weeks, all the three freedoms came about, and, on 28th of April 1991, I flew in my own plane to Prague for my first visit to Czechoslovakia in 43 years. It would have been too dangerous for me to go whilst the Communists were in power as I had fought with the Western Allies in the last war. That journey took us from Jersey to Liege and then to Prague Ruzyne. My normal comfortable descent rate for landing is 500 feet a minute, so that if flying at 10,000 feet I like to descend 20 minutes beforehand. Soon after entering Czech airspace with just over 20 minutes to landing, I requested descent.

The controller came back with a heavily accented "What is the reason for your request?"

I had never been asked this before or since. Anyway I just replied "I want to get down and land at your airfield."

After a silence I got my descent clearance. I had a great week in the wonderful city of Prague which was in a very unmaintained condition (since rectified and again the most beautiful city in Europe). I broke off the return journey in Beyreuth, just across the border in Germany to refuel before flying home. In those days, only Russian aviation fuel was available in Czechoslovakia, and I had been recommended not to use it.

In 1991, there followed several trips to Prague, Brno, Budapest and Vienna all of which were connected with our help to the newly formed Rotary Club in Znojmo in Moravia in the Czech Republic. When the Znojmo Rotarians came to Jersey in May, 1992, to take part in the Jersey Liberation Day celebrations, I flew several trips for them around Mont St. Michel, southeast of Jersey, on the French Brittany coast.

On 11 September 1992, the French section organised a Flying Rotarian trip very nearby with hardly three quarters of an hour's flying from Jersey to La Baule in France. This also happened to be the Rotary Club that the Jersey Rotary Club is twinned with, and I took along my French-speaking Rotarian friends, John and Jean King, from the Rotary Club of Jersey.

The last IFFR fly-ins of 1994 were in September. The French section organised it to Bourges. It was at the home airfield of the then long-serving President of the French Section of IFFR, Jean Recoulet. The Benelux section organised theirs to Middenzeeland. I took along my friends, Rotarian Jim and Jenny Hollywood, from the De La Manche Club in Jersey.

In late May of 1996, we flew to a German section IFFR fly-in in Lubeck, Germany. We flew there via Maastricht, Holland on the German and Belgium border and came back via Groeningen, Holland, and Le Touquet, France, where we had lunch on the way back to Jersey.

In September 1996, the French section of IFFR organised a fly-in to Toulouse, the famous place where Airbus, the European competitor of Boeing, has their main aircraft assembly factory. The French section of the Rotarians arranged a very extensive visit around this factory. We saw aircraft in assembly and test aircraft. We were able to go inside and see all the different measuring equipment used while the aircraft were being tested in the air. On that trip, my passengers were Rotarians John King from the Jersey Club and Roger Thebault from the De La Manche Club. My good friend, Rotarian Graeme Le Quesne, also went on this fly-in with his Piper Lance, and he took along Rotarian David Beaugeard from the De La Manche Club. We had a whale of a time together.

One particularly memorable incident was when we came back to our hotel. It was on a Saturday night after extensive celebrations with the French Rotarians. We all went in the lift together only to find that it got stuck between floors, and there we were without any means of contacting help. Graeme found a way of opening the doors even between floors. (Maybe he was a lift engineer in a previous life.) We were between floors, so we climbed up to the opening on the next floor, got out and quickly went to our bedrooms. We don't know what happened to the lift after that. We recounted that experience on a number of occasions. Particularly some years later when on a visit with De La Manche Club, we went to a newly-opened HSBC bank building in Jersey and got stuck in a lift again for about an hour. It became a joke that whenever somebody came in a lift with me, there was always a danger they'd get stuck.

The last trip that year 1996 was in October, again to the Benelux section to a place called Koksijde in Belgium. On that occasion, Rotarian David Reynolds came with us and became a member of IFFR.

In January 1998, we had a great holiday in Thailand. I wanted to fly in Thailand and found out you can only rent an aircraft there if you get a Thai pilot's licence. Unlike Barbados and other places who just want the money and give you a licence based on your UK or US licence, in Thailand they wanted you to pass a flying test as well. I did that on the 4th of January in an AA5 aircraft and got a Thai pilot's licence to add to my collection. From the IFFR directory of members I found two Flying Rotarians in Thailand, and I met them both during my visit there.

One was Flying Rotarian Krisda Arunvongse who had at one time been the Governor of Bangkok—not the Rotary District Governor but the actual political Governor. He was an architect and extremely respected in Bangkok. He took us to his home and was also helpful—because he had his own aircraft—in introducing me to a flying instructor examiner at an airfield called Bangphra. I got the licence and then flew with Krisda to a very nice vacation town called Huahin. Krisda had a summer house there which we stayed at. Later, I flew another flight locally from Bangkok over another holiday island called Samet.

The second Flying Rotarian we met was Ophas Kanchanavijaya who very kindly took us on a tour of Bangkok that included a boat trip to view the Royal Family fleet. At the end of the holiday, I hosted a dinner party for my new friends and their wives, and we have exchanged Christmas cards ever since. Needless to say, they are also on my CGS Round Robin e-mails list. This is an irregular e-mail of humour and even some wisdoms and computer tips, sent to 551 friends and acquaintances at the press of a button.

In April 1998, the French IFFR fly-in was to the city of Reims where we landed at an airfield called Pruney. I had a very good weekend there visiting one of the most famous cathedrals in Europe not to mention the surrounding wine country.

The German section of the Flying Rotarians organised a trip—the first one outside their own country—to the Czech Republic. I flew from Jersey on my first direct flight to the Czech Republic without landing somewhere for refuelling. We landed at Karlovy Vary (Karlsbad), a spa town in Northwest Bohemia. The flight took four hours and 32 minutes. Normally in a small plane which hasn't got a toilet and where you can't get up to walk about and stretch your legs, if the journey is likely to take more than three hours, I make an intermediate landing somewhere to have what I call a tea and pee stop for the passengers. But this was too good an opportunity to miss and we did it direct.

The organising Rotarians had arranged a coach trip from Karlovy Vary to Prague. Unfortunately, it was raining heavily, but we still went sightseeing at the famous Hradcany Castle, the Charles Bridge and all the other tourist venues. We returned to Jersey, this time doing a fuel stop at Augsburg in Germany.

In May 1999 was the usual Hanover CeBit flight and also the UK section IFFR fly-in to Norwich, another cathedral town this time in England, and home of the very famous UK insurance company, Norwich Union.

In April of 2000, was the French IFFR fly-in, this time to an airfield at a place called Tarbes. This is the nearest airfield to Lourdes, the famous religious town where people make pilgrimages to get blessings and be healed. There is a well there, where you are supposed to be able to take the water and throw away your crutches. There are one or two crutches upon the wall where people may have done that, but the hundreds I saw walking and being wheeled past there unfortunately didn't seem to have benefitted other than spiritually.

Also at Tarbes is the EADS Socata aircraft factory, which makes the small General Aviation TB aircraft. Because of that, I took along with me Bob Wright, the chief engineer of Channel Island Aero Services in Jersey, the company that looks after my aircraft.

Also, an old friend, pilot and ex-employee of mine, Ian Rosewell joined us, and we made a long weekend of it.

In May of that year, the Benelux section of the Flying Rotarians organised a fly-in to a place called Hasselt, which is a grass strip. I hadn't landed on grass for a long time, but I had no problems.

At the end of May and beginning of June 2000, the German/Austrian section organised a fly-in to Austria. As a result of that fly-in, they decided to re-name the German section of the Flying Rotarians to become the German-Austrian section. The flight went from Jersey to Manston, England, to Luxembourg, to Colmar, France and to Salzburg, Austria. Salzburg is the famous city where Wolfgang Amadeus Mozart lived for a large portion of his life. It has a beautiful opera house there where many opera festivals are held. After that very cultural weekend, we flew back via Luxembourg to Jersey.

In 2001, we had a memorable time with the Flying Rotarian UK section fly-in to Scotland. The fly-in was to Perth, an airfield north of Edinburgh, home territory of long serving member Flying Rotarian Feroz Wadia and his wife Raye. It also included a fly-about over the Scottish Islands. On the way back, we landed at Oban, a small town municipal airfield with an interesting approach. It is a non-controlled airfield. Other than that there is a very pleasant man there who just collects the landing fees in a little caravan. We said on the radio that we were approaching and asked if there was any other traffic?

He said, "No. You land at your own discretion. We've got the kettle on for a cup of tea for you."

That was a nice thing to hear over the radio. Our tea was ready when we landed. We flew back to Jersey on 28th of May.

In May, 2002, there was a UK fly-in to a small airfield in Cornwall on the southwest tip of England, a very short flight from Jersey, to a place called Perranporth. The German IFFR fly-in at the end of May and the beginning of June, was to a town called Flensburg in Northern Germany, very close to the Danish border. We flew across to a place called Sonderborg, Denmark as well, where the aviation fuel was much cheaper. On the way out, we flew through

Hamburg. On the way back, we flew through Antwerp, Belgium famous for its diamond cutting and very good restaurants specialising in moules and chips.

The 2002 German IFFR fly-in took place from 8th to 14th of August, and this time it was in Weimar, a town that used to be part of Eastern Germany and, in history, famous as the capital of the Weimar republic and the home of Goethe. We decided to land at the nearby airfield of Erfurt because that was an instrument landing airfield and a German Flying Rotarian kindly picked us up there. We joined the rest of the group at the hotel in the centre of the town. Very few of the guide books mention the proximity of the town to the site of the notorious concentration camp of Buchenwald on the slopes above the town. The Elephant Hotel in the market square of Weimar has a "Fuhrer balcony," a favourite spot from which Hitler used to give speeches. We paid a visit to the memorial site of Buchenwald and took along a couple of our German Rotarian friends to see and learn of the atrocities that went on there during the Nazi regime. (It is still difficult for me to believe the usual German excuse from the generation of that day that they did not know what was going on in their midst.) Because it's not that far away from Berlin, we extended the weekend and spent a couple of days in Berlin and then went back to Jersey via Antwerp.

In May 2003, we flew to Waterford in Ireland where the UK section had organised a full programme including a visit to the famous Waterford Glass Factory. In September the German/Austrian section had organised a fly-in to Nuremberg which brought back many memories for me. I showed the British participants around the famous courtroom where the international military tribunal had been held in 1945/6. As the French section fly-in to Marseilles was the following weekend we flew to Karlsruhe and spent four days in Baden-Baden, one of Europe's most fashionable spas.

In May 2004, the UK section held its fly-in in the university town of Cambridge. Later in the month for a German/Austrian section fly-in we went from Jersey to Moenchen Gladbach to Bauzen on the Polish border. As this was not far from Prague we flew to

My Press Scoop—the dramatic picture taken in the severe winter of 1947 of the Halifax crash after the plane was attempting to drop food in canisters for allegedly starving villagers in the Leek Moorlands. I was the only photographer there, having arrived on skis—read the full story in chapter 14.

Another picture of the tragic Halifax crash in the winter of 1947 (chapter 14).

Probably the most dramatic picture of my press scoop of the tragic 1947 Halifax crash in Grindon. Taken within minutes of the crash with fires still raging and things exploding and showing some of the food canisters in the foreground. This photograph was reproduced front page in every UK newspaper the following day (chapter 14).

Death in the blizzard

Every year on the anniversary of the Halifax crash in Grindon (on the 13th February 1947) the Staffordshire "Evening Sentinel" publishes a reminder of the event using my photographs. This one is from the 50th anniversary in 1997 and they still pay me reproduction fees (chapter 14).

Hercules flies over as cairn is unveiled for snow heroes

Story: Roger Houldcroft
Photos: Dave Randle

A GIANT Hercules swooped low over the spot where eight men perished while on a mercy mission to drop food to snowbound families in the bleak Staffordshire Moorlands.

Below the graceful aircraft stood relatives of those killed when the Halifax crashed into the hillside and burst into flames.

They had turned up together with representatives from the RAF and those who had helped at the tragedy on February, 13 1947 at Grindon, near Leek.

They gathered, along with villagers, to watch the Lord Lieutenant of Staffordshire, James Hawley, unveil a commemorative cairn which had been made by Blue Circle and was erected on behalf of the Leek branch of the RAF Association.

The son of the pilot, Squadron Leader Donald McIntyre, whose name is also Donald, travelled from his home in Halifax.

Also present was 72-year-old Charles Strasser who was working as a freelance photographer and had been sent to take pictures of the food drop.

He said: "I was working for a photographic dealer in Hanley when a call came through from the Daily Herald and they said they had got a photographer on board to do the food drop.

●Charles Strasser

●Standards raised for the fly-past

The plane was exploding and burning when I took my photographs.

First of all I got an axe out of the back of the plane and started to hack away.

"All the crew, except for a guy who was in the rear of the plane, had been thrown clear and were dead."

A press cutting of the commemoration ceremony and unveiling of a memorial cairn on the spot where the Halifax crashed in the Leek Moorlands in the terrible winter of 1947 (chapter 14).

The memorial cairn organised by the Leek branch of the RAFA, erected by Blue Circle Cement Co. and unveiled in 1997 by the Lord Lieutenant of Staffordshire on the 50th anniversary of the Halifax crash (chapter 14).

The Press cuttings of the crash of the Halifax in 1947, my scoop, mounted on a hardboard panel and presented by me to the chairman of the Leek branch of the Royal Air Force Association on the 50th anniversary of the tragic event (chapter 14).

The Spitfire unveiling party with the Lord Mayor of the City of Stoke-on-Trent Clr. William Austin, Air Chief Marshall Sir Neil Wheeler, the Lady Mayoress, Town Clerk L.K.Robinson and Charles Strasser (chapter 83).

The unveiling of the memorial tablet by Air Chief Marshall Sir Neil Wheeler KCB CBE DSO DFC AFC commemorating the donation of a Spitfire to the city of Stoke-on-Trent by the initiative of the Stoke Spitfire Appeal Committee which I had founded. The Spitfire was designed by Reginald Mitchell, a Son of the City (chapter 83).

The Mitchell Spitfire Memorial Fund limited edition plate kindly made by Wedgwoods for the Stoke Spitfire Appeal Committee (chapter 83).

Surrounded by Past World Presidents of IFFR from left to right, Marcus Crotts 78/80, Vactor Stanford 82/84, Ned Poyser 84/86, Charles Strasser 86/88, John Linford 88/90, Federico Compean 90/92, Don Bymaster 92/94 (chapter 73).

My personal pennant used for presentations during my two years, 1986/88, as World President of IFFR, at that time still called chairman (chapter 73).

The IFFR history up to my World Presidency in 1986/88. I was the first non-North American Flying Rotarian elected to that office (chapter 73).

IFFR HISTORY

The International Fellowship of Flying Rotarians (IFFR) was organized in Seattle, Washington, U.S.A. on January 1, 1965, through the efforts of E. Edison Kennell IFFR #1.

A directory is published each year which contains the names and addresses of all "IFFR Pilots" as well as their Rotary Club affiliation and its meeting day. The cross country pilot, with the IFFR directory in his cockpit, his virtually 2,000 additional flight service stations at his disposal, and many lasting friendships have begun through this "Rotarian mutual aid society."

IFFR had 67 "Fly-Ins" in 1974, held all over the world. Many of these provided the local Rotary Clubs with record attendance. At Vacaville, California, in 1974, 641 Rotarians lead by Edwin I. Power IFFR #89 in 150 individual airplanes met at the Nut Tree Restaurant.

"Bridge the Gap Tour" was made to Central America in 1974; where a group of Rotary Pilots in their aircraft visited numerous Rotary Clubs in Mexico and Central American Countries. This event was headed by Vic Bracher, IFFR #377.

The utility of IFFR was shown by flying, in private aircraft, past R.I. President, Bill Carter of Berkshire, England, and his family, on an eleven state tour in 1975 in the U.S.A. Marcus B. Crotts IFFR #1170 and Jim Lambeth IFFR #2291 arranged this event.

In 1978, Vermillon County Airport, Danville, Illinois, was renamed Clarence Carter Airport, honoring Rotarian Clarence Carter IFFR #902, in recognition of his outstanding contribution to aviation.

Larry Hirschinger IFFR #488, Muncie, Indiana, U.S.A., conducted their 1978 Annual "Fly-In" in Muncie with Mr. John Baker, President AOPA, as the principle speaker. Each year the Muncie Club Sponsors a major "Fly-In."

Herbert Pigman, a private pilot, assumed the position of general secretary of Rotary International on January 1, 1979, and was made an honorary member of IFFR. At the same time, Rotary International President-Elect James L. Bomar, Jr. of Shelbyville, Tennessee, U.S.A., who is also a private pilot, was made an honorary member of IFFR.

In 1980, IFFR in co-operation with the Yachting Rotarians, and The Caravaning Rotarians, held an "Air-Land-Sea" rendezvous in Chicago, Illinois, U.S.A. in conjunction with the Rotary International convention held in McCormick Place, Miggs Airport and The Chicago Yacht Club. This function was arranged by R.I. President Jim Bomar, and Marcus B. Crotts IFFR #1170.

In 1981, two of our members and their wives flew a single engine Cessna #210 from the U.S.A., across the Caribbean Sea to Sao Paulo, Brazil, to attend the International Convention. Ned Poyser IFFR #1276, and his Rotary Ann Betty arranged the flight.

In 1984, five light aircraft, piloted by flying Rotarians, flew from the U.S.A. to Birmingham, England to attend the International Convention.

In 1987, seven general aviation aircraft flew from the U.S.A. to the Rotary International Convention in Munich, Germany. In route, the convoy stopped at Jersey Island to visit IFFR chairman Charles Strasser IFFR #652.

The Past IFFR Chairmen are:

1965-1972---E. Edison Kennell,* Seattle, Washington, U.S.A.
1972-1976---Victor C. Bracher,* Houston, Texas, U.S.A.
1976-1978---Pablo Campos Lynch, Mexico City, Mexico
1978-1980---Marcus B. Crotts, Winston-Salem, N.C., U.S.A.
1980-1982---William A. Barnes, Muncie, Indiana, U.S.A.
1982-1984---Vactor H. Stanford, Dallas, Texas, U.S.A.
1984-1986---H. Edward Poyser, Hot Springs, VA, U.S.A.
1986-1988---Charles G. Strasser, Channel Islands, via UK

* Deceased

The International Fellowship of Flying Rotarians is a member of the World Fellowship Activities of Rotary International.

—MARCUS B. CROTTS
May 23, 1988

Pinning the IFFR Wings on the lapel of the then Lieutenant Governor of Jersey, His Excellency Air Marshal Sir John Cheshire KBE CB, when inducting him as an Honorary member of the International Fellowship of Flying Rotarians in June 2001 (chapter 73).

With Flying Rotarian Krisda Arunvongse, ex-Governor of Bangkok and famous Thai architect and member of the Rotary Club of Bangkok (chapter 74).

Sworn in and inducted, together with Flying Rotarian John Ritchie, as a D'Echevin D'Honneur of the order of St. Emilion during a fly-in to the Bordeaux region organised by the French section of the Flying Rotarians.

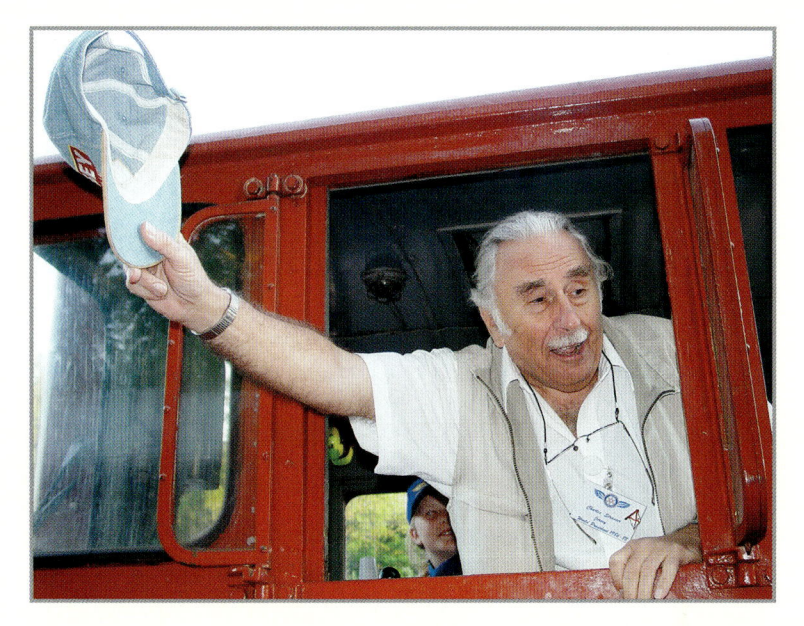

In June 2006 on the Scandinavian post-convention fly-about with 22 other IFFR aircraft. Every little boy of my generation dreamt of becoming an engine driver. My dream came true (chapter 73).

In Skagen, the most northerly point of Denmark where the North Sea ferociously meets the Baltic Sea. With one foot in each of the two seas during the 2006 IFFR Scandinavian post-convention fly-about (chapter 73).

IFFR world presidents, left to right, Angus Clark UK 2004/6, Charles Strasser Jersey 1986/8, Tony Watson USA 2002/4, Federico Compean Mexico 90/92, Marcus Crotts USA 78/80, Ned Poyser USA 84/86, Ern Dawes Australia 1998/2000, Sam Bishop USA 2000/02 (chapter 73).

Meeting Phil Boyer President of AOPA USA at an AOPA-IFFR luncheon at the AOPA Expo 2005 in Florida.

Taken at the Charter dinner of the Rotary Club de la Manche in 1985. First row left, "Godfather" Charles Strasser, centre John Averty founder President and far right Rtn. Wally Winchcombe the District Extension Officer (chapter 76).

"Jersey Evening Post" press cutting of the 2005 20th Charter anniversary dinner of the Rotary Club de la Manche of which I am an Honorary member. Due to my absence in Florida I surprised them with a huge birthday cake from their "Godfather" (chapter 76).

A presentation of a Rotary Club of Znojmo souvenir by the President of their club to Rotarian David Watkins of the Rotary Club of Jersey during our fellowship visit to our adopted club in the then Czechoslovakia (chapter 72).

Wearing two hats. Together with Cynthia Rumboll receiving a cheque on behalf of the St. John Ambulance Appeal Committee from Rotarian Derek Short of the Rotary Club of Jersey (chapter 83).

My day out with the Jersey Police. Bid for in a Jersey Christmas Charity appeal auction organised by the Rotary Club de la Manche and BBC Radio Jersey. This turned out to be an incredibly interesting day visiting all departments (chapter 85).

Always game for a bit of fun. On one of many Jersey Rotary Club fellowship visits which I arranged, this time to Morocco, being taught the art of partnering the local belly dancer.

With Allan Smith (at back) and the President of the then Czechoslovakia, Vaclav Havel on a walk-about in the grounds of Hradcany Castle during a Jersey Rotary Club fellowship visit to Prague (chapter 74).

Success after years of correspondence with Rotary International to recognise Jersey as a country and display its flag. An example at the International Convention in Chicago (chapter 75).

An anthem out of tune with our constitution

● From Charles Strasser.

CONGRATULATIONS to Senator Frank Walker for proposing a national anthem for Jersey. I hope he will be more successful than I was when I made the some proposal 18 years ago.

On my return from a very pleasant family holiday in the Netherland Antilles island of Aruba in February 1988, I wrote a letter to the then editor of the JEP. I mentioned the many similarities between our two islands in our relationship to the UK and theirs to Holland. I also mentioned how impressed I was when attending their Rotary Club meeting to see their flag proudly displayed and the singing of their national anthem. This prompted me to suggest a competition for the words and the music for a national anthem for Jersey, and I offered prizes to encourage entries.

Your predecessor, instead of publishing my letter, sent a reporter to interview me, and you will find in your JEP archives for February 1988 the quite lengthy article on that subject that appeared there.

However, the project was nipped in the bud when, on the day following publication, I received a letter from the then Bailiff, the late Sir Peter Crill. He informed me that I was obviously not aware of the constitutional position of Jersey and that we already had a national anthem for Jersey, which was God Save the Queen, and that my proposal for a national anthem was out of order.

The Cottage, Anne Port, St Martin.

My letter to the editor of the "Jersey Evening Post" re my resurrected proposal of a national anthem for Jersey by Chief Minister Senator Frank Walker. I wished him better success than my attempt some 18 years before (chapter 78).

The Canadian Mounties "Get Their Man" after the huge parade preceding the Rotary International Convention in Chicago in which they and five members of the Jersey Rotary Club participated (chapter 75).

Just one of the many Jersey flags exchanged with Rotary Clubs all over the world. This one is with the president of the Kowloon Rotary Club. I also presented him with a unique first day cover of a Jersey stamp with the Rotary wheel (chapter 79).

President Bob Marshall of the Rotary Club of Jersey presenting the 40 years of Rotary Service Award to me in July 2006.

The second aircraft I owned, a Piper Tri-pacer G-APXM, 'Mothers Blessing' which was based at Meir in Stoke-on-Trent, pictured here at the Jersey International Air Rally in 1967 (chapter 58).

My first twin engined aircraft, a Cessna Super Skymaster 337 G-ATNY with central thrust engines. This picture taken in Minorca with Peter Faktor of AICO to whom I sold it subject to this demo flight (chapter 58).

My Piper Seneca II G-PLUS, a six-seater turbocharged twin, bought new in 1980 and still going strong after 27 years but now on a second set of engines, a repaint and re-registration onto the US register as N37US (chapter 58).

the nearby factory airfield of Vodochody where the famous Czech Let Aircraft are built, returning home to Jersey via Maastricht. In June we did two fly-ins, one by the Benelux section to Middleburg and the other by the Italian section to Rome. We landed at a small airfield almost in the middle of Rome called Urbe and enjoyed fabulous sightseeing of this ancient city, of course including a visit to the Vatican. A July weekend was spent in Sheffield, the home town of the then IFFR World President Angus Clark who entertained us at his home.

In August, 2005, we had a fly-in to Lelystad, a small airfield north of Amsterdam. In September we were off to Hagenau in France.

In April, 2006, the Benelux section took us to Charleroi, quite a large airport south of Brussels. In May we went with the German/Austrian section to Saarbruecken, a town in Saarland the disputed territory between France and Germany which changed hands numerous times over the years, now being German. The town is famous for its extensive coal mines, many of which are now disused, and one of which we visited on our tour. The last trip in 2006 was in September with the UK section to the small airstrip used by flying Rotarian James Alexander and stayed at his Best Western Hotel in Kendal. This is part of the picturesque Lake District National Park and we therefore did a coach tour of many of the lakes and one by boat on Lake Windermere, the largest natural lake in England. In fact I landed in Blackpool, an instrument airfield.

❖ 75 ❖

Jersey Pride

I HAVE IMMENSE PRIDE IN everything Jersey. It sometimes seems that the expatriates in Jersey are more patriotic and loyal than the Jersey-born. An early opportunity to express my pride in Jersey presented itself after I visited my second Rotary International Convention in Birmingham, England, in 1984. I flew there in my own plane and took with me two other Jersey Rotarians, Sam Senett and Allan Smith. The first day's normal session is preceded by the opening event which has a very impressive parade of the flags of the countries in which Rotary has a presence. There was no Jersey flag in the parade.

This grievous omission had to be corrected for future conventions and all other Rotary occasions where flags are shown. Immediately upon getting back to Jersey, I started corresponding with Rotary International in Evanston. They at first didn't recognise that Jersey was an independent country with its own flag. However, after more facts from me and further investigations by them with the British Consulate in Chicago, I got them to agree that in the future the Jersey flag would be flown at opening ceremonies, and included with other flags wherever all Rotary nation flags were displayed. That omission was corrected, and whenever the Jersey flags were flown at Rotary International Conventions all over the world, I got someone to take a picture of me with the Jersey flag in the background.

Much later, I discovered from an incoming District Governor, Ron Lucas, a member of my old club in Newcastle-under-Lyme, that he had been to a Governors' assembly in Boca Raton and the Jersey flag was not present. I wrote yet another letter to Evanston to get that put right as well. Then in 2005, when the Rotary International convention was in Chicago and those of us from Jersey took a side trip to Evanston, I noticed that all the Rotary nation flags were the static centrepiece in the foyer—yet again with the omission of Jersey, so that had to be put right and it was. Proudly, I can now claim that Jersey is recognised as being a member country of Rotary in its full right.

The above held good until the 2006 Copenhagen/Malmo Convention, when presumably because of the ever growing number of Rotary countries, the flag display in the opening ceremony was taking too long. On this occasion only the Union flag was paraded with the accompanying tortuous loudspeaker announcement: "Anguilla, Bermuda, British Virgin Islands, Cayman Islands, Channel Islands Guernsey, Channel Islands Jersey, England, Gibraltar, Isle of Man, Montserrat, Northern Ireland, Scotland, Turk and Caicos Islands and Wales". So they have jumbled up The United Kingdom and Northern Ireland with the British Crown Dependencies and the British Overseas Territories into one alphabetical but politically totally incorrect list. Conceivably the Scots have complained that if Jersey has its own flag displayed they want to have the same treatment for theirs. Anyway it seems that more correspondence will be needed.

Whenever I attend a Rotary Club meeting away from Jersey, be it in Buenos Aires or in Sydney, besides exchanging the usual club banner, I also give them a short talk on Jersey.

❖ 76 ❖

Godfather

AFTER A FOURTH REQUEST, THE Rotary Club of Jersey finally gave permission for a second club to be formed at an Annual General Meeting. The club notified the District Governor, who gave the job of forming the club to District Extension Officer Rotarian Wally Winchcombe. He in turn asked the President of the Jersey Club to appoint a member of the Rotary Club of Jersey as his aide. The appointed member would have to be the extension officer because of the expense which would have been involved in somebody from the mainland commuting to Jersey every week to get the new club off the ground. The President of the Rotary Club of Jersey at that time, Richard Wade, appointed me to be the de facto extension officer for the formation of the new club. I worked extremely well with Wally Winchcombe. He was my mentor in procedures of forming a new club, and he was also a true gentleman.

The first move in forming a new club is to find six potential new members for Rotary. I sat down with a blank sheet of paper and put down the names of people I thought would qualify. Those six had to be not only potentially good Rotarians but they had to act as the first officers of the new club and get it off the ground. My six chosen founding members were John Averty (Interim President), David Beaugeard (Senior Vice-President), Richard Jeune (Junior Vice-President), Bob Norman, Barry Simpson and David Witherington (Secretary).

It was my job to choose and interview them, and they all agreed to join and serve. I didn't have to go to more than those six.

The next procedure is to choose a minimum of 18 other members with the help of the six new "officers". A new club has to have

24 new members to start with. We started off with 34. We chose the others, and I again had to interview them individually and inform them of what Rotary was all about. These were councillors Ian Toole (Treasurer), David Beuzeval, Albert Brown, Clive Henderson, John Hutchins, Ralph Robbins, Barry Simpson, and members David Arden, Ian Barnes, Richard Blampied, Ian Campbell, Peter Daniell, John Day, Maurice des Forges, Royan Ellis, Jerry Glynn, John Gready, Alan Guy, Tom Hart, Henry Head, Jim Hollywood, Paul Kuhn, Derek Mason, Robert Norman, Harry Swift, Sidney Simpkin, Peter Townend, and Michael Vibert.

Because it was now still only an interim Rotary Club, one didn't have to go through the usual approval procedures, it was entirely up to me to decide whether somebody could become a Rotarian or not. That is why I got the title of "godfather," which seems to have stuck to this day.

In fact, and this is the first time I have disclosed this, I had to make final membership decisions. In the nomination of prospective members for the new club, I got a phone call from a member of my club telling me that he had heard that a certain person had been nominated and that for reasons he would not elaborate on, I must under no circumstances let that name go forward. I ignored that request and the nominated member became an active member of the club and a good Rotarian.

After the new club was formed and chartered, I continued to go to their meetings as well as to those of my club and they very kindly made me an honorary member of the club. So I have what is probably quite a rare distinction in Rotary, to be an honorary member of three different Rotary Clubs besides being a member of the Rotary Club of Jersey. The first one was the Rotary Club of Znojmo in the Czech Republic, the second one was the Rotary Club De La Manche and the third was the Rotary Club of Newcastle-under-Lyme.

The new Rotary Club in Jersey then chose a name. They wanted a French-sounding name, so they chose "Rotary De La Manche," which in English means "Rotary of the Channel." The club meets weekly at the Victoria Club on a Tuesday evening. By the very nature of being a new club and being an evening club at that, the average age, on formation, was under 40—very much younger than in the Jersey Club. We picked a fantastic team, and they had an excellent charter evening attended by the RIBI (Rotary in Britain and Ireland) President, the District Governor and the Deputy Bailiff of Jersey. Many visiting Rotarians from the mainland, for whom we had devised a special holiday package, also attended.

On 26th November 2005, they celebrated the 20th birthday of their charter with a party at the Jersey Potteries. At the time, I was on Marco Island, Florida, and unfortunately had to miss this important event. To help with the celebrations, I secretly arranged the presentation on the evening of a huge "Happy Birthday from your Godfather" cake to surprise them. It shows how well we picked the first lot of members because in the first eight years of its existence, they didn't lose a single member. We lost the first one because his job transferred him to the UK. It is a really happy club.

They have their own charities to support, but some things went on a joint basis between the two clubs. The first major joint initiative was a celebration of Jersey's Liberation from German occupation (see the next chapter). The celebration combined a day of commemoration, a fun-filled day out and successful fundraising for the international Rotary charity Polio Plus.

A Rotarian has to attend at least 60% of the meetings of a Rotary Club to retain his membership. For the first time, the creation of Rotary De La Manche gave an opportunity to the members of the Rotary Club of Jersey to make up their attendance at another club without leaving the island. Members of both clubs can now visit each other and make up their attendances.

❖ 77 ❖

Liberation Day

ONE OF THE MORE INTERESTING of several major events organised under the auspices of the Rotary Club of Jersey was the celebration of Liberation Day. Jersey is not part of the United Kingdom of Great Britain and Northern Ireland, but is part of the British Isles. The Channel Islands were the only part of the British Isles occupied by the Germans during the Second World War. Jersey is only 14 miles away from the French Coast but 100 miles south of England, so it was not considered to be a defendable island.

Jersey was occupied by the Germans in 1940. They bombed the island, gave an ultimatum demanding surrender and German troops arrived on July 1. In 1942, 1,186 English were deported to Germany. On 30th December 1944, the first Red Cross supply ship Vega arrived, and on 9th May 1945, Jersey was liberated by the arrival of British forces followed by a visit on 7th June 1945, of King George VI and Queen Elizabeth. D-day, the Allied invasion, started on 6th June 1944, on the Normandy beaches. Shortly after, the Cherbourg peninsula, 14 miles across the sea from Jersey, was liberated by American troops. It was to be another 11 months before the Channel Islands were freed from the Occupation, which had lasted almost five years.

Liberation Day, May 9, in Jersey was made into a national holiday. The schools are closed and many shops are closed, but it never was a day of active commemoration nor particularly one of celebration. I suggested to the Rotary Club that it should raise the profile of Liberation Day to give people something to do on this day which was already a holiday anyway. As happens so often when somebody suggests something, they are given the job of carrying it through. So the President at the time, Advocate Brian Troy, appointed me the chairman of the newly formed Liberation Day Celebration Committee.

I was pleased to accept, as the organisation involved was going to be quite a challenge. I was determined to make it a success which would be the catalyst for similar functions in the years to follow. I put together a committee. At that stage, the second Rotary Club, De la Manche, of which I had been the godfather, had already been formed. So I decided that this should be a joint venture for the two clubs and got some of their members on the committee also. We decided to use the biggest most central available open space in St. Helier known as People's Park, and to divide it into commemoration and celebration activities. The Connetable of St. Helier was most co-operative. Besides permissions, we also got much help from the parish.

On the commemoration side, we planned to invite the Jersey Occupation Society and the local media to provide exhibits. We also planned to invite the local Second World War vehicle collectors to bring their vehicles and exhibit them and to generally remind people—particularly the younger ones—of things as they were during the occupation. We planned activities for both adults and children, with a massive open air ox roast, a lot of amusement stalls, tea and beer tents and candy floss. We organised it for people to have an afternoon out with competitions and a variety of participation activities.

I needed a central feature, something really special that had never been done before. Although the main purpose was to commemorate and to celebrate, we also wanted to use the opportunity to raise money for Rotary charities. I didn't want to charge an entrance fee because it was an open public area. We needed something besides the ox roast and stalls to make money. We needed something innovative and different, so I hit on the idea that, because it was Liberation Day, we would liberate balloons on a massive scale. I wanted to release 10,000 balloons in one go, which meant first blowing up 10,000 balloons. I looked into the logistics of this, and it was no easy task. But that was my aim.

If we sold each ticket for the balloon liberation for a pound, we'd make 10,000 pounds if we could get sponsorship for the costs. In return for the beer concession we got a substantial sponsorship from Ann Street Brewery. Then we hit a problem. The concept was good, but the States of Jersey ran a national lottery. To avoid any competition to this, the law stated that any raffle or lottery could have tickets to the value of up to 20 pence or over £5. Everything in between was reserved for the Jersey States Lottery. Other charity organisers holding a raffle overcame this law by having 20 pence tickets, but selling five for a pound. That was allowed because the face value of the ticket was only 20 pence and that was the limit in the law. We couldn't do that because the balloon costs themselves were over 20 pence.

Since we needed to sell the balloon liberation tickets for a pound each, I had to go and see the lady in charge for the Gambling Control Committee of the States of Jersey. She said, "No, that's the law and what you're proposing can't be done." Well, one of my mottos is never accept at face value what you get told by a bureaucrat, particularly when it seems illogical and unreasonable, so I had to overcome this. Since this was an important event and the first time that Liberation Day was going to be celebrated—in my opinion, in a proper fashion—I thought it was appropriate to have the top man in Jersey, the Bailiff, perform the mass liberation of the balloons. We also needed good advance publicity. So I thought about the best way of doing this.

I came to the conclusion that we needed the Bailiff not only to liberate the balloons but also, in all our publicity beforehand, to get him to welcome this initiative and to ask people to support it. I thought, "Now, this is a busy man and rather than brief him, I'll write his little article, to use in our publicity, for him." I thought rather than an article, he could send me a letter which we could reproduce. I wrote to him inviting him to open the Liberation Day festivities on People's Park and liberate the 10,000 balloons on this important day, which I believe is the most important day in the Jersey calendar. I also asked him if he could commend our initiative and write a letter which we could publish in our advertising and publicity. "I know you are a busy man, and I've taken the liberty of drafting it for you. Please either approve it or amend it as you think fit or throw it in the waste paper basket and write it yourself."

He accepted the invitation but told me it was a "one off" as it coincided with his wedding anniversary and I was not to ask him again. He also returned my proposed letter accepting exactly what I had drafted for him and crossed out only the last two words in the last paragraph where I had repeated myself. Now I had a letter from the Bailiff of Jersey which we could quote and use in our advance publicity and advertising. I had an attractive poster prepared announcing Liberation Day activities and the one pound tickets for the balloon competition. Prizes were given for the balloons that had travelled the furthest distance. I then went back to the Gambling Committee lady and said we've got to find a way of doing this. The Bailiff is coming to release these balloons, here is the poster containing his letter and we better have the balloons to sell. I suggested that as he is supporting it, then it must be within the law. At first she said, "Well, he just doesn't know the law." I reminded her that he was the chief judge of Jersey but, I said, "Let's try and find a way that satisfies everybody."

I suggested that we say that the value of the tickets which we're selling is 20 pence for the gambling control purposes and the other 80 pence of the pound which we're asking people to pay for the ticket is a contribution to local Rotary charities. It would be deemed to be voluntary although we would just say to people that the tickets are a pound. She said I would need to draft something that I can actually print on the tickets which will be acceptable to her. I did that and in the end it stated on the ticket, "80 pence of the value of this ticket is a donation to Rotary charities." She said, "Right, we'll accept that for this year. Here is your official approval number which has to be put on every ticket sold. Every year you will have to come back for individual approval."

I said "That's fine" and we did it.

Now we could go ahead. We printed the 10,000 tickets. We got 10,000 balloons with blow-up valves in them. We got the helium gas cylinders donated by the local distributor. We got the volunteer soldiers from the local Territorial Army unit to erect several tents and blow up the balloons inside these tents. We set it up so that when the Bailiff pulled the first string on the first balloon, the sides of the tents would open and 10,000 balloons would be liberated.

It wasn't just a balloon liberation. We also made it a competition of which balloon would fly and land at the furthest distance away from Jersey. When somebody bought a ticket for a balloon, they would put their name and phone number on the numbered counterfoil. A postcard pre-addressed to me, with the same number, would be tied to the balloon, asking whoever found that balloon to please return it to me in Jersey. If it was the winning balloon, the balloon's finder would also win a prize of a visit to Jersey, which I persuaded the Tourism Committee to fund.

Bailiff Sir Peter Crill liberated the 10,000 balloons in front of a huge cheering crowd. In the first year we got back an unbelievably large number of nearly 800 postcards. The furthest one away had landed in what then was East Germany, a remarkably long way of over 800 miles from Jersey. It turned out that it was a set of twin teenage girls who had sent this in. We invited them to come to Jersey the following year to release the next year's Liberation Day balloons. David Reynolds, a Rotarian from the Jersey Club, flew over and picked them up.

This great Liberation Day balloon liberation, my "baby," was carried on for quite a number of years to the same formula. I was chairman of the organising committee only in the first year. Rotarian Derek Mason, an architect and my vice-chairman from the Rotary Club De La Manche, took over as chairman of the joint committee the following year.

Rotary-organised Liberation Day festivities carried on for a number of years. Each year, the files outlining procedures were passed to the next committee. The balloon tickets, of course, always caused the biggest problem because permission from Gambling Control had to be requested every year. The lady who was the Gambling Control committee controller left the job, and a new controller took over. He was very friendly towards the established system but again insisted that he must be asked for approval every year. One year they forgot to ask him. They had an approval number for the ticket sale, but the printing on the tickets had not been agreed. Many of these tickets were usually sold outside department stores in the main street in the four weeks prior to Liberation Day. Members of both Rotary Clubs volunteered to sell these tickets and, of course, they were charging a pound. They still had the relevant donation statement on them although it had been slightly varied that year for reasons I don't know.

One day I got a panic phone call saying, "We've just had the gambling controller stop the sale of the tickets outside Marks and Spencers in St. Helier because apparently permission had not been sought or granted." Apparently, proper procedure had not been followed. They asked if I would come and help. I went to the gambling controller and he insisted that the varied wording made it illegal. He said, "You must have big posters at every point of sale stating that the face value of the ticket is 20 pence and that it's entirely voluntary whether people pay the other 80 pence to make it into a pound." Furthermore, before the tickets could continue to be sold, they had to change the "one pound" to "20 pence" on each one of the tickets still to be sold. They didn't make the same mistake again the following year. It was done correctly as agreed, applied for and granted. Each year as long as both the Rotary Clubs carried this on, it was a very successful event in the calendar in Jersey. I'm quite proud of the fact that the high profiling of Liberation Day originated with me.

◆ 78 ◆

Words with the Bailiff

TRADITIONALLY, THE BAILIFF OF JERSEY requests in the local newspaper, the "Jersey Evening Post", that flags, Jersey or Union, be hoisted or displayed from public and other buildings on days like the Queen's Birthday. Never had such requests been published for Liberation Day, which I thought was the most important date for Jersey. This motivated me to write a letter to the Bailiff, Sir Peter Crill. I wrote, "I think that there is something wrong here. You request that we hang out the flags on all sorts of occasions but not on Liberation Day." I suggested that in future he should also publish that flags should be hung on Liberation Day. I didn't get a reply to that letter, but every following year, in advance of 9th of May, there was the traditional request in the paper from the Bailiff for people to please hang out flags on Liberation Day. I was pleased to read that.

When I was on a family holiday in Aruba in 1989, I went to the local Rotary Club meeting there. They opened the meeting by facing the Aruba flag and singing the Aruba National Anthem. There are quite a number of similarities between Aruba and Jersey. First, it has a relationship with the Netherlands very much like Jersey has a relationship with the United Kingdom. Aruba is part of the Netherland Antilles in the Caribbean and, as Jersey is 14 miles away from France, Aruba is about 16 miles away from Venezuela. Like Jersey, it is an island and has a partial dependence on tourism. It has its own government and its own taxation system. It is also an off-shore finance centre, like Jersey.

I was impressed at the local Rotary Club meeting in Aruba that they have a national anthem, which Jersey doesn't. When I got back to Jersey, I thought this is something we ought to have too. So I wrote a letter to the "Jersey Evening Post". Instead of just publishing my letter to the editor, they sent a reporter to interview me and do an article. I suggested a competition be started through the local paper and volunteered to give a substantial prize for the best words and music, together or separately, for a Jersey National Anthem. It was published as a half-page in the JEP.

Well, I didn't get any entries for the music. I got two entries for the words and a letter from Bailiff Sir Peter Crill. He wrote to say that he'd noted with interest my proposals in the local paper but I was obviously not aware of the constitutional position of Jersey and there is no way that Jersey was entitled to have a national anthem of its own. He wrote, "We use the British National Anthem of 'God Save the Queen.' We can't possibly have a national song because we already have one. Yours sincerely." I only had two entries, so I diplomatically let the whole thing die of natural causes.

Interestingly, in 2006, I read in the JEP that the Chief Minister of the States of Jersey, Senator Frank Walker, came up with the same proposal of having a Jersey National Anthem. I wrote a letter, which was published in the JEP, that I had a similar proposal rejected many years earlier by the then Bailiff and I wished him better success in bringing the matter to fruition.

⬥ 79 ⬥

Persistent Optimism

AT ONE OF THE ROTARY conventions I went to, I found that there was a fellowship called "Rotary on Stamps". Further inspection revealed that a German Rotarian had published a book in colour in the form of a printed stamp album depicting all the national stamps from anywhere in the world which had a Rotary emblem on them. I was intrigued, so I bought one of these books.

When I got home, I saw that there had never been a Rotary emblem on a stamp for the United Kingdom. So I made inquiries about this from the Jersey Director of Posts, who happened to be a member of the Rotary Club in Jersey. He told me that there were protocol problems. He said they had tried once, but it was politely turned down. Still, he saw no reason why I shouldn't go ahead with an application to the Jersey Postal Committee—part of the States of Jersey—to see if I could persuade them to have a Rotary stamp issued in Jersey, but he held out no hope. The whole story was told in an article published in the magazine "Rotary" in the United States. After 11 years, I finally got Jersey a postage stamp with a Rotary emblem on it, which was therefore the first stamp in the British Isles with a Rotary wheel on it. Here is the story, as submitted in the form of a press release to Rotary magazines. This press release was also included in the envelopes of my limited edition first day covers.

"NOW IT CAN BE TOLD "

The full story of the first postage stamp in the British Isles with a Rotary emblem.

In 1987, Charles Strasser, a member of the Rotary Club of

Jersey in the Channel Islands, and a regular attender at Rotary International Conventions, attended the one in Munich.

For two reasons 1987 is memorable to him. As the then world President of IFFR, the International Fellowship of Flying Rotarians, he was honoured to receive from them a Paul Harris Fellowship award and he accepted a new self imposed challenge, the subject of this story.

At the Munich convention he naturally also visited the stands of the many other Rotary Fellowships. It was on the stand of the "Rotary on Stamps" Fellowship, that he saw and bought an exquisite and fascinating book, compiled by Ernst-Theodor Juergens of Augsburg in Germany, containing a colour replica of most of the stamps of the world and first day covers ever issued containing a Rotary emblem.

When Charles studied this in more detail at home, he noticed that although there were actual postage stamps with Rotary emblems from Australia, France, USA and over a hundred other countries, including many from members of the British Commonwealth, there was not a single one from the British Isles.

As a result he made it his ambition to remedy this and achieve the issue of a stamp with a Rotary emblem.

He thought it would be easy and started the process of trying to get such a stamp issued in Jersey.

In the event it was a laborious, frustrating and lengthy eleven year path and only endless patient persistence and perseverance finally brought the desired result.

The first approach to the then Director of Posts, a member of the Jersey Club, brought a pessimistic response to the effect that he had tried it before, on the occasion of the 50th Anniversary of the Jersey Club and although a design was prepared, it was sunk without trace before publication. He held out no hope of success in any new attempts.

Never one to accept no as an answer, Charles awaited the election of a new Postal Committee of the States of Jersey and the appointment of a new Director of Posts. In 1990, with the explicit authority of the Council of the Rotary Club of Jersey, he made a new application with a well reasoned lengthy letter. Alas, another negative reply was received, explaining that an application could only be considered if it consisted of a very special event of national importance to celebrate by local organisations, societies, etc. A personal interview with the President of the Committee whilst friendly and sympathetic, having seen the album of Rotary stamp replicas, produced no better result.

Also in 1990, at the RI Convention in Portland, Oregon, Charles met PDG Rtn. Michael Gosney, on the "Rotary On Stamps" booth. He is the Curator of the RIBI Wallis Philatelic Collection and a most knowledgeable philatelist, whose expertise and advice has been taken advantage of ever since.

Having copied all these letters to Michael, he wrote "I too am disappointed at the response but I have grown used to the negative attitude to anything concerning a stamp featuring Rotary (or any other Service club) within the British Isles. Over the last ten years, if not longer, there have been numerous attempts to get Rotary featured on British stamps. We have used the most influential people within our organisation but to no avail."

The Jersey Postal Administration got its total independence from the British Post Office in 1969 and formed a substantial Philatelic department. A next step was to research all the stamp issues since 1969 to see which local organisations and for what event a stamp had been issued. In the main this was for "milestone" anniversaries and a forward application was therefore submitted for a Rotary stamp to celebrate the 70th anniversary of the Jersey club in 1993, giving also a lot of background information on Rotary, the Jersey club and its achievements in the 70 years.

The May 1991 reply advised that "the Postal committee does not feel that such an issue fits into its plans for the next few years . . . of course there is no reason why Rotary, as a topic, should not be considered again at some time in the future—1998 (75th. anniversary) or 2023 (100th. anniversary) and it will be for the committee of the day to decide."!

Clearly no point in knocking your head against the proverbial brick wall. Charles advised the council of the club to diary another application for 1995/6, in time for a 75th anniversary issue.

The new club council gave Charles full authority to take up battle again after this 5 year pause.

Yet another Postal Director and Postal Committee President were now in office and rather than regurgitate past events, it was decided to make a completely new application, supported by the book of Rotary stamp replicas.

Charles also invited the President of the Postal Committee, Senator Frank Walker, an elected representative to the Jersey legislature, to a Rotary lunch, to explain to him in further detail the importance of this matter to the club. An assurance of support for a Rotary stamp issue in 1998 was the outcome.

Never count your chickens before they are hatched.

Now the Postal Authority advised that under new policy, every issue had to be profitable and they work to strict financial targets. They therefore wanted a guarantee of the sale of 40,000 sets amounting to £87,000! Understandably, neither the Jersey club nor even RI in Evanston could provide such a guarantee. It seemed we were back to square one.

Every lock has a key—you just have to find the right one.

Extensive further discussions were required and took place with the Philatelic and Marketing Managers of the Postal Authority.

Charles suggested widening the scope of the issue, to include three other major service clubs, thereby increasing interest and sales to a wider audience world wide. This was accepted subject to research. It was then decided to build it into the annual Jersey Christmas four stamp set, as a theme. This is particularly appropriate as the four clubs together with the local newspaper, have been running a Joint Christmas Charity Appeal for many years. Charles advised the Presidents of the three other clubs of their unsolicited philatelic present.

Home and dry at last? Don't believe it. Now the Rotary frustrations started.

The Jersey Postal Authority prepared designs and artwork for the four stamps, a first day of issue envelope and a presentation pack, the latter two featuring one each of the four stamps. All this was dispatched to RI in Evanston for approval, mainly for the accuracy of the Rotary logo.

Then started a new and totally unexpected saga. RI

approved the 31p stamp with the Rotary logo. However, they advised that because the first day cover and the presentation pack had the emblems of Lions, Round Table and Soroptimists next to and with the Rotary emblem, they could not be approved. The reason given was RI Bylaw XVIII section 18.020, which says, "... the RI emblem can not be combined with the name, emblem, badge or other insignia of other organisations."

Locally this decision seemed incredible, particularly as there were many examples of such joint logos in the Book of Rotary stamps. Furthermore it was thought that such a bylaw was not framed to prevent genuine joint efforts of service clubs and as endorsed from the platform at the last RI Convention in Glasgow, but was probably framed to prevent a combination of the Rotary wheel with commercial logos in adverts.

Despite many letters and phone calls with RI in Evanston, no one even at the highest level, was willing to act to prevent a potential cancellation of the whole Jersey Rotary stamp issue. The Jersey Postal Authority exercised great patience but they were perplexed at this turn of events. The other three service club HQ's had all approved the artwork. RI was even prepared to accept leaving out the Rotary emblem and leaving an empty space in the line of four, with the undoubted flood of queries resulting from this action.

What possible logic is there in having four separate stamps on the top right hand corner of the first day cover, each with a separate service club emblem and not allowing the same four emblems to be reproduced together as part of the Christmas theme design on the bottom left corner of the envelope? The book of Rotary on stamps shows numerous such examples even on the stamps themselves and RI agree this is the case, but that it was done without their knowledge or approval and apparently subsequent sanction.

Through the good offices of Rotarian Michael Gosney, British RI Board Director Tony Moore was approached and agreed to have an emergency resolution included in the next RI Board meeting which was to take place imminently. Even the Board, although again sympathetic, felt they could not go against an existing Bylaw. It was suggested that an amendment to this bylaw should be tabled for the next Council on Legislation in two years!

Luckily the Jersey Postal Authority adopted a more enlightened attitude and took off all the four club logos, despite this spoiling the aesthetic design of the artist on the first day cover and the presentation pack and are going ahead with the issue. Sales will commence on the 10th November 1998.

So Charles has finally achieved his ambition, after many hurdles, of the issue of the first British Isles postage stamp with a Rotary emblem. Additionally he has arranged a hand stamping on the day of issue of the first day cover envelope, which has the four denomination stamps on it, to commemorate the 75th Anniversary of the founding of the Rotary Club of Jersey. Thanks are also due to Andree Valentine, the Philatelic Manager of Jersey Post.

The Jersey Post Philatelic Bureau, Jersey JE1 JAB, Channel Islands (Via UK) have available a coloured leaflet on the Christmas 1998 issue, with an order form for the stamps and the first day cover and presentation packs or even sheets of the 31p Rotary stamps only. What wonderful Christmas presents for any Rotarian!

It pays to be a persistent optimist after all.

(Just in case any readers might want to get some of these stamps or first day covers, I am advised by the Jersey Post Philatelic Bureau that, regretfully, they are no longer available from them. They can now only be obtained through philatelic stamp dealers. The one in Jersey is G. Robbe Ltd. at robbestamps@hotmail.com.)

❖ 80 ❖
The Paul Harris Award

IN ROTARY, THERE IS AN international award called the Paul Harris Fellowship (PHF), named after the founder of Rotary in Chicago in 1905. Just as cultural differences affect Rotary in different countries, the method of awarding it or even the meaning of that award differs according to country. In the United States, it is looked on as, in the main, a means of collecting $1,000 for the Rotary Foundation, and a Rotarian can personally buy one or more PHFs. A club can buy it and give it to somebody. I know of instances where it was even bought in the name of a dog. That is not taken kindly by European Rotarians because we look on it as a great honour, a distinction, an award for exceptional services rendered and not to be given lightly. So even though a club has to donate the $1,000 to the Rotary Foundation if it wants a PHF, it can do that from a reserve it has built up from past donations. A club like Jersey probably has 40 PHFs it could award because it has given that much to the Rotary Foundation. It doesn't do so because it keeps it as a very precious award. My PHF wasn't given to me by the Rotary Club of Jersey. It was awarded to me by the International Fellowship of Flying Rotarians (IFFR). About 4 years ago Rotarian John Ritchie, the UK Flying Rotarians section long-serving secretary/treasurer was also awarded a well deserved Paul Harris Fellowship from IFFR. This was his second one as he had already previously received one from his own club.

I was elected the World President of the IFFR in 1986 and was in fact the first non-North American President of the Flying Rotarians. In the first year of my two years in office, I organised, for the first time, for all Flying Rotarians to stay together in one hotel for increased fellowship during the annual Rotary International

Convention. This convention usually takes place around June every year in a different country. It goes back to the United States about every third or fourth year. In my first presidential year, the convention was to be held in Munich, Germany.

Normally, Rotarians apply to participate at these conventions and also apply to the organising convention committee for hotel accommodation. This is allocated randomly. I wanted all the Flying Rotarians to be together. But I found when I wanted to book a hotel for that purpose that, in their contract with the hosting town, Rotary International insists that all hotel accommodation within a certain radius of the town during the period of the convention must be allocated through Rotary and nobody can make direct bookings. Rotary International was not prepared to accept the allocation of a particular hotel for a fellowship.

So in 1986, the year before the RI Convention to be held in Munich, another Rotarian and I flew in my plane to Munich to see whether we could find a suitable hotel just outside the radius where hoteliers had to commit to book only through Rotary International. We found one just on the outside of that boundary, a little local brewery which had a hotel attached to it, and I booked the whole of that hotel for the Flying Rotarians.

That was the first time the Flying Rotarians—who go to conventions to be together, have their Annual General Meeting and have their dinner dance—were able to be in the same hotel and enjoy that special fellowship. During the social occasion in that brewery, I was quite unexpectedly presented with a Paul Harris Fellowship in recognition of my services to IFFR. For the very first time in my life, I was totally speechless. The PHF is considered, in Europe anyway, a very highly prized award, the highest in Rotary, rather than just a sign of a $1,000 pledge.

Besides the Paul Harris Fellowship awarded me by IFFR in 1987, there is another internationally recognized award which is given at the discretion of the local club President. That is the Rotary International Four Avenues of Service Award. It is, as the name suggests, a recognition that you have been active in all the four avenues of Rotary Service. My Jersey Rotary Club awarded that to me in 1999.

◈ 81 ◈

Rotary Fellowships

BECAUSE I HAD BEEN THE World President of the Flying Rotarians from 1986 to 1988, I was invited by the President of Rotary International to be a member of the Rotary International World Fellowship Activities (WFA) Committee from 1988 to 1990. The main task of that committee was to find a way to get Rotary to understand and recognise internationally the purpose or even just the existence of fellowships, and then advise the Board of Rotary International of its findings and recommendations. Very few Rotarians know about fellowships. When I talk to Rotary Clubs about them, I always say they are the best kept secret within Rotary. There are over 50 Rotary Fellowships ranging from Golf to Esperanto, from Home Exchange to Flying, from Skiing to Yachting, from Philately to Chess.

Originally there were two separate groupings of fellowships—one for recreational fellowships like the ones I've just mentioned and the others for vocational fellowships, like doctors, travel agents, and police officers. In later years, that was combined, and they are now known as the Rotary Recreational and Vocational Fellowships. They are international in concept, and they identify a particular group of common interests within Rotary. But they are not well-known enough.

The chairman of that WFA committee convened a committee meeting in Evanston, Illinois, the headquarters of Rotary International. This turned out to be the longest committee meeting of any sort I've ever attended. It lasted four days. We met in the Board Room of Rotary International and discussed ways and means to get fellowships better known and accepted within Rotary. We had a professional committee clerk with us who also was knowledgeable in how to phrase any recommendations we might make to the Rotary International Board. We discussed existing rules, regulations and structure of Rotary at length. The conclusion we came to, and our recommendation, was that the organisation of Fellowships had to be understood and activated at club level. Therefore, we recommended that, just like every club has a Rotarian who is responsible for Youth Exchange and a Rotarian who is responsible for Rotary Foundation, there ought to be in every club a Rotarian responsible for Recreational and Vocational Fellowships. That was the gist of our recommendation, and we gave many reasons for it.

Although we'd been there for four days, the Board did not accept any of our recommendations. Therefore, the existence of these Fellowships today is just as little known, by ordinary Rotarians at club level, as it ever was. When we had completed our work, we were invited as the guests of Rotary International to go on what is known in Evanston and Chicago as the "Rotary Trail" tour. The tour took us to the birthplace of Paul Harris, where he's buried, and to the room where the first Rotary meeting was held. I became a member of the 711 club, which was the number of that room in the Unity Building in Chicago, and I received a key to it. (You pay a subscription and become a member.) Since my visit, that building was demolished, but the actual room was taken down brick by brick in the building where it was in Chicago and is now replicated in Rotary Headquarters in Evanston.

As with any organisation, you only get out of it what you're prepared to put into it. I have enjoyed my participation in Rotary tremendously. I've always considered it to be an avenue for doing good unto others and as a means of good fellowship, fun and enjoyment. And of course one of the great pleasures I derived from Rotary has been through membership of the International Fellowship of Flying Rotarians.

❖ 82 ❖

Community Service: Trade and Professional Associations

WHETHER YOU ARE A BUSY man or not, you owe it to your fellow men and the community you live in to serve it in some capacity. You can contribute to the well-being of the community by giving of your expertise and profitability for the benefit of that community. It's just as important to give service—indeed, sometimes more important to give service—than to give money. Everybody can give service; not everybody can give money. Once you get to a stage in life where you've got money to give, that should become an important part of community service as well. Besides contributing to your community through various associations, it is also useful to be involved because you get to know people and enrich your circle of friends. You see what makes people tick, and you learn what other people's views are.

My first involvement with community service was with the Chamber of Trade in Newcastle-under-Lyme. I had just bought the W. Parton Photographers business when I became a member of the Chamber. Very soon I was asked to become a member of its committee, to which I readily agreed. In that committee, I met the Ramsbotham family. John Ramsbotham had been a Mayor of the Loyal and Ancient Borough of Newcastle-under-Lyme. He ran a gents' outfitters shop and his wife a very good restaurant in the town. The other family I met were the Boormans, Reg and Lily Boorman. The reason I mention these two families is they were locally well respected and influential. Reg Boorman was the factory manager of the local BTH factory, which made fractional horsepower motors in a big way for building into appliances. They were both very active in local and civic affairs. They both had children of my generation. I was one of the younger people on this committee, as in most instances in my life. I also made friends with the children of the Ramsbothams—their son, Ian, and his wife, Pamela. Unfortunately, that friendship didn't last long. He was a surveyor in the planning department of the local council and at the age of only 28, he suddenly collapsed dead one day on the street without any previous warning, because of a stroke or heart attack. It was a very sad and most unfortunate event. Pamela came from another part of England, and after his death she moved back to where she'd been brought up.

In the same office of the local borough surveyor's office in town, there worked a young man by the name of Gordon Johnson, who had a wife by the name of Mary. He later set up a very successful business, first as a civil road building engineer and later a housing developer and builder. They became our best friends, and Gordon later also became a Rotarian. We visited many places all over the world together. Both Mary and Maureen were active in Inner Wheel, the organisation for wives, partners and widows of Rotarians. Interestingly, when we became friends, it turned out that years beforehand I had taken their wedding photographs as the professional photographer in town.

From my acquaintance with the Boormans at the Chamber of Trade, I met their daughter, Sheila, who married David O'Brien. Through them, I met his brother, Paul O'Brien, and his wife, Ireen. They were my generation, so that enlarged our circle of friends. Unfortunately, some years later, Paul died in an unfortunate motor accident, so once again we had a sad loss in our friendships.

Once I started importing and distributing on a national basis and became well-known locally as an employer, the next local organisation that requested my services was the North Staffordshire Chamber of Commerce and Industry, who asked me to join its council.

The proprietor of the largest office supply organisation in North Staffordshire, Francis Bosson, decided to form a local branch of what was then called the Incorporated Sales Managers Association.

Because of my well-known marketing activities, I was asked to be one of the founder members. It later changed its name to the Institute of Marketing and later still became the Chartered Institute of Marketing. We organised regular meetings with talks on marketing and were then granted a local branch status. In due course, I became its Chairman. We had as President, the Lord Stafford, and he was President for many years. When he decided to resign, I followed him in the presidency, but I changed the rules so that a President like the Chairman could only serve for two years. I felt that in any elected office there should be a limit to the number of years you serve so as not to block the progress path of younger people.

During my term in office in the North Staffordshire Branch of the Institute of Marketing, I organised a very big theme Ball one year that became an annual event. The theme I chose that particular year was Arabian Nights. I wanted this Ball to become the most sought-after function to attend in the local social calendar, and I succeeded in doing that. Each year, we just had more applicants than tickets available—a sign of good marketing. We always had a complete box full of goodies in the evening to give to every person there. We wrote to many local and national companies, particularly those where we had members who were on their staff, to give us things for giveaways as individual presents and prizes—particularly samples of their products or promotional items for the goodie boxes. Secondly, we always provided an item of head gear or ornament suitable for the theme of the evening.

In the year that I organised it, I found a government war surplus organisation which had thousands of different sized fezzes for sale. These were good quality, having originally been made for the regiment in the British Army that served somewhere in the Arabian Gulf or Middle East. So we bought 200 of these. For the ladies, we had some Arabian-style tiaras. It was a very memorable occasion. The idea of these themed balls carried on for quite a number of years. They became so popular that if you didn't get your tickets early, you just couldn't participate.

As far as trade associations were concerned, when we started importing I moved from the purely local ones to the national scene and finally became a member of the British Photographic Importers Association. They asked me to become a council member, and later I also became the Chairman. In particular, I was the delegate for the British Photographic Importers Association to the committee of the Photographic Industry Association and delegate to the Joint Taxation Committee. I negotiated with the government departments on behalf of the entire photographic industry on questions of taxation—particularly regarding Purchase Tax and Customs duties. Later, when we expanded our import line from photographic equipment to include electronic products, we joined the International Consumer Electronic Association in London, which was largely composed of Japanese companies like Sony, National Panasonic and JVC (Japan Victor Company, the inventor of VHS system for VCRs). In fact, the Chairman was from JVC and I became the Vice Chairman of that organisation.

All of these bodies were national ones with meetings in London requiring quite a number of trips there. It was a three-hour train journey or four-hour road journey from Stoke-on-Trent, but the trip got quicker as the motorways and train services improved.

Besides the Jersey Computer Association (see next chapter), I was also a member of the Jersey Chamber of Trade and Commerce, a member of the Jersey Branch of the Institute of Directors, and a member of the Jersey Branch of the Chartered Institute of Marketing. When I was a member of the North Staffordshire branch, I gained my FCIM—Fellowship of the Chartered Institute of Marketing.

⋄ 83 ⋄

Making a Difference: The Joy of Giving

AFTER BEING A PILOT AND later group coordinator for the Midland Region of St. John Ambulance Air Wing and transporting kidneys for transplants in Europe, I was asked to become a council member of the Staffordshire County Committee of St. John Ambulance Brigade. Its meetings were held in the county town of Stafford. I served on that for a number of years, together with Lady Stafford, the Chief Constable of Staffordshire and many other worthy individuals. When I relocated to Jersey, I became a member of the St. Johns Ambulance Appeals Committee which achieves outstanding results from a number of fundraising events. I am presently the only man on this committee.

Then I was asked to become a member of the BBC Radio Stoke-on-Trent Advisory Council. This is one of many regional broadcasting stations of the British Broadcasting Corporation. They decided in the early 1950s not only to have national stations but also local ones. There is one in Jersey known as BBC Radio Jersey. A three-year appointment is like being a Governor of the local radio station. You deal with reports from executive management, deal with possible complaints from listeners and generally advise on local policy. The national policy of the BBC is regulated from London. That was an interesting three-year experience.

As a result of my photographic activities, I supported the local camera club and also became friendly with all the professional photographers in the area. It came to light that one of the inventors of photography—besides the well-known names of Fox Talbot and the Frenchman Daguerre—was a local person who researched the chemistry of photography at that time. He was a man called Wedgwood, which is a famous name in the pottery field. This Wedgwood was Tom Wedgwood, the youngest son of Josiah Wedgwood the potter, who lived at Etruria Hall, the home of the Wedgwoods. Tom Wedgwood is credited with a major contribution to photography for being the first man to think of a method to copy visible images chemically to permanent media, though he could never make those images permanently fix on the media. He chemically stained an object's silhouette to paper by coating the paper with silver nitrate. He then exposed the paper, with the object on top, to natural light. Then he preserved it in a dark room. Doing this was, essentially, the birth of photography.

We decided to form a Society of Staffordshire Photographers in Etruria, which is in Stoke-on-Trent, to uphold the honour and tradition of photographers in the area, but also with the aim of getting recognition for Tom Wedgwood. I was its founder Chairman. Local author, historian and photographer Ernest Warrilow became a member of the committee. He is well-known in Stoke-on-Trent and the surrounding area for his book *A Sociological History of Stoke-on-Trent*, which chronicles the development of the area in great detail. Lord Lichfield, a relative of the Queen, who was also into photography, was on the committee as well.

I approached the council of the City of Stoke-on-Trent and asked them to provide us a suitable area in one of the city parks with good visibility from a main road where we could erect a memorial to Tom Wedgwood. They gave permission for a memorial wall, appropriately in Etruria Park facing the main road from Hanley to Newcastle. I got the Wedgwood Factory to make and donate a three-foot diameter black basalt plaque with Tom Wedgwood's silhouette portrait on it. The descriptive bronze tablet underneath showed that this was a local lad who was one of the inventors of photography. The wall with the plaque was erected around 1954 and is still there in good condition to this day.

In those days, I'd always been interested in driving. (Although today, I don't like driving long distances at all. I prefer to fly and rent a car when I get to the intended destination.) The North Staffordshire branch of a national organisation called the Disabled Drivers Club was formed, and they asked me to become its President. We had regular events, some competitive and some social, at which disabled drivers could meet. We also helped when people became disabled and wanted to continue driving and had to have special adaptations made to the cars to enable them to use controls by hand, if they had a leg amputated or the like. That was very rewarding and also a very useful activity. It is always a good way to increase social activity to arrange a get-together of people of any sphere of life who have common interest.

Then the Staffordshire County Council, the authority embracing the whole of the County of Staffordshire, decided to build a factory for the disabled in Newcastle-under-Lyme. They were seeking advice on how to go about the layout of the factory—what sort of activities could be most readily performed, what product, and particularly its sale, could be most easily achievable. I was in on that, right from the foundation stone onwards. I took on the chairmanship, formed a small management committee and appointed a professional manager to run the place. Then we started taking in people with all sorts of disabilities to enable them to lead, as far as possible, a normal personal life but within sheltered employment. Work places were adapted to their particular disabilities. Some people came to work in wheel chairs and again disabled drivers came into the picture. With care and thought, you can find a way of doing things, maybe not at the same speed as an able bodied person, but certainly we gave employment to quite a number of disabled people in this new factory. Our research showed that a lot of potential activity would be of an assembly and packaging nature, so we called the factory Newpak. I stayed with that for about three years until it was well-established and growing. Then I handed the reigns over to my vice chairman.

I then found another interesting challenge—the provision of an actual Spitfire fighter plane for the City of Stoke-on-Trent. Now, why would I want to do something like that? The Supermarine Spitfire, which played such a crucial part in the Second World War Battle of Britain in the 1940s, was designed by an aeronautical engineer named Reginald Mitchell. He was born in the village of

Talke in Stoke-on-Trent. In 1917, he joined the Supermarine Aviation Works at Southampton, where the plane was also built, and in 1918 was appointed chief designer. He was promoted to chief engineer in 1920, and in 1927 he was promoted to technical director. He was so valuable to the project that when Vickers took over Supermarine in 1928, one of the conditions of their contract was that he stay as a designer for five more years. Both the City of Stoke-on-Trent and the City of Southampton claimed the fame of Reginald Mitchell. Being in Stoke-on-Trent, I was interested in perpetuating, like we did with Tom Wedgwood, Mitchell's local connection. The best way to do that was to get an ex-RAF Spitfire and mount it on a plinth somewhere in the city. Quite a lot of money would be needed to be able to purchase a Spitfire, so we set up a Stoke Spitfire Appeal Fund.

I found an ex-Battle of Britain pilot, a retired solicitor who lived in the city. With him and other people who were interested in aviation, we formed a committee and set about organising a public appeal for money. I again enlisted the help of Wedgwoods. The Wedgwood factory produced for us a commemorative basalt plate with a Spitfire painted on it in gold. This was a plate which we could sell as a limited edition item for quite a lot of money to help to raise funds. We did many other fund-raising activities as well. When we got to the stage when we thought we had enough money, we got in touch with the Royal Air Force to see how they could help us. Fate was on our side. They actually had a Spitfire Mark XVI available and were prepared to donate it to us as long as we undertook to look after it and display it in a prominent place. That's exactly what we had set out to do. They told us to build the plinth and they would transport the plane and mount it.

We figured that a Spitfire on a plinth is not going to be there for a long time because it will deteriorate and corrode in the weather. So we designed and built a glass bubble to house it. The City of Stoke-on-Trent agreed that this could be done in front of the Hanley town hall. There was a ceremonial opening in 1969 with a RAF Air Vice Marshal, the City of Stoke-on-Trent Town Clerk and all the organising committee. [See photograph for names] I was not the Chairman of that committee. We made the ex-Battle of Britain pilot the Chairman. I was a founder member and committee member. That's the sort of committee where you want someone with a suitable image to be Chairman. An ex-Battle of Britain pilot had a better image for that purpose than an owner of a small private aircraft.

I also belonged to some organisations and bodies who simply wanted a name to put on their letterhead and usually some financial help to go with it. I became a Patron of the Newcastle-under-Lyme String Orchestra. This always gave me great pleasure because I like associating with people and encouraging their many voluntary causes. I also became President of the Trentham Scout Troop. Through the Rotary Club, I was asked also to lend my name to the New Staffordshire Heart Research Fund, a pure charity, and I became a Vice President of it.

I'm also a duly initiated Councillor of the Ancient Corporation of Hanley—a grand title and an organisation that has been going since 1783. It consists of Aldermen and Councillors who meet once a year for a formal meeting and social occasion. This is called the Venison Feast, and each year the Duchess of Sutherland sends venison from her estate in Scotland. It has to be specially prepared by the chef in whichever hotel the feast takes place, and it is brought in ceremoniously and then becomes part of the menu. The traditional speeches are always extremely full of local interest. Besides the Mayor and the Aldermen, the organisation also has a Recorder, who at the feast reads out (hopefully in a humorous vein) the events both locally and nationally that have taken place in the previous 12 months since his last report. New Councillors have to be nominated and seconded by an existing Alderman or Councillor and approved by a meeting of Aldermen convened for that purpose. Once they have been accepted, on the evening in question they are initiated by two of the tallest Councillors present holding a yard glass of champagne—not the usual yard of ale—up to the opened mouth of the initiate. They then gradually increase the number of degrees of inclination of the yard glass to a vertical position, whether or not the initiated is capable of absorbing the flow. Some people are able to do it; others just have the champagne all over their dinner suit instead. No mercy is shown.

On the evening I was initiated, very many years ago, I had been delegated to make the speech on behalf of the initiates of the evening. After my yard of champagne, I didn't remember a word of what I had carefully prepared, but I made, I'm told, quite a good speech anyway. I'm also pleased to say that I did manage to absorb the whole yard of champagne without spilling a drop.

Before I left North Staffordshire in November of l980, I founded a charitable trust known as the "Strasser Foundation". Once a non-discretionary trust is created, the person who has made the funds available can no longer decide how the trust is to be administered, because this must be entirely up to the trustees. However, it is possible for the person establishing the trust to deposit with the trustees a letter of wishes, and these are usually adhered to. I decided against the trust being administered, as is often the case, by solicitors or accountants who would require quite large fees which would drain from the monies available. I asked my Rotary Club of Newcastle-under-Lyme to set up a small committee to make recommendations, within the terms of the wishes, to the trustees, who also were to be members of the Newcastle-under-Lyme Club. In this way, the trust could remain free of expenses. I must say that the then President and the whole of the club were enthusiastic in accepting that duty I thrust upon them. The letter of wishes basically was that the capital was to be preserved and that the income from interest was to be used for the benefit of people and organisations from and in North Staffordshire who needed some help in achieving worthwhile ambitions or to help fund worthwhile projects. Although it is not part of the requirement of the trust for me to be kept in the picture, every year the trustees send me the audited accounts and the quite extensive list of names and amounts of the disbursements to chosen people and organisations. The original trustees were Geoffrey Snow and Rotarian Bruce Goode. Alan Booth took over from Geoffrey Snow and when Bruce died Tony Bell replaced him. I am grateful to them and the recommendations committee of the Newcastle-under-Lyme Rotary Club for giving of their time and expertise over the years.

After my move to Jersey, I established a similar trust in Jersey with very similar aims but for the beneficiaries to be Jersey people or causes. In this case, my letter of wishes was not as precise as the one for North Staffordshire and did not bind or suggest to the trustees that they must retain the capital intact and only use the interest. They decided that with some financial advisors they would invest some of the money in stocks and shares and try to get some capital appreciation as well as interest and dividend income. Again, I'm pleased that the Rotary Club of Jersey agreed to provide the advisory committee. In their case, the trustees formed that committee as well. The trustees were Rotarians Reg Jeune, Richard Wade, David Watkins, Ian Bravery, Bernard Dubras. Richard and Bernard retired and were replaced by John King. Again my thanks are due to them for the meticulous way they administer the trust.

Once charitable trusts become known, they get their names published in national lists, and the appeals for funds from charities seem to grow year by year. Although in both cases it is made very clear in the aims and objects of the trusts that the money is only available for applicants for use in North Staffordshire and in the second case in Jersey, appeals still come in for all sorts of possibly worthy causes, but which don't fall into the set parameters.

As inflation and/or lowering interest rates made the total interest from the capital less valuable, I have topped up the capital amounts in the North Staffordshire Strasser Trust and the Jersey Strasser Trust. Sometimes they use the name "foundation"; sometimes they use the name "trust." Very often, as in the case of the Jersey Trust, we get a recipient of some funds for service overseas or a student wanting to do a research project coming to talk to the club on what achievements they've made resulting from the contribution. Not necessarily the whole of the funding they required came from the trust.

As of this writing a total of £707,621 has been distributed. These distributions, per the terms of the two trusts, continue to be made on a monthly basis to worthy individuals and organisations who need assistance to further their educational, cultural and research aspirations.

◈ 84 ◈
Other Clubs & Charities

MUCH ENJOYMENT CAN BE HAD through participation in clubs and charities. Here are a few more that I have found worthwhile.

Probus is from the first letters of the two words, Professional and Business, and its membership is made up from retired professional and business men. Quite a number of its members are ex-Rotarians. These are people who no longer want to be committed to a Rotary meeting or the charitable monetary and service requirements. The Probus Club is a luncheon club, effectively a social club only. It meets once a month in a nice restaurant for a lunch which invariably takes three hours or more, usually has a good speaker and just has good fellowship with no duties. A lot of people join it when they leave Rotary. I decided that when I was retired, I could be a member of both, and I kept my Rotary membership. I meet many ex-Rotarians there, and it's a pleasant social occasion.

The Ordre des Anysetiers is another one of these worldwide ceremonial clubs. It started in France and is to celebrate the drink produced from anise seed known as Pastis. It meets once a year formally with due ceremony for an intronisation meeting when new members are initiated. There are about three social events a year with spouses and partners.

The Jersey Wildlife Preservation Trust runs, amongst its many other activities, the Jersey Zoo, now to be known as "Durrell" with a newly branded logo. It was founded by the prolific author, Gerald Durrell, and is now one the biggest tourist attractions in Jersey. The wildlife preservation part of it is very active in ensuring that endangered species are helped to breed, first in Jersey and then in their own countries. Particularly active areas are Madagascar and St. Lucia—the former with lemurs and the latter with the St. Lucia parrot. They certainly need support. With Jersey tourism having suffered a downturn, their income from gate money has decreased, and they are looking to other forms of funding.

The Jersey Speakers Club, of which I was a founder member, goes back to 1980. The initial moves to form the club were made by the late Rotarians Sam Senett and Allen Clerk and me. We put an advertisement in the local "Jersey Evening Post" that we proposed to form such a club to help people learn the art of public speaking. We had a surprising number of people come to that first investigative meeting, which encouraged us to form the club. Sam Senett became its first Chairman, I became its Vice Chairman, and we held regular weekly or fortnightly meetings. We started teaching people, first by a short talk from experience, how to compose speeches, how to present themselves, how to get rid of shyness, how to carry on when suddenly they run out of words, how to address a meeting, how to finish a speech and all that goes on in between. We then had a person responsible for choosing a variety of subjects on which members had to come to the front of the audience and make a two-minute speech about. This subject was only disclosed to them when they stood in front of the audience. It was of course allowed that they could invent things. It didn't have to be factual but was designed to show that they could talk about anything. We had a time keeper with three coloured lights—a start light, a 30-seconds-to-end light and an end light. The timing of the speeches was important. Immediately afterwards, one of the experienced speakers gave them an analysis of how their presentation came over and points where they could improve. It's the sort of club which will never retain the same membership because once people have achieved what they came for, they leave for other things. We had that type of turnover and a constant flow of new people, including a number who were or became members of the States of Jersey, and we vastly improved their standard of public speaking.

We also had social occasions with meals and after-dinner speakers. As people got more experience, they wanted to speak for longer than two minutes on a previously unknown subject, so we gave them a subject to prepare themselves for the next meeting and to talk for five minutes. We intermingled the two-minute and five-minute sessions. This was of more interest to the audience because people were given or chose themselves subjects about which they were experts. We all learned a lot from people passing on their knowledge. Sam Senett and his wife, Rita, were extremely active and came to most meetings. He was subsequently, at my suggestion, made Life President. When he died, the committee decided to make Rita Life President. When she died, I was made Life President. The club did a tremendous job teaching many people to speak. Even if they used it only for making a speech at their daughter's wedding reception, they learned not to be shy, to get up at a public meeting and ask a question to the speaker. You'd be amazed that some people just can't do that. The club went from success to success, and when Sam passed away, Allan Smith took over the Chairmanship and then it passed to others. When we started, the States Education Committee made school rooms, lecture halls and assembly halls available to us, when they weren't being used. When those facilities were no longer available, and the only place the then committee could find was a church hall way out of town—far too inconvenient to get to—so the numbers started dwindling. In the end, it died.

    I was also a founder member of the Jersey Computer Association. A meeting was called in the St. Helier Town Hall for anybody interested in joining such an organisation. At this first meeting, the formation was formally proposed by ex-Senator John Averty, later to become a Rotarian, and I seconded the proposition. This was in the very early days of computing on the PC platform when for the first time it became of interest to individuals and small business users. The association was formed, and I was a committee member for many years. In the main, we had meetings with lectures on how to use computers and individual member's comparison stories. Ultimately, computing became just another leisure or business activity which hardly needed an association. Finally it died a natural death through lack of interest.

During the years it was still alive, we staged an annual exhibition of the latest in computers, hardware, software, peripherals and accessories, either at Fort Regent or in the Pomme d'Or Hotel. I volunteered to organise the first few exhibitions, selling and allocating the space, doing the publicity and really being responsible for the whole exhibition from start to finish. After some years, Dr. Steven Chiang, also a very enthusiastic member of the Jersey Computer Association, took over from me. He is now the most senior IT man for the States of Jersey and still a good friend. The two of us were both awarded the only two honorary life memberships of the association for the services given to it. The association annually awarded a prize for the best commercial programme produced by a member. My programme, Navtor, to create computerised flight plans, was awarded the first prize in the first year of the programme's existence. We proudly proclaimed that in the advertising and on the box for the product itself.

Another charity I supported was the Royal Air Force Association in Jersey. This is for ex-members of the Royal Air Force. It gives them a club to belong to and also collects money for ex-Royal Air Force servicemen or their families who fall on hard times. Once a year they had a charity dinner with an auction which has valuable donated prizes and raises a lot of money. This is quite a popular way of raising money in Jersey because it combines a social activity with a fund-raiser where you have a captive audience of people who know why they've come. Usually, the Royal Air Force Association dinner auctions had a lot of original paintings by painters specialising in painting aircraft in battle actions and also aircraft pictures autographed by Battle of Britain pilots. I was always tempted to buy these, so I have a number of them at my home.

At a similar charity dinner auction for Rotary charities the organiser, Rotarian Allan Smith, was fortunate enough to be able to get the well-known Chinese TV Chef, Ken Hom, who broadcasts nationally on the BBC, to come over as the principal guest speaker. Hom auctioned quite a number of his recommended cooking utensils and also his autobiography, which is also a Chinese cookbook. He was happy to dedicate that for people in the front of the book. In my case he signed it "To the second best Chinese Chef, my friend Charles." This was quite a nice memento to have and treasure.

Another function of this nature, which takes place every two years and is organised by the Rotary Club of Jersey, is an "AMIRA" dinner. AMIRA is an international organisation of Italian maitre d's and there is a Jersey section. We jokingly call it "the local Mafia," and they probably don't like that. When this joint event first started many years ago, I was the Chairman of the organising committee. We had joint meetings before the event to arrange all the details. Their members own or work at different well-known eating establishments in Jersey, and the venue for that evening is usually provided by the Pomme d' Or Hotel, the biggest hotel in the centre of the town, which makes a suitable huge ballroom available to us. The maitre d's set up separate tables and cook different specialty Italian foods at each one. Once you've bought your ticket—and they are quite hard to come by because the event has become so popular and is always oversold—you stay for the whole evening. You can go as many times as you like to the different tables and get served by the maitre d's and their assistants, anything from hors d'oeuvres to soups to steak to Italian specialties, right down to the tiramisu at the end and coffee and drinks. It's all included. It provides a lot of money for local charities. "AMIRA" provides all of that on a voluntary basis. During the proceedings, either an auction or raffle takes place to further swell the charity kitty or for a specific charity. On one of these, a baseball cap personally worn by and signed by Ferrari's Michael Schumacher, the world's best and fastest racing driver, was auctioned. I dearly wanted to add this to my quite large collection of baseball caps, but someone else wanted it too. Believe it or not, the bidding went up to £600 before I finally claimed this dear possession. The charity did well that evening.

To keep me young I decided to have birthdays only every five years and then host a really good party for family and friends in Jersey and for ex-Photopia employees in Newcastle-under-Lyme. The latter also serves as a reunion party and is held at Keele University.

The invitations always read "The only presents I would like is your presence." I also make the suggestion that if they so desire, in lieu of presents, a donation be made to one of my three favourite charities. This practise is a frequent request in the case of "the dear departed". My thought was, why wait. These charities have varied over the years but for the celebration in 2007, my eightieth, they are: 1) The Jersey Hospice Care, 2) The Channel Island Air Search and 3) St. John Ambulance. I have always been pleasantly amazed at the wonderful amounts received by these charities.

⬥ 85 ⬥

The Jersey Joint Christmas Appeal Auction

IN JERSEY, WE HAVE WHAT is called a "Joint Christmas Appeal" which collects money for the elderly and poor to be given as Christmas benefits. Many of the service organisations operate it, including the two Rotary Clubs, with tremendous support from the "Jersey Evening Post" newspaper. The committee is a joint committee of the different organisations, and each of the service organisations that participate provide the chairman in alternating years.

The contribution in terms of service by the Rotary Club De La Manche is a radio auction together with, originally, BBC Radio Jersey and, latterly, with the commercial FM 103 local broadcast station. It needs 12 people all sitting round a table to man 12 incoming telephone lines. The broadcaster takes the items to be auctioned in lots of eight and gives them numbers and describes what they are. People then phone in, the incoming calls are routed sequentially to the 12 different phones, and the volunteers answer them. Bidders give their names, the amount of the bid and their telephone number. After five minutes, that particular section of the auction is closed, and whoever has made the highest bid for any one of those articles is then telephoned and told that they've been successful, and they are asked for their credit card number. They can then pick up the goods or the voucher at the radio station. To have a successful auction we needed attractive lots to bid for. These are donated by different business organisations, by different individuals and even States departments. Usually, because they're not allowed to give goods or money, the States departments offer a visit to their department, like the police station for a day or for a visit to the fire station or the airport for a day.

Besides helping to man the phones, I also always tried to buy something at the auction. Obviously, I didn't want something like a permanent wave at a local hair dresser or a tool kit given by a local hardware store, so I usually went for one of the States of Jersey lots. The first one I bid for and got was a day at the Jersey Police Headquarters, and that was fantastic.

I was picked up from home in the morning in a police car, chauffeured to the police station, shown every department from finger printing to financial fraud to the prison cells, and had a good few minutes with the head of each department and was made very welcome. I then had lunch with the then Chief of Police, David Parkinson, in the police canteen. After that, I was taken in the police car to the shooting range. I was allowed to practise on rotating targets, some of which had women with children in their arms and others terrorists with machine guns, and I had to make sure I shot only the right one. Then they brought the dog handlers out to that countryside area, and I had a live demonstration of how these K9 police dogs caught people trying to escape. We then did some live checking for traffic speeding and finished off by going back to the police station. There, I was again presented to the Chief of Police and given a Jersey police tie, badge and wall plaque. That was a great day out and well worth the donation to charity.

The next year, at the same auction, one of the lots was donated by the Bailiff of Jersey and was for a visit to his Chambers, to the Royal Court Room and to the States Chamber where the members of the States sit to deliberate on the laws and welfare of Jersey. I kept that for quite a long time because when I got the envelope containing the letter of invitation, it read that I could bring up to eight people with me. I didn't want to use it until I had some suitable visitors to take with me. That occasion arose when United Kingdom AOPA (Aircraft Owners and Pilots Association) Chairman George Done and his wife came over to Jersey to award me the AOPA Safety Prize. As he also stayed with us at our home, I thought this would be a good opportunity to use it for the visit to the Bailiff. So I arranged a suitable date and time.

When we got there, the Bailiff himself, Sir Philip Bailhache, welcomed us and really went out of his way to show us around personally. In the States Chamber, he explained to us the political and constitutional position of the Bailiwick of Jersey and gave us its history and some leaflets for my guests. That again was an extremely worthwhile charitable donation at the Christmas Auction.

The following year I was away for Christmas and couldn't help at the auction. Still wanting to donate some money, I gave instructions to a Rotary friend to make a bid on my behalf. Since I'd always done extremely well with bidding for lots given by a States department, I told him to do that again for another one. When I got back, he'd done just that. This time he had bid and won for me a visit into the sewers under the town of St. Helier, which apparently is a privilege to be able to do. In all honesty, it didn't excite me, so I gave that particular voucher to a friend of mine who was more likely to benefit from it.

The following year I was there again helping to man the phones, and I bid, of course, for a States department lot. This time it was from Customs and Excise. Their prize was for a trip in their rigid inflatable Customs boat used for patrolling the territorial waters around Jersey. Our trip was to go round the island and then to Les Écrehous islands halfway between Jersey and the west coast of the Cherbourg peninsula of France, where they had made provision to bring a picnic hamper with them that included champagne.

Since Tony Renouf, the Chief of Customs at that time, was a Rotarian in the De La Manche Club, I had managed to arrange that he be a member of the party on the boat. A Customs boat is not all that easy to arrange. It depends on the availability of the boat from an operational point of view, on the weather being suitable, on the people who intend to go in the party, both from the Customs side and from my side, being available. It took about a year and a half before we got synchronised, but when it did finally happen, it was a fantastic day out. We all had to put on wetsuits, because this was a very exposed, very fast boat which had to be able to catch people in situations where they were not supposed to be.

We took these suits off when we got to the island and had our picnic on the rocks. Les Écrehous is a granite reef about six miles off the northeast corner of Jersey and eight miles from Cap de Carteret, the nearest point on the coast of Normandy. There are a few buildings on three of the tiny islands of Maitre Ile, the largest, Marmotier, where most of the houses are sited, and Blanche Ile. These three and a number of isolated rocks in the area remain above high-water sea level. These rock islands belong to Jersey and are part of my Parish of St. Martin. There is no main water nor main sewerage, nothing other than some rocks, and they are used mainly by boating people for recreation and fishermen for shelter. In one of the houses is a very sparsely furnished room which Customs and Excise use if they are ever caught overnight in that situation. I was invited to use that house and room any time in the future if I wanted to. I again enjoyed another States department day out.

❖ 86 ❖
Keele University

IN 1962 I WAS INVITED to be a member of the Arts Advisory Committee of the Newcastle-under-Lyme College of Further Education. That was my first experience of being involved with an educational body. I really saw the different way academics think from business people. Maybe as a result of my contribution to that body, in 1968-69, I was asked to become involved with the University of Keele.

Established in 1949, as a result of an initiative by the City of Stoke-on-Trent, as the University College of North Staffordshire on land bought from the Sneyd family, it became the University of Keele in 1962. This remains the official name, though Keele University is now the name used by the university itself.

Keele is on the hill just outside Newcastle-under-Lyme. It started with 600 students. Its difference from most other Universities was its constitution, which provided that all students and staff must live on campus. Secondly, it was a minimum four-year course with the first year being the foundation year of interdisciplinary study for everybody, without specific academic subjects, and with everybody deciding after the first year which faculty they wanted to go to and which subjects they wanted to read. That was quite a novel concept at that time. Unfortunately, mainly because of financial constraints, not everybody lives on campus now, but the majority still do. Students can now opt for a three-year course.

In the year 2000, after many years of trying, it finally got its own medical faculty with the local hospital being the training hospital for the University.

The Vice-Chancellors were H.M. Taylor CBE (1962-1967), Professor W.A.C. Stewart (1967-1979), Dr. D. Harrison (1979-1984),

Professor B.E.F. Fender CMG (1985-1995), Professor J.V. Finch CBE DL (1995-)

Its first registrar was John Hodgkinson, and he started as the University Administrator and later became its Registrar, a position he was appointed to in 1953.

Keele was founded in a time of severe post-war austerity, and the government initially limited its size because of its unwillingness to fund growth in its four-year degree courses. Keele was the first new UK University of the 20th century, and with its 617 acres it has the largest University campus in Europe. The University was also anxious to foster a spirit of "town and gown". The University had a huge physical wall around it, as it was in grounds previously owned by the Sneyd family. The central feature was and still is the 19th century Keele Hall. A lot of the buildings were from that era but were subsequently added to by new buildings like the library, the chapel, the various faculty buildings and a thriving student union building.

It was also part of this town and gown philosophy that motivated the University to get more local professional and business people involved in the running of the University. That's how my name came to be put forward as the Chief Executive of one of only two publicly quoted companies in Newcastle-under-Lyme at that time.

I first became a member of the finance committee. Tony Hayek was the honorary Treasurer of the University for many years and I served with him on the finance committee. We had many discussions at his house in connection with University projects. Tony was of Austrian origin, a very well-qualified and respected management consultant and a head hunter in Stoke-on-Trent. He gave many hours of service every week to the University.

As time passed, I was asked to join more of the governing bodies, and in due course I was a member of the Council of the Court, the highest body. I then took over the chairmanship of the Estates and Buildings Committee, which had responsibility for all the buildings and the contents thereof, including new buildings, maintenance and dealing with quite a large staff to achieve the targets set.

One year there was a severe water shortage, and the whole

country was asked to save water. The government suggested that people should limit their bath water to five inches and then use it afterwards to water the garden. Cartoonists had a heyday suggesting, "Save water. Shower together." We discussed how to go about this because, in my view, there was no point in just issuing leaflets to students to use less water. We had to do something that would actually save water without it being obvious that we were doing so. Since every toilet on the University—and there were hundreds of them—disposed a tremendous amount of water every time it was flushed, I hit on the idea that because there was no means by which one could control whether to use a full flush or not, that we should limit the amount of water per flush. I decided to get the maintenance department to put a common brick into every one of these cisterns for the toilet. We worked out how many thousands of gallons of water that would save, and it was an astounding figure, achieved by such a simple solution. We forgot to take these bricks out again when the water shortage was over, and the University is probably still using less water to this day.

Another thing we had to decide was whether to have maintenance contracts on the many machines and utilities. That is always an interesting question as to whether or not it makes the most economical sense to have a maintenance contract, or to wait for a breakdown and pay for its repair when it happens. The same applies to insurance, because maintenance contracts are a form of insurance. As the organisation was so large and the likelihood of everything going wrong at the same time was not likely, we decided we would not have maintenance contracts on anything other than where it was a statutory requirement, such as on elevators and lifts.

We had to decide on maintenance of the old wartime Nissen huts which were leftovers from the days when the Sneyd Estate was used as an army officers' training ground during the war. A Nissen hut was made out of curved corrugated steel or asbestos sheeting based on a foundation wall up to about four feet high and this becomes a semi-circular roof. In the army days, each one of these had beds inside or even bunk beds and a stove with a chimney going right through the centre of it. It was a traditional army camp accommodation—not really best practise for Universities.

Initially, they came in handy as student accommodation, lecture rooms and even kindergartens for staff children. But clearly they didn't fit in with the modern image of the University. As new buildings were built, we dismantled these Nissen huts until only two were left, and they were kept as museum pieces and a reminder of how it all started.

Maintenance and Services was a very good committee. The chief architect and the chief development officer of the University were members of my committee. There were also some University academic staff with us. It became a good mixture of academic thinking and business and professional input and experience. The debate was good, and almost always the resultant conclusions were right.

Another body I was asked to join, on an ad hoc basis, was a selection board when a new Vice Chancellor was to be appointed. A standard advertising procedure in the academic and national press produced quite a number of applicants, and a short list was built up. I was a member of the Interviewing Board of the four final short-listed applicants for the post. The Vice Chancellor is the executive head of the University. The titular head is the Chancellor who, in the case of Keele, for many years was HRH Princess Margaret. She came regularly to Keele to chair degree ceremonies and to balls and student functions. A lot of etiquette and protocol was always explained before any member of the Royal Family arrived anywhere. I was at a number of dinners where she always was quite informal. In later years, as security risks increased, much more vetting of attendees took place. I met her not only at Keele but also when, as member of the Council of the St. John Ambulance Brigade for Staffordshire, she came on a number of occasions to open buildings and events. It was always made very clear in the briefing for HRH Princess Margaret that she did not want to have any pictures taken with any glass in her hand—presumably any glass of alcohol in her hand. (She did like her gin and tonic.) Similarly, she didn't like pictures with a cigarette—although she was an inveterate smoker. She always had a cigarette in a long cigarette holder. Consequently, whenever you saw pictures of her, you would never have seen her with either a cigarette or a glass in her hand. She was indeed, as I believe all members of the Royal Family are, as it is part of their upbringing, an extremely good conversationalist. Certainly, she was genuinely interested in her position as the Chancellor of Keele University.

Another appointment of mine in the early days was as a member of a disciplinary appeals committee which adjudicated, if called upon to do so, on any disciplinary measures taken against an undergraduate by the Vice-Chancellor. Only twice was I called upon to listen to an undergraduate appeal. One was in the case of a degree being denied by the Vice Chancellor for examination cheating. The other case involved thirteen students who had been sun bathing in the nude. Thirteen were fined £10 and eleven were also banned from living on campus for one term. Three of the thirteen appealed the charge. In both cases our committee upheld the decision of the Vice-Chancellor.

Most Universities in the 1970s went through a period of student anger when a lot of protests and sit-ins and all sorts of signs of discontent arose. Keele certainly didn't escape from this national movement, and I remember one in particular where the Registrar, John Hodgkinson, who was a very popular figure at Keele, had this anger vented against him and the Registry Building. It was broken into, occupied and partly set on fire. They even attacked his house.

Yet, to quote from his obituary (he died 4th January 2004), *"he remained good humoured and, had the radical students but realised it, he was more inclined to be sympathetic than to be hostile . . . he also had a firm belief in the importance of academic freedom and the independence of universities. When the University Grants Committee sought to develop techniques of comparative analysis of university costs, he exposed the exercise in a letter to the Times in 1965 as both dangerous and useless."*

He certainly could speak his mind. Students and graduates were important to him. He was the chairman and mainstay of the Keele

Society for many years. Certainly, my knowledge of him over the 12 years I was associated with Keele was that he was a great asset and a great administrator. He was ably assisted in that by Dr. David Cohen, who was the Senior Tutor and who later took over as the Registrar when John Hodgkinson retired.

Keele was a great experience for me. It gave me an insight into academic thinking and into the growth potential of education in Staffordshire, of which the University made maximum use. On average, during the time that I served, I would spend almost two days a week at Keele in one activity or another. I was very honoured in 1979 when I was awarded an honorary degree of Master of Science by the University. At the degree ceremony, which was attended by all graduates and others who received degrees in that year, the citation that was read out to Chancellor HRH Princess Margaret and the congregation by Dr. David Cohen, the Senior Tutor, was as follows:

> When in the ancient world in drama there was need for a miraculous intervention, the deus ex machina appeared in the air before an appreciative and possibly startled audience.
>
> In our times we almost take for granted the modern miracle of the descent from the skies by dedicated men bearing organs such as human kidneys which are transplanted to give new life to men and women who formerly had little hope of survival.
>
> There stands before you today a man devoted to this service; who is a pilot and a Co-ordinator of the St. John Ambulance Air Wing for the transport within Europe of kidney transplants; and for whom this is only one of the many charitable causes which he has served. The range of his activities is the more remarkable in that it has grown at the same time as he has created and fostered the development and growth of an imposing and diversified company which has helped to bring to our homes those very latest products in the fields of photography and electronics which seem so often to originate in the Orient. Perhaps as he returns to this country from one of his visits to Tokyo with the newest microminiaturised television set in his hands he feels like Wordsworth's youth "who

daily farther from the East must travel . . . and by the vision splendid is on his way attended". It might be going too far, however, to suggest that he arrives "trailing clouds of glory"!

That such a man should have time to spare for other things would in itself be noteworthy but that, in addition to his work both locally and nationally with many professional and trade associations, he has served the University of Keele as a member of its Court, its Council and its Finance and Estates and Buildings Committees (and has been the Chairman of its Maintenance and Services Committee for many years) is astonishing and from our viewpoint extremely fortunate.

In the course of the past three years Your Royal Highness has conferred the degree of Bachelor of Arts on each of his two daughters. Today in one characteristic stride he overtakes them.

Your Royal Highness and Chancellor I present to you Charles Strasser, Serving Brother of the Order of St. John, Fellow of the Institute of Marketing, Fellow of the Institute of Directors, Fellow of the Royal Society of Arts, to be admitted to the degree of Master of Science, *honoris causa*.

In the same year I was awarded my honorary degree, the infamous Austrian Secretary General of the United Nations, Kurt Waldheim, was also awarded an honorary degree. Unfortunately, he was unable to attend the main degree ceremony. He came on a separate visit to which I was also invited, and he was shown round the university and awarded his honorary degree in a private ceremony by the Vice Chancellor.

My interest in Keele was also in part due to the fact that my two daughters, Suzanne and Dianne, had both opted to go to Keele when they finished their pre-university schooling. They put it as their first choice on their UCCA forms, and they both were fortunate enough to obtain their first choice. They attended Keele for four years. Both got their degrees from Keele in different years. So there are three members of the Strasser family with Keele degrees—two genuine ones and one honorary one.

After my time at Keele, the University badly needed the upgrading and refurbishment of one of the main lecture auditoriums and the three associated lecture rooms. It was suggested that I might fund the costs involved in bringing these facilities up to date, and I willingly acceded to this request. When completed, the four rooms were re-launched by County Councillor Elsie Ashley in the presence of the then Vice Chancellor, Professor Sir Brian Fender, CMG MA PhD (Lond) and myself. The auditorium was named the Charles Strasser Lecture Theatre. The three rooms were named the Maureen Strasser, Suzanne Strasser and Dianne Strasser lecture rooms.

Keele had excellent sports grounds and facilities but no swimming pool, and I was keen to remedy this. I tried very hard to get people interested in this project. I succeeded in getting interest, but we just could not get enthusiasm for funding it in favour of what were then considered to be more important priorities. With the help of Dr. David Cohen, an appeal for a swimming pool was started among staff and students. It got to a certain stage when, through insufficient funds raised, it was thought not to be a feasible proposition and put into moratorium.

I then thought it needed a push to get it off the ground again. I suggested that I would provide, if and when it was ready to be built, a quite appreciable amount of money as the seed corn for the project and that amount is still guaranteed to this day. There were lots of further negotiations from time to time. One suggestion was that the swimming pool ought to be a joint venture between the Borough of Newcastle-under-Lyme and the University, but that fell by the wayside.

I visited the indoor pool built at nearby Market Drayton and suggested it for a model and that, by using the same architect and builder, substantial savings were possible. I'm told that there are now plans afoot in the next phase of development for a swimming pool to be included. I was told again that it would be called the Strasser Swimming Pool, and I look forward to the day when I can launch it—not by the traditional way of cutting the opening tape with scissors, but by swimming the first length. I hope I'm still around when that happens. In any event, even if I am not and have left for the hangar in the sky, I have made provision for the promised sum in my will.

I wanted to help potential University students leaving Czechoslovakia in 1968 during the period of the "Prague Spring", when it was easier for people to leave from behind the Iron Curtain, as far as Czechoslovakians were concerned anyway. At that time, I provided a temporary home for Paul Strass and his family in our house. Because of my involvement with Keele, I then also undertook to provide money for a scholarship for an undergraduate student who had left Czechoslovakia during studies there and wanted to take them up again in the UK. As it so happens, that money was never used. It became part of my will, and I'll have to think again now as to which is the best way to alter the terms of this scholarship so that it can get a wider potential and therefore a more likely list of applicants.

Since September 1995, the university has been under the most progressive and active Vice Chancellorship of Professor Janet Finch, CBE, DL, AcSS, professor of Social Relations. She is the first woman Vice Chancellor Keele has had. She wrote to me recently to say the student population is now over 7,000 and that in the summer of 2005, 1,600 degrees were awarded over a three-day period in 13 degree ceremonies. These were awarded to undergraduate and post-graduate students attending the ceremonies in the famous Keele University chapel.

Keele is now also a leading conference centre, attracting 100,000 visitors a year. I, too, am a customer of this excellent facility, holding my ex-Photopian staff reunion dinner party there every fifth birthday.

… 87 …

Marco Island

I DECIDED THAT THE WINTERS in Jersey were getting rather cold and damp. (It was actually me rather than the weather that changed.) As a result I decided to winter in warmer climes. I set myself five parameters which had to be satisfied. Firstly, the climate had to be such that for all the six winter months I could swim outdoors every day. Secondly, it had to be in an English speaking country but American was acceptable. Thirdly, it had to have good medical services. Fourth, the transportation access had to be easy, frequent and competitive. And fifth, a country with all the basic human freedoms. Particularly because I like islands and the community spirit generally found there, I decided on Marco Island, Florida which amply fulfilled all the criteria.

It was in the year 2002 that I made my first acquaintance with the paradise of Marco Island, Florida, which has now become my winter abode. I now spend six months in Jersey and still travel and fly in Europe. I spend the other six months (in two three-month segments) on Marco Island. Any visit to the United States longer than three months requires a visa. Also, my annual holiday insurance stipulates that no one holiday may be longer than 90 days. It includes good insurance that allows me private flying, and I don't want to risk upsetting that. I had two check rides at Marco Island airport in a Marco Aviation Cessna 172 aircraft and a Piper Arrow, which they rent out. My check rides were made with Ed Welch, a very able flying instructor, who on his visiting card has the inscription, "Pilot Extraordinaire." Despite that, I passed my check rides and am now able to rent aircraft whenever I want to at Marco

Island Airport. That's where we fly out of nowadays when doing Florida trips.

There are so many winter time Rotary visitors to the Marco Island Rotary Club that the club has welcomed them as Kingfishers, a species of birds that migrates south in the winter. We enjoy all the privileges and fellowship of membership in that club.

There are in fact a number of Jersey families who are regular visitors to, and even residents of, Marco. The doyen of them all is undoubtedly Peter Marek and his wife Penny. Peter was the head chef of the L'Horizon Hotel in Jersey and the winner of many culinary contests. They have established a fine food restaurant in an old Collier house on Marco and made a huge success of this venture.

At a Rotary meeting in Marco I sat by a local Rotarian whose classification on his badge proclaimed him as an Author. Further conversation with Wade Keller established that he was in fact a publisher of private autobiographies and had already at that time published about a dozen. Fate once again had brought me to the ideal person to work with in the publishing of this autobiography. Wade and his wife Sue have also become friends.

❖ 88 ❖

My Business and Life Philosophy

MY DETERMINATION TO SUCCEED, MY perseverance and my confidence in the ability to achieve success were all the factors that led to my attaining business success. Also, it could be that originally having to stand on my own feet at a very early age had something to do with it. Having to leave my own country for strange surroundings with strange new "parents" could have had a lot to do with building my determination. Being in the army had a huge influence in changing me from a boy into a man who saw and grasped opportunities. When I came out of the army, the photographic opportunity was there. This later brought me to my theory of the "conveyor belt of opportunities."

I believe that we are all given a conveyor belt of opportunities, which is constantly moving along in front of us with different parcels of opportunity on it. Some who don't want any responsibility in life will never take a parcel off. Other people who take too many risks will take every parcel off. Clearly, it is not good to take more than one can cope with at any particular time in life. The conveyor belt theory is the basis of my having taken opportunities in my life and enlarged on them. No opportunity is in itself anything other than the definition of opportunity—a means to an end that needs development, hard work and a target to achieve all its possibilities.

Another one of my pet theories is that one shouldn't accept everything at face value. If it isn't logical or reasonable, then challenge it, especially if it comes from a bureaucrat. Certainly, don't believe everything you read in a newspaper.

The often-used word "entrepreneur" is of French origin. One of its various definitions in English is "anybody who shows a more than average ability to take opportunities and convert them into achievements." That is also my definition of entrepreneur. Another definition of the word, that I like and would subscribe to, was used in a book I read. To quote "the dictionary tells us it is derived from the French word 'entrepredre', which means an undertaking with risk. The entrepreneur is always willing to take a significant risk in order to achieve his objective. He is also capable of using trail blazing, or non-conforming strategies in the quest. These are not characteristics in people easily accommodated by large corporations."

I always wanted to "do my own thing", be an entrepreneur and run my own business. That led me to open my own photography studio. Yet I came to realise when I was a photographer that I could never really make a lot of money just by taking photographs. You can become famous, but you can't become rich. I came to realise, looking around me, that successful people are those who buy and sell, whether goods or services. Similarly there is a limit to what you can achieve on your own without also creating employment for others. I started on my own and finished giving employment to hundreds of people.

It's important for an entrepreneur to always remember four classes—effectively, four partners—in his business, to whom he owes primary loyalty. The first class is the customer. Without him, the other three cannot exist. The other three classes are the investors, the staff and the suppliers. Without any one of these classes, you cannot run a successful business. Another one of my basic principles is to keep your accountant, banker, lawyer and insurance broker fully informed and updated with your activities and plans. Communication in this, as in any other field, will pay dividends.

✦ 89 ✦

More Quotes & Personal Observations

HERE ARE A FEW OF the mottos that I live by.

Why say it with 100 words, when 10 will do? (Obviously, I'm not going to enlarge on that.)

My word is my bond (dictum meum pactum). This has been the motto of the London Stock Exchange since 1801, where bargains are made with no exchange of documents. In terms of believing in someone's word, there can be no stronger recommendation.

The slogan "Add value" is important and not paid heed to sufficiently. Whether you are giving a service, manufacturing a product, or selling a product, the best way to ensure continued loyalty is to add value.

Enthusiasm is infectious. Any leader must possess a mountain of enthusiasm.

It is very important to lead by example. That doesn't mean that one has to be at work at exactly 7 a.m. every day and be there at all times. It means showing willingness to perform any duty and showing people how they can perform their function better.

In reading other people's success stories, you can see that they grew by giving employment to others. The whole theory of capitalism is based on the employment of people. The old contention of the anti-capitalist would be that you exploit other people, but you can employ other people without exploiting them. The basic concept has always got to be to create wealth. Wealth creation gives job opportunities. Of course, you can also go bankrupt, and that's the risk of the capitalist, or of the entrepreneur, as I prefer to name him. Provided it has been set up correctly, the more sales people you employ in a selling organisation, the more wealth you create for everyone involved.

I had profit sharing for all staff even before going public. Usually it was a percentage of sales. It was paid out in the form of a Christmas bonus. The size of it was dependent on the sales of the previous year. It was a good payout once a year, but we called it a Christmas bonus, because of tax advantages. It was always based on gross sales rather than profits.

Another one of my policies is that it's totally management's responsibility to turn sales into maximum net profits. People in the work place have very little control of keeping costs and overheads down. Things like that are purely functions of management. You can say to people, "Switch the lights off when you go out of the room," but whether they do it or not is a management training and control function. It's an educational process. Doing things in-house is also a function of management.

Other principles, philosophies and practices of mine include the following:

- I would never ask anyone to do what I am not prepared to do myself.

- Never to go back on an incentive arrangement with any employee regardless of earnings produced or benefits. A lot of ill will has been created in other companies when salesmen were deemed to earn too much money and the basis of their remuneration was changed so they wouldn't earn so much money. That's the most terrible thing you can do to a salesman, because once you've agreed on a system of percentages, bonuses, etc., the more they earn, the more the employer should be pleased because he in turn is going to earn a lot more as a result of that.

- Always personally answer letters addressed to you. (Ask for the facts from the relevant department heads.)

- Never have Board meetings during normal working hours. Whenever I phoned up another company, nothing annoyed me more than being told the person I wanted to speak to wasn't available because he was in a Board meeting. Board meetings should not prevent important people in the company from speaking to customers, and they should always be held out of working hours.

- Always have your door open and be accessible to anybody at any time.

- Never blame employees for what are management shortcomings and failures. I've heard many organisations and managers complain about things being done wrongly or badly which they were responsible for. The higher in the organisation an executive rises, the more responsibility he must assume for teaching people at lower levels how he wants things done, rather than blaming them for things not being done in that way.

- Here is a tried and true saying: "Trust and reputation take a long time to acquire, but can be lost in minutes."

- You have to pay for your own mistakes, but you don't have to pay for the mistakes of others. In practical terms, if we lost money because we've made mistakes on invoicing or over delivery and nobody ever pointed it out to us, that's our problem for lack of control, and we have to pay for that. Similarly, when other people in business make mistakes, it's not up to us to point out their mistakes to them resulting from their inefficiency. That is a thing that other people may disagree with. But I believe that the one cancelled out the other—the mistakes we made and the mistakes they made.

- Most important is my one-word slogan: "Anticipate."
- As I've said many times, "Persistence and gentle persuasion achieve results."
- Every lock has a key—you just have to find the right one.

I particularly dislike management consultants and employment agencies. They are both, in my opinion, totally unnecessary and redundant to the running of a sound business. I know large businesses and government departments use them extensively, but I have never used either of them. They exist for organisations with officers who lack the confidence of making decisions and need the protection of being able to blame somebody else if things don't go according to plan.

In management terms, consultants sell good ideas and practices obtained from one client at expensive fees to another client. Employment agencies exist to turn over staff, and that is how they earn their fees. They send an employee to a prospective employer but believe that once that employee is on their books they own him or her. Very often before they have even settled down in their new job, they are approached again by that employment agency to suggest a change of jobs. This is purely so the employment agency can earn more fees.

Any self-respecting employer or government department, however small, should have a person or department responsible for recruitment and have a proper method of selection without needing outside help for it. Similarly, regarding consultants, any company should ensure they employ experts in their particular field or get advice from their trade association. In the case of government, they should employ people from other departments within or outside their organisation who have already had similar experiences.

Invest to accumulate. That has been a large part of my success. If you want to build up a big business, then it is important in the initial stages to live frugally and to reinvest all profits of the business into it to enlarge it. Take out only a minimum amount of salary, dividends, bonuses, and thereby prevent any drain on the capital available for expansion. Don't take anything out of the business for quite a time until it can properly stand on its own feet.

We had a standard costing formula and cost cards for every one of our products. That formula was given to the shipping and buying departments. We tended not to sell products at a high price just because we were the only ones with it on the market. Every little item, whether it was a £1 item or a £1,000 item, was costed on that standard basis without discretion to vary it. The costing formula was a function of management from budget control and the like. If a psychological or break point price was needed, if the item costed out at say £103 and you wanted to be able to sell it at £99, you couldn't sacrifice that percentage out of your margin. Therefore, you'd have to go back to the manufacturer and make a good case for getting a price reduction. You had to explain to them that you'd sell a lot more at £99 than you would at £103. The same procedure arose if a product was no longer competitive. Then the maker had to be persuaded to reduce the price to that of a competitor or accept a drop in sales.

I have a theory about partners in business. First of all, an enterprise is like a ship and can only have one captain. You need a good team of officers and a good crew, but you can only have one captain. Even in consensus management every company needs to have one person who makes the final policy decision. Usually the more equity he or she owns, the more responsible he or she will be about making those decisions. The partnership side comes into that as well. You can have sleeping partners who provide money and know-how, but there must still only be one captain, even in a partnership. I don't believe in business partnerships. Sooner or later they will fall out. Then you have opened a whole can of worms in trying to decide who should own what. Often the business falls apart.

A government that levies taxes becomes a partner in your business. They are taking money from your business out of all proportion to what services they provide. Their ever increasing regulations just make life more difficult for you. So they are, in my language, a sleeping partner. You give them money every year, but they don't actively do anything for it. I'm prepared to accept a sleeping partner. But if I do all the work, I'm the active partner and I want at least 50% of the share. It is unacceptable, in my view, for any government to take more than 50% in cumulative taxation—that is, income tax, sales tax, social security taxes, etc. During Harold Wilson's government in England, we had a lot more than 50% in taxation. Any government which takes more than 50% taxation will, in my opinion, not sustain a successful economy.

A successful government is one that leaves as much freedom as possible to the people and business. It is the government's responsibility to provide education, social and health care and internal and external security, and to provide the freedom for businesses to create employment and wealth. All the other things will then follow automatically from that. There should be a minimum amount of government regulation and interference with business. The more time companies and their management are required to spend on the two vexing problems of over-taxation and over-regulation, the less time they are able to spend on wealth creation for the benefit of their company, the employees, the community and the country in general. What I'm looking for are politicians courageous enough to challenge and do something about the constant burden of over-taxation and over-regulation.

It is fair that people who earn a lot of money should pay a lot more income tax than people who earn less. There doesn't necessarily need to be a cap in terms of amount either, as long as the percentage levied is the same for all taxpayers.

A sales tax at a very low level, no higher than 3 percent, is better than a Value Added Tax. A Value Added Tax, particularly at varying rates, takes too much collection and supervision cost. A universal sales tax is easier as long as there are no exceptions whatsoever. It's easier, but then you get people arguing that there shouldn't be a sales tax on children's clothing or food or the like because that's taxing the poor. There should be one very low rate across the board. Then, if you want to—and you should—support people who are genuinely in need, then you should give them financial support rather than stop taxation for certain goods or services. In other words, help the genuine needy as required.

If somebody, for a length of time, sells goods under the price he buys them for in order to kill a competitor, that is unfair competition. Both companies can't continue business on that basis. If you allow a situation where people can bribe or corrupt officials, that's also unfair. But the fewer officials you have, the fewer opportunities for bribing. So, again, the government should be hands-off as much as possible. Then you can have discussions on what is fair and what is unfair.

I don't have a sufficient amount of patience for politics. I've been asked many times to stand for election for a seat on my town council in my original home town in England and also for a seat in the States of Jersey. I might be successful at it, but to continue to debate things over and over again is not my forte. I like quick decisions based on research and facts. I also don't like large committees. In any organisation some people always do most of the work while others do little or nothing. I call it the "20/80 ratio." 20% of the people do 80% of the work.

A quote I like is by Calvin Coolidge on persistence. He said, "Nothing in the world can take the place of persistence. Talent will not. Nothing is more common than unsuccessful individuals with talent. Genius will not. Unrewarded genius is almost a proverb. Education will not. The world is full of educated derelicts. Persistence and determination alone are omnipotent."

❖ 90 ❖

Charles G. Strasser OBE

WHEN THE QUEEN'S BIRTHDAY HONOURS LIST or the Queen's New Year Honours List is published, most people believe that the people listed therein did not know they would receive the award. Although the award winners express surprise, they actually knew about the receipt of the honour one month ahead of time. On a date in May 2000, I got a buff envelope marked "On Her Majesty's Service." I immediately thought it was an income tax demand, because that's the usual envelope they use. But when I opened it, it was a letter from the Prime Minister's Office advising me that my name had been put forward for receipt of the Order of the British Empire and I had the option to accept it or refuse it.

The final paragraph then said, "We look forward to hearing from you, but until you hear officially in the published lists, it is by no means certain that you will get the award, and you will be well advised not to talk to anybody about it before that date."

You are effectively in the know of exciting information but bound to secrecy—not by having been sworn to secrecy, but by the very fact that you might be embarrassed by your name not being on the list, and then you really would look silly if you told anyone beforehand. It was a long month for me, but I kept the information completely to myself. Shortly before the proposed list was published, I got another letter to say there would be local and national publicity and that the Press required a little advance information so they could publish the list on the day in question.

Therefore, the letter read, I might be approached by the media up to 24 hours before the event and to be ready for that, and that is what happened. On the day before, I received phone calls from all the media in Jersey—from the "Jersey Evening Post", BBC Radio Jersey, and Channel Television—all of whom arranged an immediate appointment to come and see me at my house. They came with television cameras, reporters and recorders, and took videos and statements which were then released on the actual day of the award being published.

On the two dates in the year when these honours are published, a very long list appears in various newspapers but specifically in very detailed fashion in "The Times" of London. Included are all the honours, from KBEs (Knighthoods) to MBEs (Member of the Order of the British Empire) as well as Police Medal Awards, Diplomatic Service Awards, etc. All the honours are given for services rendered of one sort or another, from a lollipop school traffic warden to a senior ambassador in another country, on behalf of Her Majesty the Queen. These awards are published in the order of seniority of the award and then in alphabetical order.

At the time of the Queen's Birthday Honours in the middle of the year, the Lieutenant Governor of Jersey, who is the Queen's representative in Jersey, also arranges a garden party at Government House. Although this is on the evening before the official publication date of the honours, the Lieutenant Governor has always used the occasion to announce the local names within the honours list. Normally, those people have been invited to be present at the garden party amongst hundreds of people. The garden party is partly by invitation but is advertised in the local press as being open house, and anyone is welcome to go to Government House, which is not guarded in any way, to take part in the Queen's Birthday garden party.

So it was that on Friday 16th of June 2000, I attended Government House for this party. The point came when the Lieutenant Governor, His Excellency General Sir Michael Wilkes, KCB, CBE, announced the three local people whose names appeared in that year's birthday honours. They were, firstly, Pierre Horsfall, who was a senior Senator in the States of Jersey, the Parliament of Jersey. At that time, he was the President of the Finance and Economics Committee, the equivalent of the Chancellor of the Exchequer in the UK. The second name was an MBE, Wendy Hurford, who had been a headmistress in Jersey for many years and in particular had done tremendous work with special needs children. The third one, an OBE, went to yours truly.

The awards which are all made within "the most excellent order of the British Empire" are in the following classes: The Knight Grand Cross, which is known as the KBE and entitles the recipient to a Knighthood and be called Sir, or Dame in the case of a lady. Next is the CBE, which is the Commander of the Order of the British Empire and entitles the person to put CBE behind their name. Then comes the Officer of the Order of the British Empire, which entitles the person to put OBE behind their name. Last, but by no means the least honour, is the MBE, which is the Member of the Order of the British Empire. There are also some military equivalents of these orders.

Once the local publicity, festivities and celebrations are finished, one waits to get another letter to be invited to go for the actual investiture of the honour, by Her Majesty the Queen at Buckingham Palace. The three local recipients had hoped that we could go to the Palace together, but it was not to be. The dates are entirely decided by the organising authorities. Once the news was published on the front page of the "Jersey Evening Post" about the three local honours, I received a tremendous number of letters of congratulations. Later, once the news filtered to other parts of the United Kingdom and the world, I received even more letters.

The first such letter I received was hand delivered by the chauffeur of the Lieutenant Governor, His Excellency General Sir Michael Wilkes, KCB, CBE. It was handwritten by him, from Government House and still dated 16th of June, the day before the official announcement. It read, *"It is my privilege to be one of the first on the Island to congratulate you on your award of the OBE on the Birthday Honours List. Your services to Keele University in Staffordshire and to Jersey are all well documented and serve as testimony to your generosity and far-sightedness. Your life has been a remarkable tale of adventure and fortitude. Recognition at the National Level does not come easily but I can think of no one who deserves it more than you do. All Jersey will, I know, be delighted. With very warmest best wishes, yours sincerely, Michael Wilkes."*

That is a very treasured letter.

In my case, the letter advising me of the date of the investiture arrived quite late in the year. It was fixed for the 5th of December, 2000. I decided to invite my two daughters to be my official guests, and we made a social occasion of the trip. I flew out of Jersey in my Piper Seneca II for Southampton, on Saturday 2nd of December. I stayed with my daughter and son-in-law at their house in West Tytherley until Monday 4th of December and then we went in Dianne's car to Southampton Airport. From there, we hired an airport limousine to take us to the Mayfair Intercontinental Hotel in London's West End. Suzanne had already come on the plane with me from Jersey, so now there were three of us at the hotel.

The investiture is a very formal affair and has a very strict dress code. Since I was likely to wear the outfit only on this occasion, I decided to hire it for the day. All the measurements had been sent to Moss Bros and, on the afternoon of the Monday, I picked up the coat, trousers, special waist coat, top hat and all the accessories. We had a dress rehearsal at the hotel. Everything fitted perfectly. For my daughters, it was an opportunity for new outfits also, but in their cases I bought the dresses and hats of their choosing. In the evening we went to a Japanese restaurant.

The invitation to the Palace requested arrival at 10 a.m., and we had been provided with car identification stickers, security passes and invitations. If you went with your own car or in a chauffeured car, you could drive into the courtyard of the Palace. We decided to go the short drive by taxi and were dropped off at the gate and walked from there.

On the way in, right by the gate, Suzanne suddenly said, "Hey, dad, somebody is shouting, 'Mr. Strasser, Mr. Strasser.'" I couldn't believe it, but the next minute I saw three ladies whom I recognised as ex-employees of mine from North Staffordshire in the Photopia Company. They had come up specially that morning just to wish me well on this great day. They'd got green and yellow- Photopia colours—balloons and were so excited and joyful. Considering that they'd got up very early in the morning and made the coach journey to London to be there from 9:30 a.m. to catch me on the way in shows real lasting loyalty and affection. I was very moved. Although I couldn't talk to them at length at that particular point, they said that they would still be there after the ceremony and that I would see them then.

We went into the Palace. The award recipients part company from their guests, who are shown into the auditorium of the Great Hall where the investiture takes place. The recipients are marshalled into a picture gallery within the Palace to have explained to them and be instructed in the very precise procedure that has to be followed. This is to make sure that everybody goes in the right order so there is no chance that they get the wrong medal. This is all done very professionally by household staff, usually ex-military officers, who do it in a most clear-cut manner, partly laced with humour.

They explain that once you come to the point of entry into the Great Hall, you are held by an Air Vice Marshal until it is your turn. Once he taps you on the shoulder, you go forward to the middle of the hall, where you see a small dais. If you go there to receive a Knighthood, you would have to kneel to have the sword put on your shoulder. In the case of other classes of awards, like CBEs, OBEs, and MBEs you would go forward to a marked point. Her Majesty the Queen would then hand the honour to you. In the case of the KBE and the CBE, the award is in the form of a ribbon which goes around your neck. In the case of the OBE and the MBE, it is a medal which she pins to your lapel. You are taught that she will speak to you and that you address her purely as "Ma'am", not "Your Majesty" or anything of the sort.

When she's finished, she will shake your hand, and that signals that it is the end of your turn, your moment of glory. You then must remember to walk backwards until you are back in the line from where you went forward, turn smartly to the right, and go out through the exit at the other end of the hall. It is not easy under those circumstances to remember that you must walk backwards.

It came to my turn. I did as instructed, and Her Majesty the

Queen pinned the OBE on my lapel and started talking about my experiences and service to Keele University. I was quite amazed at her personal knowledge, and I said to her that, yes, it had been my pleasure and that I'd given service there to repay the tremendous amount of help and assistance and support that I received when I first came to that area as a refugee. That was the point at which I got the handshake. I went only a small number of paces, and I nearly forgot to walk backwards. I started to turn, then I caught myself and walked backwards and proceeded to exit.

The ceremony carries on, and you wait until it is finished and then you join up again with your guests and go outside in the courtyard, where the official photographers are busy taking photographs. These are then used in the local papers where the recipients had come from, and the pictures, no doubt, adorn their albums and picture frames.

As we were standing in the courtyard waiting for our turn with the official photographer, I saw that also waiting in the courtyard were four Yeomen Warders, or Beefeaters, who had been part of the ceremony and who live in the barracks at the Tower of London. Wearing their extremely ceremonial red and gold uniforms, they are always used for all sorts of ceremonial occasions, and they stand during the investiture ceremony at the back of the platform behind Her Majesty the Queen and her entourage. They get brought to the Palace in a covered horse-drawn carriage, and they were waiting for that carriage to take them back again to the Tower.

As a photographer and as someone who is not backward in coming forward, I could see a wonderful opportunity of a unique picture here. I went over to one of them and asked him whether it would be possible please to have a picture quickly taken with them. They immediately acceded to the request. I believe they were quite pleased for that sort of an opportunity as well.

I immediately gave my Minolta digital camera to my daughter, Suzanne. I quickly stood in an appropriate position amongst them, and she took the picture. It was only just in time because she had taken two shots when their horse-drawn carriage came, and they had to quickly embark. The "Jersey Evening Post" printed that picture in full colour. The picture was and is, as far as I am aware, unique. I also used it in the following year, 2001, as the cover of my annual photographic Christmas Card and now as the cover picture of this book.

When we got back outside the Palace about two and a half hours later, we had not forgotten my three ex-employees, Christine Sutton (nee Bengry), who was for many years my secretary, Anne Davies (nee Conyon), who was for many years staff supervisor, and Phyllis Bayley, who was for many years a senior typist and some of the time also stood in as my secretary. They had all joined the company straight from school, all now retired, and here they were having come up by coach to London for the day to see me and wish me well. We stayed and chatted, and I expressed my deeply felt gratitude and appreciation of their having gone to so much trouble to make the day an even bigger event than I had anticipated.

Before the event, I had received an invitation from my long-standing friend, Stanley Kalms—by that time Sir Stanley —and his wife, Pamela Kalms—by that time Lady Pamela. Sir Stanley had already gone through the same experience of an investiture to get his Knighthood. He invited us to come direct from the Palace as his guests for a celebration luncheon at the Ritz Hotel. This is booked by many for such celebrations, and unless you do it early enough, you stand no chance of getting in. He had very graciously said that I could bring whoever I wanted to that luncheon. Since Keele had been so much involved in part of the reason for the award, I had invited Professor Janet Finch, the Vice Chancellor of Keele University, and her husband, Professor David Morgan, to join us. Sir Stanley and Lady Pamela brought their eldest son, Richard, along. He and his brother Steven and my daughters had spent some holidays together with us when they were children, and this was their first reunion since then.

Needless to say, it was a wonderful lunch. Stanley was on his best form. We always sparred quite a lot on occasions of this nature, and this lunch was no exception.

It was at this point that I announced my intention to do my autobiography, and Stanley said that he was already busy doing his and that he wouldn't mention anything in his book about me that I might not like if I gave him the same undertaking which, of course,

I immediately did. The champagne and wine were appropriate to the occasion, and they were flowing liberally. As you, dear reader, will see from the photograph of my daughters at the Palace, they both had, as any lady would expect, brand new outfits for the occasion. I must say they looked very smart indeed. I was very proud to have been accompanied by them on this memorable day.

I found out subsequently that the delightful menu at the Ritz had been personally chosen by Pamela. The specially printed menu for our table read "Luncheon in Honour of Charles Strasser OBE given by Pamela and Stanley." The delectable menu was smoked salmon and caviar, cannon of lamb, Lyonnaise potato, chocolate fondant or strawberry cheesecake, coffee and petit fours. Most people present put little remarks on the back of my copy of the menu as a souvenir. Stanley wrote, "Charles, an invaluable friendship, long may it last. We have shared many happy days. Stanley." Pamela wrote, "Dear Charles, You do so very much for others, it gives us great pleasure to share this moment with you. Pamela." That is a very moving sentimental memento, as you can imagine.

Also as a souvenir of the occasion—besides the official photograph and the unique photograph with the Beefeaters—there is made available a video of the investiture. It lasts about 45 minutes, and it is produced in such a way that it appears that the ceremony features you as the main star. It is, in fact, a standard video of an investiture with carefully spliced unique shots of the individual featured in that video which one can buy afterwards. This shows one receiving the award and already includes some snippets taken from entering the steps of the Palace and again joining up with one's guests and even shots being instructed on procedure in the Picture Gallery. When the video comes, it is a really wonderful souvenir of the occasion that captures forever the full pomp and ceremony that one felt on the day.

After our lunch at the Ritz, we went back to the hotel and all met again at 6:30 p.m. to have an evening out at the Apollo Theatre. On Wednesday morning, we went back to Southampton in the airport limousine. Sue got a commercial flight back to Jersey, and Dianne went home by car. I flew to Coventry Airport and stayed with my friends, Gordon and Mary Johnson, at their house in Maer

Heath near Newcastle-under-Lyme, because on Thursday the 7th of December was the Annual Venison Feast of the Ancient Corporation of Hanley at the North Stafford Hotel in Stoke. Gordon and I were both councillors of this corporation, so I was able to, as they say, kill two birds with one stone. I had also arranged for us to sit with Councillor Geoffrey Snow and this was an added pleasure. A very enjoyable evening was spent among many old friends, and on Friday morning I left Coventry Airport to fly myself back to Jersey.

❖ Epilogue ❖

IN COMPLETING THIS AUTOBIOGRAPHY I am reminded of the story of a reporter interviewing the oldest man in a small village on his 100th birthday.

The reporter asked, "Have you lived here your whole life?"

To which the man replied, "No, not yet."

It has been good to reflect back over the 80 years that have passed since I first arrived on the scene. I agree with Socrates when he said "The unexamined life is really not worth living." I've done much examining in writing this autobiography. When you look back over a long journey you can see many forks in the road and decisions made. And when you look just a little deeper I think you have to agree with the following quote from Buddha:

> All that we are is the result of what we have thought: it is founded on our thoughts, it is made up of our thoughts.
>
> If a man speaks or acts from an evil thought, suffering follows him as the wheel follows the foot of the ox that draws the carriage.
>
> If a man speaks or acts from a pure thought, joy follows him as his own shadow that never leaves him.

My thoughts from the earliest days have led me to the person I am today. So, who is Charles Strasser? And how would I like to round out my time here on earth? Those are the questions I will address in this epilogue.

First of all I'm cosmopolitan. I feel comfortable in many different regions of the world, different cultures and spheres of interests. Part of this may have been the result of being uprooted at an early age from my Czechoslovakian culture and plopped down in the English Midlands. But more importantly I embraced the change. Even before leaving my homeland I was fluent in both Czech and

German. In the Czech Army attached to the American Army at Nuremberg I soaked up American culture and indeed decided to take the name Charles at the suggestion of a G.I. friend. Later two of my best friends (who led me to Maureen) were Indian and Pakistani. And as my business grew it was necessary to travel the world, first Europe and then Asia, in pursuit of agencies.

My religious journey also has a cosmopolitan nature. My parents were living in the Bet Alfa kibbutz in the British Mandate of Palestine when I was born. Disillusioned, they returned to Czechoslovakia four months after my birth and I was raised in a secular household. When adopted by foster parents in England, I easily became a part of the Church of England and am today a parishioner of St. Martin's Parish Church in Jersey. My wife Maureen is buried in the church cemetery and I expect to be also.

But religion to me takes on a much broader concept than church buildings or dogma. My true religion is best expressed in the ideals of Rotary with its emphasis on *Service Above Self* and its objective of world peace and understanding.

Politics is another area for self examination. A quote often attributed to Winston Churchill sums up my path. "If a man is not a socialist by the time he is 20, he has no heart. If he is not a conservative by the time he is 40, he has no brain."

I was an ardent socialist in my youth. The siren call was strong. Socialism embraced the noble concept of altruism as the basis for government policy. It claimed that wars were caused by capitalism and only with socialism could we have world peace. That sounded good and reasonable. But the reality is that human nature is not suited to collectivism. To grow as individuals and as a society we need the sparks of individual initiative.

While I have been successful in building a business and fully taking advantage of the opportunities in a largely capitalist, free enterprise environment, I have also strived throughout my life to serve the larger community. My charitable endeavours are well documented in this autobiography.

Like the old man in the small village, I can still say, "Not yet."

There are no more mountains in my future. But the opportunity to enjoy all the blessings of civil society are very pleasant and rewarding. Where I can use my negotiating skills to benefit others, I will do so. Where I can fund worthwhile charities, I will do so. Where I can enjoy a pleasant conversation, the good company of men and women, I will do so. Where I can provide guidance to my children and grandchildren, I will do so.

And of course there is flying which I still enjoy and which reminds me of a zestful—although premature—obituary that was written for me by an American Flying Rotarian friend, Herman Hassinger, a retired architect and still active pilot from Block Island, RI.

Charles was happy when he could fly
To go with the birds in the sky.
Humble but regal
He was our silver eagle.
That Strasser was a helluva guy.
His hair was silver but his heart was gold
Eternally young no matter how old.
Ran life as a race
With a smile on his face.
After God made Charles
He broke the mould.
His like we will never again see
A man like Charles Strasser OBE.
His silver moustache,
His style and panache,
He was one of a kind, you'll agree.
With regard to these words we have penned
We realise that all good things must end.
In heaven or hell
We all wish Charles well.
Farewell dear Charles, our good friend.
Now here is what I really think.
He went with a smile and a wink.
In heaven or hell,
We all wish him well.
Let's lift our glasses and drink.

Appendixes

Appendix A

Offer Document to Become a Public Company

PF-PL 72   **PHOTOPIA INTERNATIONAL LIMITED**   **PHO**

(Incorporated under the Companies Act, 1948)

Photopia REGISTERED TRADE MARK   **Japanese Cameras Ltd**

A Copy of this Advertisement (having attached thereto the documents specified below) has been delivered to the Registrar of Companies for registration.

This Advertisement is issued in compliance with the Regulations of the Council of The Stock Exchange, London, for the purpose of giving information to the Public with regard to the Company. The Directors collectively and individually accept full responsibility for the accuracy of the information given and confirm, having made all reasonable enquiries, that to the best of their knowledge and belief there are no other facts the omission of which would make any statement in the Advertisement misleading.

Application has been made to the Council of The Stock Exchange, London, for permission to deal in and for quotation for all the 1,000,000 Ordinary Shares in the capital of the Company.

SHARE CAPITAL

Authorised   Issued and Fully Paid
£250,000   in 1,000,000 Ordinary Shares of 5s. each   £250,000

Neither the Company nor either of its subsidiaries has any mortgages, debentures, loan capital, bank overdrafts or guarantees outstanding, apart from an inter-company guarantee in respect of bank overdraft facilities.

GRESHAM TRUST LIMITED
Barrington House, Gresham Street, London, E.C.2.
has agreed, pursuant to Contract No. (2) below, to purchase 250,000 Ordinary Shares of 5s. each.

Directors: CHARLES GAD STRASSER, " Montrose ", Parkway, Dairyfields, Trentham, Staffordshire. (Chairman and Managing Director.)
RUPERT JAMES HENRY CARTLIDGE, " White Gables ", Seabridge Lane, Newcastle-under-Lyme, Staffordshire. (Assistant Managing Director.)
JOHN ERNEST BATTISON, " Oysters ", Poplar Drive, Alsager, Cheshire. (Advertising Director.)
JEFFREY AMOR PICKFORD, " Marice ", Fowlers Lane, Light Oaks, Milton, Staffordshire. (Shipping Director.)

Bankers: MARTINS BANK LIMITED, Ironmarket, Newcastle-under-Lyme, Staffordshire.

Brokers: COLEGRAVE & CO., Clements House, 14-18, Gresham Street, London, E.C.2, and The Stock Exchange, London, E.C.2.

Solicitors: ROBERTSON, WORTHINGTON & BRODIE, 13, Brunswick Street, Newcastle-under-Lyme, Staffordshire.
RICHARDS, BUTLER & CO., Stone House, 128-140, Bishopsgate, London, E.C.2.

Auditors: A. B. SNOW, WOOD & CO., 10, Pall Mall, Hanley, Stoke-on-Trent, Staffordshire. (Chartered Accountants.)

Accountants Reporting to Gresham Trust Limited: PEAT, MARWICK, MITCHELL & CO., 11, Ironmonger Lane, London, E.C.2. (Chartered Accountants.)

Secretary and Registered Office: CYRIL SMITH, Hempstalls Lane, Newcastle-under-Lyme, Staffordshire.

Registrars and Transfer Office: GRESHAM TRUST LIMITED, Barrington House, Gresham Street, London, E.C.2.

HISTORY AND BUSINESS.—Photopia International Limited (" the Company ") was incorporated in England as a private company on the 12th November, 1962. On the 19th November, 1962, it acquired, under Contract No. (1) below, the issued share capitals of Photopia Limited (" Photopia ") and Japanese Cameras Limited (" Japanese Cameras "). These two companies have operated in close association, having had similar directorates and shareholders. The Company became a public company on the 19th November, 1962.

Photopia and Japanese Cameras were incorporated respectively on the 1st May, 1957, and the 8th May, 1957, to acquire from Mr. C. G. Strasser, trading as " North Staffs. Photographic Services ", the business of importers and distributors of cameras and photographic equipment founded by him in 1951. The acquisition was effected in two stages in May, 1957, and May, 1958, respectively. Since 1957, both companies have expanded rapidly and are now leading importers and distributors to the photographic trade in the United Kingdom.

Photopia imports mainly from Western Germany and also from Italy, Liechtenstein and U.S.A. The products imported include the " Edixa ", " Edixamat ", " Regula " and " Felica " cameras ; the " Plaubel " mono-rail cameras ; the " Carena " autoload cine cameras ; the " Durst " photo-technical enlargers ; the " Steinheil " lenses and binoculars ; the " Multiblitz ", " Regula-Variant ", " Ariosa " and " Photopia " flash units and accessories ; the " Felitor " slide projector ; the " Aurora " projection screens ; the " Watameter " range finders ; the " Photopia " gadget bags, exposure meters, editor-viewers and tripods ; and a wide range of other photographic equipment and accessories. Photopia's chief suppliers are Gebr Wirgin, Regula-Werk King K.G., Edmund Wateler and Plaubel Feinmechanick and Optik, all of Western Germany ; Durst A.G. of Italy ; and Carena S.A. of Liechtenstein. Photopia is the sole distributor in the United Kingdom for these manufacturers, with whom it has five year agreements, all of which were entered into this year with the exception of one which was entered into in 1961. Photopia at present has 24 overseas suppliers. There have been no import quota restrictions on European photographic goods since November, 1959.

Japanese Cameras imports, exclusively from Japan, a comprehensive range of cameras, cine cameras, slide and cine projectors, binoculars, flash units, lenses, colour transparency viewers, exposure meters, and other photographic equipment. These include the " Minolta ", " Pal " and " Mycro " cameras ; the " Minolta " and " Kopil " fully automatic cine cameras ; the " Minolta ", " Nipole " and " Pal " slide projectors ; the " Aroca " cine projector ; the " Atlas " binoculars ; the " Kako " flash units ; the " Palinar " lenses ; the " Pal ", " Nipole " and " Minette " slide viewers ; the " Pal " and " Minette " exposure meters ; the " Minolta " enlarger ; the " Shinwa " and " Nipole " tripods ; the " Pal " gadget bags and the " Minette " and " Atlas " editor-viewers. Japanese Cameras at present has 17 suppliers. The chief suppliers include Minolta Camera Co. Limited, Minato Shokai Co. Limited, Kobayashi Seiki Seisakujo Limited, Kako International Corporation and Taiyo Co., Limited. Japanese Cameras is the sole distributor in the United Kingdom for these manufacturers pursuant to five year agreements, of which three were entered into this year and two were entered into in 1961.

Although sales of products imported by Photopia have represented the greater part of the total turnover of the two companies up to the 30th April, 1962, the sales of Japanese imports have increased sharply during the two years ended on that date. The import quota restrictions on Japanese photographic goods were finally removed in January, 1962 ; and, mainly as a result of this, imports by the two companies are now assuming approximately equal importance.

The products imported by both companies are distributed and sold in the United Kingdom to wholesalers and over 3,500 retailers, including well-known multiple stores and mail order houses. Photopia, through its industrial and graphic arts division, also sells to hospitals, government departments, newspapers and industrial concerns. Both companies have sales representatives covering the whole of the United Kingdom. Illustrated catalogues for dealers and the public are published annually, and the products are advertised regularly in photographic and other journals.

There is a technical and service department, which tests new equipment and provides " after sales " service.

PREMISES.—In view of the expanding turnover, the present freehold premises at Hempstalls Lane, Newcastle-under-Lyme, were acquired early in 1960. These premises, which were extensively modernised in that year, contain the main offices, stores, packing and despatch departments, service department, and demonstration showrooms. There is a total floor area of approximately 12,100 square feet. Nearby at Meir airfield, Photopia rents, at a ground rent of £10 per annum, a small hangar, which houses its aircraft ; the aircraft is flown by Mr. C. G. Strasser, who is a qualified pilot, to visit customers in the United Kingdom and suppliers in Western Europe.

There is also a London office and showroom at No. 21, Noel Street, W.1, held on a lease at an exclusive rental of £1,350 per annum for a term expiring in 1979, the landlord or the tenant having the option to terminate the lease in 1972. Japanese Cameras has an office in Tokyo, which is managed by its resident representative.

MANAGEMENT AND EMPLOYEES.—All the Directors are full-time working directors. Mr. C. G. Strasser, the Chairman and Managing Director, is the founder of the business ; he is now 35 years of age. Mr. R. J. H. Cartlidge, the Assistant Managing Director, is 30 years of age and has been with the business for 8 years. Mr. J. E. Battison, the Director in charge of advertising, is 32 years of age and joined the business in 1955. Mr. J. A. Pickford, who is 36 years of age, joined the business in 1959 and is the Director in charge of shipping.

All the Directors have entered into full-time Service Agreements under Contracts No. (3) below.

There are over 80 employees and no difficulty is experienced in obtaining suitable staff. There is a contributory pension scheme in operation for male employees over 21 years of age.

WORKING CAPITAL.—Having regard to the bank facilities available, the Directors are of the opinion that there is adequate working capital for current requirements.

PROFITS, PROSPECTS AND DIVIDENDS.—Turnover has increased annually throughout the period covered by the Accountants' Report set out below. There was a particularly sharp increase in turnover in the year ended the 30th April, 1960, while overheads for that year were at a comparatively low level. In the subsequent two years, however, the level of overheads increased mainly as a result of higher advertising expenditure and the move to the more extensive premises at Hempstalls Lane referred to above.

On the basis of the profits statement in the Report, the combined net profits of Photopia and Japanese Cameras for the year ended the 30th April, 1962, were £95,006, subject only to taxation. Having regard to the increased turnover for the first six months of the current year

WORKING CAPITAL.—Having regard to the bank facilities available, the Directors are of the opinion that there is adequate working capital for current requirements.

PROFITS, PROSPECTS AND DIVIDENDS.—Turnover has increased annually throughout the period covered by the Accountants' Report set out below. There was a particularly sharp increase in turnover in the year ended the 30th April, 1960, while overheads for that year were at a comparatively low level. In the subsequent two years, however, the level of overheads increased mainly as a result of higher advertising expenditure and the move to the more extensive premises at Hempstalls Lane referred to above.

On the basis of the profits statement in the Report, the combined net profits of Photopia and Japanese Cameras for the year ended the 30th April, 1962, were £95,006, subject only to taxation. Having regard to the increased turnover for the first six months of the current year 1st May, 1962 to the 30th April, 1963, the Directors are of the opinion that, in the absence of unforeseen circumstances, the combined net profits of the Group for the current year, calculated on the same basis, should be not less than £100,000, subject only to taxation. The whole of such combined net profits for the current year will be regarded as available for the payment of dividend on the shares of the Company; and accordingly, on the realisation of the above-mentioned profit estimate for the current year, the Directors would propose to recommend a dividend of 14 per cent. actual (less income tax) on the 1,000,000 Ordinary Shares of the Company in respect of its first financial period ending on the 30th April, 1963. The Annual General Meeting to declare this dividend will be held in or about September, 1963.

If, from the above estimated figure of £100,000, there are deducted income tax at 7s. 9d. in the £ (£38,750) and profits tax at 15 per cent. (£15,000) there would remain a sum of £46,250. A dividend of 14 per cent. (less income tax) on the 1,000,000 issued Ordinary Shares of 5s. each in the Company would absorb £21,438, leaving a balance of £24,812.

ACCOUNTANTS' REPORT.—The following is a copy of a Joint Report by Messrs. A. B. Snow, Wood & Co. Chartered Accountants, the Auditors of the Company (and of Photopia Limited and Japanese Cameras Limited in respect of their last three financial years ended on the 30th April, 1962) and by Messrs. Peat, Marwick, Mitchell & Co., Chartered Accountants :—

To the Directors of
    PHOTOPIA INTERNATIONAL LIMITED, and
    GRESHAM TRUST LIMITED.   19th November, 1962.
GENTLEMEN,

We have examined the audited accounts of Photopia Limited and of Japanese Cameras Limited ("the subsidiary companies") for the periods from the 1st May and the 8th May, 1957, their respective dates of incorporation, to the 30th April, 1962. We have also examined the audited accounts for the year ended the 30th April, 1958, of the business carried on by Mr. C. G. Strasser, trading as North Staffs. Photographic Services ("North Staffs"), which was transferred to Photopia Limited as from the 1st May, 1958.

The whole of the issued share capitals of the subsidiary companies was acquired on the 19th November, 1962, by Photopia International Limited in consideration of the issue, credited as fully paid, by that company of 999,998 Ordinary Shares of 5s. each.

We report as follows :—

    I. **Profits.**—The combined profits of the subsidiary companies and North Staffs, arrived at on the basis stated below, were :—

Year ended the 30th April	Profits before Directors' emoluments and Taxation	Directors' emoluments	Profits before Taxation
(1)	(2) £	(3) £	(4) £
1958	9,833	1,250	8,583
1959	21,712	3,500	18,212
1960	89,729	10,000	79,729
1961	76,717	10,550	66,167
1962	100,006	5,000	95,006

NOTES.—(1) The profits set out in column (2) above are arrived at before charging Taxation and Directors' emoluments but after charging all other working expenses, including depreciation and interest, and after making such adjustments as we consider appropriate.
    (2) The profits shown in column (2) above for the year ended the 30th April, 1958, include £6,159 relating to that part of the present business of Photopia Limited which was carried on during that year by North Staffs and which was transferred to Photopia Limited as from the 1st May, 1958.
    (3) The emoluments of the persons who have been appointed Directors of Photopia International Limited amounted, for the year ended the 30th April, 1962, to £8,411, of which £4,000 is charged in column (3) above and the remaining £4,411 is charged in arriving at the profit set out in column (2) above; under the arrangements now in force the emoluments of these persons for that year would have amounted to £11,843.

    II. **Net Tangible Assets.**—The combined net tangible assets of the subsidiary companies at the 30th April, 1962, based on their audited Balance Sheets at that date, and before deducting the amount of £37,145 due to Mr. C. G. Strasser referred to in Note (3) below, were :—

	Cost £	Depreciation £	£
FIXED ASSETS			
FREEHOLD PROPERTY	14,811	811	14,000
PLANT AND EQUIPMENT	10,712	2,497	8,215
VEHICLES AND AIRCRAFT	17,197	6,312	10,885
	42,720	9,620	33,100
CURRENT ASSETS			
STOCK, at lower of cost and net realisable value		66,495	
DEBTORS AND PREPAYMENTS		182,289	
CASH AT BANK AND IN HAND		27,540	
		276,324	
LESS:			
CURRENT LIABILITIES			
BANK OVERDRAFT (see Note (1))		33,891	
CREDITORS		46,408	
TAXATION		17,278	
AMOUNTS DUE TO DIRECTORS (since paid)		10,112	
DIVIDENDS (since paid)		2,450	
		110,139	
NET CURRENT ASSETS			166,185
			199,285
LESS:			
AMOUNTS SET ASIDE FOR FUTURE TAXATION			
INCOME TAX 1962/63 (11/12ths)		22,700	
INCOME TAX 1963/64		37,900	
			60,600
NET TANGIBLE ASSETS			£138,685

NOTES.—(1) The Bank Overdraft at the 30th April, 1962, was secured by a charge on the freehold property, which charge has since been released.
    (2) No provision has been made in the above Statement of Net Assets for Irrevocable Letters of Credit and Acceptances totalling £32,718, which had been issued at the 30th April, 1962, in respect of goods ordered, but not received, at that date.
    (3) The above Net Assets are arrived at before deducting an amount of £37,145 due to Mr. C. G. Strasser at the 30th April, 1962, which amount has since been satisfied by the issue, credited as fully paid, of 900 shares of £1 each of Photopia Limited at a total premium of £36,245.

    III. **Accounts.**—No audited accounts have been made up by the subsidiary companies in respect of any period subsequent to the 30th April, 1962.

    IV. **Photopia International Limited.**—Photopia International Limited was incorporated on the 12th November, 1962. No accounts have been made up and no dividends have been paid.

        Yours faithfully,
            A. B. SNOW, WOOD & CO.
            PEAT, MARWICK, MITCHELL & CO.
                              Chartered Accountants.

This card is circulated in The Exchange Telegraph Company's Daily Statistics Service in conformity with the requirements of the Council of The Stock Exchange, London, and is printed by The Times Publishing Company, Limited

GENERAL INFORMATION.—The Company was incorporated on the 12th November, 1962, with an authorised share capital of £100 divided into 400 Ordinary Shares of 5s. each, of which 2 shares were issued for cash at par to the subscribers to the Company's Memorandum of Association. On the 19th November, 1962, (*a*) the authorised share capital of the Company was increased to £250,000 by the creation of a further 999,600 Ordinary Shares of 5s. each, and (*b*) 999,998 Ordinary Shares of 5s. each in the Company were allotted, credited as fully paid, as consideration for the acquisitions of the entire issued share capitals of Photopia and Japanese cameras pursuant to Contract No. (1) below.

Subject to the Council of The Stock Exchange, London, granting permission to deal in and quotation for all the 1,000,000 Ordinary Shares of 5s. each in the Company not later than the 30th November, 1962, the persons named in Contract No. (2) below have agreed to sell to Gresham Trust Limited (" Gresham Trust ") a total of 250,000 Ordinary Shares of 5s. each in the Company at the price of 9s. 6d. per share.

The Special Commissioners of Income Tax have stated that they do not propose to take any action under the provisions of Section 245 of the Income Tax Act, 1952 (relating to surtax) in respect of the income of Photopia and Japanese Cameras for the periods from their respective dates of incorporation to the 30th April, 1962.

The following Contracts (not being contracts in the ordinary course of business) have been entered into within the two years preceding the date of this Advertisement and are or may be material :—

(1) Dated the 19th November, 1962, between (i) the persons named below and (ii) the Company whereby such persons between them agreed to sell and the Company agreed to purchase the entire issued share capitals of Photopia (109,000 fully paid Ordinary Shares of £1 each) and Japanese Cameras (1,000 fully paid Ordinary Shares of £1 each) for an aggregate consideration consisting of the allotment, credited as fully paid, of 999,998 Ordinary Shares of 5s. each in the Company, the numbers of (*a*) Ordinary Shares of £1 each in Photopia and (*b*) Ordinary Shares of £1 each in Japanese Cameras sold by, and (*c*) Ordinary Shares of 5s. each in the Company issued to, each such person being specified after his (or her) name :—Charles Gad Strasser (*a*) 89,000, (*b*) 900, (*c*) 824,862 ; Maureen Jane Strasser (*a*) 10,000, (*b*) 100, (*c*) 92,568 ; and Arthur Bernard Snow and John Paterson Brodie (as Trustees under family settlements made by Mr. C. G. Strasser) (*a*) 10,000, (*b*) nil, (*c*) 82,568. These purchases have been completed. Under the terms of the Contract these purchases take effect from the 1st May, 1962, no part of the purchase considerations being attributable to any profits of Photopia and Japanese Cameras since the date of their respective last audited Balance Sheets dated the 30th April, 1962. Under this Contract, Mr. C. G. Strasser has covenanted to indemnify the Company, Photopia and Japanese Cameras against death duties and surtax as therein mentioned.

(2) Dated the 19th November, 1962, between (i) the persons named below and (ii) Gresham Trust, whereby such persons between them agreed to sell and Gresham Trust agreed to purchase a total of 250,000 Ordinary Shares of 5s. each in the Company at 9s. 6d. per share, the number of shares agreed to be sold by each such person being specified after his (or her) name :—Charles Gad Strasser, 206,216 ; Maureen Jane Strasser, 23,142 ; and Arthur Bernard Snow and John Paterson Brodie (as Trustees under family settlements made by Mr. C. G. Strasser), 20,642. This Contract is conditional upon permission to deal in and quotation for all the 1,000,000 Ordinary Shares of 5s. each in the Company being granted by the Council of The Stock Exchange, London, not later than the 30th November, 1962, and provides for payment to be made for the 250,000 Ordinary Shares agreed to be purchased by Gresham Trust within 10 days after the said permission to deal and quotation are granted.

(3) Dated the 19th November, 1962, between the Company and (*a*) Charles Gad Strasser, (*b*) Rupert James Henry Cartlidge, (*c*) John Ernest Battison and (*d*) Jeffrey Amor Pickford, appointing them as (*a*) Managing Director, (*b*) Assistant Managing Director, (*c*) Advertising Manager and (*d*) Shipping Manager respectively for a period of 5½ years from the 1st November, 1962, at an aggregate remuneration (inclusive of Directors' fees) of £10,500, plus commissions amounting in the aggregate to 9½ per cent. of the excess over a sum at the rate of £80,000 per annum of the aggregate net profits of the Company and its subsidiaries for each financial period, such profits to be calculated before taxation and otherwise as therein provided.

(4) Dated the 19th November, 1962, between (i) the Company and (ii) Gresham Trust, appointing the latter as Transfer Registrars of the Company for a period of three years from the 19th November, 1962, at a remuneration as therein mentioned.

(5) Dated the 23rd October, 1962, between (i) Pitrie Limited and (ii) Photopia being the Assignment of a Lease of office premises at 21, Noel Street, London, W.1, for a term of 21 years from the 25th March, 1958, at an exclusive rental of £1,350 per annum. These offices are referred to under " Premises " above.

The Chairman, Mr. C. G. Strasser, is interested under Contracts Nos. (1), (2) and (3) as stated above. All the Directors are directors of Photopia and Japanese Cameras. After the completion of Contract No. (2) above, Mr. C. G. Strasser, his wife and the above mentioned trustees will together own 75 per cent. of the issued share capital of the Company.

The 250,000 Ordinary Shares agreed to be purchased under Contract No. (2) above will be placed privately by Gresham Trust directly and through the Brokers. Gresham Trust is paying to the Brokers the normal Stock Exchange rates of commission in respect of the Ordinary Shares placed through them. No part of the proceeds of this placing is payable to the Company, and no amounts are to be provided out of such proceeds for any of the matters referred to in Paragraph 4 of Part I of the Fourth Schedule to the Companies Act, 1948.

The promoters of the Company are Mr. C. G. Strasser and Gresham Trust. The preliminary expenses of the Company, including the costs of and incidental to the formation of the Company and its acquisitions of the share capitals of Photopia and Japanese Cameras, and the duty payable on the increase of capital of the Company referred to above, are estimated at £3,600 and are payable by the Company. The costs of preparing and publishing this Advertisement, a fee of £2,100 to Gresham Trust, the fees payable to the Brokers, Solicitors, Auditors and Reporting Accountants, the printing charges and the cost of obtaining the said permission to deal and quotation, are estimated at £10,700 and are also payable by the Company. The above-mentioned commission to the Brokers, estimated at £1,050, is payable by Gresham Trust.

The Articles of Association of the Company include provisions to the following effect :—

(*a*) The remuneration of the Directors shall be £500 per annum for each Director. The Directors shall also be entitled to such further sum (if any) as shall from time to time be voted to them by the Company by Ordinary Resolution, and any such further sum (unless otherwise determined by the resolution by which it is voted) shall be divided amongst the Directors as they shall agree, or, failing agreement, equally. The Directors' remuneration shall be deemed to accrue *de die in diem*.

(*b*) The Directors shall be entitled to be paid all travelling, hotel and other expenses incurred by them respectively in and about the performance of their duties as Directors, including their expenses of travelling to and from meetings of the Directors or Committees of the Directors or General Meetings.

(*c*) Any Director who serves on any Committee or who devotes special attention to the business of the Company or who otherwise performs services which in the opinion of the Directors are outside the scope of the ordinary duties of a Director may be paid such extra remuneration by way of salary, commission, participation in profits or otherwise as the Directors may determine.

(*d*) The Directors may from time to time appoint one or more of their body to be the holder of any executive office on such terms, at such remuneration and for such period as they think fit.

(*e*) The Directors may make such arrangements as may be thought fit for the management of the Company's affairs in the United Kingdom or abroad, and may for this purpose appoint local boards and fix their remuneration.

(*f*) The Directors may establish and maintain pension or superannuation funds for the benefit of and grant pensions or the like benefit to (*inter alia*) any persons who are or were at any time Directors of the Company or of any company which is a subsidiary of the Company or is allied to or associated with the Company or any such subsidiary or which is a predecessor in business of the Company or of any such other company as aforesaid and the wives, widows, families and dependants of any such persons (provided that, without the sanction of an Ordinary Resolution of the Company, such powers may not be exercised in favour of any Director who does not hold or has not held any salaried employment or office in the Company or in any such other company as aforesaid). A Director may vote as a Director upon any resolution in respect of any such matter notwithstanding that he is personally interested in such matter.

(*g*) The Directors may exercise all the powers of the Company to borrow money and to mortgage or charge its undertaking, property and uncalled capital or any part thereof and to issue debentures and other securities. The Directors shall exercise such powers and shall exercise or procure to be exercised all rights or powers of control directly or indirectly exercisable by the Company in relation to its subsidiaries so as to ensure that the aggregate of the amounts borrowed or secured by the Company and its subsidiaries and remaining outstanding at any one time (excluding inter-company loans) shall not, without the previous sanction of an Ordinary Resolution of the Company exceed an amount equal to the aggregate of (1) the amount paid up on the share capital of the Company, plus (2) the amount standing to the credit of the consolidated capital and revenue reserves (including share premium account) plus (3) the amount standing to the credit or minus the amount standing to the debit of the consolidated profit and loss account, all as shown in the latest audited consolidated balance sheet of the Company and its subsidiaries (having upon consolidation allowed for any amounts attributable to outside shareholders in subsidiaries), but (i) adjusted as may be necessary in respect of any variation in the paid up share capital or share premium account of the Company since the date of that balance sheet, and (ii) excluding any amounts set aside for taxation ; but no such sanction shall be required to the borrowing of any moneys intended to be applied in the repayment (with or without premium) of any moneys then already borrowed and outstanding notwithstanding that the same may result in such limit being exceeded.

(*h*) A Director may hold any other office or place of profit under the Company (except that of Auditor) in conjunction with his office of Director, and may act in a professional capacity to the Company, on such terms as to remuneration and otherwise as the Directors shall arrange.

(*i*) A Director may be or become a director or other officer of, or otherwise interested in, any company promoted by the Company or in which the Company may be interested as member or otherwise, and no such Director shall be accountable for any remuneration or other benefits received by him as a director or officer of or from his interest in such other company. The Directors may also exercise the voting power conferred by the shares in any other company held or owned by the Company in favour of any resolution appointing them or any of their number directors or officers of such other company or voting or providing for the payment of remuneration to the directors or officers of such other company. A Director may vote in favour of the exercise of such voting rights in manner aforesaid notwithstanding that he may be or be about to become a director or officer of such other company and as such or in any other manner is or may be interested in the exercise of such voting rights in manner aforesaid.

(*j*) Subject to any special rights or restrictions as to voting attached to any class of shares, every member who is present in person shall have one vote on a show of hands and upon a poll every member present in person or by proxy shall have one vote for every share held by him.

Photopia and Japanese Cameras were incorporated in England as private companies on the 1st May, 1957, and 8th May, 1957, respectively. On the 16th November, 1962, 900 Ordinary Shares of £1 each in Photopia were issued, credited as fully paid, to Mr. C. G. Strasser in satisfaction

The promoters of the Company are Mr. C. G. Strasser and Gresham Trust. The preliminary expenses of the Company, including the costs of and incidental to the formation of the Company and its acquisitions of the share capitals of Photopia and Japanese Cameras, and the duty payable on the increase of capital of the Company referred to above, are estimated at £3,600 and are payable by the Company. The costs of preparing and publishing this Advertisement, a fee of £2,100 to Gresham Trust, the fees payable to the Brokers, Solicitors, Auditors and Reporting Accountants, the printing charges and the cost of obtaining the said permission to deal and quotation, are estimated at £10,700 and are also payable by the Company. The above-mentioned commission to the Brokers, estimated at £1,050, is payable by Gresham Trust.

The Articles of Association of the Company include provisions to the following effect :—

(a) The remuneration of the Directors shall be £500 per annum for each Director. The Directors shall also be entitled to such further sum (if any) as shall from time to time be voted to them by the Company by Ordinary Resolution, and any such further sum (unless otherwise determined by the resolution by which it is voted) shall be divided amongst the Directors as they shall agree, or, failing agreement, equally. The Directors' remuneration shall be deemed to accrue *de die in diem*.

(b) The Directors shall be entitled to be paid all travelling, hotel and other expenses incurred by them respectively in and about the performance of their duties as Directors, including their expenses of travelling to and from meetings of the Directors or Committees of the Directors or General Meetings.

(c) Any Director who serves on any Committee or who devotes special attention to the business of the Company or who otherwise performs services which in the opinion of the Directors are outside the scope of the ordinary duties of a Director may be paid such extra remuneration by way of salary, commission, participation in profits or otherwise as the Directors may determine.

(d) The Directors may from time to time appoint one or more of their body to be the holder of any executive office on such terms, at such remuneration and for such period as they think fit.

(e) The Directors may make such arrangements as may be thought fit for the management of the Company's affairs in the United Kingdom or abroad, and may for this purpose appoint local boards and fix their remuneration.

(f) The Directors may establish and maintain pension or superannuation funds for the benefit of and grant pensions or the like benefit to (*inter alia*) any persons who are or were at any time Directors of the Company or of any company which is a subsidiary of the Company or is allied to or associated with the Company or any such subsidiary or which is a predecessor in business of the Company or of any such other company as aforesaid and the wives, widows, families and dependants of any such persons (provided that, without the sanction of an Ordinary Resolution of the Company, such powers may not be exercised in favour of any Director who does not hold or has not held any salaried employment or office in the Company or in any such other company as aforesaid). A Director may vote as a Director upon any resolution in respect of any such matter notwithstanding that he is personally interested in such matter.

(g) The Directors may exercise all the powers of the Company to borrow money and to mortgage or charge its undertaking, property and uncalled capital or any part thereof and to issue debentures and other securities. The Directors shall exercise such powers and shall exercise or procure to be exercised all rights or powers of control directly or indirectly exercisable by the Company in relation to its subsidiaries so as to ensure that the aggregate of the amounts borrowed or secured by the Company and its subsidiaries and remaining outstanding at any one time (excluding inter-company loans) shall not, without the previous sanction of an Ordinary Resolution of the Company exceed an amount equal to the aggregate of (1) the amount paid up on the share capital of the Company, plus (2) the amount standing to the credit of the consolidated capital and revenue reserves (including share premium account) plus (3) the amount standing to the credit or minus the amount standing to the debit of the consolidated profit and loss account, all as shown in the latest audited consolidated balance sheet of the Company and its subsidiaries (having upon consolidation allowed for any amounts attributable to outside shareholders in subsidiaries), but (i) adjusted as may be necessary in respect of any variation in the paid up share capital or share premium account of the Company since the date of that balance sheet, and (ii) excluding any amounts set aside for taxation ; but no such sanction shall be required to the borrowing of any moneys intended to be applied in the repayment (with or without premium) of any moneys then already borrowed and outstanding notwithstanding that the same may result in such limit being exceeded.

(h) A Director may hold any other office or place of profit under the Company (except that of Auditor) in conjunction with his office of Director, and may act in a professional capacity to the Company, on such terms as to remuneration and otherwise as the Directors shall arrange.

(i) A Director may be or become a director or other officer of, or otherwise interested in, any company promoted by the Company or in which the Company may be interested as member or otherwise, and no such Director shall be accountable for any remuneration or other benefits received by him as a director or officer of or from his interest in such other company. The Directors may also exercise the voting power conferred by the shares in any other company held or owned by the Company in favour of any resolution appointing them or any of their number directors or officers of such other company or voting or providing for the payment of remuneration to the directors or officers of such other company. A Director may vote in favour of the exercise of such voting rights in manner aforesaid notwithstanding that he may be or be about to become a director or officer of such other company and as such or in any other manner is or may be interested in the exercise of such voting rights in manner aforesaid.

(j) Subject to any special rights or restrictions as to voting attached to any class of shares, every member who is present in person shall have one vote on a show of hands and upon a poll every member present in person or by proxy shall have one vote for every share held by him.

Photopia and Japanese Cameras were incorporated in England as private companies on the 1st May, 1957, and 8th May, 1957, respectively. On the 16th November, 1962, 900 Ordinary Shares of £1 each in Photopia were issued, credited as fully paid, to Mr. C. G. Strasser in satisfaction of an amount of £37,145 due to him by Photopia on loan account on the 30th April, 1962. On the 19th November, 1962, (a) a further 98,100 Ordinary Shares of £1 each in Photopia were allotted, credited as fully paid, by way of capitalisation of reserves, and (b) 900 Ordinary Shares of £1 each in Japanese Cameras were allotted, credited as fully paid, by way of capitalisation of reserves. Following these issues, Photopia has an issued and fully paid share capital of 109,000 Ordinary Shares of £1 each and Japanese Cameras has an issued and fully paid share capital of 1,000 Ordinary Shares of £1 each.

Except as specifically mentioned above, (a) no sums have been paid, or agreed to be paid, to any Director of the Company, or to any firm of which he is a member, in cash or shares or otherwise by any person either to induce him to become or to qualify him as a Director or otherwise for services rendered by him or by his firm in connection with the promotion or formation of the Company ; (b) no cash, shares, securities or other benefits have been paid or given to any promoter during the two years preceding the date of this Advertisement, nor is it proposed to pay or give any cash, shares, securities or benefits to any promoter ; (c) no share or loan capital has been issued by the Company or either of its subsidiaries during the said two years or is proposed to be issued ; (d) no property has been purchased or acquired on capital account by the Company or either of its subsidiaries during the said two years (otherwise than in the ordinary course of business) nor, except as aforesaid, does the Company or either of its subsidiaries propose to purchase or acquire any property on capital account ; (e) no shares in or debentures of the Company or either of its subsidiaries are under option or agreed conditionally or unconditionally to be put under option ; (f) no commissions, discounts, brokerages or other special terms have been granted in connection with the issue or sale of any shares in or debentures of the Company or either of its subsidiaries and, except as aforesaid, no commissions, discounts, brokerages or other special terms will be granted to any person in connection therewith ; and (g) there are no life or long-term service agreements with the Company or either of its subsidiaries. Neither the Company nor its subsidiaries has any litigation or claim of material importance pending or threatened against it.

Messrs. A. B. Snow, Wood & Co. and Messrs. Peat, Marwick, Mitchell & Co. have given and have not withdrawn their written consents to the issue of this Advertisement with the inclusion therein of their Report set out above in the form and context in which it is included.

The documents attached to the copy of this Advertisement delivered to the Registrar of Companies for registration are copies of the letters under which the above mentioned 250,000 Ordinary Shares of 5s. each will be placed privately, the written consents referred to above, copies of the Contracts listed above and a written statement by Messrs. A. B. Snow, Wood & Co. and Messrs. Peat, Marwick, Mitchell & Co. setting out the adjustments made in their Report and giving the reasons therefor.

Copies of the Memorandum and Articles of Association of the Company, the above-mentioned consents and statement, the Contracts listed above (except Contract No. (1) above) and the audited accounts of Photopia and Japanese Cameras for their last two financial periods, and the originals of Contract No. (1) above and the Report set out above may be seen at the office of Messrs. Richards, Butler & Co., Stone House, 128-140, Bishopsgate, London, E.C.2, during usual business hours (Saturdays excepted) for a period of fourteen days from the date of publication of this Advertisement.

Dated 19th November, 1962.

Appendix B

Extract from Chairman's 1969 Report and
Accounts of Government Impositions

Chairman's Statement

Review

My Statement last year ended with the prophecy that "This will undoubtedly be the most difficult year we have had to face, and whilst your Directors and Staff will exert their utmost endeavours..."

Unfortunately my forecast was, if anything, an understatement. The already quite catastrophic Government measures were further added to, and despite your Board's constant endeavours, the rewards are most disappointing. I make no apology for our results, they arise directly as a result of, and solely because of, the indefensible level of taxation imposed by the Government on our Industry.

My Seventh Annual Report of the progress of Photopia International Limited, is therefore the first one in which I have to announce a drop in turnover compared with the previous year, resulting in a sharp drop in profitability.

The profit before tax for the year was £12,702, compared with £140,221 for the previous year. After taking account of tax recoverable and previous tax provisions no longer required, the Group profit after tax was £24,702 compared with £102,721 last year.

You will remember that in my Interim Statement on the 4th March, I stated that "Despite this gloomy state of affairs, it is our intention to maintain last year's level of final dividend, making use of retained profits from previous years if necessary." Your Board therefore recommends a final dividend of 9d. per share (15%), making with the interim of 3d. per share (5%) already paid, a total of 1/- per share (20%), which is the same as last year. I have again, for the seventh year in succession, waived the majority of my entitlement to the dividends.

The Group total turnover table, split as regards Net Sales and Purchase Tax for the last two financial years, tells its own story.

	Year to April 1969	Year to April 1968
Net Sales	£1,087,597	£1,419,057
Purchase Tax	£329,857	£258,504
Total Turnover	£1,417,454	£1,677,561
	(Incl. £32,777 export)	(Incl. £81,753 export)

(The 1969 figures include Citizen Watches Ltd. which commenced trading in May 1968).

It does not need a trained economist to perceive that at the top end of turnover, after all the overheads have been covered, gross profit becomes almost the same as net profit. Thus, the loss of the top 23.4% of our net sales (£331,460) almost wiped out our net profit. Naturally we immediately re-investigated most thoroughly all our overheads, which had been correctly geared to our previous levels of turnover. This resulted in a cut-back in staff and unfortunately we had to declare some redundancies. These and other savings, however, came only at the tail end of our financial year and later, as we still had hopes of some justice in the form of relief as regards re-classification of Purchase Tax grouping, right up to the April 1969 National Budget. No such relief came, and we must continue to struggle under the accumulation of the existing burdensome legislation and conditions—some common to all business, but others penal only to the Photographic Trade. I have listed already the effects on us and similarly I tabulate the causes.

September 1966
Selective Employment Tax introduced—cost to Company £6,000 per annum.

August 1967
Hire-Purchase Deposit on photo equipment for the first time higher than on radios, cars, domestic appliances, etc., and re-payment period also shorter.

November 1967
Sterling devalued—most of our products increased in cost by 16⅔% resulting in similarly increased retail prices.

March 1968
Purchase Tax on still and cine cameras, enlargers, etc. increased from 27½% to 50% and on slide and movie projectors, screens and viewers etc. from nil to 50%.

September 1968
Selective Employment Tax increased 50%—total cost to Company now almost £10,000 per annum.

October 1968
To avoid up-valuation of the German Mark, the German Government introduced 4% Export Tax—increasing cost of our German imports by that amount.

November 1968
Purchase Tax further increased on photographic equipment from 50% to 55%.

November 1968
Import Deposit introduced, whereby we have to deposit with H.M. Customs at the time of importation 50% of the value of the goods. This is held by them for 6 months without interest.

And since the end of our financial year:—

July 1969
Selective Employment Tax increased by 28%.

August 1969
Industrial Training Levy for distributive trades announced at ½% of total wages bill.

In addition to the above, we also pay the highest rates of import duty in the British Customs Tariff.

Regretfully I can see no improvement for us in the situation, possibly until the Budget in April 1970. In the meantime rising costs and lower sales will undoubtedly further increase the end consumer prices of our products and those of our competitors.

6

Noteworthy events of the year.

Having first acquired from our U.S. minority partners their loan and share capital at no cost, we sold our former subsidiary, Docustat Limited, at favourable terms.

Our wholly-owned subsidiary, Paul Plus Limited, signed contracts with Vega of Ljubljana, Yugoslavia. These give Paul Plus Limited sole selling rights for the whole of the Western World, in their slide and overhead projectors, episcopes and epidiascopes, etc. A most pleasing start has already been made with the slide projectors and for the other items we are forming a visual aid division to market in the U.K. to educational establishments and industry as the items are particularly suited for the Industrial Training Act.

Citizen Watches Limited has now operated for a full year and the watches which have proved of outstanding quality are gaining trade and public acceptance. The necessary extent of our launch and initial advertising expenditure have not yet made a profit contribution possible.

To enlarge our share in the lucrative Channel Islands market, we opened an office, showroom and stores in Jersey.

To consolidate after sales service—a feature common to all our operating companies—a new company, Interserve Limited, was formed to carry out this function for the Group.

We congratulate the Minolta Camera Company Limited of Osaka, Japan, for whom our subsidiary, Japanese Cameras Limited, is the sole agent in the U.K., on having one of their exposure meters selected by NASA for the Apollo 8 orbit and the Apollo 11 Moon landing. This, together with the Hi-Matic Camera chosen for the first manned Space Flight, confirms the reliability and excellence of their products. We are now also actively negotiating the sale of Minolta Planetariums in the United Kingdom.

Comment

To my colleagues on the Board, our staff, our dealers and our suppliers, I wish to express my personal appreciation for their outstanding efforts and co-operation and, not least, understanding during a most difficult year.

For the reasons already outlined, it is impossible for me to make a forecast as to when our curve of progress will start climbing again as this is entirely dependent on Government measures. Naturally, both directly and through my membership of the Joint Purchase Tax Action Committee of the British Photographic Manufacturers Association, the Photographic Dealers' Association and the Photographic Importers Association, I shall spare no effort to bring that time nearer.

Charles G. Strasser
Chairman.

Appendix C

Photopia International Ltd Dealer Charter

Most companies publish a "Terms of Trading", usually a very one sided document prepared by lawyers to protect the company. I decided to compose and issue a complementary document, a "Dealer Charter" to spell out what our obligations were to our customers. Today you would, I suppose, call it a mission statement.

Photopia International Ltd.

Dealer Charter.

Intent. A Company's Terms of Trading sets out its conditions of sale and is therefore a document which restricts its liability in a legal and businesslike form for the information of its customers. This Dealer Charter is complementary to our Terms of Trading, its intention being to set out the numerous services and benefits which we solemnly undertake to provide for our dealer customers. This Dealer Charter applies to all our wholly owned operating subsidiary companies, Photopia Limited, Japanese Cameras Limited, Paul Plus Limited, Mayfair Photographic Limited and Citizen Watches Limited.

Products. WE WILL use all our resources and endeavours to find, test and if found satisfactory in every way, purchase for distribution, at most competitive retail selling prices, photographic, cinematographic and horological apparatus and accessories, irrespective of country of origin.

Distribution. WE WILL, as bonafide importers and distributors, refrain from owning either directly or indirectly retail shops, so as not to compete with our customers. WE WILL supply only bona-fide retail accounts and will permit our strategically placed wholesalers, where these have been appointed, to supply only such accounts also.

Prices. WE WILL continue our policy of stable prices in the interests of the consumer, at the most competitive levels possible. WE WILL, in the case of price reductions, excepting reductions in tax or levy or Government surcharge over which we have no control, credit dealers with the full amount of such a reduction for goods they still have in stock and which they have purchased from us up to three months previous to the date of reduction.

Discounts. WE WILL ensure that any discounts we offer shall apply equally to all dealers large and small.

Credit. WE WILL give, to satisfactorily opened and conducted accounts, credit to the end of the month following date of invoice.

Advertising. WE WILL consistently advertise our products throughout the whole of the year in the photographic and horological press and during selected months in the National press. WE WILL continue to publish Catalogues and Price-Lists showing all our products and automatically supply these to all dealers and keep them up to date. WE WILL supply to dealers, free of all charge, on request, leaflets, showcards, posters and camera and watch stands subject to availability, also advertising blocks and dealer advertisment layouts. WE WILL do everything possible to create a demand for our products and, in furtherance thereof, also participate in all major National Photographic and Horological equipment exhibitions. WE WILL pass to dealers all enquiries received as a result of our advertising. WE WILL courteously, efficiently and expeditiously answer all letters from dealers and the public with enquiries or technical queries. WE WILL, wherever possible, support dealers own advertising and participate in dealer sponsored Exhibitions.

Representation. WE WILL employ only sound technically qualified Representatives to call on dealers. WE WILL equip them with a full range of samples and keep them up to date with information, so as to enable them to render the best possible service to assist dealers with their sales efforts.

Despatch. WE WILL ensure that all equipment sent to dealers is correctly and safely packed and accompanied by a Delivery Note showing suggested retail selling prices. Should, despite this, equipment be damaged or pilfered in transit, WE WILL immediately arrange replacement, subject only to the recipient (a) notifying us immediately in writing, (b) notifying the carrier immediately in writing, (c) in the case of damage, keep the packing for inspection. WE WILL, at our expense, cover by a currently valid insurance policy, all outgoing despatches for transit risks.

Replacements. WE WILL, as a further service to our dealers, as an expression of confidence and so as to avoid inconvenience to dealers, in future replace immediately any camera, exposure meter, time-piece or other piece of equipment which, despite inspection and care, still arrives in a faulty condition. This offer holds good subject only to (1) the goods having been supplied by us direct to the dealer, (2) the goods are inspected immediately on arrival by the dealer, (3) the equipment to be replaced is returned to us within three days from date of receipt, together with our blue Delivery Note (which will be returned) stating the fault found and requesting a replacement, (4) our having a replacement in stock, otherwise a priority repair, within three days of receipt, will be carried out. To ensure that only brand new goods are exchanged, we regret that this replacement service cannot be extended beyond the three days period under any circumstances. For administrative reasons, where a replacement is authorised, we will credit and re-invoice.

Guarantees. WE WILL, so as to give a satisfactory after sales service, maintain a service department staffed by fully skilled mechanics and equipped with the latest machines and test equipment and stocked with regularly required spare parts. WE WILL issue with each piece of numbered equipment a twelve months written Guarantee and with electronic flashguns a six months written Guarantee. WE WILL acknowledge immediately in writing, any equipment sent to us for servicing. WE WILL service free of all charge to the dealer or his customer, goods found to have a manufacturing fault within the Guarantee period applicable, subject only to these not having been misused. WE WILL service, free of all charge to the dealer, any unsold item of ours from his stock shown to have a manufacturing fault and not discovered on inspection as provided for in the paragraph titled "REPLACEMENTS", subject only to it not having been misused. WE WILL accept dealer's written confirmation that goods fall into one of the above two categories, subject only to inspection of the equipment, showing misuse or other evidence to the contrary. WE WILL strive to maintain a speedy repair service both for Guarantee and charge repairs, giving priority service to Guarantee repairs. WE WILL, on request, in the case of chargeable repairs, send an estimate first and make no charge for this service. WE WILL, at our expense, cover by a currently valid insurance policy, all customers' goods whilst in our possession for goods in trust risks.

Contra Support. WE WILL, in all our activities and through every member of our staff, give such a service to dealers as to warrant an being entitled to expect the wholehearted support of all dealers in stocking, recommending and selling our equipment with complete confidence.

for PHOTOPIA LIMITED
JAPANESE CAMERAS LIMITED
PAUL PLUS LIMITED
MAYFAIR PHOTOGRAPHIC SUPPLIERS (LONDON) LIMITED
CITIZEN WATCHES LIMITED

p.p. PHOTOPIA INTERNATIONAL LIMITED

Charles G. Strasser,
Chairman and Managing Director.

Appendix D

List of Clubs & Associations Past and Present

- AOPA UK—Aircraft Owners and Pilots Association.—Board member and Chairman of the Channel Island Region of AOPA
- PPL/IR EUROPE—Club for private pilots holding an instrument rating.
- Jersey Aero Club which used to be the Channel Island Aero Club—Life member and past Vice-Chairman
- Rotary Club of Jersey—awarded 4 Avenues of Service
- Rotary Club de la Manche—Honorary member
- Rotary Club of Newcastle-under-Lyme—Past President and Honorary life member
- Rotary Club of Znojmo in the Czech Republic—Honorary member
- IFFR—The International Fellowship of Flying Rotarians—Director and past World President 1986-1987—awarded Paul Harris Fellowship 1987
- St. John Ambulance—Serving Brother of the Order of St. John and member of Jersey Appeals Committee
- CIM—Chartered Institute of Marketing—Fellow
- IoD—Institute of Directors—Fellow

- BIPP—British Institute of Professional Photography—Licentiate
- Jersey Chamber of Trade and Commerce—Member
- The Ancient Corporation of Hanley—Councillor
- Jersey Wildlife Preservation Trust—Life member
- Probus Club of Jersey—Member
- Ordre International des Anysetiers—Member
- St. Emilion—D'Echevin D'Honneur
- Jersey Speakers Club—Past President and Chairman
- Jersey Computer Association—Honorary life member and past committee member and exhibition organiser
- Rotary International—Past committee member World Fellowship activities
- St. John Ambulance Air Wing—Past Midland Region Group Co-ordinator and volunteer pilot for European kidney transplant transport service
- BPIA—British Photographic Importers Association—Past Chairman
- North Staffs Chamber of Commerce and Industry—Past council member
- Newcastle-under-Lyme Chamber of Trade—Past committee member
- ICEA—International Consumer Electronics Association—Past Vice Chairman
- ISMA—Institute of Sales Management North Staffs Branch—Past President and Chairman
- BIM—British Institute of Management North Staffs Branch—Past Vice Chairman and founder member

- St. John Ambulance Brigade for Staffordshire—Past council member
- BBC Radio Stoke—Past member advisory council
- North Staffs. Heart Research Fund—Past Vice President
- Society of Staffordshire Photographers—Past President
- Disabled Drivers Club North Staffs. Branch—Past President
- Stoke Spitfire Appeals Committee—Past founder and committee member
- Newpak Products (Factory for the disabled)—Past Chairman of the management committee
- Newcastle-under-Lyme String Orchestra—Past Patron
- Trentham Scout Group—Past President

Appendix E

List of Aeroplanes Flown

Charles Strasser, holder of UK CAA Private Pilot's Licence with twin-engine and Instrument Rating and US FAA Commercial Pilot's Licence with multi-engine and Instrument Rating. Those owned by me shown in bold with an asterisk.

AUSTER	G-AIBW
	G-HCM
	G-AGVN
	G-AJPU
	G-AGYH
	G-AHAP
	G-AGTO
	G-ANRP *
MAGISTER	G-AIUA
PIPER TRI-PACER PA22	**G-APXM ***
	G-ARGY
	G-APZL
CESSNA SKYMASTER C336	N17072
	G-ASLL
C337	**G-ATNY ***
	N59N
PIPER PA28	G-ASLV
	G-ASSW
	G-ASWX
	G-BEYL
	G-BOXC
	N56672
	N222CC
	G-BOXB
	N38599
	N9102K

PIPER APACHE	G-ARYP
CESSNA 310	G-ATPS
PIPER AZTEC PA27	G-ATDC
	G-HLFF
CESSNA C172	N1188M
	N84515
	N39366
	N7569G
	N7085G
	N7004G
	N65268
	N733RL
	N1729V
	N4915D
	N91903
	N729SP
	N3521A
	N54859
	N215FR
	VH-BYR
PIPER SENECA II PA34-200T	G-BEYO
	G-BEVG *
	G-BFKO *
	G-PLUS *
	N37US *
	N1026U
	G-BFHL
	N3252G
	N21847
	N2840X
	VH-IOZ
	VH-IEE
CESSNA 150	VQ-SAF
	G-BDBU
	G-BCPE
	N6662S
	N714CD
	N18063
	8P-BAW
	G-BTYC

GRUMMAN AA5 A AND B	G-BEVW
	G-BHLX
	HS-ATG
	HS-ATH
CESSNA 182	8P-ASK
	G-BGAJ
	N21297
	D-EGLF
	N756CS
BN TRISLANDER	5YBBR
CESSNA C152	N69218
	G-BHAI
	N757HB
	N757EQ
	N444QA
CESSNA 177	N52668
PIPER CHIEFTAIN PA31-350	N32794
PIPER MALIBU	G-BLIZ
PIPER SENECA III PA34	G-BLYK
CESSNA 210	XBCQJ
	N732PH
	VH-5DU
PIPER SARATOGA PA32	N83052
	N58881
CESSNA SKYNIGHT C320	N269WP
CESSNA C207	N802AN
	N1675U
MOONEY 203	N322DB
ROCKWELL COMMANDER	G-GOIBM
BEECH BONANZA B36	N6467X
SOCATA TOBAGO TB10	VH- ???
CIRRUS SR22	N436CD
DIAMOND TWIN STAR DA42	N35AL

Appendix F

"Strasser Scheme" Press release

AOPA
Aircraft Owners & Pilots Association
CHANNEL ISLANDS REGION
CHARLES G. STRASSER OBE SBStJ MSc FCIM
CHAIRMAN AOPA C.I. REGION
DIRECTOR AOPA UK

The Cottage, Anne Port	Tel. ++44 (0)1534 851681
St. Martin, JERSEY, JE3 6DT	Fax ++44 (0)1534 854559
Channel Islands, (Via UK)	E-mail strasser@propilots.net

1st September 2006—NOW 193!

Hardwick airfield in Norfolk (on ½" map) just joined Charles Strasser's campaign on behalf of AOPA to get all airfields to accept CAA CAP 667 9.2(c) recommendation and not to charge GA aircraft making an emergency or precautionary diversion landing there is still growing.

To the 1st of September 2006, no less than 193 airfields have agreed this potentially life saving measure.

The 157 civil airfields, in alphabetical order, are—Aberdeen, Aberporth, Alderney, Andrewsfield, Ashcroft, Audley-End, Bagby, Barra, Barrow, Barton, Belfast-City, Belle-Vue, Bembridge, Benbecula, Beverley, Blackbushe, Bodmin, Bourn, Bournemouth, Breighton, Brimpton, Bristol-Intl., Brough, Bruntingthorpe, Caernarfon, Cambridge, Campbeltown, Chalgrove, Charterhall, Chester-Hawarden, Clacton, Compton-Abbas, Coventry, Cranfield, Cromer, Cumbernauld, Davidstow-Moor, Denham, Derby, Dornoch, Dunsfold, Duxford, Eaglescott, East-Midlands, Eday, Eddsfield, Edinburgh, Elmsett, Elstree, Enniskillen, Enstone, Fair-Isle, Fairoaks, Farnborough, Farway-Common, Fenland, Fife, Finmere, Fowlmere, Full-Sutton, Glasgow, Glenforsa, Goodwood, Guernsey, Hanley,

Hardwick, Haverfordwest, Henstridge, Hinton/Hedges, Inverness, Islay, Isle-of-Gigha, Isles-of-Scilly, Jersey, Kemble, Kingsmuir, Kirkwall, Lamb-Holm, Lands-End, Langar, Lasham, Lashenden-Headcorn, Lee-on-Solent, Leicester, Little-Gransden, Liverpool, Londonderry, Ludham, Lydd, Manston, Maypole, Netherthorpe, Newcastle, Newquay, Newtownards, Nort-Ronaldsay, North-Weald, Northampton-Sywell, Nottingham, Oaksey-Park, Oban, Old-Sarum, Old-Warden, Oxford, Panshanger, Papa-Westray, Pembray, Perranporth, Perth, Peterborough-Conington, Peterborough-Sibson, Plymouth, Popham, Prestwick, Redhill, Retford-Gamston, Rochester, Sanday, Sandtoft, Seething, Sheffield, Sherburn-in-Elmet, Shipdham, Shobdon, Shoreham, Sleap, Southampton, Southend, Stansted, Stapleford, Stornoway, Stronsay, Sturgate, Sumburgh, Swansea, Tatenhill, Thruxton, Tiree, Top-Farm, Truro, Turweston, Walton-Wood, Warton, Wellesbourne, Welshpool, Westray, White-Waltham, West-Freugh, Wick, Wolverhampton, Wombleton, Woodford, Wycombe-Air-Park, Yeovil, York-Rufforth.

And all 36 MILITARY MOD airfields—ROYAL AIR FORCE—RAF Benson, RAF Brize Norton, RAF Colerne, RAF Coltishall, RAF Coningsby, RAF Cosford, RAF Cottesmore, RAF Cranwell, RAF Halton, RAF Henlow, RAF Honington, RAF Kinloss, RAF Leeming, RAF Leuchars, RAF Linton on Ouse, RAF Lossiemouth, RAF Lyneham, RAF Marham, RAF Newton, RAF Northolt, RAF Odiham, RAF St.Athan, RAF St.Mawgan, RAF Scampton, RAF Shawbury, RAF Valley, RAF Waddington, RAF Wittering, RAF Woodvale, RAF Wyton. ROYAL NAVAL AIR STATION—RNAS Culdrose, RNAS Yeovilton. ARMY—Dishforth, Middle Wallop, Netheravon, Wattisham.

This concession applies to genuine emergencies and diversions to airfields other than the destination airport.

Wide awareness means that GA pilots in a difficult situation can at least eliminate the cost factor as a potential worry. Publishers of Airfield Data have been asked to highlight this safety concession and so far Aerad, AFE and Pooleys have agreed to do this in their "VFR Flight Guide". No Response from Jeppesen/Bottlang.

Unfortunatel 17 Airports/Airfields have so far decided that they will not implement the CAP 667 9.2(c) recommendation. Hopefully they will have a change of heart and join the majority of UK airfields that have.

Belfast-Intl., Biggin-Hill, Birmingham, Blackpool, Cardiff, Carlisle, Dundee, Exeter, Filton, Gloucestershire, Humberside, Isle-of-Man, Leeds/Bradford, London-Luton, Manchester, Norwich, Teesside.

And 3 Airports have not been approached—London Heathrow, City and Gatwick.

In recognition of their outstanding contribution to UK General Aviation Flight Safety, AOPA has presented a "Flight Safety Award" Certificate to each of the 193 Aerodrome operators above, who have fully accepted CAA CAP 667 9.2(c) recommendation not to levy any fees from a General Aviation pilot who makes a genuine emergency or diversionary landing at their Aerodrome.

The full CAA CAP 667 9.2(c) recommendation states:-"There were a number of fatal accidents where a timely diversion or precautionary landing could have avoided an accident. In the UK there is a 'culture' of pressing on and hoping for the best rather than accepting the inconvenience and cost of a diversion. This 'culture' needs to be changed, firstly by educating pilots and secondly by persuading Aerodrome owners that there should be no charge for emergency landings or diversions. *It is recommended that all Aerodrome owners be persuaded to adopt a policy that there should be no charges for emergency landings or diversions by general aviation aircraft.*" Aopalh100.doc

To all Editors: It would be appreciated if you would publish for the benefit of GA private pilots, the latest list of both the 193 airports who have agreed, to waive charges for emergency and precautionary diversion landings *and the 17 airports who so far have refused to do so.*

Appendix G

Personalities of the BPIA & Photo Trade

The following names are extracted from a speech I gave in 1976 at a British Photographic Importers Association dinner to mark the retirement of its Secretary, John Annetts. The speech was published in two parts (January and February 1977) in *Photo Trader*.

The Association had been organised 25 years earlier. I spent the whole of one weekend studying and researching the BPIA history through its minutes books and included in my speech the year by year growth in the membership during the early years.

Date Joined	Company	Represented by
1951	Agfa	E. R. Napthine (elected Chair)
	Actina	M. Games
	Nebro	Neville Brown
	Cinex	Charles Fer
	Dallmeyer	H. A. Carter
	W F Dormer	W. F. Dormer
	Gevaert	J. Bracey-Gibbon & F. Eade
	Haynor	R. Hayne & S. Orski
	R F Hunter	A. Blackburn
	Johnsons of Hendon	E. S. Houghton
	Kodak	R. Freeman Wright
	Kranseder	R. Henkel

	Leitz	A. Smith
	Milbro	K. C. Bowles
	Pathescope	Dowers & Joslen
	Peeling & Komlosy	S.W. Komlosy & R. E. Peeling
	Photax	H. Jacobs
	Photo-Science	C. W. Harrison
	J J Silber	J. J. Silber
	Dawe Instruments	F. M. Savage
1952	Aparatus & Instrument Co	Faktor, Snr.
	K G Corfield	Ken Corfield
	Johnsons of Hendon	E. Reuter
	Photax	L. Dunn
1953	Chemical & Natural Products	H. K. Shephard
	Gevaert	Rafferty
1954	Photax	B. Hodges
	Pullin Optical Co	N. E. Houghton
1955	K G Corfield	Bill Webb
1956	Pullin Optical Co	S. J. Hawke
1957	Photax	F. G. Dunn
	Rank Precision Industries	J. F. Tindale
1958	Hanimex UK	John Bealey
	North Staffs Photographic Services	Charles Strasser
1960	Arrowtabs	Maurice Mindel
	Bealey & Co	John Bealey
	Rosley Products	Stanley Kramer
1961	Bush & Meissner	

	J R Distributing Co	
	Mayfair Photographic Suppliers	Freddy Weitzmann
	Northgate Cameras	
	Specto	
1963	P M Cox	
	Fasid Enterprises	
	Highgate Optical	
	Luminos	
	David Williams Cine Eqpt.	David Williams
1964	E Hill & Co	
	Ilford	
1966	Beaulieu Cinema	
1970	Pako	
	Pyser-Britex	

Some other photo-trade personalities of the era, not mentioned in the above list nor in this book, were:
Jan Horal (Mercurex & Dixons), Mark Souhami (Dixons), Boris Bennett, Maurice Bennett & Michael Bennett (Bennetts), Richard Ford & Frank Carlisle (Boots), Peter Bird (Boots & Dixons), Allan Warren (Spectrum), Barry Young (Photomarkets), Bill Pirie, Jack Jackson, David Grandison, Gerry Dingley (Rank Audio Visual), John Cashmore (Hanimex), Ron Thorne & Dennis Lascelles (J J Silber), John Armit (Pentax), Brian Hall & Mike Boon (Canon), Alan Price, Danny Churchill, Kevin Day (Konica), Peter Faktor (Aico), Len Easterbook, Garry Banks (Samsung), Laurie Moore (Minolta), Barry Taylor, Frank Hatton (Southall Bros.), Alan Jessop, Anthony Jacobs, Alex Falk, Derek Whitby, Chris Swain, Michael Heaton, Victor Blackman (Amateur Photographer & Daily Express), Dennis Taylor (P.T.W.), Derek Gardner, Bert Davies (Fallowfields), and Reg Mason (Amateur Photographer).

Appendix H

Inflation Table

Included to facilitate interpretation of values used in this book

The following table of values was taken from the Office of National Statistics website. The Office for National Statistics (ONS) is the government department that provides UK statistical and registration services.

ONS is responsible for producing a wide range of key economic and social statistics which are used by policy makers across government to create evidence-based policies and monitor performance against them.

The Office also builds and maintains data sources both for itself and for its business and research customers. It makes statistics available so that everyone can easily assess the state of the nation, the performance of government and their own position.

Example to use the table: I was employed by John Martin for my first job in 1946 for a wage of £10 per week. To compute the pounds required today (2005 latest year available) to have the same purchasing power as the £10 in 1946, multiply by the 2005 index figure (2805) and divide by the 1946 index figure (100). The answer is £280.50 per week. A note of caution is in order. This table applies to general retail purchasing power of the pound and not to specific goods or services. Real estate and probably wages also have experienced higher inflation over the years. Other items, especially those involving chip technology, have actually experienced deflation.

Year	Index	Inflation %	Year	Index	Inflation %
1946	100	3.1	1976	582	16.5
1947	107	7.0	1977	674	15.8
1948	115	7.7	1978	730	8.3
1949	119	2.8	1979	828	13.4
1950	122	3.1	1980	977	18.0
1951	133	9.1	1981	1093	11.9
1952	146	9.2	1982	1187	8.6
1953	150	3.1	1983	1241	4.6
1954	153	1.8	1984	1303	5.0
1955	160	4.5	1985	1382	6.1
1956	168	4.9	1986	1429	3.4
1957	174	3.7	1987	1489	4.2
1958	179	3.0	1988	1562	4.9
1959	180	0.6	1989	1683	7.8
1960	182	1.0	1990	1843	9.5
1961	188	3.4	1991	1951	5.9
1962	196	4.3	1992	2024	3.7
1963	200	2.0	1993	2056	1.6
1964	207	3.3	1994	2106	2.4
1965	216	4.8	1995	2179	3.5
1966	225	3.9	1996	2231	2.4
1967	231	2.5	1997	2301	3.1
1968	241	4.7	1998	2380	3.4
1969	254	5.4	1999	2417	1.5
1970	271	6.4	2000	2488	3.0
1971	296	9.4	2001	2532	1.8
1972	317	7.1	2002	2574	1.7
1973	346	9.2	2003	2649	2.9
1974	402	16.0	2004	2728	3.0
1975	499	24.2	2005	2805	2.8

North Staffs Photographic Services Christmas Party in 1954. Top row left to right: Marion Brown, Margaret Fagan, Ann Conyon, Barbara Tunnicliffe, Geoffrey Barber, Carol Barber, Second row: Joan Ashley, Nigel Cope, John Foden, Muriel Bailey, Alice Ford, Christine Bengry, Doreen Carter, Shirley Cannon, Third Row: Rupert Cartlidge, Yvonne Cartlidge, Maureen Strasser, Charles Strasser, Mrs. Vickers, Anthony Vickers, Rita Lowe (chapter 17).

Presenting a staff award. This picture from the early days of photofinishing and importing is included without names for the benefit of those featured (chapter 17).

An early sales conference of North Staffs Photographic Services at Balls Yard in Newcastle-under-Lyme, from left to right Arthur Sams, Mike Hanson, Rupert Cartlidge, Peter Gorton, A.N.Other, Charles Strasser and, in front John Ash (chapter 18).

One of the early Wirgin Edinex camera adverts from the "Amateur Photographer" of 1954. At today's equivalent price you can buy a top 6-mp digital camera! (Chapter 19).

An early Photographic Dealers Association Dinner. Facing left to right, Norman Green of JJ Silber, me, my wife Maureen, Stanley Kramer (my first freelance salesman) and Christine Bengry (now Sutton) my first secretary. Opposite to me is Henry Loebstein, founder and owner of Gnome Photographic factory in Cardiff, circa 1952.

The Photopia building in Hempstalls Lane, Newcastle, immediately after its conversion from a derelict fustian mill and before further wings were added to cope with the rapid expansion (chapter 21).

Another early Photopia sales conference, from left to right, Mike Hanson, Vic Rosewell, David Morgan, David Hire, Jack Dean, CGS, Peter Gorton, Norman Whibley, Rupert Cartlidge, Ken Kitchener, John Battison.

At an exhibition with my advertising director John Battison. Note my "trademark" pippo pipe which I always smoked with Clan aromatic tobacco, until I stopped 20 years ago. John is wearing the green Photopia blazer with the embroidered Photopia blazer badge (chapter 33).

The Photopia stand at the "Photofair" at Olympia in London, before Japanese imports started, topped by a model of the Mastra camera named after MAureen STRAsser (chapter 33).

The famous singer/comedian Harry Secombe, one of the "Goons", with me on our stand at one of the early "Photofair" exhibitions. He, like many other stars, including Harry Worth, Peter Sellars, Graham Starke and Tommy Steele, used our cameras and were friends of the company (chapter 33).

Walter Emanuel, the famous and prolific author of many books on photography and cameras, in a rare shot relaxing with his wife. He was for many years the manager of our customer Wallace Heaton, the photographic dealer in New Bond Street in London holding many Royal Warrants and it was Walters's job to go to the Palace and show the Queen how to use her newly acquired cameras. He also published the then famous WH Blue book. Retired shortly after WH was taken over by Dixons (chapter 25).

One of the early Photopia sales conferences at the new building in Hempstalls Lane with one of our German camera suppliers Willie Bauser of Regula Werk King participating. From left to right, front row David Hire, Charles Strasser, Willie Bauser, Rupert Cartlidge, John Battison, mid row Vic Rosewell, Mike Hanson, Peter Gorton, Raymond Heron, Ken Kitchener, Jack Dean, top row Norman Whibley, Mitch Thompson (chapter 24).

A PDA dinner in 1958 at the Grosvenor House Hotel, Park Lane, London, when I hosted Dixons. From left to right, Ernie Shenton, Denise Shenton, Charles Strasser, Pam Kalms, Stanley Kalms, Maureen Strasser, Ray Cooke, Barbara Morgan, David Morgan, Dilys Hanson, Mike Hanson. Stanley, with the help of Ernie and Ray, started Dixons. I hosted a replica dinner table 39 years later in 1997, alas without Maureen and Barbara.

The Photopia ten pin bowling team, from left to right, David Hire, Jeff Pickford, Rupert Cartlidge, Charles Strasser, John Battison. David Coupe, circa 1961/63.

An early Japanese Cameras Ltd. Sales Conference with my introducing a new cine camera on return from a trip to Japan. From left to right Alan Phelan, George Duerden, A.N.Other, Mike Wadsworth, A.N.Other, Max Blakeman, David Coupe, Rupert Cartlidge, Charles Strasser, David Hire.

Our sales team at a "Photofair" exhibition at Olympia in London in our green Photopia blazers from left to right back, A.N.Other, Mike Hanson, Ken Kitchener, CGS, A.N.Other, Vic Rosewell, front, Max Blakeman, David Hire, A.N.Other, Peter Gorton, John Battison (chapter 33).

The signing at Gresham Trust on the 19th November 1962 of the Photopia International placing documents when it became a public company with a London Stock Exchange quotation.
From left to right, Arthur Snow (AB Snow Wood and Co, our accountants), Maureen Strasser, Peter Wreford (M.D. Gresham Trust), John Colegrave (Colegraves our stockbrokers), Pat Grundy (Richards Butler, solicitors), John Grenside (Peat Marwick Mitchell and Co. Supervising Auditors, John later became the senior partner of PMM), standing, a Secretary, Norman Baldock (Gresham Trust), Malcolm Farrer Brown (Richards Butler) (chapter 28).

Going Public, signing the final document, from left to right, Arthur Snow, Charles Strasser and Maureen Strasser looking on (chapter 28).

The Interplan conference introducing a group dealer incentive scheme. From left to right, front row, Rupert Cartlidge, Tim Knight, David Uwins, Alan Bethel, Charles Strasser, Mike Hanson, Alan Batty, A.N.Other, David Coupe. Mid row, Ken Kitchener, David Morgan, Chris Mason, Len Roper, Roger Ayling, George Duerden, Malcolm Douglas, Alan Phelan. Top row, A.N.Other, John Cooke, John Kirk, Vic Rosewell, Max Blakeman, Mike Smith, Frank Wilkinson (chapter 45).

Our first entry into Audio with a portable record player and reel-to-reel tape recorders. A demonstration in Tokyo by two Japanese makers' representatives to Peter Gorton and me (chapter 39).

Yugi Kobayashi, the boss of Kobayashi Seiki Seisakusho, and his export manager Ken Ichihashi on a visit to our house in Trentham with myself and Peter Gorton. They made Kopil and Kobena Zoom cine cameras and many models exclusively for us under our brands for Europe (chapter 39).

"Samurai" Mr. Otake of Orion with his two export department managers on a visit to our head office in Newcastle with Mike Gilmore my Plustronics manager. They made our "unputdownable" portable TV's and are probably even now the world's largest OEM electronics manufacturer with factories all over the world (chapter 35).

Sam Kusumoto and his wife Kumiko and their two daughters, and my wife Maureen on the far right, on a social visit to us. Sam has been a friend almost from our first trading relationship with Minolta when he was export manager in Japan and we spent lots of business and leisure time together (chapter 41).

Mr. Yoshikatsu Ota of the Minolta Hamburg office introducing a new model Minolta camera to us at the Minolta European sales conference at the Berlin Hilton in 1970. Mr. Ota later progressed to become the first non-Tashima family member to head the Board (chapter 42).

K.Tashima (KT) founder and President of Minolta giving his welcoming speech in English at a Minolta European sales conference. I am sitting puffing at my pippo by his temporarily empty seat (chapter 42).

K. Tashima (KT) the founder and President of Minolta inspecting some of our UK advertising on my annual visit to the Minolta head office in Osaka (chapter 42).

A Geisha party hosted by Minolta (chapter 42).

At a "Photokina" reception in Cologne Mrs. Mayumi Moriyama presented me with a signed copy of her book "What I saw in the Cabinet". Besides being the boss of the Japanese Camera Inspection Institute for many years, she became an MP, the Secretary to the Cabinet of the Japanese Government and later Minister of Justice (chapter 41).

My Japanese visiting card—a good supply of these was needed for every trip for the traditional exchange (chapter 39).

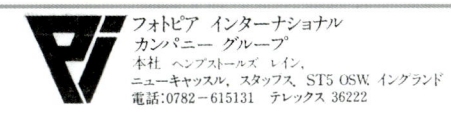

フォトピア インターナショナル
カンパニー グループ
本社 ヘンプストールズ レイン、
ニューキャッスル、スタッフス、ST5 0SW、イングランド
電話:0782-615131 テレックス 36222

社長
チャールズ G. ストラッサー

フォトピア Ltd・ジャパニーズ カメラ Ltd
メイフェアー フォトグラフィック Ltd・ポール プラス Ltd
プラストロニクス Ltd・インターサーブ Ltd

With Peter Gorton and guide on our first crossing into China from Hong Kong, circa 1957.

Benson Lee and family with Peter Gorton and myself. He made many simple promotional cameras for us in his Singapore factory (chapter 46).

After a day of business with Citizen Watch Co in Hamburg, a relaxing evening in a beer hall with the usual 'umpapa' band. If you bought them a round of beer you could conduct the band. Tim Knight performed well. On the first row Peter Holmes my Citizen Watch sales manager and yours truly and on the second row right David Morgan my sales director (chapter 51).

June 2006, a visit to my old head office in Newcastle and chatting with the then boss David Vaughan and my publisher Wade Keller of Marco Island. Florida (chapter 51).

June 2006 at the mini ex-Photopia local staff reunion at the Borough Arms in Newcastle talking with one of my ex-secretaries Kath Hire and her husband David my ex-office manager (chapter 49).

Rupert Cartlidge with me at a mini ex-Photopia local staff reunion, June 2006 at the Borough Arms, Newcastle-under-Lyme (chapter 49).

Outside Buckingham Palace. Christine Sutton (Bengry) Anne Davies (Conyon) and Phyllis Bayley who all started working for me straight from school and are now retired. They came to London for the day specially to see me and wish me well when I was presented with my OBE. Note the Photopia coloured balloons (chapter 90).

Photopia International Ltd. 1973/74 Group Catalogue front and back covers.